2-15-77

# putting money to work

# an investment primer

**YALE L. MELTZER**

*Pace University*

A SPECTRUM BOOK

PRENTICE-HALL, INC., Englewood Cliffs, New Jersey

*Library of Congress Cataloging in Publication Data*

Meltzer, Yale L.
  Putting money to work.

  (A Spectrum Book)
  Includes bibliographies and index.
  1.  Investments.    I.  Title.
HG4521.M436      332.6'78      75-43923
ISBN 0-13-744516-4

**To my wife, Annette, and my sons, Benjamin and Phillipe**

A Spectrum Book

10   9   8   7   6   5   4   3   2   1

Printed in the United States of America

Prentice-Hall International, Inc., *London*
Prentice-Hall of Australia, Pty. Limited, *Sydney*
Prentice-Hall of Canada, Ltd., *Toronto*
Prentice-Hall of India Private Limited, *New Delhi*
Prentice-Hall of Japan, Inc., *Tokyo*
Prentice-Hall of Southeast Asia, Ltd., *Singapore*

# contents

# *preface*

You will find some people who are pessimistic about the future. You will find some people who talk about the stock market crashing as it did in 1929. You will even find some writers who expound at great length about how the world is headed for a deep depression of the catastrophic dimensions of the Great Depression of the 1930s. A sober look at the economic realities, however, makes these dire forecasts appear unduly pessimistic.

A deep depression appears unlikely because of the numerous tangible changes which have taken place since 1929. Today, there are many monetary institutions, systems, and procedures which did not even exist in 1929 or, in some cases, were not as highly perfected as they are now.

It is true that some people have been shocked by the recession and unnerved by the rising inflation. The rising unemployment and declining value of the dollar hit home for many people. Low-income families have been hit very hard; middle-income families have been especially squeezed by the recession, inflation, and taxes; and even wealthy families have felt the pinch of the harsh economic realities of today. Nevertheless, there is no reason to believe that economic catastrophe inevitably awaits us.

The best way to view our present predicaments is in the light of past experiences. They will not then appear so shocking, and you can, therefore, think in terms of making your own personal adjustments.

The United States has been in seven recessions since the Second World War. It would appear that we are coming out of the seventh one right now.

Peaks in economic activity were reached in 1948, 1953, 1957, 1960, 1969 and 1973. The latest sharp decline started with the Arab oil embargo in October 1973 and rapidly accelerated in October 1974. What is necessary is that you learn to live with the business cycles and not become overly pessimistic about them. There will always be prophets of doom and gloom, but don't get taken in. Instead, think constructively and use your creative abilities.

Read newspapers and other publications carefully to become aware of what the fiscal and monetary authorities are attempting to do and when they change their policies. For example, the tax-cut is a fiscal policy which has as its purpose stimulation of the economy and the creation of more jobs. The buying of government securities by the Federal Reserve System is a monetary policy which also has as its purpose stimulation of the economy. There are many other fiscal and monetary policies which can be pursued. They will be dealt with in various chapters of the book. Please refer to the portion of the book entitled "Where You Can Get Current Information and Data on a Continuous Basis" (Appendix E) for sources of information on these matters, as well as many other important economic matters.

Above all, do not lose confidence. Become aware of how the various instruments of fiscal and monetary policy work. Understanding them is vital to sound investment decisions.

The instruments of fiscal policy are far more effective now than they were in 1929, and new ones have come into existence since then. For example, today we have built-in stabilizers in the economy, such as unemployment insurance and other social security benefits, which we did not have in 1929. Today, we have Medicare, which we did not have in 1929.

The Federal Reserve System, which was first established by Act of Congress in 1913 and opened for business in 1914, has learned a lot about monetary control since 1929. Central banks in many countries are now working together, and the Eurodollar market has developed an elaborate international monetary mechanism, as have the other Eurocurrency markets. The Federal Deposit Insurance Corporation (FDIC), first established in 1933, now insures each savings account up to $40,000. Meanwhile, the Securities and Exchange Commission (SEC) is doing a progressively better job of policing the securities industry of the United States. In 1929, the SEC did not even exist.

In addition, since 1929 a growing number of financial institutions, such as commercial banks, pension funds, life insurance companies, and mutual funds, have entered the stock market and have become stabilizing forces in the market. The past few years have also seen the growth of the money market funds, such funds as the Anchor Daily Income Fund, J.P. Cabot Short-Term Fund, Capital Liquidity, Daily Income Fund, Dreyfus Liquid Assets, Fidelity Daily Income Trust, Money Market Management, Oppenheimer Monetary Bridge, The Reserve Fund and Scudder Managed

Reserves, to name only a few. These funds offer investment opportunities in the short-term securities markets for middle-income people, who otherwise might not have enough money to get into these markets.

Furthermore, people have become better informed about economics and are demanding more value for their hard-earned money. Since 1929 many sensible middle-income people have entered the stock market and have found out what goes on there, not just speculators and a few rich people. Some of them have left the market after having won; some of them, after having lost; and some of them are still hanging on. Most of them, however, have learned something.

Another significant development, right through the recession and rising inflation, from 1973 to 1975, has been the dynamic growth of the stock options market, which in the 1960s was only beginning to get off the ground. This is a market for the speculative-minded and those who seek to shift their risks, but the options market has clearly matured and is now quite organized with the present-day operations of the Chicago Board Options Exchange and the American Stock Exchange.

On the other hand, on December 31, 1974, U.S. citizens were officially granted the right to own gold after a 41-year ban. Some "gold bugs" saw trading in gold by U.S. citizens as heralding a rapid rise in gold prices from $195 per troy ounce of gold on December 27, 1974 to $250, $300, and $400 per ounce. This surge has so far not materialized.

What the investor has to realize is that an investment in the capital markets (e.g., the stock market and the bond market) is in essence an optimistic vote for the future and the need for capital formation (e.g., new plant, new equipment, and new technologies) most of the time. In contrast, an investor in gold has to realize that he is taking a pessimistic view.

The surge in gold prices from 1971 to the end of 1974 did indicate a broad-based lack of confidence on the part of many individuals and financial institutions regarding the ability of the governments of the Western world to cope with their economic problems. The rise in gold prices during this period actually outpaced the rise in the inflationary rate.

When people lose faith in the ability and determination of governments to hold down the rate of inflation, there is a "flight from money." The classic case of such a "flight from money" took place in the hyperinflation of Germany, 1920-23. When such situations develop, people seek substitutes for currency. Gold has long been considered the best commodity substitute for currency. If countries show the ability and clear resolve to cope with their problems, the price of gold can be expected to decline.

The ability of Western governments, especially the United States Government, to cope with their problems, does exist. The tools of economic policy do exist, and innovations with those tools can be made when necessary. It is simply a matter of properly using those tools.

But what about such things as bank failures, problems in the Eurocurrency loan markets, the Arab petrodollars, the energy crisis, pollution, and the problems of the food supply, to name just a few danger points?

The Franklin National Bank failure was one outstanding case. Actually, once the problems of the Franklin National Bank were discovered they were dealt with speedily. On September 26, 1974, the Federal Reserve Bank of New York, after consultation with the Board of Governors of the Federal Reserve System, the U.S. Treasury, and other Federal agencies, acquired the foreign exchange commitments of Franklin. It was, after all, the foreign exchange commitments that were a major cause of the bank's trouble. The action of the Federal Reserve Bank of New York was swift and impressive. On October 8, 1974, the Comptroller of the Currency declared Franklin insolvent and appointed the FDIC as receiver. Bids were received for the bank, and the European-American Bank & Trust Company had the highest bid. On October 9, 1974, all of Franklin's domestic offices opened with the new name "European-American Bank" on their buildings.

Thus, the Board of Governors of the Federal Reserve System was able to report in the *Federal Reserve Bulletin* that "news of Franklin's insolvency was taken in stride by the [foreign exchange] market with no adverse impact on dollar rates."

The collapse of the West German bank Bankhaus I.D. Herstatt in 1974 did not bring on a financial and monetary panic. True, there was nervousness in the foreign exchange market as a result of the closing of Herstatt. This did weigh heavily upon the West German mark for a while, but, in spite of the strains in the West German credit markets, liquidity in the West German banking system was maintained and West Germany weathered the storm.

Regarding the problems of the Eurocurrency market, at a meeting of the central bank governors in Basel, Switzerland, on September 10, 1974, it was concluded that means were available for the provision of temporary liquidity and would be used if and when necessary.

As for the Arab petrodollars and the petrodollars of the other members of OPEC (Organization of Petroleum Exporting Countries), the Eurocurrency market has been the major place for deposit of those funds which could not be invested in actual goods and services or for grants-in-aid and loans to oil-importing countries. Then, too, there are the U.S. banks and the highly sophisticated U.S. money and capital markets to cushion the impact of the petrodolars.

As for the energy crisis, new technologies are being developed to substitute alternative forms of energy for oil, gas, and the fossil fuels in general. Pollution-control processes have been developed, while high-protein foods and application of the "Green Revolution" offer great promise for providing the growing world population with its needed nutrition.

If it is likely that we will avert a 1929-type stock market crash, if we can avoid a deep worldwide depression like that of the 1930s, and if we can cope with the other problems, what should that mean to you? It means that you should put your money to work.

This book is designed to help you do just that. You yourself can wage war against the two enemies: *Inflation and Recession.* There are things that you can do in addition to the actions of the governmental fiscal and monetary authorities.

This book will explain the details of fixed-income securities, which were so profitable in 1974 and right into early 1975. It will explain what the money market is, as well as the bond market. It will delve into the mysteries of the stock market and the Eurodollar market. It presents and discusses the alternatives of how you can put your money to work and what lies behind the financial and monetary institutions whose authorities often make decisions that directly affect you.

Remember this. You are not alone. There are all sorts of organizations, institutions and professionals at your service.

There are rating services for bonds and commercial paper (e.g., Fitch, Moody's, and Standard & Poor's). There are services that supply information on stocks and companies (e.g., Dun & Bradstreet, Moody's, Standard & Poor's, Value Line). There are publications that can keep you up with the latest developments (e.g., *Barron's, Business Week, Fortune, Newsweek, The Journal of Commerce, The New York Times, The Wall Street Journal, The Wall Street Transcript, The Washington Post, Time,* and *U.S. News & World Report*). In addition, an enormous amount of information can be obtained from publications of the Federal Reserve System, the U.S. Treasury, and other governmental agencies.

For stocks, the investor is advised to look for good balance sheets and income statements, that is, to look for a solid financial position and good earning power. This book can help you make the necessary analyses by yourself.

Realize that money represents a bridge to the future. That future can be one of great enjoyment for you. Much depends upon what you decide to do.

Seek to constantly humanize money. You humanize money when you take pride in the fruits of your labor. You humanize money when you draw satisfaction from your hard work, strenuous efforts, and accomplishments, when you see them showing up in ever greater value and then see that value transmuted into money terms. You humanize money when you eliminate waste. You humanize money when you equate the time you put in on-the-job with the things you need and want, such as the groceries, the rent, clothing, a vacation, a theater ticket, a concert performance, a movie, a baseball game, or other things. You humanize money when you think in such terms as "one hour on-the-job equals one theater ticket" or one ticket to a baseball game, or something else that you want.

When you think in these terms, money then becomes saturated with a sense of human vitality, human significance, and human values. Money is not then something cold, unfeeling, and inhuman. In emphasizing value and equating value with money, think of your hopes, aspirations, and ambitions.

In conclusion, I wish to express my appreciation to the many individuals who were so helpful when I was preparing this book, especially those at the World Bank, the Federal Reserve Banks, and U.S. government agencies. I wish to express my gratitude to Professor John R. Ward, Chairman of the Department of Accounting, Finance and Management at Pace University, for reading portions of the manuscript and making many helpful suggestions. In particular, I wish to express my deepest appreciation to my wife, Annette Meltzer, for the enormous aid which she gave me.

Yale L. Meltzer

# *introduction*

Your financial goals are inextricably bound up with your personal goals. Therefore, basic questions to ask yourself are:

What are my personal goals?
What are my financial goals?

In considering your personal goals, you have to decide such things as:

What kind of education do I want?
What kind of career do I want?
Do I want to get married?
Do I want to have children? If so, how many?
Where do I want to live?
Do I want to rent an apartment or buy a home?

Your decisions regarding your personal goals will affect how much money you spend, how much money you save, how you will spend your money, and where you will spend your money.

After establishing what your personal goals are—and it's a good idea to jot them down on paper to fix them in your mind—you should examine just what your financial goals are in the light of those personal goals. You should consider the following questions or combinations of them:

Do I want to invest for income?
Do I want to invest for long-term growth?
Do I want to engage in speculative situations?

Decide on your personal and financial goals for different time periods. Write them down for the following time periods:

Up to six months
Six to twelve months
One year to five years
Five years and over

## WHAT IS YOUR NET WORTH?

You should determine your net worth right now, in order to know just how much wealth you possess.

If you have a positive net worth, that means that you own more than you owe. A negative net worth means just the opposite.

In order to compute your net worth, fill in the "Financial Statement" that follows. If you have a positive net worth, which you feel is sufficiently high and not tied up, then you can afford to make investments.

You should be sure, however, that you have funds to take care of regular expenses (e.g., the groceries, the rent, clothing, and the like) and enough money to take care of unexpected emergencies.

Financial Statement

| *Assets* | *Liabilities* |
|---|---|
| Cash on hand | Notes payable to banks (secured) |
| Money in checking accounts | Notes payable to banks (unsecured) |
| Total in savings accounts | Notes payable to others (secured) |
| Money market securities | Notes payable to others (unsecured) |
| Notes receivable | Accounts payable (if applicable) |
| Accounts receivable (if applicable) | Debit balances on margin accounts with brokers |
| Real estate | Mortgages payable on real estate |
| Mortgages owned | Loans against life insurance |
| Common stock | Other liabilities |
| Preferred stock | TOTAL LIABILITIES |

|                   *Assets*              |                *Liabilities*            |
| Bonds                                   | NET WORTH                               |
| Cash value of life insurance            |                                         |
| Other assets (e.g., car, furniture)     |                                         |
| TOTAL ASSETS                            | TOTAL LIABILITIES AND NET WORTH         |

*Notes:*

1. Your Net Worth is equal to Total Assets minus Total Liabilities, or Total Assets equals Total Liabilities plus Net Worth.

2. The latest market value should be used for common stock, preferred stock and bonds. In considering these values, you should think about how much money you could get if you had to sell the securities right now. The closer you get the value to the present point in time the better. Such newspapers as *The New York Times, The Wall Street Journal,* and *The Washington Post* can be used to determine current values, if you do not have access to a quotation machine or a ticker tape.

3. You should obtain the very latest cash value for your life insurance policy (if your life insurance policy has one). You can obtain the "cash value of life insurance" by contacting your life insurance company.

4. Traditional accounting practice requires that the cost principle be applied (i.e., that the assets, liabilities, and net worth be stated at the original cost incurred). You should, however, also state assets, liabilities, and net worth at the current market value for comparison purposes. Thus, for example, such assets as common stock, preferred stock, and bonds should be stated at the original cost to you, as well as at the latest (or current) market value (see Note 2).

Carefully analyze your net worth and overall financial position and then decide whether you feel that you are in a position to invest.

## THE NEXT STEP

If you feel that you are in a position to invest, you then have to decide whether you want to put your money in savings deposits or keep your money in savings deposits or whether you want to invest in securities or in other forms of investment (e.g., gold, other commodities, real estate).

If you want to invest in securities, you have to decide whether you want a fixed income from your investment or whether you want growth (i.e., appreciation in the value of the securities or, putting it another way, capital gains). The following lists classify investment possibilities from these points of view.

In evaluating investments and potential investments, you have to learn to think in terms of liquidity, safety, structure, yields, and growth. Liquidity tells you how readily you can convert your investment into cash. Safety tells you how well protected your investment is or, from another point of view, the degree of risk that you are taking with a certain investment. Structure tells you the degree of organization that you are getting with a certain investment or market. Some investors like a high degree of structure, whereas others don't care. A high degree of structure exists where you have formal, well-organized agencies (e.g., U.S. government agencies). Yields tell you what your rates of return are (e.g., if you buy a bond for $1,000 and you get $50 per year in interest, your annual yield is $^{50}/_{1000}$ or 5%). Growth, for an investment, occurs when you buy low and sell high.

### Fixed Income Investments

Money Market Securities (or Money Market Instruments):

> U.S. Treasury bills: For great liquidity and safety ($10,000 minimum investment).

> U.S. Treasury notes: For great liquidity (but less than for U.S. Treasury bills) and great safety, but the minimum investment is only $1,000 as opposed to $10,000 for U.S. Treasury bills.

> U.S. government agency securities and related securities: Fair degree of liquidity and safety, but high degree of structure and generally higher yields than for U.S. Treasury bills and U.S. Treasury notes. There is considerable variation in the minimum investment required.

> Commercial paper: The yields can be quite high, but one has to be very cautious about the financial soundness of the issuer. Remember the defaults of the Penn Central and others.

> Negotiable certificates of deposit: Generally high yields with good liquidity and safety, although less liquidity and safety than for U.S. Treasury bills. Be sure to check the financial soundness of the commercial bank issuing the certificate of deposit.

> Bankers' acceptances: Generally good yields with reasonable liquidity and safety.

Common Stocks: The common stock of some companies is bought for high dividends (i.e., income). Usually, common stock is bought, however, for growth.

Preferred Stocks: A lot depends upon the rights and privileges of the particular issue of preferred stock which you may be considering. In general, preferred stock is not a very attractive form of investment.

Bonds:

> Corporate bonds: There are many types of corporate bonds. The yield is an important factor in considering these as investment vehicles, but even more important than the yield is the credit-worthiness and financial soundness of the issuing corporation. Ratings by such services as Fitch, Moody's, and Standard & Poor's can be helpful.

> Municipal bonds: Attractive as investment vehicles, because of the exemption from Federal income taxes (and often from state and local income taxes, but exemption from state and local income taxes has to be checked for the particular issue). You have to be just as careful in checking the credit-worthiness and financial soundness of the municipality as of a corporation. Ratings by Fitch, Moody's, and Standard & Poor's can be helpful here, too. Whether these securities are really for you depends upon your particular income tax bracket and the actual yield as against other bonds (see the coverage of municipal bonds in this book for the necessary computations).

U.S. government bonds:

*U.S. Treasury bonds:* Great safety (they are backed by the U.S. Government) and liquidity. They offer you a broad range of maturity periods, generally 7 to 35 years.

*U.S. savings bonds:* Series E and H bonds have recently become great favorites for the small investor, because of the increase in the average interest rate from 5½% to 6% plus the safety feature of the backing of the U.S. Government (see the discussion in this book of Series E and H bonds for the details).

U.S. government agency and U.S. government-sponsored agency bonds: There are some highly attractive issues.

Foreign bonds: These are bonds for foreign governments and foreign corporations. They often offer high yields, but you have to be very wary of political developments. Governments may be overturned or corporations nationalized, and you may lose all your money.

World Bank bonds: These are substantial bonds. They have the backing of the member countries of the World Bank and provide good investment vehicles.

Funds:

Money market funds: They are also referred to as "monetary bridges" and "liquid asset funds." These funds specialize in the money market instruments. They offer income and permit the small investor to take advantage of a pooling of funds with other small investors, so that he can buy the money market instruments, which might otherwise be too expensive for him and investment possibilities only for very wealthy families, financial institutions, large corporations and others with large investment funds. *A note of caution:* With regard to the money market funds, try to anticipate which way interest rates are headed, and from your readings of the financial press see which way the Federal Reserve System wants to move interest rates. If interest rates are headed sharply downward, avoid these funds.

Income funds: These funds seek out securities with high dividends. The objective is not growth but income, and the investment situations are often not known to the ordinary investor.

Bond funds: These funds specialize in bonds and seek a balance of safety and yield. Some will concentrate on high-grade bonds, some on medium-grade bonds and some on low-grade bonds. Movements in interest rates are very significant in their performance.

Eurodollar Market and Eurocurrency Market—These markets generally offer high yields, often higher than other yields, but they are for the very wealthy. There are many Eurocurrencies, but the most important is the Eurodollar. A Eurocurrency deposit has to be created. For example, a Eurodollar deposit is created when a person with a checking account in a commercial bank located in the United States has this bank transfer money from his checking account to a foreign branch of this U.S. bank or to a foreign bank, in which the deposit is denominated in the currency of the foreign country. The usual trading unit is one million units of the particular currency (e.g., one million U.S. dollars). In Eurocurrency trading, the emphasis is on high yields and not on liquidity.

### Growth Investments

Common stocks: These securities represent a risky form of investment. *Nothing is guaranteed.* There is no fixed income. You may or may not receive any dividends. Many growth-oriented companies, in fact, pay no dividends, in order to use the cash for corporate projects. The potential is there, however, for growth and capital gains. In other words, you are hoping that you will buy low and sell high.

For example, if you bought one share of common stock of Company XYZ for $10 and you sold it at $100, your capital gains would be $90. On the other hand, Company XYZ might go bankrupt, in which case you would be the last to receive any of the assets upon liquidation, and you might receive nothing.

You should also be aware that some common stocks are riskier than others. There are various analytical services (e.g., Standard & Poor's and Value Line), in addition to security analysts at brokerage firms and various financial institutions, that assess degrees of risk. There are also what are called "blue chip" stocks, i.e., high-quality stocks (e.g., AT&T, General Electric, and Texaco), but even with the blue chips you should realize that nothing is guaranteed.

Bonds: With convertible bonds, you can take advantage of obtaining a fixed income, but if the common stock does appreciate in value, you can convert into the common stock (check first, however, whether conversion is into common stock or some other security) and can then take advantage of the growth. There are also other situations with bonds where you have the possibility of capital gains.

Investment companies: The purpose of an investment company is to provide you with professional management and more diversification than you would otherwise get for your investments. There are many types of investment companies, e.g., some are speculative and some are conservative, some specialize in certain industries and some cover all industries. You should decide which one you want (if any). The guiding legislation is the Investment Company Act of 1940.

The fundamental concept is for many small investors to pool their money, to take advantage of large block trading of securities, and to get diversification (i.e., to avoid putting all your eggs in one basket).

There are two main types of investment companies:

The open-end investment company (also called a "mutual fund")

The closed-end investment company

The mutual fund has to stand ready to buy back the shares you bought whenever you demand it. With a closed-end investment company, the shares already bought do not have to be bought back. The shares of a closed-end investment company sell on stock exchanges (e.g., the New York Stock Exchange), just like other stocks, and have to be bought and sold in the open market with a regular commission paid by you.

There are two types of mutual funds:

The "load fund"

The "no-load fund"

The "load fund" requires an extra charge (or "load") when you buy into the mutual fund. The "no-load fund" makes no extra charge. A large part of the extra charge of the load fund goes to the paying of a commission. There is no particular advantage to either type. What ultimately counts for *you* is the ability of the management. Will your mutual fund shares appreciate in value. What you have to know is whether the fund is profitable, what its potential is, how it compares with others, and whether it fits in with your goals.

## KEEP GOOD RECORDS

Keep a daily record of all your expenses. Set up a sheet of paper for each month and draw columns to itemize expenses for food, clothing, transportation, medical treatment, dental treatment, membership dues, recreation, and miscellaneous expenses.*

Keep a record of future expenses by month and type of expense. Keep a careful record of any fixed payments that will have to be made. For example:

Rent or mortgage payments
Auto loan payments
Personal loan payments
Installment payments (e.g., for appliances, furniture, TV sets)
Credit card payments
Membership dues
Educational expenses
Insurance premiums
Estimated income tax payments (if applicable)

Keep a careful record of all incoming money and try to live, as much as possible, on the money coming in without drawing down your savings accounts.

### Using Your Records

Be sure to use your records. They should not just be collected and stared at. Look for trends (daily, weekly, monthly and annual trends) in your expenses and income. Break up your income into predictable and unpredictable income. Predictable income would be, for example, your salary or interest income from bonds. Unpredictable income would be, for example, the income you get from the sale of stock or an unexpected fee for special work. Try to use the predictable income for paying for regular

---

*In strict accounting practice, a distinction is drawn between an expenditure and an expense. An expenditure refers to the acquisition of an asset, while an expense refers to the consumption of an asset.

expenses (e.g., the groceries) and to save as much of the unpredictable income as you possibly can. Records can help you in these ways and many other ways.

Ask yourself these simple questions:

Do I know where my money is going?
Am I getting what I want for my money in all cases?
Am I getting value for my money?

You should also be sure to know where you keep your valuable papers.

## SAFE DEPOSIT BOX

Use a safe deposit box for your valuables and keep an accurate record of what you keep in your safe deposit box.

Such things as the following should be kept in the safe deposit box:

Money market instruments (keep a record at home of the date on which you bought each money market instrument, its maturity date and its yield)

Stock certificates (keep a record at home for each stock certificate of the number of shares covered, the par value, if any, the certificate number, the date on which you acquired the stock, and the price you paid for the stock)

Bond certificates (keep a record at home of the par value, maturity date, interest rate, certificate number, the date on which you acquired the bond, and the price you paid for the bond).

U.S. Savings bonds (keep a record at home, for each bond, of the names in which it is registered, the beneficiaries, if any, the series, the face amount, the date of issue, the price you paid, the maturity date, the bond number and the date on which you cashed it in)

Leases

Deeds

Tax receipts

Income tax records

Legal documents

Any important cancelled checks

Birth certificates

Marriage certificates

Military service discharge papers

Citizenship papers

Social Security cards

Wills

Jewelry

## CONCLUSION

In conclusion, be wary, at all times, of "get rich quick" schemes. Invest your money carefully and wisely. Be sure that your investment fits in with your goals, not somebody else's, whether that person is a broker, investment counselor, banker, or another person. Others can help and give advice, but your investment must fit in with your goals. You have to make the decisions.

To help you formulate your decisions and consider the alternative courses of action, information is essential. For that, you would do well to look at the various sources of information listed in Appendix E, under the title "Where You Can Get Information and Data on a Continuous Basis." Keep up with the latest developments.

It is important to set goals for yourself and to make plans, but don't become a slave to your goals and plans. It is absolutely essential, however, to keep up with the latest information and data. You may have to change your goals and plans when conditions change. Be flexible!

# money markets

# 2

In newspaper and magazine articles and on television programs, the money markets are often referred to as the "money market." As you shall see, there are several markets, encompassed by the financial securities involved. Nevertheless, the use of the term "money market" does emphasize an important point, that the various money markets operate with a considerable degree of unity. Thus, their patterns and responses to economic conditions are quite similar. This unity often contrasts with the variations in movements found in the capital markets (i.e., the world of stocks and bonds), where the common stock of different industrial groups and different types of bonds often deviate quite widely.

Differences do exist in the various money market instruments, but, because their patterns and responses are quite similar, these securities are close substitutes for each other in investment portfolios. Consequently, the yields (or rates of return) on these securities usually fluctuate together. A particular money market instrument may deviate from the pattern of the other instruments; however, over time, strong pressure is exerted on it to fall into line with the others.

At this point, let us define our terms. Money market instruments are short-term securities. They are generally thought of as securities with maturities of up to one year, although the maturities do extend up to five years. Securities with maturities of five years or over are considered part of the capital markets.

Money market instruments are also securities which usually possess a high degree of safety and liquidity (i.e., they are readily converted into cash).

The following list gives you the order in which the money markets will be dealt with. Each of the markets is thoroughly described.

*U.S. Treasury bills:* These securities are the most liquid of investments. They also possess a very high degree of safety, because they are backed by the U.S. government. They are very popular forms of investment. Maturity periods range up to one year.

*U.S. Treasury notes:* These securities are not quite as liquid as U.S. Treasury bills, but they have the same degree of safety, because they are also backed by the U.S. government. Maturity periods range from one year to seven years.

*U.S. government agency securities and related securities:* These securities have become increasingly popular over the past few years. This market is characterized by a very high degree of structure. The growing popularity of these securities is due to the fact that, although the safety and liquidity features are somewhat less than for U.S. Treasury bills and U.S. Treasury notes, they usually offer higher yields. Many financial innovations have taken place in this market.

*Commercial paper:* This is the oldest of the U.S. money market instruments. Its long history has resulted in a highly sophisticated market. During the stock market decline of 1969 to the end of 1974, commercial paper represented an important investment alternative to common stock (the usual type of stock bought). Maturity periods range up to nine months.

*Negotiable certificates of deposit:* These have been great favorites as investments for many money market funds. They are issued by commercial banks. Their appeal has been rates of return generally higher than for other U.S. money market instruments and the existence of a fairly substantial secondary market, although certainly thinner than that for U.S. Treasury bills, combined usually with the safety of financially solid commercial banks.

*Bankers' acceptances:* These securities are used primarily in connection with international trade. Maturity periods usually range from 30 to 180 days (with 90 days the most common). Maturities can be tailored to the periods necessary for the shipping and disposal of goods. There is considerable safety and liquidity, although they are not as high as for U.S. Treasury bills.

*Federal funds market:* This market is extremely important. It lies at the very heart of the money markets. As it exerts an influence over all the money markets, you must understand it in order to fully appreciate the significance of the money markets and the effects of national monetary policy. Thus, the

Federal Reserve System in the second half of 1974 and in early 1975 exerted strong pressure to bring down the highly critical Federal funds rate. The Federal Reserve System was successful, which helped prevent the recession from becoming worse. In the absence of the action of the Federal Reserve System, the United States might have been thrown into a depression of the catastrophic dimensions of the 1930s. (See Appendix A for details on the Federal funds market.)

# U.S. Treasury Bills

*What are U.S. Treasury bills?*

They are IOUs of the U.S. Treasury Department, which are backed by the full faith and credit of the United States government. New Treasury bills are currently issued with maturities of three months, six months and one year.

*In what form are U.S. Treasury bills available?*

*They are available only in bearer form.* This means that they are bought without the investor's name on them, which makes them easily transferable from one owner to another. For this reason, Treasury bills must be *safeguarded as carefully as cash. They can be given away, sold or redeemed (turned in for repayment from the U.S. Treasury Department) without your signature or knowledge.* Your Treasury bills cannot be registered in your name at the U.S. Treasury Department.

*Do U.S. Treasury bills bear interest?*

*U.S. Treasury bills do not bear interest. They are sold at discount.* This means that they earn a return for you only when you buy them at

*In what denominations are U.S. Treasury bills currently issued?*

less than the face value (the issued denomination).

Currently, new Treasury bills are issued in the following denominations:

$10,000
$15,000
$50,000
$100,000
$500,000
$1,000,000

You can buy Treasury bills in multiples of $5,000 above the minimum purchase of $10,000 by combining $10,000 and $15,000 denominations.

*Why are U.S. Treasury bills sold?*

They are sold as one means by which the U.S. Treasury Department can obtain the money it needs to finance programs of the United States government.

*At what prices are new U.S. Treasury bills sold?*

They are sold at prices determined by the competitive bidding of investors at scheduled U.S. Treasury auctions. *Prices are not set by the U.S. Treasury Department.* Inasmuch as Treasury bills do not bear interest, investors must bid prices lower than the face value of the Treasury bills in order to get a return. The return is simply the difference between the price paid and the amount received.

*What are the alternative courses of action for you to obtain a return on your money?*

You have the following alternatives for obtaining a return on your money:

holding the Treasury bills until maturity, so that your return is the difference between what you originally paid and what you obtain at maturity, or

accepting the difference between what you originally paid and the market value, if you sell the Treasury bills before maturity.

*How can you buy new U.S. Treasury bills at an auction?*

You can submit either a *competitive or a noncompetitive bid* (called a "tender"):

*If you submit a competitive tender,* you must specify the price that you are willing to pay. With a competitive tender you risk not getting any Treasury bills by bidding too low, because the U.S. Treasury can accept or reject any tender.

*If you submit a noncompetitive tender,* you do not have to specify a price. You agree to pay the average price of the competitive tenders accepted by the U.S. Treasury. You are very likely to have your tender accepted, because the U.S. Treasury normally accepts all noncompetitive tenders.

*Are there any limits on the amount of each new U.S. Treasury bill issue that you may buy?*

There is no limit on the amount of each new Treasury bill issue that you may buy in any one name by competitive tender. Noncompetitive tenders in any one name, however, are limited to a maximum of $200,000 for each new Treasury bill issue.

*Where can you submit a noncompetitive tender?*

You can submit a noncompetitive tender directly to the Federal Reserve Bank in the district in which you live (see the chapter entitled "Federal Reserve System and the U.S. Banking System" for the address of the Federal Reserve Bank in your district). Each Federal Reserve Bank acts as the U.S. Treasury Department's agent in Treasury bill transactions with investors in the Bank's district. There is no change when you submit a noncompetitive tender directly to a Federal Reserve Bank. A commercial bank can also submit a noncompetitive tender for you, but the bank may charge a fee for this service.

*Where are auctions held for U.S. Treasury bills?*

Auctions for new three-month and six-month Treasury bills are held weekly on Mondays (the previous Friday if Monday is a bank holiday). Auctions for new one-year Treasury bills are held approximately every four weeks. The announcement usually appears in the financial pages of local newspapers.

*When can you submit a noncompetitive tender?*

You can submit the tender in person (between 9 A.M. and 3 P.M.) or by mail. To make sure it is received in time for the auction, submit the tender any business day before the auction. You can submit it on the auction date, but it must be received by 1:30 P.M. (New York City time) by the Federal Reserve Bank on the date of the auction. A tender received after 1:30 P.M. (New York City time) on the auction date will be held for the next weekly auction, unless you specifically request that it be returned to you.

*How can you pay for new U.S. Treasury bills?*

There are two ways:

Submit payment for the full face value of the Treasury bills with your tender.

A Federal Reserve Bank check for the difference between the purchase price and the face value of the Treasury bills (called a "discount check") will then be mailed to you on the issue date. For example, you would receive a check for $150 if the purchase price turns out to be $9,850 for a $10,000 Treasury bill.

Submit partial payment of 2% of the face value ($200 on a $10,000 Treasury bill, for example) with your tender. Make this partial payment in one of the acceptable forms (as indicated in the answer to the following question). The balance of the purchase price ($9,650 if the purchase price is $9,850 for a $10,000 Treasury bill) must also be made in an acceptable form. Payment in U.S. currency, by Federal funds check, or in maturing Treasury bills may be made on the issue date. Payment by certified personal check or by official bank check must be made before the issue date and must be made at least three business days before the issue date to avoid delaying delivery of your Treasury bills until the check is collected.

Note: If you fail to make final payment in an acceptable form on the issue date, your tender will be cancelled and your partial payment will either be kept or returned to you, at the U.S. Treasury Department's option.

*What are the acceptable forms of payment?*

The following are the acceptable forms of payment:

U.S. currency

certified personal check

official bank check (for example, a commercial bank's cashier's check or treasurer's check or a savings bank's teller's check)

Federal funds check (a check drawn

by a commercial bank on its Federal Reserve account)
Treasury bills maturing on or before the issue date of the new Treasury bills

NOTE: The check must be drawn in U.S. dollars and collectible at par; the check must be payable on its face to the Federal Reserve Bank (endorsed checks cannot be accepted); print your name on the check if it is not a certified personal check so it can be identified with your tender.

*What are the issue dates for new U.S. Treasury bills?*

New three-month and six-month Treasury bills are issued on the Thursday following the weekly auction (Friday if Thursday is a bank holiday). New one-year Treasury bills are issued on the Tuesday following the auction (Wednesday if Tuesday is a bank holiday).

*When can you take delivery of your new U.S. Treasury bills?*

There are two classifications for the time of delivery depending on the time and form of payment:

There is no delay in delivery. The new Treasury bills may be picked up between 11 A.M. and 3 P.M. on the business day following the issue date or between 9 A.M. and 3 P.M. on any of the next five business days when there is:

full payment with the tender.

partial payment with the tender and full payment in U.S. currency, by Federal funds check or in maturing Treasury bills on the issue date.

partial payment with the tender and full payment by certified check or official bank check at least three business days before the issue date.

There is a two-day delay in delivery. The new Treasury bills may be picked up between 9 A.M. and 3 P.M. on the third through eighth business days after the issue date when there is partial payment with the tender and final payment by certified personal check or official bank check one or two business days before the issue date.

*How can you take delivery of your new U.S. Treasury bills?*

There are two ways to take delivery:

You, or a representative authorized in writing by you, can pick them up at the Federal Reserve Bank. Make sure a sample of your representative's signature appears in your letter, because your representative must sign for your new Treasury bills.

You do have the option of having your Treasury bills mailed to you. If mailed, the Treasury bills will be sent registered first class mail and insured at the U.S. Treasury Department's expense. Delivery may take two to four weeks. The Treasury bills will be delivered to you or someone authorized in writing by you in your tender to accept delivery. They become your responsibility once delivery is accepted.

NOTE: Once you submit your tender with delivery instructions, you cannot change them and you cannot leave your Treasury bills with the Federal Reserve Bank. If they are not picked up within the time specified or accepted by mail, your tender will be canceled and all or part of your money will be returned at the U.S. Treasury Department's option.

*How do you submit a noncompetitive tender?*

Before the auction, you must submit:

either a letter or a Federal Reserve Bank tender form specifying the Treasury bills you want and payment in an acceptable form (as already indicated).

*Who can submit a noncompetitive tender?*

You can submit the tender yourself. If, however, you are unable or do not wish to submit the tender yourself, you can have a friend, relative or financial institution submit it for you. A U.S. Treasury regulation requires that you sign the tender. The only exception is that a commercial bank is permitted to submit a tender in its own name to buy new Treasury bills for you. This regulation is partly for your protection, because the check for the discount will be payable to the person who signs the tender and the new Treasury bills will be delivered according to the signer's instructions.

*What information should you give if you submit a letter for a noncompetitive tender?*

If you submit a letter, be sure to type or print carefully and give the following information:

the face amount of the Treasury bills that you want

the maturity that you want (three months, six months or one year)

the mailing address for the discount check

the delivery instructions for the Treasury bills

the date and your name below your signature

*Where can you obtain forms for noncompetitive tenders?*

You can obtain forms for noncompetitive tenders by writing to:

Securities Department
Federal Reserve Bank of New
York
33 Liberty Street
New York, N.Y. 10045

A sample form for a noncompetitive tender for three-month Treasury bills is shown in Figure 2-1.

**FIGURE 2-1**

```
              NONCOMPETITIVE TENDER FOR 3-MONTH TREASURY BILLS

                                    Date _____


                               ┌─────────────────────────────────┐
                               │ FOR FEDERAL RESERVE USE ONLY     │
                               │                                  │
                               │ Series dated_____    │
                               │ Date issued_____     │
  Securities Department        │ Maturity date_____     │
  Federal Reserve Bank of New York └───────────────────────────────┘
  33 Liberty Street
  New York, N.Y.  10045

  Gentlemen:

  This noncompetitive tender is submitted in the amount of $_____
                                                            $10,000 or multiple
  for the next auction of 3-month Treasury bills.


  Payment for the full face amount of the bills is enclosed in the form of

            ☐  a certified personal check or a bank (cashier's) check payable
               to the Federal Reserve Bank of New york;

            ☐  cash;

            ☐  Treasury bills maturing on or before the issue date.


  On issuance, the bills

            ☐  should be mailed to the bidder;

            ☐  will be picked up by the bidder between 11 a.m. and 3 p.m. on
               the business day following the issue date.


  The check for the discount will be mailed to the bidder.


  The bidder's name and complete address are


      _____      _____
             Print or type                  Bidder's signature

      _____

      _____

      _____
```

*Where should your tender and payment be sent?*

Mail your tender and payment to the Securities Department at the above indicated address or to the Federal Reserve Bank in your district.

NOTE: Print or type "Tender for Treasury bills" along the bottom of your envelope.

*What are the major steps for buying new U.S. Treasury bills?*

Decide on the total amount and the maturity that you want.

Decide whether to submit a competitive tender and where and when to submit your tender.

Decide how to pay.

Decide when and how to take delivery.

Decide how to submit your tender.

Submit your tender and payment.

Take delivery of your Treasury bills. Remember to safeguard them as carefully as cash.

*How can you make a denominational exchange?*

You can exchange denominations (for example, one $50,000 Treasury bill for five $10,000 Treasury bills or vice versa) at any time. The exchange can be processed at a Federal Reserve Bank without a charge or through a commercial bank, which may charge a fee for the service. If you exchange denominations at a Federal Reserve Bank, deliver the Treasury bills or mail them (registered and insured at your expense) to the Federal Reserve Bank (for example, the Federal Reserve Bank of New York). The new denominations will be sent to you by registered first class mail and insured at your expense (you will be billed for the postage and insurance).

*How can you cash U.S. Treasury bills before maturity?*

You must sell them privately or in the securities market through a commercial bank or a securities broker. You cannot cash them at a Federal Reserve Bank or at the U.S. Treasury Department before maturity.

*What does it mean to "roll over" maturing U.S. Treasury bills?*

To "roll over" Treasury bills means to reinvest the proceeds of maturing Treasury bills for new Treasury bills.

*How can you roll over maturing U.S. Treasury bills?*

You can roll over maturing Treasury bills for new Treasury bills by following the procedures for buying new Treasury bills (as already outlined). A discount check for the difference between the purchase price of the new Treasury bills and the face value of the maturing Treasury bills will be mailed to you first class on the issue date of the new Treasury bills. You can take delivery of the new Treasury bills in the same way as for your first purchase of Treasury bills.

*How can you redeem maturing U.S. Treasury bills?*

You can redeem maturing Treasury bills at a Federal Reserve Bank (for example, the Federal Reserve Bank of New York) without a charge or through a commercial bank, which may charge a fee for the service. The redemption is made by Treasury check, not in cash. The check can be cashed in person at the U.S. Treasury Department's Washington, D.C., office (but not at a Federal Reserve Bank) or it can be deposited in a checking account or a savings account for collection. If you redeem Treasury bills at a Federal Reserve Bank, deliver the Treasury bills or mail them (*registered and insured at your expense*) to reach the Federal Reserve Bank at least two business days before the maturity date. The check can be picked up on the maturity date if your Treasury bills are received by the Federal Reserve Bank at least two business days before that date. If not picked up, the check will be mailed to you first class on the maturity date.

*How can you calculate the rate of return of your Treasury bills?*

Inasmuch as Treasury bills are purchased at less than face value and are redeemed at face value without interest at maturity, your return is the difference between the purchase price and the face value (assuming that you hold them to maturity). This difference is called the "*discount.*" For example, the discount is $150 if the purchase price was $9,850 for a $10,000 Treasury bill. If the Treasury bill has a three-month maturity, the approximate annual rate of return can be calculated by first dividing the discount of $150 by the purchase price of $9,850 and then dividing the result by the fraction $\frac{3}{12}$, which represents the Treasury bill's three-month maturity over twelve months. Thus:

$$\frac{\$150}{\$9,850} = 0.0152$$

$$\frac{0.0152}{3/12} = 0.0608 = 6.08\% \text{ per year}$$

If the Treasury bill has a maturity of six months or one year, the fraction 3/12 becomes 6/12 or 12/12, respectively. The 6.08% per year is the approximate annual rate (within a few hundredths of a percentage point). The actual rate can be calculated by using precise figures in the formula (i.e., the exact discount and purchase price in dollars and cents and the exact number of days to maturity over a 365-day (or 366-day) year.

*Where and how are the results of U.S. Treasury bill auctions reported?*

The results of Treasury auctions are reported in the financial pages of many local newspapers the day after the auction. Two rates are given for the average purchase price of new Treasury bills, a discount rate and a coupon-equivalent rate. The coupon-equivalent rate is your rate of return if you submitted a non-competitive tender.

*Does the Federal Reserve Bank or the U.S. Treasury Department notify you of your rate of return?*

No. Neither the Federal Reserve Bank nor the U.S. Treasury Department notifies you of your rate of return.

*What is the tax status of U.S. Treasury bills?*

The income from Treasury bills is subject to Federal income taxes, but is exempt from state and local government income taxes. The income is defined as the difference between the purchase price and either:

the face (maturity) value of the Treasury bills if they are held to maturity, or

the market value of the Treasury bills if they are sold, given away, or otherwise disposed of before maturity.

The income is considered earned during the year the Treasury bills are redeemed, sold, given away, or otherwise disposed of. Since Treasury bills are not considered capital assets under the Internal Revenue Code, any gain or loss on them is considered ordinary gain or loss, even if they are held for more than six months.

Treasury bills are also subject to Federal and state inheritance, estate, gift, and other excise taxes.

## INFORMATION IN DEPTH

U.S. Treasury bills are the best-known and most popular of the money market instruments. As short-term investment vehicles, they traditionally account for the largest dollar volume outstanding. The Treasury bill, however, does not offer the highest yield of the money market instruments. The great prestige accorded the Treasury bill lies rather in its liquidity, which is a particularly relevant consideration these days. An asset possesses the property of liquidity when it can be converted into cash very quickly and easily without any serious risk of capital loss.

Of the financial assets, there is no other, in general, which can be sold as easily as a Treasury bill. In addition, it possesses the highest credit rating, because the full faith and credit of the United States government stands behind it. Its liquidity is further enhanced by the fact that there is a highly developed secondary market for selling Treasury bills before maturity, because government securities dealers stand ready to buy and sell U.S. Treasury bills.

Other important factors regarding Treasury bills are:

They provide an excellent medium for the U.S. Treasury Department to raise large amounts of money without disturbing the money markets very much and

they are the main means by which the Federal Reserve System influences the bank reserves on a day-to-day basis and enforces monetary policies.

### Development of the Market

Treasury bills have grown in significance since they were first issued. In June 1929, Congress enacted legislation which authorized the issuance of Treasury bills. The first public offering of U.S. Treasury bills was made in December 1929, with a total offering of $100 million sold at an average discount of 3.30%.

### Types of Treasury Bills

Below are listed some of the types of Treasury bills that have been issued:

The three-month Treasury bill is the oldest type of bill issued by the U.S. Treasury. It is the best known for the small investor.

The six-month Treasury bill was first introduced on a regular weekly basis in December 1958, with an initial offering of $400 million. Attempts were made to sell six-month Treasury bills in 1934 and 1935, but no further attempts were made until 1958, because a strong preference for the three-month bill had been observed. After 1958, a strong market for six-month Treasury bills opened up.

The nine-month Treasury bill was started in September 1966 on a regular basis. As with the six-month bill, attempts were originally made in 1934 and 1935, but were abandoned due to the public's strong preference for the three-month bill. This type is not offered at the present time.

The one-year (12-month or 52-week) bill was offered for the first time on a regular monthly cycle basis in September 1963, when the monthly issue was set at $1.0 billion. Treasury bills with one-year maturities had been sold before 1963, but on a quarterly rather than a monthly basis. In three separate auctions during 1959, the U.S. Treasury sold bills with maturities of 9½ to 12 months. During 1960, the one-year series was "regularized" on a quarterly basis, with $1.5 billion worth of bills issued in January, April, July, and October.

The tax-anticipation bill ("tax bill") was first started in October 1951 for the specific purpose of attracting the money that corporations accumulate for income tax purposes. Tax bills serve to smooth out the U.S. Treasury's uneven flow of tax receipts while providing corporations with an investment vehicle. Maturity dates on tax bills are set for a week after quarterly corporate tax-payment dates. Thus, bills that can be turned in to pay for taxes due on June 15 will be scheduled to mature on June 22. Holders also have the option of redeeming tax bills for cash on the maturity date, but this option is not exercised very often, because tax bills are accepted for tax payments at the full maturity value of the bills.

Most of the tax bills (especially before 1966) were scheduled to mature in March and June and were usually sold between August and December of each year. U.S. Treasury cash receipts generally exceed cash payments during the January-June period. The sale of tax bills in the second half of the year was synchronized well with the U.S. Treasury's cash management. In 1966, tax legislation changed the pattern of corporate tax payments and, as a result, the scheduled maturity distribution of tax bills. This change has served to make tax bills maturing in April and September somewhat more popular. Most tax bills, however, still run off in the first half of the calendar year and most sales take place in the second half of the year.

Tax bills are not offered on a regular basis (i.e., weekly or monthly). They are instead coordinated with the U.S. Treasury's estimates of cash income and outgo. (See Appendix C for data on U.S. Treasury bills.)

## U.S. DEPARTMENT OF THE TREASURY
## CALCULATION OF THE BOND-EQUIVALENT YIELD
## FOR U.S. TREASURY BILLS
### (Formulas for Calculating the True Yield)

There are two formulas for calculating the true yield of U.S. Treasury bills. Which one you use depends upon the maturity period you are considering.

The formula for calculating the true yield for U.S. Treasury bills with a term of a half year or less is as follows:

$$\frac{\text{Discount (100 minus average price)} \times 365 \text{ (number of days in a year)}}{\text{Average price} \times \text{number of days for the issue}}$$

The method and formula for calculating the true yield for U.S. Treasury bills with a term of more than a half year and less than a whole year are as follows, together with an illustrative example.

### The Meaning of the Symbols

$P$ = price (average price of issue)

$I$ = true yield of issue at simple interest, i.e.:

$$\frac{\text{Discount} \times \text{number of days in the year}}{\text{Price} \times \text{number of days for issue}}$$

expressed as a decimal.

$C$ = number of interest periods to be compounded

N = number of days in excess of a half year.

S = number of days in semi-annual period (normally 182.5 days, but, if the term of the U.S. Treasury bill includes February 29th, the period would be 183 days)

## The computations

1. Calculate the true yield at simple interest (I).
2. Arbitrarily select two yields several basis points below the yield at simple interest, as determined in Step 1 (e.g., if the yield is 2.91996%, you can use 2.86% and 2.90%).
3. For both numbers selected in Step 2, compute the answer to the following formula (using each selected number in turn for "I"):

$$\left(1 + \frac{I}{C}\right)\left(1 + \frac{N}{S} \times \frac{I}{C}\right) \div \frac{100}{P}$$

*Note:* Although it is unlikely that the result of either calculation will be exactly 1.00, if this does happen, the interest yield used to arrive at 1.00 would be the true yield compounded, and it would not be necessary to make any further computations.

4. a. Compute the difference between the two figures obtained in Step 3.
   b. Subtract the lesser of the two figures obtained in Step 3 from 1.00.
   c. Divide the difference found in Step b by the difference found in Step a.
   d. Multiply the quotient found in step c by the difference between the two yields selected in Step 2 (e.g., 0.0290 − 0.0286 = 0.0004).
5. Add the product of Step 4d to the lesser of the two yields selected in Step 2. The sum will be the true yield for the issue compounded semi-annually.

*Note:* In making the computations, carry out the calculations to seven decimal places.

## An Illustrative Example

To find the true yield of a U.S. Treasury bill issue of 252 days at an average price of 98.023864:

1. $\dfrac{1.976136 \times 365}{98.023864 \times 252} = 0.0291996$ (or 2.91996%)

2. 2.86% and 2.90% (expressed as decimals, 0.0286 and 0.0290)

3. a.
$$\left(1 + \frac{0.0286}{2}\right)\left(1 + \frac{69.5}{182.5} \times \frac{0.0286}{2}\right) \div \frac{100}{98.023864}$$
$$= (1 + 0.0143)(1 + 0.03808219 \times 0.0143) \div 1.0201597$$

$$= (1.0143)\,(1.0054458) \div 1.0201597$$
$$= 1.0198237 \div 1.0201597$$
$$= 0.9996706$$

b.

$$\left(1 + \frac{0.290)}{2}\right)\left(1 + \frac{69.5}{182.5} \times \frac{0.0290)}{2}\right) \div \frac{100}{98.023864}$$
$$= (1 + 0.0145)\,(1 + 0.3808219 \times 0.0145) \div 1.0201597$$
$$= (1.0145)\,(1.0055219) \div 1.0201597$$
$$= 1.0201020 \div 1.0201597$$
$$= 0.9999434$$

4. a.

$$\begin{array}{r} 0.9999434 \\ - 0.9996706 \\ \hline 0.0002728 \end{array}$$

b.

$$\begin{array}{r} 1.0000000 \\ - 0.9996706 \\ \hline 0.0003294 \end{array}$$

c.

$$\frac{0.0003294}{0.0002728} = 1.2075$$

d.

$$1.2075 \times (0.0290 - 0.0286)$$
$$= 1.2075 \times 0.0004$$
$$= 0.00048300 \ (\text{or expressed as a percent, } 0.048300\%)$$

5. Take the lower value of the two values chosen (i.e., 2.86%)

$$\begin{array}{r} 2.86 \quad \% \\ + \ 0.048300\% \\ \hline 2.908300\% \end{array}$$

## Notes

1. The foregoing material or yield calculation has been presented with the permission of the U.S. Department of the Treasury.
2. At the time of writing, the U.S. Department of the Treasury was considering proposals for changing the manner in which it calculates and presents the yields on its debt obligations. These proposals, from the securities and banking industries, have been the subject of several meetings between U.S. Treasury officials and committees from those industries.
3. Maturity periods can be quoted in different ways. Thus, a one-year Treasury bill can be quoted as a one-year, 12-month, or 52-week bill. Maturity periods can be given in months (e.g., 3 months, 6 months, 9 months, 12 months) or weeks (e.g., 13 weeks, 26 weeks) or days (e.g., 91 days, 182 days, 252 days).

# U.S. Treasury Notes

*What are U.S. Treasury notes?*

U.S. Treasury notes are direct obligations (IOUs) of the United States government.

*How often is the interest paid?*

The interest is payable semi-annually.

*In what form is the interest paid?*

The interest is paid either by coupon or by check.

*In what denominations are U.S. Treasury notes issued?*

Treasury notes are issued in the following denominations:

$1,000
$5,000
$10,000
$100,000
$1,000,000

*What is the minimum amount that you can purchase of new U.S. Treasury notes?*

$1,000

*How can you buy new U.S. Treasury notes?*

You may subscribe, in person, on the days of the offering at the Federal Reserve Bank in the district in which you live (See the chapter entitled "Federal Reserve System and the U.S. Banking System" for the address of the Federal Reserve Bank in your district). If you cannot come in person, your subscription and payment may be mailed to the Federal Reserve Bank. Your subscription must be received in the

Federal Reserve Bank no later than the time indicated in the offering notice. Late subscriptions are not accepted.

*How can you pay for new U.S. Treasury notes?*

There are two ways:

(1) The simpler way is to make payment for the full face value of the Treasury notes with your subscription, in one of the following forms:

(a) in U.S. currency (if you appear in person).

(b) by certified personal check or by official bank check (i.e., a cashier's check); the check must be payable on its face to the Federal Reserve Bank (e.g., "Federal Reserve Bank of New York"). Endorsed checks are not accepted. Print your name on the check if it is not a certified personal check, so that it can be associated with your subscription.

(c) in maturing U.S. government securities (only as provided in the offering circular).

(2) The more difficult way to pay is to submit partial payment of the face value of the Treasury notes subscribed to (usually 10%, i.e., $500 for a $5,000 subscription). The partial payment must be submitted with your subscription form on the days of the offering. Final payment must be made on or before the issue date. Only a Federal funds check or U.S. currency will be accepted from individual subscribers on the issue date. If you fail to make final payment on or before the issue date, your subscription will be cancelled and your partial payment will

either be kept or returned to you, at the U.S. Treasury Department's option.

*How do you complete the subscription form?*

The form should be completed to show all the information requested. The back of the form should be completed if you want registered notes and only the front if you want bearer notes. Be sure to complete the lower portion with your name, address, telephone number, and personal signature.

Sample forms are shown in Figures 2-2 and 2-3.

*What is a bearer note?*

A bearer note is payable to anyone who has possession (just like currency). It must be safeguarded as carefully as cash. It carries interest coupons that are clipped and redeemed for cash as they mature every six months. *They may be cashed through a commercial bank or through a Federal Reserve Bank.*

*What is a registered note?*

A registered note is registered as to principal and interest and bears the owner's name on its face. It cannot be negotiated without the owner's written assignment on the back. The signature to the assignment must be certified by an officer of a commercial bank or trust company and must bear the corporate seal (or savings bond validating stamp) of the attesting officer's bank. Interest is mailed semi-annually by check from the U.S. Treasury Department.

## FIGURE 2-2

GB 635 9/74

**NONCOMPETITIVE TENDER FOR SHORT-TERM TREASURY NOTES**

*THIS INFORMATION MUST BE SUPPLIED ON ANY TENDER FOR NOTES OR BONDS*

| DATE | ← | | SUBSCRIPTION NO. |
|---|---|---|---|

**IMPORTANT**

IF THIS SECURITY IS SOLD AT AUCTION THE INVESTOR MAY PAY **MORE OR LESS** THAN FACE VALUE. THIS TENDER WILL BE ACCEPTED SUBJECT TO THE TERMS AND CONDITIONS STATED IN THE OFFICIAL OFFERING CIRCULAR. THE INVESTOR AGREES NOT TO BUY OR SELL, OR TO MAKE ANY AGREEMENTS WITH RESPECT TO THE PURCHASE OR SALE OR OTHER DISPOSITION OF ANY NOTES OF THIS ISSUE AT A SPECIFIC RATE OR PRICE, UNTIL AFTER THE TIME SPECIFIED IN THE OFFICIAL OFFERING CIRCULAR.

TO: FEDERAL RESERVE BANK OF NEW YORK,
Fiscal Agent of the United States

I HEREBY SUBMIT THIS NONCOMPETITIVE TENDER FOR CURRENTLY OFFERED SHORT-TERM TREASURY NOTES IN THE FACE AMOUNT OF

(in multiples of $1,000) → $ *12000*

TYPE OF SECURITIES TO BE ISSUED (CHECK ONE)
☒ BEARER ☐ REGISTERED (Complete Registration Instructions)

DELIVERY INSTRUCTIONS (CHECK ONE)
☒ By Mail ☐ Over the counter to the undersigned

SPECIAL INSTRUCTIONS

**Complete Denominations for Bearer Securities Only**

| Pieces | Denomination | Maturity Value | |
|---|---|---|---|
| 2 | $ 1,000 | 2 | 000 |
| | $ 5,000 | | |
| 1 | $ 10,000 | 10 | 000 |
| | $100,000 | | |
| 3 | Total | 12 | 000 |

**FOR FRB USE ONLY**

| TYPE OF PAYMENT SUBMITTED WITH TENDER | AMOUNT |
|---|---|
| ☐ Check Payable to the Fed. Res. Bk. of N. Y. | $ |
| ☐ Cash | $ |
| ☐ Eligible Maturing Securities | $ |

| Rate | Descript. | Dated | Due | |
|---|---|---|---|---|
| | | | | Teller's Signature |

PLEASE *PRINT* ALL INFORMATION, EXCEPT YOUR SIGNATURE

| Name of Subscriber | J O H N   S M I T H |
|---|---|
| Street Address | 1 2 3   M A I N   S T R E E T |
| City | B R O O K L Y N    State N Y    Zip 1 0 0 0 9 |
| Home Phone | 2 3 4 5 6 7 8    Business Phone |
| Signature of Person Completing this Form | *John Smith* |

**REGISTRATION INSTRUCTIONS**

COMPLETE FOR REGISTERED SECURITIES ONLY

Name(s) Print Only

ID or S.S. No.

Street Address

City            State            Zip

| No. of Pieces | Denomination | Amount | Serial Nos. (Leave Blank) |
|---|---|---|---|
| 30 | $ 1,000 | | |
| 32 | $ 5,000 | | |
| 34 | $ 10,000 | | |
| 38 | $ 100,000 | | |
| 99 | TOTAL | | |

FOR FRB USE ONLY

TR. CASE NO.

TO BE USED FOR SECOND REGISTRATION

Name(s) Print Only

ID or S.S. No.

Street Address

City            State            Zip

| No. of Pieces | Denomination | Amount | Serial Nos. (Leave Blank) |
|---|---|---|---|
| 30 | $ 1,000 | | |
| 32 | $ 5,000 | | |
| 34 | $ 10,000 | | |
| 38 | $ 100,000 | | |
| 99 | TOTAL | | |

FOR FRB USE ONLY

TR. CASE NO.

**SPECIMEN**

| TRANS. ACCOUNTING DATE | ISSUE AGENT 12 | LOAN CODE | INTEREST COMP. DATE | 110—0I |
|---|---|---|---|---|

**TENDER COPY 1**

**FIGURE 2-3**

GB 636 9/74

## NONCOMPETITIVE TENDER FOR LONG-TERM TREASURY NOTES

*THIS INFORMATION MUST BE SUPPLIED ON ANY TENDER*
*FOR NOTES OR BONDS*

| DATE | ← | SUBSCRIPTION NO. |
|------|---|------------------|

**IMPORTANT**

IF THIS SECURITY IS SOLD AT AUCTION THE INVESTOR MAY PAY **MORE OR LESS** THAN FACE VALUE. THIS TENDER WILL BE ACCEPTED SUBJECT TO THE TERMS AND CONDITIONS STATED IN THE OFFICIAL OFFERING CIRCULAR. THE INVESTOR AGREES NOT TO BUY OR SELL, OR TO MAKE ANY AGREEMENTS WITH RESPECT TO THE PURCHASE OR SALE OR OTHER DISPOSITION OF ANY NOTES OF THIS ISSUE AT A SPECIFIC RATE OR PRICE, UNTIL AFTER THE TIME SPECIFIED IN THE OFFICIAL OFFERING CIRCULAR.

TO: FEDERAL RESERVE BANK OF NEW YORK,
Fiscal Agent of the United States

I HEREBY SUBMIT THIS NONCOMPETITIVE TEN-
DER FOR CURRENTLY OFFERED LONG-TERM
TREASURY NOTES IN THE FACE AMOUNT OF

(in multiples of $1,000) → $ 7000

TYPE OF SECURITIES TO BE ISSUED (CHECK ONE)
☐ BEARER    ☒ REGISTERED (Complete Registration Instructions)

DELIVERY INSTRUCTIONS (CHECK ONE)
☒ By Mail    ☐ Over the counter to the undersigned

SPECIAL INSTRUCTIONS

**Complete Denominations for Bearer Securities Only**

| Pieces | Denomination | Maturity Value |
|--------|--------------|----------------|
| | $ 1,000 | |
| | 5,000 | |
| | $ 10,000 | |
| | $100,000 | |
| **Total** | | |

FOR FRB USE ONLY

| TYPE OF PAYMENT SUBMITTED WITH TENDER | AMOUNT |
|---|---|
| ☐ Check Payable to the Fed. Res. Bk. of N. Y. | $ |
| ☐ Cash | $ |
| ☐ Eligible Maturing Securities | $ |

| Rate | Descript. | Dated | Due | |
|------|-----------|-------|-----|--|
| | | | | Teller's Signature |

**PLEASE *PRINT* ALL INFORMATION, EXCEPT YOUR SIGNATURE**

Name of Subscriber: J O H N   S M I T H
Street Address: 1 2 3   M A I N   S T R E E T
City: B R O O K L Y N   State: N Y   Zip: 1 0 0 0 9
Home Phone: 2 3 4 5 6 7 8   Business Phone:
Signature of Person Completing this Form: *John Smith*

### REGISTRATION INSTRUCTIONS

| COMPLETE FOR REGISTERED SECURITIES ONLY | TO BE USED FOR SECOND REGISTRATION |
|---|---|
| Name(s) Print Only<br>JOHN SMITH | Name(s) Print Only |
| ID or S.S. No.<br>123 - 04 - 5678 | ID or S.S. No. |
| Street Address<br>123 MAIN ST. | Street Address |
| City  BROOKLYN  State N.Y.  Zip 10009 | City  State  Zip |

| No. of Pieces | | Denomination | Amount | Serial Nos. (Leave Blank) | No. of Pieces | | Denomination | Amount | Serial Nos. (Leave Blank) |
|---|---|---|---|---|---|---|---|---|---|
| 30 | 2 | $ 1,000 | 2 000 | | 30 | | $ 1,000 | | |
| 32 | 1 | $ 5,000 | 5 000 | | 32 | | $ 5,000 | | |
| 34 | | $ 10,000 | | | 34 | | $ 10,000 | | |
| 38 | | $ 100,000 | | | 38 | | $ 100,000 | | |
| 99 | 3 | TOTAL | 7 000 | | 99 | | TOTAL | | |

FOR FRB USE ONLY | FOR FRB USE ONLY

# SPECIMEN

| TR. CASE NO. | | TR. CASE NO. |
|---|---|---|

| TRANS. ACCOUNTING DATE | **ISSUE AGENT 12** | LOAN CODE | INTEREST COMP. DATE | **110 — 01** |
|---|---|---|---|---|

**TENDER COPY 1**

*In what forms can a U.S. Treasury note be registered?*

A Treasury note can be registered in the following forms:

*One Name:* John Smith (Social Security number)

*Two Names:* John Smith (Social Security number) *or* Mrs. John Smith.

John Smith (Social Security number) *and* Mrs. Jane Smith

*Note:* either party's Social Security number is acceptable.

*Minors:* John Smith as natural guardian of Benjamin Smith, a minor (Social Security number of natural guardian)

John Smith, as custodian for David Smith, a minor (Social Security number of custodian) under the New York State Uniform Gifts to Minors Act.

*Note:* A Treasury note may not be registered with only the name of a minor appearing on it.

1947698

*How are U.S. Treasury notes delivered?*

You may take possession of the Treasury notes, in person, at the Federal Reserve Bank or request that they be sent to you by registered mail, at the expense of the U.S. Treasury Department. In either case, allow several weeks for delivery.

*What is the tax status of U.S. Treasury notes?*

The income from Treasury notes is subject to Federal income taxes but is exempt from state and local government income taxes. Treasury notes are also subject to Federal and state inheritance, estate, gift, and other excise taxes.

## INFORMATION IN DEPTH

Private individuals have become increasingly interested in U.S. Treasury notes over the past few years, because the minimum purchase is only $1,000 as compared to a minimum purchase of $10,000 for U.S. Treasury bills. In addition, the liquidity of Treasury notes runs very close to that of Treasury bills.

While Treasury bills have maturities ranging up to one year, Treasury notes are issued in maturities which vary from one year to seven years. They are sold with fixed interest rates, unlike Treasury bills, which are sold at discount. In addition, unlike Treasury bills, the U.S. Treasury Department has to take into account market conditions and national and international economic developments when setting the interest rates on Treasury notes.

Commercial banks have historically purchased large amounts of Treasury notes and have intentionally varied the maturity periods of their Treasury note portfolios, in order to achieve flexibility in future financing situations. Private individuals can operate in a similar manner.

A breakdown of the ownership of Treasury notes is shown in Appendix C.

**FIGURE 2-4**

---

FEDERAL RESERVE BANK
OF NEW YORK
Fiscal Agent of the United States

$$\left[\begin{array}{l}\text{Circular No. } \textbf{7526} \\ \text{December 16, 1974}\end{array}\right]$$

## Auction of $2 Billion of New Treasury Notes

*To All Banking Institutions, and Others Concerned,*
*in the Second Federal Reserve District:*

The following statements were issued on December 13 by the Treasury Department:

### TREASURY TO ROLL OVER NOTES IN QUARTERLY CYCLE

The Treasury will refund $1.9 billion of notes held by the public maturing December 31, 1974, by selling $2.0 billion of 2-year notes maturing December 31, 1976. Additional amounts of these notes may be issued at the average price of accepted tenders to Government accounts and to Federal Reserve Banks for themselves and as agents of foreign and international monetary authorities.

The notes will be sold at auction, on a yield basis, on Monday, December 23. Bidders must state the yield they will accept on the basis of a percentage to two decimal places. The coupon rate will be set, after the auction, at the ⅛ of one percent which is nearest to the average yield on accepted tenders and which produces an average price at or below par. The minimum denomination of these notes will be $5,000.

The payment date for the notes will be December 31, 1974. Payment may not be made by credit to Treasury tax and loan accounts.

This is the second rollover of notes in the quarterly cycle of 2-year maturities started in 1972.

### DETAILS OF TREASURY ANNOUNCEMENT OF AUCTION OF $2 BILLION OF NOTES

The Treasury will auction under competitive and noncompetitive bidding $2.0 billion, or thereabouts of 2-year notes to raise cash for refunding $1.9 billion of notes held by the public maturing December 31, 1974. The coupon rate for the notes will be determined after tenders are allotted. Additional amounts of the notes may be issued to Government accounts and to Federal Reserve Banks for themselves and as agents of foreign and international monetary authorities.

The notes to be issued will be Treasury Notes of Series K-1976 dated December 31, 1974, due December 31, 1976 (CUSIP No. 912827 EB4) with interest payable semiannually on June 30 and December 31. They will be issued in registered and bearer form in denominations of $5,000, $10,000, $100,000 and $1,000,000, and in book-entry form to designated bidders. Delivery of bearer notes will be made on or about January 6, 1975. A purchaser of bearer notes may elect to receive an interim certificate on December 31, which shall be a bearer security exchangeable at face value for Treasury Notes of Series K-1976 when available.

Tenders will be received up to 1:30 p.m., Eastern Standard time, Monday, December 23, at any Federal Reserve Bank or Branch and at the Bureau of the Public Debt, Washington, D. C. 20226; provided, however, that noncompetitive tenders will be considered timely received if they are mailed to any such agency under a postmark no later than Sunday, December 22. Each tender must be in the amount of $5,000 or a multiple thereof, and all tenders must state the yield, if a competitive tender, or the term "noncompetitive", if a noncompetitive tender. The notation "TENDER FOR TREASURY NOTES" should be printed at the bottom of envelopes in which tenders are submitted.

Competitive tenders for the notes must be expressed in terms of annual yield in two decimal places, e.g., 7.75, and not in terms of a price. Tenders at the lowest yields, and noncompetitive tenders, will be accepted to the extent required to attain the amount offered. After a determination is made as to which tenders are accepted, a coupon yield will be determined to the nearest ⅛ of 1 percent necessary to make the average accepted price 100.00 or less. That will be the rate of interest that will be paid on all of the notes. Based on such interest rate, the price on each competitive tender allotted will be determined and each successful competitive bidder will pay the price corresponding to the yield he bid. Price calculations

**FIGURE 2-4** *(Continued)*

will be carried to three decimal places on the basis of price per hundred, e.g., 99.923, and the determinations of the Secretary of the Treasury shall be final. Tenders at a yield that will produce a price less than 99.501 will not be accepted.

The Secretary of the Treasury expressly reserves the right to accept or reject any or all tenders, in whole or in part, including the right to accept more or less than the $2.0 billion offered to the public, and his action in any such respect shall be final. Subject to these reservations, noncompetitive tenders for $500,000 or less will be accepted in full at the average price of accepted competitive tenders, which price will be 100.00 or less.

Commercial banks, which for this purpose are defined as banks accepting demand deposits, and dealers who make primary markets in Government securities and report daily to the Federal Reserve Bank of New York their positions with respect to Government securities and borrowings thereon, may submit tenders for the account of customers, provided the names of the customers are set forth in such tenders. Others will not be permitted to submit tenders except for their own account.

Tenders will be received without deposit from commercial and other banks for their own account, Federally-insured savings and loan associations, States, political subdivisions or instrumentalities thereof, public pension and retirement and other public funds, international organizations in which the United States holds membership, foreign central banks and foreign States, dealers who make primary markets in Government securities and report daily to the Federal Reserve Bank of New York their positions with respect to Government securities and borrowings thereon, Federal Reserve Banks, and Government accounts. Tenders from others must be accompanied by payment of 5 percent of the face amount of securities applied for. However, bidders who submit checks in payment on tenders submitted directly to a Federal Reserve Bank or the Treasury may find it necessary to submit full payment for the securities with their tenders in order to meet the time limits pertaining to checks as hereinafter set forth. Allotment notices will not be sent to bidders who submit noncompetitive tenders.

Payment for accepted tenders must be completed on or before Tuesday, December 31, 1974, at the Federal Reserve Bank or Branch or at the Bureau of the Public Debt in cash, 5⅞% Treasury Notes of Series F-1974, which will be accepted at par, in other funds immediately available to the Treasury by December 31, or by check drawn to the order of the Federal Reserve Bank to which the tender is submitted, or the United States Treasury if the tender is submitted to it, which must be received at such Bank or at the Treasury no later than: (1) Friday, December 27, 1974, if the check is drawn on a bank in the Federal Reserve District of the Bank to which the check is submitted, or the Fifth Federal Reserve District in case of the Treasury, or (2) Tuesday, December 24, 1974, if the check is drawn on a bank in another district. Checks received after the dates set forth in the preceding sentence will not be accepted unless they are payable at a Federal Reserve Bank. Where full payment is not completed on time, the allotment will be canceled and the deposit with the tender up to 5 percent of the amount of securities allotted will be subject to forfeiture to the United States.

Commercial banks are prohibited from making unsecured loans, or loans collateralized in whole or in part by the securities bid for, to cover the deposits required to be paid when tenders are entered, and they will be required to make the usual certification to that effect. Other lenders are requested to refrain from making such loans.

All bidders are required to agree not to purchase or to sell, or to make any agreements with respect to the purchase or sale or other disposition of the notes bid for under this offering at a specific rate or price, until after 1:30 p.m., Eastern Standard time, Monday, December 23, 1974.

The terms of this offering are set forth in Treasury Department Circular No. 16-74, Public Debt Series, dated December 16, 1974, a copy of which is printed on the following pages.

This Bank will receive tenders up to 1:30 p.m., Eastern Standard time, Monday, December 23, 1974, at the Securities Department of its Head Office and at its Buffalo Branch, except that noncompetitive tenders mailed to this Bank or its Branch postmarked no later than Sunday, December 22, will be considered timely. Please use the enclosed tender form to submit a tender, and return it in the enclosed envelope marked "Tender for Treasury Notes." Tenders not requiring a deposit may be submitted by telegraph, subject to written confirmation; no tenders may be submitted by telephone. Settlement for accepted tenders may be made in cash, 5⅞% Treasury Notes of Series F-1974, or other immediately available funds; *settlement cannot be made by credit to Treasury Tax and Loan Accounts.* If payment is made by check, the check must be a certified personal check or an official Bank check, payable on its face to the Federal Reserve Bank of New York; *checks endorsed to this Bank will not be accepted.*

The notes will be auctioned on a yield basis, rather than the conventional price basis. Competitive tenders for these new notes must be expressed in terms of an annual yield in two decimal places, e.g., 7.75, rather than in terms of a price. Tenders at the lowest yields, and noncompetitive tenders, will be accepted to the extent required to attain the $2 billion offered. After a determination is made as to which tenders are accepted, a coupon yield will be determined to the nearest ⅛ of 1 percent necessary to make the average accepted price 100.00 or less. That will be the rate of interest that will be paid on all of the notes. Based on such interest rate, the price on each competitive tender allotted will be determined and each successful competitive bidder will pay the price corresponding to the yield he bid. Price calculations will be carried to three decimal places on the basis of price per hundred, e.g., 99.923, and the determination of the Secretary of the Treasury shall be final. Tenders at a yield that will produce a price less than 99.501 will not be accepted.

Telephone inquiries regarding this offering may be made by calling Telephone No. 212-791-5823, 212-791-6616, or 212-791-5465.

**Alfred Hayes,**
*President.*

**FIGURE 2-4** *(Continued)*

# UNITED STATES OF AMERICA
## TREASURY NOTES OF SERIES K-1976

Dated and bearing interest from December 31, 1974

Due December 31, 1976

DEPARTMENT CIRCULAR
Public Debt Series — No. 16-74

DEPARTMENT OF THE TREASURY,
Office of the Secretary,
*Washington, December 16, 1974.*

### I. INVITATION FOR TENDERS

1. The Secretary of the Treasury, pursuant to the authority of the Second Liberty Bond Act, as amended, invites tenders on a yield basis for $2,000,000,000, or thereabouts, of notes of the United States, designated Treasury Notes of Series K-1976. The interest rate for the notes will be determined as set forth in Section III, paragraph 3, hereof. Additional amounts of the notes may be issued by the Secretary of the Treasury to Government accounts and Federal Reserve Banks for themselves and as agents of foreign and international monetary authorities at the average price of accepted tenders. Tenders will be received up to 1:30 p.m., Eastern Standard time, Monday, December 23, 1974, under competitive and noncompetitive bidding, as set forth in Section III hereof. The 5⅞ percent Treasury Notes of Series F-1974, maturing December 31, 1974, will be accepted at par in payment, in whole or in part, to the extent tenders are allotted by the Treasury.

### II. DESCRIPTION OF NOTES

1. The notes will be dated December 31, 1974, and will bear interest from that date, payable semiannually on June 30, 1975, December 31, 1975, June 30, 1976, and December 31, 1976. They will mature December 31, 1976, and will not be subject to call for redemption prior to maturity.

2. The income derived from the notes is subject to all taxes imposed under the Internal Revenue Code of 1954. The notes are subject to estate, inheritance, gift or other excise taxes, whether Federal or State, but are exempt from all taxation now or hereafter imposed on the principal or interest thereof by any State, or any of the possessions of the United States, or by any local taxing authority.

3. The notes will be acceptable to secure deposits of public moneys. They will not be acceptable in payment of taxes.

4. Bearer notes with interest coupons attached, and notes registered as to principal and interest, will be issued in denominations of $5,000, $10,000, $100,000 and $1,000,000. Book-entry notes will be available to eligible bidders in multiples of those amounts. Interchanges of notes of different denominations and of coupon and registered notes, and the transfer of registered notes will be permitted.

5. The notes will be subject to the general regulations of the Department of the Treasury, now or hereafter prescribed, governing United States notes.

### III. TENDERS AND ALLOTMENTS

1. Tenders will be received at Federal Reserve Banks and Branches and at the Bureau of the Public Debt, Washington, D. C. 20226, up to the closing hour, 1:30 p.m., Eastern Standard time, Monday, December 23, 1974. Each tender must state the face amount of notes bid for, which must be $5,000 or a multiple thereof, and the yield desired, except that in the case of noncompetitive tenders the term "noncompetitive" should be used in lieu of a yield. In the case of competitive tenders, the yield must be expressed in terms of an annual yield, with two decimals, e.g., 7.75. Noncompetitive tenders from any one bidder may not exceed $500,000.

2. Commercial banks, which for this purpose are defined as banks accepting demand deposits, and dealers who make primary markets in Government securities and report daily to the Federal Reserve Bank of New York their positions with respect to Government securities and borrowings thereon, may submit tenders for account of customers provided the names of the customers are set forth in such tenders. Others will not be permitted to submit tenders except for their own account. Tenders will be received without deposit from banking institutions for their own account, Federally-insured savings and loan associations, States, political subdivisions or instrumentalities thereof, public pension and retirement and other public funds, international organizations in which the United States holds membership, foreign central banks and foreign States, dealers who make primary markets in Government securities and report daily to the Federal Reserve Bank of New York their positions with respect to Government securities and borrowings thereon, and Government accounts. Tenders from others must be accompanied by payment (in cash or 5⅞ percent Treasury Notes of Series F-1974 which will be accepted at par) of 5 percent of the face amount of notes applied for.

3. Immediately after the closing hour tenders will be opened, following which public announcement will be made by the Department of the Treasury of the amount and yield range of accepted bids. Those submitting competitive tenders will be advised of the acceptance or rejection thereof. In considering the acceptance of tenders, those with the lowest yields

**Figure 2-4** *(Continued)*

will be accepted to the extent required to attain the amount offered. Tenders at the highest accepted yield will be prorated if necessary. After the determination is made as to which tenders are accepted, an interest rate will be established at the nearest ⅛ of one percent necessary to make the average accepted price 100.00 or less. That will be the rate of interest that will be paid on all of the notes. Based on such interest rate, the price on each competitive tender allotted will be determined and each successful competitive bidder will be required to pay the price corresponding to the yield bid. Price calculations will be carried to three decimal places on the basis of price per hundred, e.g., 99.923, and the determinations of the Secretary of the Treasury shall be final. The Secretary of the Treasury expressly reserves the right to accept or reject any or all tenders, in whole or in part, including the right to accept more or less than $2,000,000,000 offered to the public, and his action in any such respect shall be final. Subject to these reservations, noncompetitive tenders for $500,000 or less without stated yield from any one bidder will be accepted in full at the average price (in three decimals) of accepted competitive tenders.

4.   All bidders are required to agree not to purchase or sell, or to make any agreements with respect to the purchase or sale or other disposition of any notes of this issue at a specific rate or price, until after 1:30 p.m., Eastern Standard time, Monday, December 23, 1974.

5.   Commercial banks in submitting tenders will be required to certify that they have no beneficial interest in any of the tenders they enter for the account of their customers, and that their customers have no beneficial interest in the banks' tenders for their own accounts.

#### IV.  PAYMENT FOR AND DELIVERY OF NOTES

1.   Settlement for accepted tenders in accordance with the bids must be made or completed on or before December 31, 1974, at the Federal Reserve Bank or Branch or at the Bureau of the Public Debt, Washington, D. C. 20226. Payment must be in cash, 5⅞ percent Treasury Notes of Series F-1974 (interest coupons dated December 31, 1974, should be detached), in other funds immediately available to the Treasury by December 31, or by check drawn to the order of the Federal Reserve Bank to which the tender is submitted, or the United States Treasury if the tender is submitted to it, which must be received at such Bank or at the Treasury no later than: (1) Friday, December 27, 1974, if the check is drawn on a bank in the Federal Reserve District of the Bank to which the check is submitted, or the Fifth Federal Reserve District in the case of the Treasury, or (2) Tuesday, December 24, 1974, if the check is drawn on a bank in another district. Checks received after the dates set forth in the preceding sentence will not be accepted unless they are payable at a Federal Reserve Bank. Payment will not be deemed to have been completed where registered notes are requested if the appropriate identifying number as required on tax returns and other documents submitted to the

Internal Revenue Service (an individual's social security number or an employer identification number) is not furnished. In every case where full payment is not completed, the payment with the tender up to 5 percent of the amount of notes allotted shall, upon declaration made by the Secretary of the Treasury in his discretion, be forfeited to the United States. When payment is made with notes, a cash adjustment will be made to or required of the bidder for any difference between the face amount of notes submitted and the amount payable on the notes allotted.

2.   Delivery of notes in bearer form will be made on or about January 6, 1975. Purchasers of bearer notes may elect to receive interim certificates on December 31, 1974, which will be exchangeable for the notes when available at any Federal Reserve Bank or Branch or at the Bureau of the Public Debt, Washington, D. C. 20226. The interim certificates must be returned at the risk and expense of the holder.

#### V.  ASSIGNMENT OF REGISTERED NOTES

1.   Registered notes tendered as deposits and in payment for notes allotted hereunder are not required to be assigned if the notes are to be registered in the same names and forms as appear in the registrations or assignments of the notes surrendered. Specific instructions for the issuance and delivery of the notes, signed by the owner or his authorized representative, must accompany the notes presented. Otherwise, the notes should be assigned by the registered payees or assignees thereof in accordance with the general regulations governing United States securities, as hereinafter set forth. Notes to be registered in names and forms different from those in the inscriptions or assignments of the notes presented should be assigned to "The Secretary of the Treasury for Treasury Notes of Series K-1976 in the name of (name and taxpayer identifying number)." If notes in coupon form are desired, the assignment should be to "The Secretary of the Treasury for coupon Treasury Notes of Series K-1976 to be delivered to . . . . . . . . . . . . . . . . . . . . ." Notes tendered in payment should be surrendered to the Federal Reserve Bank or Branch or to the Bureau of the Public Debt, Washington, D. C. 20226. The notes must be delivered at the expense and risk of the holder.

#### VI.  GENERAL PROVISIONS

1.   As fiscal agents of the United States, Federal Reserve Banks are authorized and requested to receive tenders, to make such allotments as may be prescribed by the Secretary of the Treasury, to issue such notices as may be necessary, to receive payment for and make delivery of notes on full-paid tenders allotted, and they may issue interim receipts pending delivery of the definitive notes.

2.   The Secretary of the Treasury may at any time, or from time to time, prescribe supplemental or amendatory rules and regulations governing the offering, which will be communicated promptly to the Federal Reserve Banks.

**STEPHEN S. GARDNER,**
*Acting Secretary of the Treasury.*

# U.S. Government Agency Securities and Related Securities

*What are these securities?*

They are debt obligations of U.S. Federal agencies and U.S. government-sponsored agencies. These securities fall in both the money and the capital markets. Most of them, however, lie in the maturity range of the money market (one year to five years).

*Why do these securities appeal to investors?*

They appeal to investors because they generally have higher yields than U.S. Treasury bills, are almost as safe and liquid as U.S. Treasury bills and are highly structured.

*How safe are these securities as investments?*

The interest and principal of most U.S. government agency securities and U.S. government-sponsored agency securities are guaranteed only by the issuing agency.

*How liquid are these securities?*

As there is a secondary market for these securities, the investor can usually sell the securities before maturity. The investor, however, should be aware that some agency securities have more active secondary markets than others (see the latter part of this chapter for additional coverage of the secondary market).

*In what sense is this market highly structured?*

This market is highly structured by virtue of the fact that it consists of many U.S. Federal agencies and U.S. government-sponsored agencies, which are themselves highly structured.

*What U.S. government agencies and U.S. government-sponsored agencies does this market include?*

Banks for Cooperatives ("Bank for Coops," "Bank for Co-ops" or "COOPS")

District of Columbia Armory Board

Environmental Financing Authority

Export-Import Bank of the United States ("Ex-Im Bank" or "Eximbank")

Farmers Home Administration (FHDA)

Federal Financing Bank (FFB)

Federal Home Loan Banks (FHLB)

Federal Home Loan Mortgage Corporation ("Freddie Mac" or FHLMC)

Federal Housing Administration (FHA)

Federal Intermediate Credit Banks ("FIC Bank")

Federal Land Banks

Federal National Mortgage Association ("Fannie Mae" or FNMA)

General Services Administration (GSA)

Government National Mortgage Association ("Ginnie Mae" or GNMA)

Maritime Administration

Rural Electrification Administration

Rural Telephone Bank

Small Business Administration (SBA)

Student Loan Marketing Association ("Sallie Mae" or SLMA)

Tennessee Valley Authority (TVA)

U.S. Postal Service (USPS)

U.S. Railway Association

Washington Metropolitan Area Transit Authority

## INFORMATION IN DEPTH

### Development of the Market

U.S. Federal agency securities and the securities of U.S. government-sponsored agencies were great favorites with investors in 1974, and their appeal continued into 1975. The appeal resides in the fact that these securities offer relatively high yields, when compared to U.S. government securities (i.e., U.S. Treasury bills, U.S. Treasury notes and U.S. Treasury bonds), and, in addition, almost as much safety and liquidity as U.S. government securities.

This market provides the investor with a broad range of investment possibilities. The securities offered actually fall in both the money and the capital markets. Thus, there are securities with maturities under one year, one year to five years, five to ten years, and even over ten years.

The overall market has grown rapidly. With the volume outstanding at only $1.5 billion in 1950, it grew to $16.3 billion in 1965, to $68.2 billion by September 30, 1973, and to $84.7 billion by September 30, 1974.

The history of this exciting market has been marked with continual financial innovations. Various U.S. government agencies and U.S. government-sponsored agencies issue securities to finance their operations. They were originally established, by law, to implement lending programs of the United States government. The "Big Five" in this market are the Banks for Cooperatives, the Federal Home Loan Banks, the Federal Intermediate Credit Banks, the Federal Land Banks, and the Federal National Mortgage Association ("Fannie Mae").

These agencies were originally financed by the U.S. Treasury, in that the U.S. Treasury subscribed to most of their capital stock. Treasury holdings in these "Big Five" have now been redeemed, and ownership has passed to member organizations and the general public.

The Federal Home Loan Banks are owned almost 100% by savings and loan associations, while the other four agencies passed to private ownership as a result of legislation enacted in 1968.

An agency to watch closely for growth in this market is the Federal Financing Bank (FFB). While most securities in this market are not guaranteed by the United States government, FFB securities are guaranteed. The FFB first came into existence by legislation passed in 1973.

### Types of Securities

The following are broad classifications of U.S. government agency and government-sponsored enterprises securities:

Participation Certificates (PCs)
Notes
Debentures
Bonds
Certificates of Beneficial Interest (CBIs)
Certificates of Beneficial Ownership (CBOs)

*Participation Certificates (PCs).* These are securities issued against a "pool" of assets (usually loans) of the participating agencies. The interest obtained from the pooled loans is used to pay the interest on the PCs. They became an important debt-marketing technique in the financial markets of 1964, when "Fannie Mae" issued $300 million worth of fully marketable PCs. The Export-Import Bank actually sold PCs against a pool of loans in 1962, but they were small in dollar volume and not marketable.

PCs fall in both the money and the capital markets (i.e., there are both short-term and long-term maturity periods). The Internal Revenue Service (IRS) has ruled that PCs qualify savings and loan associations, savings banks, and real estate investment trusts (REITs) for special tax benefits.

*Notes.* "Fannie Mae" has sold notes to finance its secondary market purchases. Short-term notes are discounted at published rates that are closely fixed above U.S. Treasury bills rates. They are marketed in a manner similar to commercial paper and bankers' acceptances. Secondary market rates on "Fannie Mae" notes are published for different maturities, usually 30 days to 270 days. On the other hand, obligations of the Federal Home Loan Banks (FHLB) with a one year maturity or less are called notes. The FHLB notes have the added difference from "Fannie Mae" notes that they carry a fixed (coupon) rate of interest, while the "Fannie Mae" notes are sold at discount.

*Debentures.* "Fannie Mae" debentures typically have two to five year maturities. The Federal Intermediate Credit Banks (FICB) and Banks for Cooperatives (COOPS) issue short-term debentures that mature within one year, while FHA debentures are usually long-term obligations which the Secretary of the Treasury has authority to redeem before maturity. Debentures are securities which are not secured by any specific asset.

*Bonds.* The Federal Land Banks (FLB) issue bonds usually secured by first mortgages on farm properties. Federal Home Loan Banks (FHLB) securities with original maturities of over one year are classified as bonds, with FHLB securities issued against guaranteed mortgages, U.S. government securities, or cash assets. TVA issues long-term bonds (e.g., due in 1994).

*Certificates of Beneficial Interest (CBIs).* These securities have been issued by the Export-Import Bank in the past and have not always been fully guaranteed by the Bank.

*Certificates of Beneficial Ownership (CBOs).* These securities are issued by the Farmers Home Administration (FHDA) and is a marketing method which the FHDA employs for selling its Insured Notes in trusts.

### Types of Markets

For classification purposes, two broad types of markets can be distinguished. This classification applies not only to the U.S. government agency and U.S. government-sponsored agency markets, but to the entire money market and to the capital market.

One market is known as the "primary market" and the other is known as the "secondary market." The primary market refers to the market where new securities are issued, while the secondary market refers to the market where previously issued securities are traded.

What is the importance of a secondary market to an investor? The importance of a secondary market to an investor is that, if he wants to sell his securities before the maturity date, he can do so. It is, therefore, essential to know whether a secondary market does exist for a particular security and, if it does, how active that secondary market is.

### The Primary Market

Most Federal agencies have a Fiscal Agent in New York City under contract, in order to promote sales in the primary market. Some agencies may employ the services of the same Fiscal Agent.

The Fiscal Agent organizes a selling group, which consists of banks, brokerage firms, and specialized securities dealers. The members of the selling group, unlike syndicates formed for the issuance of stocks and bonds, do not bid against each other. In order to set the price of the agency issue, the Fiscal Agent discusses the pertinent points with the members of the selling group, the U.S. Treasury, the Trading Desk at the Federal Reserve Bank of New York, and the agency issuing the securities. The Fiscal Agent allocates the portions to the members of the selling group.

This is the general procedure used by the "Big Five" agencies. There are other procedures. The Farmers Home Administration sells notes directly to investors, the TVA uses an auction method, and other methods are employed by other agencies.

### The Secondary Market

The Banks for Cooperatives, Fannie Mae, the Federal Home Loan Banks, the Federal Intermediate Credit Banks, and the Federal Land Banks have well-established secondary markets. Some agencies do not have active secondary markets.

Pursuant to an act of Congress, the Federal Open Market Committee of the Federal Reserve System authorized the use of repurchase agreements for U.S. government agency securities in its open-market operations in 1966, which served to buttress the agency market and expand the secondary market.

## U.S. GOVERNMENT AGENCIES AND U.S. GOVERNMENT-SPONSORED AGENCIES

### Banks for Cooperatives

Banks for cooperatives ("Bank for Coops," "Bank for Co-ops," or "COOPS") operate under the authority granted by Title III of the Farm Credit Act of 1971.

The Banks for Cooperatives were organized in 1933 for the purpose of making loans to cooperatives engaged in marketing farm products, buying farm supplies, or providing farm business services.

There are 12 district Banks for Cooperatives. All of the capital stock of the 12 district banks is held by borrowing cooperatives. There is a Central Bank for Cooperatives and all of its stock is held by the district banks.

The Central Bank for Cooperatives is controlled by a Board of Directors consisting of thirteen persons. Twelve of these directors are elected, one each by the district boards. The other director is appointed by the Governor of the Farm Credit Administration with the advice and consent of the Federal Farm Credit Board.

Any association of farmers, ranchers or producers or harvesters of aquatic products or any federation of such associations which operates on a cooperative basis and provides marketing and processing functions for its members may be eligible to borrow from a Bank for Cooperatives.

Eighty percent of the voting control of such associations must be held by bona fide farmers, ranchers, producers or harvesters of aquatic products, or federations of such associations. The cooperative must also do as much business with or for members as it does with or for nonmembers. Excepted from this requirement is business transacted with the U.S. government and services and supplies furnished by the cooperative as a public utility.

The Banks for Cooperatives make three basic types of loans which are adapted to the particular needs of cooperatives, seasonal loans, term loans, and loans secured by commodities.

The Central Bank for Cooperatives participates with the district banks on very large loans. Interest rates are determined by the Board of Directors with the approval of the Farm Credit Administration. Distributions of earnings by the Banks for Cooperatives to their borrowers have the effect of reducing the rate of interest.

The Banks for Cooperatives obtain the bulk of their loan funds through the sale of consolidated bonds to investors.

The bonds are not guaranteed by the U.S. government. They are issued in bearer form. The minimum denomination of the bonds is $5,000.

### District of Columbia Armory Board
### (or District of Columbia Stadium Fund)

The District of Columbia Armory Board was authorized by the District of Columbia Stadium Act of 1957 to construct, operate, and maintain a stadium from 1960 to 1990. The District of Columbia Armory Board offered 4.20% bonds (December 1970-1979) in 1960. These bonds are guaranteed by the U.S. government, and they are issued in registered form. The minimum denomination for the bonds is $10,000.

### Export-Import Bank of the United States

The Export-Import Bank (Eximbank) was first established in 1934 under the name "Export-Import Bank of Washington," as a banking corporation organized under the laws of the District of Columbia (Executive Order 6581, February 2, 1934). It was made an independent agency of the U.S. government by the Export-Import Bank Act of 1945, which was subsequently amended in 1947 to reincorporate the Bank under Federal charter. The name was changed to the "Export-Import Bank of the United States" by act of March 13, 1968. The Export Expansion Finance Act of 1971 removed the receipts and disbursements of the Bank from the budget of the U.S. government and increased its overall lending authority.

Its purpose is to aid in financing and facilitating exports and imports and to aid in the exchange of commodities between the United States and any foreign country. The Export-Import Bank Act of 1945, as amended, expresses the policy of Congress that the Bank should supplement and encourage and not compete with private capital; that loans should generally be for specific purposes and offer reasonable assurance of repayment; and that, in authorizing loans, account should be taken of the possible adverse effects upon the U.S. economy.

The Eximbank is authorized to have outstanding at any one time dollar loans, guarantees, and insurance in an aggregate amount not in excess of $20 billion. It is also authorized to have a capital stock of $1 billion and to borrow from the U.S. Treasury on its own obligations not more than $6 billion outstanding at any one time.

The Foreign Credit Insurance Association (FCIA) is an association of commercial insurance companies which was formed by the Eximbank and the insurance industry in 1961 to provide credit protection for U.S. exporters. Policies issued by FCIA insure repayment in the event of default by a foreign buyer and may be used as collateral for bank loans to U.S. exporters. FCIA policies cover both short-term and medium-term transactions.

The Eximbank also guarantees repayment to commercial banks which finance medium-term transactions for exporters. It also issues guarantees to exporters covering service contracts, leases, and other special situations.

The Eximbank issues debentures and Participation Certificates (PCs) which are guaranteed by the U.S. government. These securities are issued in both bearer and registered forms. The minimum denomination for the debentures is $50,000, and the minimum denomination for the PCs is $5,000.

### Farmers Home Administration

The Farmers Home Administration (FHDA) is an agency within the U.S. Department of Agriculture which provides credit for those in rural areas of the United States who are unable to get credit from other sources at reasonable rates and terms. It operates principally under the Consolidated

Farm and Rural Development Act of 1921 and Title V of the Housing Act of 1949.

Loans are made with funds borrowed from the U.S. Treasury. These loans are then sold to private lenders under an insurance agreement, and the U.S. Treasury is repaid.

The FHDA issues "Insured Notes," which are guaranteed by the U.S. government. These notes are issues in both bearer and registered forms. The minimum denomination for the Insured Notes is $25,000.

### Federal Financing Bank

The Federal Financing Bank (FFB) can be expected to become highly important in the U.S. government agency securities market. It was established under the "Federal Financing Bank Act of 1973" (Public Law 93-224, 93rd Congress, H.R. 5874, December 29, 1973). The purpose of this act is stated as follows:

> The Congress finds that demands for funds through Federal and federally assisted borrowing programs are increasing faster than the total supply of credit and that such borrowings are not adequately coordinated with overall Federal fiscal and debt management policies. The purpose of this Act is to assure coordination of these programs with the overall economic and fiscal policies of the Government, to reduce the costs of Federal and federally assisted borrowings from the public, and to assure that such borrowings are financed in a manner least disruptive to private financial markets and institutions.

The Bank was created as follows:

> There is hereby created a body corporate to be known as the Federal Financing Bank, which shall have succession until dissolved by an Act of Congress. The Bank shall be subject to the general supervision and direction of the Secretary of the Treasury. The Bank shall be an instrumentality of the United States Government and shall maintain such offices as may be necessary or appropriate in the conduct of its business.

Regarding the Board of Directors, the act stated:

> The Bank shall have a Board of Directors consisting of five persons, one of whom shall be the Secretary of the Treasury as Chairman of the Board, and four of whom shall be appointed by the President from among the officers or employees of the Bank or of any Federal agency.

Regarding the obligations of the Federal Financing Bank, the Act states:

> The Bank is authorized, with the approval of the Secretary of the Treasury, to issue publicly and have outstanding at any one time not in excess of

$15,000,000,000, or such additional amounts as may be authorized in the appropriations Acts, of obligations having such maturities and bearing such rate or rates of interest as may be determined by the Bank. Such obligations may be redeemable at the option of the Bank before maturity in such manner as may be stipulated therein. So far as is feasible, the debt structure of the Bank shall be commensurate with its asset structure.

The Bank may require the Secretary of the Treasury to purchase the obligations of the Bank . . . in such amounts as will not cause the holding by the Secretary of the Treasury resulting from such required purchases to exceed $5,000,000,000 at any one time.

The overall concept behind the Federal Financing Bank is to aid in the financing of Federal agencies and some other establishments, with federally related programs, which might have difficulty obtaining funds on their own and to reduce financing costs without disrupting the money and capital markets.

The principal Federal agencies or programs eligible to use FFB are:

Amtrak
Department of Defense military credit sales
Department of Health, Education, and Welfare
    Medical facilities
    Student Loan Marketing Association
Department of Housing and Urban Development
    Government National Mortgage Association
    New community debentures
    Public housing
    Urban renewal
Environmental Financing Authority
Export-Import Bank
Farmers Home Administration
General Services Administration
Maritime Administration
Overseas Private Investment Corporation
Rural Electrification Administration
Rural Telephone Bank
Small Business Administration
Tennessee Valley Authority
U.S. Postal Service
U.S. Railway Association

Government-sponsored agencies not eligible to use FFB include:

Banks for Cooperatives
Federal Home Loan Banks
Federal Home Loan Mortgage Corporation

Federal Intermediate Credit Banks
Federal Land Banks
Federal National Mortgage Association

FFB obligations are like Treasury obligations in that they are:

Available in book-entry, registered, and bearer forms.

Eligible for Federal Reserve wire transfer at all Federal Reserve Banks or Branches.

Exempt from state and local government taxation to the same extent as Treasury securities.

Lawful investments and acceptable as security for all fiduciary, trust, and public funds (including Treasury Tax and Loan accounts), the investment or deposit of which is under the authority of any officer of the United States.

Eligible as collateral for Federal Reserve Bank advances.

Eligible for Federal Reserve open market purchases.

Payable as to principal and coupon interest at Federal Reserve Banks or at the Treasury.

Payable by Treasury check for interest on registered securities.

Eligible for denominational exchanges, transfer, and interchanges among book-entry, registered, and bearer forms at the Federal Reserve Banks or at the Bureau of Public Debt of the Treasury.

Eligible for relief in the event of loss, theft, or destruction in the same manner as Treasury securities.

Eligible for purchase by national banks without restriction.

Eligible for investment by federal credit unions and small business investment companies.

Countable as liquid assets by members of the Federal Home Loan Bank System.

All FFB bills are subject to Federal taxation to the same extent that obligations of private corporations are taxed. They are exempt, however, from state and local taxation to the same extent as Treasury securities.

Each FFB bill will be paid its face amount upon presentation and surrender to any Federal Reserve Bank or Branch or to the

Department of the Treasury
Bureau of the Public Debt
Securities Transaction Branch
Washington, D.C. 20226

If a FFB bill is presented and surrendered after it has become overdue, the FFB may require satisfactory proof of ownership as provided in section 30C-25 of Department of the Treasury Circular No. 300, current revision.

Tenders were received for the FFB's first offering of securities on July 23, 1974. The announcement stated: "The Federal Financing Bank, with the approval of the Secretary of the Treasury, by this public notice invites tenders for $1,500,000,000, or thereabouts, of 244-day Federal Financing Bank bills to be dated July 30, 1974, and to mature March 31, 1975.''

The bills were issued on a discount basis under competitive and noncompetitive bidding. The tenders were received at the Federal Reserve Banks and Branches and not at the Federal Financing Bank itself, which is located in Washington, D.C.

The bills were issued in bearer and book-entry form only in the following denominations:

$10,000
$15,000
$50,000
$100,000
$500,000
$1,000,000

The total actually issued was $1,500,010,000 at an average yield of 8.048%.

### Federal Home Loan Banks

The Federal Home Loan Banks (FHLB) are also referred to as the "Federal Home Loan Bank System." These banks were created by authority of the Federal Home Loan Bank Act (approved July 22, 1932). The purpose of the banks is to provide at all times a flexible credit reserve for member savings institutions engaged in home mortgage lending.

There are twelve regional Federal Home Loan Banks in the System. The Federal Home Loan Bank Board (FHLBB) supervises the Federal Home Loan Bank System (as well as the Federal Savings and Loan System and the Federal Savings and Loan Insurance Corporation). The Federal Home Loan Bank Board was made an independent agency in the Executive Branch of the U.S. government under section 109(a)(3) of the Housing Amendments of 1955.

The capital stock of the district Federal Home Loan Banks is entirely owned by member institutions, each of which is required to purchase stock. The banks obtain other lendable funds through the issuance of consolidated obligations in the money and capital markets, through time and demand deposits accepted from member institutions and from other Federal Home Loan Banks.

The types of institutions which are eligible to become members of the Federal Home Loan Banks are savings and loan associations, building and loan associations, homestead associations, savings banks, cooperative banks, and insurance companies. Every savings and loan association is required to become a member of its regional Federal Home Loan Bank and to qualify for insurance of deposit accounts. Close to 100% of the membership is held by savings and loan associations.

Consolidated Federal Home Loan Bank obligations are the joint and several liabilities of all the Banks. They are issued by the Federal Home Loan Bank Board in the form of notes and bonds. Although the banks are instrumentalities of the United States, their securities are not obligations of the U.S. government and are not guaranteed by the U.S. government.

Nevertheless, the Secretary of the Treasury is authorized, in case of need, to purchase consolidated Federal Home Loan Bank obligations up to an aggregate amount of $4 billion outstanding at any one time.

Bonds issued with maturity periods of one year or less are called "notes". Like the bonds, they are not guaranteed by the U.S. government. They differ as to the existence or lack of existence of a guarantee by the U.S. government and the minimum denomination. "Consolidated Notes" are also issued, which are not guaranteed by the U.S. government. The bonds, "notes" and "Consolidated Notes" are issued in bearer form. The minimum denomination for old bonds and "notes" is $5,000. The minimum denomination for new bonds and "notes" is $10,000. The minimum denomination for "Consolidated Notes" is $100,000.

### Federal Home Loan Mortgage Corporation

The Federal Home Loan Mortgage Corporation (Freddie Mac or FHLMC) was created by an Act of Congress on July 24, 1970, under Title III of the Emergency Home Finance Act of 1970. Its specific purpose is ". . . to increase the availability of mortgage credit for the financing of urgently needed housing . . . ." The legislative history of the Act indicates that this objective was to be accomplished through the creation of a viable secondary market for conventional residential mortgages (those mortgages not insured or guaranteed by an agency of the U.S. government).

FHLMC has worked to establish a truly secondary market (i.e., a market in which mortgages are sold as well as bought) for residential mortgages; a market that will increase the ability of mortgages to compete for capital on an equal basis with other investment instruments in the capital market; and a market which will increase the availability of mortgage credit. From January 1, 1974, to July 31, 1974 (a period of extremely tight mortgage credit), FHLMC issued approximately $4.3 billion in contracts and commitments to purchase residential mortgages. Marketing is engaged in for the purpose of selling or otherwise financing the mortgages acquired by FHLMC. The FHLMC has utilized four methods to accomplish this purpose. These methods are:

borrowings from the Federal Home Loan Banks
the issuance of GNMA guaranteed mortgage-backed bonds
the sale of Participation Sale Certificates (PCs)
the direct sale of mortgage holdings

The following table shows the amount of capital obtained under each method as of June 30, 1974:

Sources of Capital to Fund Mortgages Acquired and Operations
(in millions)

| | | |
|---|---|---:|
| Borrowings from the Federal Home Loan Banks | | $3,136 |
| GNMA Guaranteed Mortgage-backed Bonds | | 1,782 |
| Participation Sale Certificates | | 919 |
| Direct Sale of Mortgages | | 50 |
| | TOTAL | $5,887 |

*Source:* Federal Home Loan Mortgage Corporation

The sale of Participation Sale Certificates meets the conditions of ease of evaluation and administration. The certificates are classified as mortgages for regulatory and tax purposes with timely payment of interest and collection of principal guaranteed by FHLMC. The certificates are easier to administer than mortgages because the investors receive only one monthly check from FHLMC and receive interest at the coupon rate on the unpaid principal balance of the certificate regardless of the status of the underlying loans.

Monthly remittances in themselves, however, cause difficulties for many investors. Therefore, complete ease of administration has not been attained. The element of standardization has been attained only to the degree that the certificates are issued and guaranteed by FHLMC, and certificates issued against the same pool of mortgages will receive an equal pro rata share of principal and interest depending on the denomination of the certificate. The principal and interest payment will, however, normally differ in amount from month to month. There is thus a lack of the standardization which many investors like. If the monthly pass-through of the principal and interest in irregular amounts is unusual and cumbersome for many investors, this would certainly work against a certificate's competitiveness. Traditionally, bond buyers have therefore not bought such certificates unless they offered a substantially higher yield than that available on comparable bonds. A standard mortgage-backed bond could be issued, but this would serve to fragment the market between the traditional mortgage investors who would prefer securities to be classified as mortgages for regulatory and tax purposes. FHLMC is currently working on a concept of a mortgage investment for regulatory and tax purposes while also permitting a more traditional method of remitting payments to the investors.

The Participation Sale Certificates (PCs) are only guaranteed by the FHLMC and not by the U.S. government. The bonds, however are guaranteed by the U.S. government. They are issued in bearer or registered form. The minimum denomination of Participation Sale Certificates varies. The minimum denomination of the bonds is $25,000.

### Federal Housing Administration

The Federal Housing Administration (FHA) was created by the National Housing Act (approved June 27, 1934). It was grouped with other agencies to form the Federal Loan Agency by Reorganization Plan 1 (effective July 1, 1939). Its functions were transferred to the Federal Housing Agency (by Executive Order 9070 of Feb. 24, 1942). The FHA was transferred to the Housing and Home Finance Agency by Reorganization Plan 3 (effective July 27, 1947). Its functions, powers, and duties were transferred to the Department of Housing and Urban Development (HUD) by an act approved September 9, 1965).

Its purpose is to give assistance to home builders, home buyers, and mortgage-lending institutions. The FHA issues debentures which are guaranteed by the U.S. government. They are issued in registered form. The minimum denomination for the debentures is $50.

### Federal Intermediate Credit Banks

The Federal Intermediate Credit Banks (FIC Banks) operate under the authority of Title II of the Farm Credit Act of 1971.

The Federal Intermediate Credit Banks make loans to production credit associations, state and national banks, livestock loan companies, agricultural credit operations, and similar organizations. They may also make loans to the Banks for Cooperatives and the Federal Land Banks.

The Federal Intermediate Credit Banks do not generally lend directly to individuals or conduct a general banking business. They may, however, participate in loans with production credit associations. They may also invest in the capital stock or surplus of production credit associations.

The discount or interest rate charged by a Federal Intermediate Credit Bank is determined by the Board of Directors with the approval of the Farm Credit Administration.

There are twelve Federal Intermediate Credit Banks, all of the capital stock of which is owned by farmers through their 435 local production credit associations. Other financing institutions which discount the notes of farmers with the banks provide some of the necessary capital by holding Participation Certificates issued to them by the banks.

The banks obtain the funds they use in their lending operations primarily from sales to investors of consolidated bonds which are the joint and several obligations of the twelve banks. These bonds are not guaranteed by the U.S. government. They are issued in bearer form. The minimum denomination for the bonds is $5,000.

### Federal Land Banks

The Federal Land Banks operate under the authority granted by Title I of the Farm Credit Act of 1971.

These banks make loans to farmers and ranchers for any agricultural purpose or other needs of the applicant. Loans are also made to rural residents for the purpose of financing housing. Financing for rural housing must be for single-family, moderately priced dwellings in towns and villages where the population does not exceed 2,500 persons. A Federal Land Bank is limited to rural housing loans totaling 15% of the total amount of its loans outstanding.

There are 578 Federal Land Bank Associations and 12 Federal Land Banks. The Federal Land Bank Associations own all the stock of the Federal Land Banks. Federal land bank loans may be obtained only with the endorsement of the Associations. When a loan is granted, the borrower purchases stock in the Association equal to at least 5% of his loan. The Association purchases a like amount of stock in the land bank. When the loan is repaid, the stock in the bank and in the association is retired.

Each Association is controlled by a Board of Directors, which is elected by and from the membership. Each Association member is entitled to one vote in the election of directors and in other matters regarding the Association.

Federal Land Bank loans may be made to persons who are or become members of Federal Land Bank Associations and who are bona fide farmers or ranchers, who furnish farmers or ranchers services directly related to on-farm operating needs, or who are owners of rural homes. Loans may be made for periods of 5 to 40 years.

Federal Land Bank loans may be made in amounts up to 85% of the appraised value of the real estate security and are secured by first liens on such real estate. Additional security may be required to supplement the real estate security and credit factors other than the ratio between the amount of the loan and the security value are given due consideration.

Loan funds are obtained primarily through the sale of "consolidated bonds" to investors. These bonds are called "consolidated" because they are the joint obligations of all twelve Federal Land Banks. These bonds are not guaranteed by the U.S. government. They are issued in bearer form. The minimum denomination for the bonds is $1,000.

### Federal National Mortgage Association

The Federal National Mortgage Association ("Fannie Mae" or FNMA) is a U.S. government-sponsored private corporation pursuant to Title VIII of the Housing and Urban Development Act of 1968.

The FNMA was originally chartered on February 10, 1938, as a U.S. government agency pursuant to Title III of the National Housing Act.

With rechartering under the Housing Act of 1954, it was made a constituent agency of the Housing and Home Finance Agency. It was transferred with the functions, powers, and duties of the Housing and Home Finance Agency to the Department of Housing and Urban Development (HUD) by an Act approved September 9, 1965. It was converted to private ownership pursuant to provisions of the Housing and Urban Development Act of 1968 (P.L. 90-448), effective September 30, 1968.

FNMA is sometimes referred to as a secondary market for mortgages. Its Charter Act of 1954, however, actually states that "Congress declares that the purposes of the (Act) are to establish secondary market facilities . . ." rather than a secondary market.

A secondary market implies that there are buyers and sellers with quite different motives for holding securities or whatever commodity is being traded and that therefore there are frequent or almost continuous purchases and sales of the security or commodity being discussed.

There is, however, a basic dilemma in the mortgage market. It stems from the fact that deposits at thrift institutions (e.g., savings and loan associations and savings banks) and the funds available to other mortgage lenders tend to move in the same way over the credit cycle. Thus, in periods of tight credit availability, funds available for mortgage lending tend to decline concurrently at all mortgage lenders, while in periods of easy credit availability, these funds tend to increase. In addition, those mortgage lenders which have the authority to lend or invest in other investment areas tend to shift to these other markets in periods of tight credit. Thus, the secondary market facilities such as FNMA can supply are very important.

FNMA supplies supplementary liquidity by purchasing mortgages during periods of credit stringency and sells mortgages during periods of credit ease.

In order to understand FNMA, it is necessary to understand the investment characteristics of a mortgage. From one point of view, a mortgage represents one of the symbols of "the American way of life," home ownership. From the point of view of an investment, however, whoever puts up the money to build or buy whatever the mortgage was given for expects to get a return, a profit, on his investment. He expects to get back not only the original money he put up, but some interest.

Just like other investments, mortgages can be bought and sold. In many cases, the person whose home is covered by the mortgage does not even know that his mortgage has been sold. He may continue to make payments to the same mortgage company or savings and loan association through which he originally obtained the loan. The mortgage company or savings and loan association collects the monthly payments and sends the money on to the owner of the mortgage, a procedure called "servicing" the mortgage. FNMA deals with more than 1,500 servicers throughout the United States.

It is generally understood that the prices of stocks on the stock market will change from day to day. Land prices, mortgages, and bonds fluctuate just like the prices of stocks. For purposes of understanding FNMA, however, one has to remember that the prices of bonds and mortgages are quoted in percentages. A $1,000 bond with a price quotation of 97.50 could be bought for $975. The buyer would get the bond for a $25 discount (2.5%). Similarly, a $10,000 mortgage offered for sale at 97.50 yields a discount of $250 (2.5%).

There is, however, an important difference between bonds and mortgages. A $1,000 bond remains a $1,000 bond until it is paid off. If you bought it for $975, you would still get $1,000 for it if you held it until maturity. In the case of a mortgage, however, a balance of $10,000 at purchase does not stay at $10,000. As the homeowner makes his monthly mortgage payments, the outstanding principal balance of the mortgage is reduced and if the mortgage is sold, the 97.5% must be applied to the reduced amount rather than the $10,000.

It has to be further realized that there is a big difference in the way in which FNMA finances its mortgage purchases and the way in which mortgage purchases are financed by commercial banks, thrift institutions, and life insurance companies. The latter work with quite a steady supply of funds, while FNMA has to obtain its funds on its own. FNMA does not have depositors or policy-holders. Although FNMA has common stock which trades on the New York Stock Exchange, the Pacific Coast Stock Exchange, and the Midwest Stock Exchange, by far its most important source of funds is borrowing.

FNMA issues four types of securities in its borrowings, discount notes, subordinated capital debentures, debentures, and mortgage-backed bonds.

*Discount Notes.* The discount notes range in maturities from 30 to 270 days. They are distributed through dealers, who also provide a secondary market for the notes. They are not guaranteed by the U.S. government. Redemption is made on maturity, at face value, at the Federal Reserve Bank of New York. The notes are issued in bearer form only.

*Subordinated Capital Debentures.* FNMA's subordinated capital debentures are evidences of general obligations of FNMA and some contain stock conversion provisions. Principal and interest are subordinated to any payments due on debentures and the discount notes. They are not guaranteed by the U.S. government and are issued in registered and bearer forms.

*Debentures.*   Debentures are general obligations of FNMA. The total amount of debentures and discount notes which may be issued and outstanding at any one time, as presently authorized by the Secretary of Housing and Urban Development, may not exceed 25 times the corporation's capital, capital surplus, general surplus, reserves, and undistributed earnings. They are not guaranteed by the U.S. government and are issued in bearer form.

*Mortgage-backed Bonds.*   FNMA bonds are general obligations of FNMA, based on and backed by mortgages which FNMA has set aside and conveyed in trust. They are guaranteed as to principal and interest by the Government National Mortgage Association. With respect to the mortgage-backed bonds, the full faith and credit of the U.S. government is pledged to the payments of all amounts which may be required to be paid under the guarantee.

The minimum denomination for the discount notes is $5,000 (minimum order by investor is $50,000). The minimum denomination for the subordinated capital debentures is $10,000. The minimum denomination for the debentures is usually $10,000, but does vary. The minimum denomination for the mortgage-backed bonds is $25,000.

### General Services Administration

The General Services Administration (GSA) was established by section 101 of the Federal Property and Administrative Act of 1949 (effective July 1, 1949).

GSA establishes policy and provides an efficient system for the U.S. government's management of government property and records. Included in GSA operations is the construction and operation of buildings, the procurement and distribution of supplies, and the utilization and disposal of property, as well as the management of transportation, the stockpiling of strategic materials, and the management of the U.S. government's ADP (Automatic Data Processing) resources program.

The programs operating under the GSA Administrator's office represent a wide range of activities:

1. The Federal Management Policy Program involves certain functions transferred to GSA from the Office of Management and Budget (by Executive Order of May 9, 1973). These functions include formulating, prescribing,

and assuring compliance with U.S. government-wide policies in financial management systems, automated data processing management, and other areas.

2. The Preparedness Program is the U.S. government-wide civil emergency preparedness program. Some of the responsibilities involve emergency availability of manpower, materials, industrial capacity, transportation, and communications; civil defense policy; emergency organization of Government; emergency stabilization of the civilian economy; rehabilitation after enemy attack; continuity of Federal, state, and local governments administration and coordination of the National Defense Executive Reserve Program; participation in NATO and other international civil emergency planning activities; and the determination and plans for the stockpile maintained under the Strategic and Critical Materials Stock Piling Act of 1946.

   These functions were transferred to GSA (by Executive Order 11725, effective July 1, 1973) from the Office of Emergency Preparedness, Executive Office of the President of the United States.

3. The Stockpile Disposal Program manages the disposal of certain stockpiled materials due to age, changes in requirements, or the need to rotate materials.

4. The Consumer Product Information Program includes two major activities: (a) encouraging Federal agencies to develop and release relevant and useful consumer information and (b) increasing public awareness of this information.

5. The Business Service Centers Program furnishes advice and assistance to businessmen interested in government procurement and disposal.

6. The Federal Information Centers (FIC) Program runs the Federal Information Centers that are clearinghouses for information about the Federal government.

7. The Bicentennial Coordination Program.

The GSA issues Participation Certificates guaranteed by the U.S. government.

The minimum denomination of the PCs is $5,000.

### Government National Mortgage Association

The Government National Mortgage Association ("Ginnie Mae" or GNMA) operates within the Department of Housing and Urban Development (HUD). Some historical background will help to explain the difference between GNMA and FNMA.

The National Housing Act was enacted on June 27, 1934. It provided for the establishment of a Federal Housing Administration (FHA) to be headed by a Federal Housing Administrator. Title II of the Act provided, as one of the principal functions of the FHA, for the insurance of home mortgage loans made by private lenders.

Title III of the Act provided for the chartering of national mortgage associations by the Administrator. These associations were to be private corporations regulated by the Administrator, and their chief purpose was to buy and sell the mortgages to be insured by FHA under Title II. Only one association was ever formed under this authority. It was formed on February 10, 1938, as a subsidiary of the Reconstruction Finance Corporation (RFC), a government corporation. Its name was "National Mortgage Association of Washington," which was changed in that same year to the "Federal National Mortgage Association" (FNMA).

By amendments made in 1948, the charter authority of the Administrator was repealed, and Title III became a statutory charter for FNMA. By revision of Title III in 1954, FNMA was converted into a mixed-ownership corporation, its preferred stock to be held by the U.S. government and its common stock to be privately held. At this time, section 312 was enacted, giving Title III the title of "Federal National Mortgage Association Charter Act."

By amendments made in 1968, FNMA was partitioned into two separate entities: one to be known as the "Government National Mortgage Association" (GNMA) and the other to retain the name of "Federal National Mortgage Association." GNMA remained in the government, while FNMA became entirely privately owned by retiring the government-held stock.

GNMA provides three programs, the Special Assistance Functions, the Management and Liquidating Functions, and the Mortgage-backed Securities Program.

*Special Assistance Functions:*

Section 301(b), Title III of the National Housing Act (12 U.S.C. 1716, et seq.) states these functions as follows:

> [to] provide special assistance (when, and to the extent that, the President has determined that it is in the public interest) for the financing of (1) selected types of home mortgages (pending the establishment of their marketability) originated under special housing programs designed to provide housing of acceptable standards at full economic costs for segments of the national population which are unable to obtain adequate housing under established home financing programs, and (2) home mortgages generally lending and home building activities which threatens materially the stability of a high level national economy.

*Management and Liquidating Functions:*

Section 301(c), Title III of the National Housing Act (12 U.S.C. 1716, et seq.) states these GNMA functions as follows:

> [to] manage and liquidate federally owned mortgage portfolios in an orderly manner, with a minimum of adverse effect upon the home mortgage market and minimum loss to the Federal Government.

*Mortgage-backed Securities Program:*

Section 306(g), Title III of the National Housing Act provides for a guarantee by GNMA of mortgage-backed securities. This guarantee bears the guarantee of the full faith and credit of the U.S. government.

The GNMA mortgage-backed securities program includes two types of securities, the bond type and the pass-through type.

The pass-through type of security should be of particular interest to pension funds and other funds which want to invest in mortgages from a certain geographical area.

There are three types of pass-through securities:

The straight pass-through, which provides for monthly payment of principal and interest as collected on the mortgages in the pool backing the securities.

The partially modified pass-through, which provides a fixed payment of interest each month whether or not colleced.

The fully modified pass-through, which provides a fixed payment of principal and interest each month whether or not collected on the mortgage.

Under all three types of pass-through securities prepayments on the mortgages are passed through to the security holder. All three types are fully guaranteed by GNMA.

*The Issuer*

A FHA-approved mortgagee obtains authority from GNMA to issue a certain amount of securities to be collateralized by a pool of a specified amount of FHA, VA, or Farmers Home Administration mortgages. The pool must be in a minimum amount of $2 million and the mortgages cannot be more than twelve months old. The issuer services the mortgages and makes all payments due to the investor.

*The Custodian*

When the specified amount of mortgages has been accumulated in the pool, they are submitted to an approved custodian (usually a bank) where they are examined. After examination and appropriate certification, GNMA issues its guarantee on the mortgage-backed security or certificate, which is then sold to the investor. Mortgages are held in safekeeping by the custodian.

The interest rate is stated on the face of the security. While the rate relates to the current VA or FHA mortgage rate (less ½% servicing fee), the price of the security is set to produce a yield to the investor competitive with current market conditions. The yield terms are negotiated between the issuer and the investor.

All of the following GNMA securities are guaranteed by the U.S. government. The mortgage-backed bonds are issued in bearer or registered form. The pass-through securities and Participation Certificates are issued only in registered form. The minimum denomination of mortgage-backed bonds is $25,000. The minimum denomination of pass-through securities is $25,000. The minimum denomination of PCs is $5,000.

### Small Business Administration (SBA)

The Small Business Administration (SBA) was created by the Small Business Act of 1953 and derives its present existence and authority from the Small Business Act, as amended. It also derives its authority from the Small Business Investment Act of 1958, as amended, Title IV of the Economic Opportunity Act of 1964, and the Disaster Relief Act of 1970.

The Secretary of Commerce has delegated to the SBA certain responsibilities and functions under section 202 of the Public Works and Economic Development Act of 1965.

The SBA has the following purposes:

To aid, counsel, assist, and protect the interests of small business.

To insure that small business concerns receive a fair proportion of government purchases, contracts, and subcontracts, as well as of the sales of government property.

To make loans to small business concerns, state and local development companies, and the victims of floods or other catastrophes.

To license, regulate, and make loans to small business investment companies.

To improve the management skills of small business owners, potential owners, and managers.

To conduct studies of the economic environment.

The SBA issues debentures guaranteed by the SBA which are general obligations of the U.S. government. They are issued in registered form. The minimum denomination of debentures is $10,000.

### Tennessee Valley Authority

The Tennessee Valley Authority (TVA) is a corporation which was created by an Act of Congress on May 18, 1933.

The purpose of TVA is to conduct a unified program of resource conservation, development, and use to advance the economic development of the Tennessee Valley region.

All functions of TVA are vested in its Board of Directors, the members of which are appointed by the President of the United States with the consent of the Senate. The offices of the Board of Directors and the General Manager are in Knoxville, Tennessee.

TVA is wholly owned by the U.S. government. Its electric power program is required to be financially self-supporting, but other programs are financed primarily by appropriations.

A system of dams built by TVA on the Tennessee River and its larger tributaries provides flood regulation on the Tennessee River and contributes to regulation of the lower Ohio and Mississippi rivers. The dams harness the power of the rivers to produce electricity. TVA is the wholesale power supplier for 160 local municipal and cooperative electric systems serving approximately 2 million customers in parts of seven states. It also supplies power to several Federal installations.

TVA is also engaged in the construction of nuclear power plants, hydroelectric projects, reservoirs, and pollution control facilities. At Muscle Shoals, Alabama, TVA operates a national laboratory for the development of new and improved fertilizers and processes. With other Federal agencies, it conducts research and development programs in forestry, fish and game, watershed protection, and health services. In the western region of the Tennessee Valley, TVA is developing "Land Between the Lakes" as a demonstration project in outdoor recreation and conservation education.

TVA issues short-term notes and bonds. The notes and bonds are not guaranteed by the U.S. government. The notes are issued only in bearer form, but the bonds are issued in both bearer and registered forms. The minimum denomination for the notes is $5,000. The minimum denomination for the bonds is $1,000.

### U.S. Postal Service

The U.S. Postal Service (USPS) was created as an independent establishment of the Executive Branch of the U.S. government by section 2 of the Postal Reorganization Act, approved August 12, 1970.

The major purpose of the Postal Service is to provide prompt, reliable, and efficient postal services to individuals and businesses in all areas of the country. Its approximately 700,000 employees handle some 90 billion pieces of mail per year.

The Board of Governors is composed of nine Governors appointed by the President of the United States with the advice and consent of the Senate for overlapping nine-year terms. The Postmaster General and the Deputy Postmaster General are named by the Board of Governors and both serve on the Board of Governors.

In addition to the national headquarters, there are five Regional organizations to which the 85 Districts report. The Districts are divided into 321 Sectional Center Manager Areas which are composed of nearly 32,000 Post Offices throughout the United States.

The Postal Service issues bonds which may or may not be guaranteed by the U.S. government. A guarantee by the U.S. government for a particular bond issue may be requested and the Secretary of the Treasury is authorized to grant such a guarantee, but it is subject to his decision. They may be issued in bearer or registered form. The minimum denomination for the bonds is $10,000.

Tables listing data about the Federal debt and securities issued by U.S. government agencies, U.S. government-sponsored agencies, and the District of Columbia will be found in Appendix C.

# Commercial Paper

*What is commercial paper?*

Commercial paper refers to short-term, negotiable, unsecured promissory notes sold by some companies with original maturities of 270 days or less.

*Why is commercial paper issued?*

It is issued as a means of raising cash. It represents an alternative to bank loans and other means of raising funds.

*What types of commercial paper are there?*

There are two broad types of commercial papers, dealer-placed paper and directly placed paper.

*Who are the dealers of dealer-placed commercial paper?*

A.G. Becker & Co., Inc.
Blyth Eastman Dillon & Co., Inc.
First Boston Corporation
Goldman, Sachs & Co.
Lehman Brothers, Inc.
Loeb, Rhoades & Co.

Merrill Lynch, Pierce, Fenner & Smith, Inc.

Paine, Webber, Jackson & Curtis, Inc.

Salomon Brothers

*Who are the main firms which sell directly placed commercial paper?*

C.I.T. Financial Corporation
Commercial Credit Corporation
Ford Motor Credit Corporation
General Electric Credit Corporation
General Motors Acceptance Corporation (GMAC)
Sears Roebuck Acceptance Corporation

*What are the denominations in which commercial paper is available?*

The following are the usual denominations, although many dealers offer commercial paper at $5000 and multiples thereof:

$25,000
$50,000
$100,000
$250,000
$500,000
$1,000,000

How low a denomination a dealer is willing to sell depends upon the dealer.

*In what form is commercial paper issued?*

Commercial paper is usually issued in bearer form (i.e., without the name of the investor). It can, however, be supplied as payable in the name of the investor.

*What is "finance company paper"?*

This is a term which has been used to refer to "directly placed" paper, because most of the issuing companies that sell commercial paper to investors without using the services of a dealer are finance companies. However, some industrial corporations also issue direct paper.

*Is commercial paper sold at a specified interest rate?*

Commercial paper is not usually sold at a specified interest rate. It is usually bought and sold at a discount. The difference between the purchase price and the redemption price tells the investor what his return is in dollars and cents. The discount rate is on a 360-day basis for commercial paper. The yield is not comparable to yields obtained on long-term bonds or interest rates paid by banks, where a 365-day-year basis is commonly used (see "THE ABCs OF CALCULATING INTEREST RATES" in the chapter "Money and Interest Rates," for a discussion of this important point).

*What is the tax status of commercial paper?*

The income from commercial paper is subject to Federal, state, and local government income taxes.

## INFORMATION IN DEPTH

### Development of the Market

The commercial paper market is a unique development of the financial and monetary system of the United States. Canada does have a commercial paper market, but it is relatively small.

Commercial paper is the oldest of the money market instruments in the United States. The very first issuance of commercial paper is lost in the annals of history, but such money market instruments were known to have been sold by brokers in New York City and Boston in 1790.

During the nineteenth century, the market became well-established and expanded. New York City became the main commercial paper market, with many other large cities setting up markets. Two developments in the early twentieth century had an important effect on the expansion of the market. During the financial panic of 1907, when high-grade corporate bonds were sold at large losses, the bulk of commercial paper notes were repaid at maturity. Later, the Federal Reserve Act of 1913 provided that commercial paper was an acceptable secondary reserve instrument for Federal Reserve member banks and was "eligible" to be discounted by the Federal Reserve.

By 1920, more than 4,000 firms were issuing commercial paper, and the outstanding volume reached $1.30 billion. During the 1920s, the volume of outstanding commercial paper declined as a result of companies acquiring working capital by issuing securities in the capital market. The Great Depression of the 1930s saw a continuing decline, with the outstanding volume falling to approximately $100 million by 1933.

Commercial paper could not adequately compete with bank loans as an alternative for companies which wished to obtain funds during the mid-1930s, because of the large build-up in excess bank reserves, which resulted in low interest rates. In 1934, the prime rate was only 1.50%.

Some consumer finance companies began to issue commercial paper during this low ebb in the market in the mid-1930s, with the entrance into the market of Commercial Credit Corporation and C.I.T. Financial Corporation. General Motors Acceptance Corporation had already entered the market in the 1920s. Finance company paper was directly placed, which eliminated the services of a dealer.

Finance company paper was, at first, not readily accepted by investors, because of the general public's fear, in the 1930s, of companies involved in consumer installment lending. After the Second World War, finance companies resorted, once again, to directly placed paper, as a result of the large growth in demand for consumer goods and financing through installment credit. By 1951, outstanding commercial paper reached $1.33 billion (surpassing the previous high of $1.30 billion in 1920), with two thirds of the outstanding paper directly placed with investors, whereas in 1920 there had been no directly placed paper.

The 1950s and 1960s saw a continued expansion of the market. By 1959, the volume of outstanding commercial paper rose to $3.5 billion (with directly placed paper accounting for approximately one half of the total volume). By the end of 1969, the total outstanding hit $31.6 billion (with directly placed paper accounting for $20 billion).

The following factors combined to result in this growth in the commercial paper market in the 1960s:

The long period of U.S. economic expansion.

The interest costs of commercial paper held at a significantly lower level than the bank prime rate through most of the 1960s.

The "credit crunch" of 1966 and 1969 forced banks to limit their lending. Several industrial companies, especially those in the electric, gas, oil, railroad, steel and telephone industries, therefore, turned to the commercial paper market for short-term funds.

Finance companies placed greater reliance on commercial paper than other forms of borrowing in the latter part of the 1960s.

In 1969, commercial banks through their subsidiaries and holding companies began to borrow heavily in the commercial paper market.

### Dealer Placement

Eight firms dominate the dealer market. During the 1960s, however, new dealers entered the market. By 1969, there were more than 30 dealers.

Companies that make use of the services of dealers will generally place their commercial paper notes in one of three ways:

By the "outright sale" method—the borrowing company is immediately paid the face value of the notes less the discount and commission. This method serves to give the borrower a definite amount of money at a specific point in time. It is the dealer who assumes the risks of the sale. This is the most popular method.

By the "bought as sold" method—the dealer markets the borrowing company's paper at the best available price and transfers the proceeds of the sale less commission to the borrower after the sale is completed. This method shifts the risks of marketing to the borrower.

The "open rate" method—combines the two other methods. The borrowing company first receives a percentage of the face amount of the commercial paper when it is delivered to the dealer. After it is sold, the dealer remits the balance less the commission to the borrower. This method also shifts the risks of marketing to the borrower.

### Direct Placement

Directly placed paper is identical to dealer paper in all respects except the manner in which it is sold. The size of the discount for both types of commercial paper depends on the interest rates prevailing for similar money market instruments of the same maturities. The discount for directly placed paper is, however, generally less than that for comparable dealer-placed paper. The size of this difference is an indication of the financial strength of the company making a direct placement.

Direct placement is especially necessary for finance companies because of their constant need for large amounts of money. Direct placement permits them to eliminate the dealer's commission.

The sales procedure for directly placed commercial paper differs from that for dealer paper. The company making the direct placement quotes an interest rate at which funds will be accepted. The investor then sets the maturity period (usually between 30 and 270 days).

If companies making the direct placement are "in funds," which means that they have all the money they want, they will temporarily lower the interest rate below the market rate, in order to discourage other investors. This technique has often served to damage investor relationships. As a result, direct-placement companies at times will make placements when they don't even need the money for the purpose of preserving good customer relationships.

### Features of Commercial Paper

Commercial paper offers certain advantages to the issuer. Interest costs are generally lower on commercial paper than on bank loans, especially when the added cost of compensating balances is considered. This feature is especially advantageous during periods of "tight money" when banks often increase the amount of compensating balances. During periods of "easy money," commercial paper rates generally decline faster than bank rates. Funds are usually readily available, particularly if the outright sales method is used. The corporate image of a company can be enhanced if it issues commercial paper, because companies with financial sophistication and good management issue "prime" commercial paper.

Despite these advantages, some firms are afraid that they will damage their existing bank relationships if they issue commercial paper. Also some firms feel that there may be too many problems in actually obtaining the funds, especially when the market is unreceptive. Others may hold back at the end of fiscal years, when financial statements are being prepared, because it shows that the company has to go into debt, which might hurt investor confidence. Unlike bank loans, commercial paper cannot be paid off before the maturity date at the discretion of the company.

Investors can usually expect a good return on commercial paper. However, there are risks, and losses can occur.

### Rating Services for Commercial Paper

Fitch Investors Service, Inc. (started rating commercial paper issues in 1971)
  *Ratings:* Fitch-1 (highest quality)
      Fitch-2
      Fitch-3
Moody's Investors Service, Inc. (a wholly-owned subsidiary of Dun & Bradstreet; took over the operations of the National Credit Office in 1971; NCO started rating the issuers of commercial paper in 1920)
  *Ratings:* Prime-1 (highest quality)
      Prime -2
      Prime-3
Standard & Poor's Corporation (started rating commercial paper issuers in 1969)
  *Ratings:* A-1 (highest quality)
      A-2
      A-3
      B
      C
      D

### Yields and Money Rates

A close relationship exists between the commercial paper yields and the yields of other money market instruments. Rates on commercial paper are usually quoted on a discount basis (i.e., a 360-day year basis). As a result, it is important to remember that on a bond-yield equivalent basis (i.e., a 365-day year basis) the yield is somewhat higher than the rate actually quoted.

Interest rates on such money market instruments as three-month Treasury bills have generally been below commercial paper rates. Cyclical patterns for commercial paper and other money market securities have usually been similar. Rates also show similar responses to monetary policies with rapid declines during periods of easy money and sharp increases during periods of tight money.

The best time to buy commercial paper and the other money market instruments is when their yields (or interest rates) are headed upward, but have not yet made their moves. The movement of yields (or interest rates) has to be gauged by the investor by his learning to be adept at understanding monetary policy and economic conditions (see the following chapters for this subject matter: "Money and Interest Rates" and "Federal Reserve System and the U.S. Banking System"; also appendices A and B).

### Significant Developments

When the Penn Central filed for bankruptcy in June 1970, it was holding $82 million in commercial paper. This default plus other defaults in commercial paper, also in 1970, by Four Seasons Nursing Centers of America and King Resources hurt the entire commercial paper market and served to make borrowers, rating services and especially investors a lot more cautious.

The period of 1970 through 1975 saw increased emphasis placed on an issuing company's liquidity (i.e., working capital or current assets minus current liabilities) rather than its total assets minus total liabilities.

Another important development in the commercial paper market has been the controversy presently raging over the financial backing for some commercial paper by letters of credit (LOCs) issued by banks. The Federal Reserve Board has raised objections to such use of LOCs because of insufficient control and insufficient disclosure by banks on their balance sheets as to the size of these contingent liabilities. Some dealers, rating personnel, money managers, and individual investors refuse to consider LOC-backed commercial paper at all.

## NEGOTIABLE CERTIFICATES OF DEPOSIT

Negotiable certificates of deposit (CDs) should not be confused with the non-negotiable types. For example, a non-negotiable type has been issued by savings banks in which the interest is paid at the rate of 7.75% per year, compounded daily, when the individual deposits $1,000 for a four-year period. Other non-negotiable types have different interest rates, depending on the amount of the initial deposit and the maturity period.

Negotiable CDs are those favored by money market funds. They require larger amounts for deposit (or investment). The non-negotiable types, however, are of great value to the small investor, because they offer him a way of directly coping with inflation. The negotiable types, however, are of particularly great value to investors, large and small, because they represent a continuous market for coping with inflation, when they offer high enough interest rates.

The small investor can invest in negotiable CDs, just as wealthy investors do, through money market funds, or through brokerage firms where the money of many small investors is pooled for the large denominations required. The market for negotiable CDs is, however, more complex than that for non-negotiable CDs.

# Negotiable Certificates of Deposit

*What is a negotiable certificate of deposit?*

It is a receipt by a commercial bank given in exchange for a deposit of money. It is sometimes called a "negotiable time certificate of deposit."

*What does a bank agree to with a negotiable certificate of deposit?*

The bank makes an agreement to pay back the amount of money deposited with interest to the holder of the receipt on a specified date.

*What significance does the fact that a certificate of deposit is negotiable have?*

The fact that a certificate of deposit (CD) is negotiable means that it can be traded in a secondary market before maturity. Nonnegotiable CDs cannot be traded in a secondary market and, therefore, have to be held to maturity.

*In what denominations are negotiable certificates of deposit issued?*

The denomination depends upon the original buyer and the issuing bank, but the range ordinarily runs from $25,000 to $10 million. It can go over $10 million, but the usual denominations are

$100,000

$500,000

$1,000,000.

The large city banks lean to the larger denominations, while the small banks lean to the smaller denominations.

*On what basis are negotiable certificates of deposit sold?*

They are sold on a bond-yield equivalent basis (i.e., on the basis of a 365-day year), unlike U.S. Treasury bills, commercial paper and bankers' acceptances, which are sold on a discount basis (i.e., on the basis of a 360-day year). Securities sold on a discount basis, therefore, have to be adjusted upwards if they are to be compared with securities sold on a bond-yield equivalent basis for the same maturity period.

*In what forms are negotiable certificates of deposit issued?*

They are issued in bearer form or registered form. The bearer form, however, is more convenient for trading in the secondary market.

## INFORMATION IN DEPTH

### Development of the Market

First National City Bank initiated the modern type of market for negotiable certificates of deposit (CDs) with an announcement in February 1961 that it would issue negotiable CDs with a large government securities dealer making a market in them.

The absence of a secondary market before 1960 had held back the growth of a CD market. CDs were rarely issued in negotiable form before 1960, although issuance of CDs actually went back to 1900. Before 1960, however, the few negotiable CDs which were issued could not be traded. From less than $1 billion outstanding before 1960, the total of CDs in denominations of $100,000 or more reached $92.8 billion on January 8, 1975 (not seasonally adjusted) for large U.S. commercial banks.

During the second quarter of 1974, credit demand was strong and banks relied heavily on the issuance of negotiable CDs to attract lendable funds. During the third quarter of 1974, however, banks greatly reduced their reliance on large CDs. Borrowing from foreign banks was discouraged during the third quarter of 1974 by the relatively large spread between Eurodollar interest rates and domestic interest rates. Large CDs outstanding increased $3.5 billion for this quarter (seasonally adjusted), and the expansion was concentrated in the large money market banks to a somewhat greater extent than it had been during comparable periods in recent years.

There was heightened concern on the part of the public regarding the stability of financial institutions and, as a result, some investors registered this concern by preferring the liabilities of a small number of very large commercial banks.

### Maturity Periods

The maturity period can range from one month to 18 months. A survey taken in December 1969 showed that slightly over 70% of total CDs outstanding at weekly reporting member banks of the Federal Reserve System matured within four months. It is especially common to follow the yields on 90-day (or three-month) CDs.

Important factors in determining the maturity period are Regulation Q of the Federal Reserve System, a bank's need for funds, and expectations of future movements of interest rates.

Regulation Q of the Federal Reserve System sets the ceiling rate that banks can pay on time deposits. Regulation Q also applies to the ceiling rates on CDs. Thus, during the early 1960s, the ceiling rate structure resulting from Regulation Q made it very difficult to issue CDs with maturities of less than six months. This structure resulted from the maximum interest rates permitted under Regulation Q, as can be seen in Table (2-1.)

An examination of the table indicates that up to July 17, 1963, for maturities of 90 days to six months only a 2.5% interest rate was permitted, while up to November 24, 1964, only a 1.0% interest rate was permitted on maturities of less than 90 days. The difficulty facing the commercial banks was that, starting in 1962, the rates on competing money market securities (e.g., Treasury bills and commercial paper) generally rose above 2.5%. As a result, new CD issues of less than six months could not compete.

**TABLE 2-1**

**Maximum Interest Rates Payable Under Regulation Q On Certain Time Deposits**

| Maturity | Effective Date | | | | | | | |
|---|---|---|---|---|---|---|---|---|
| | January 1, 1957 | January 1, 1962 | July 17, 1963 | November 24, 1964 | December 6, 1965 | July 20, 1966 | September 26, 1966 | April 19, 1968 |
| 1 year and over | 3.0% | 4.0% | 4.0% | 4.5% | 5.5% | | | |
| 6 to 12 months | 3.0 | 3.5 | 4.0 | 4.5 | 5.5 | | | |
| 90 days to 6 months | 2.5 | 2.5 | 4.0 | 4.5 | 5.5 | | | |
| Less than 90 days | 1.0 | 1.0 | 1.0 | 4.0 | 5.5 | | | |
| Denominations of $100,000 and over | | | | | | | | |
| 180 days and over | | | | | | 5.5% | 5.5% | 6.25% |
| 90 to 179 days | | | | | | 5.5 | 5.5 | 6.0 |
| 60 to 89 days | | | | | | 5.5 | 5.5 | 5.75 |
| Less than 60 days | | | | | | 5.5 | 5.5 | 5.5 |
| Denominations of less than $100,000 | | | | | | 5.5 | 5.0 | 5.0 |

*Source:* Federal Reserve Bank of Cleveland, *Money Market Instruments* (August 1970), p. 79.

On December 6, 1965, however, Regulation Q ceilings were set at 5.5% for all maturity periods. Banks then issued CDs with shorter maturity periods. Finally, on May 16, 1973, the interest rate ceilings were suspended on large negotiable CDs with maturity periods of 90 days or over.

A bank can adjust the maturity period according to its need for funds. With regard to expectations of future movements of interest rates, if interest rates are expected to decline in the near term, a bank will emphasize CDs with short maturity periods, with the expectation of renewing the maturing issues at lower rates in the future. Investors, however, would prefer long maturity periods if they expected a decline in interest rates.

### The Secondary Market

The secondary market for CDs is thinner than the U.S. Treasury bill market. A big reason for the thinness of the CD market is due to the fact that original purchasers often like to hold their CDs until maturity. In addition, CD dealers generally like to keep low inventories during periods of uncertain economic conditions and during periods of rising interest rates because of risks of capital losses. Another contributing factor regarding the size of CD inventories is the relative cost of CD inventories in comparison to the other securities (CD inventories are financed almost exclusively through short-term loans rather than equity capital).

It should be noted that CDs are not eligible for Federal Reserve repurchase agreements, although nonbank dealers often finance Treasury bills and bankers' acceptances through repurchase agreements.

The usual size of a trading unit in the secondary market is $1 million. The volatility of CD interest rates, in the secondary market, is reduced, because small denominational units, which have a broader range of interest rates are eliminated or used very little.

The heart of the CD secondary market lies in New York City. The large New York City banks figure importantly in this market because a great number of multinational corporations and other large corporations have accounts at these banks. A significant factor in the growth of the CD market has, in fact, been due to purchases by large corporations.

### CDs and Monetary Policy

The direct connection of CDs and monetary policy lies in the fact that the monetary authorities, specifically the Board of Governors of the Federal Reserve System, have the authority to set the maximum rate on new CD issues under Regulation Q.

During the 1960s, the Board of Governors of the Federal Reserve System saw fit to vary the maximum interest rates payable. At times, banks could not successfully provide CD rates which could compete with other money market instruments. On May 16, 1973, however, suspension of interest rate ceilings on large negotiable CDs with maturity periods of 90 days or over led to a mushrooming of the CD market.

Another factor to be considered in affecting CD rates is the influence which the Federal Reserve System can exert on the interest rates of other money market instruments. This monetary power was brought out very well in the pressure which Dr. Burns, Chairman of the Board of Governors of the Federal Reserve System brought to bear in the latter part of 1974 and early 1975 to bring down interest rates. The Federal funds rate, CD rates, and other money market rates came down as a result of a deliberate policy of the Federal Reserve System.

A comparison of some money market rates can be seen in Table 2-2.

**TABLE 2-2**

Money Market Rates (per year)

| Date | 90-day CDs | Prime Commercial Paper, 4-6 months | Prime Bankers' Acceptances | Three-month Treasury Bills |
|------|-----------|------------------------------------|----------------------------|----------------------------|
| January   3, 1975 | 9.36 | 8.84 | 9.08 | 6.96 |
| January 10, 1975 | 8.57 | 7.83 | 8.33 | 6.59 |
| January 17, 1975 | 7.81 | 7.53 | 7.65 | 6.54 |
| January 24, 1975 | 7.31 | 6.85 | 7.03 | 5.98 |
| January 31, 1975 | 6.78 | 6.48 | 6.59 | 5.68 |
| February 7, 1975 | 6.55 | 6.50 | 6.40 | 5.57 |

Note: The figures shown for the 90-day CDs are seven-day averages of secondary market rates for the week ending Wednesday, which is two days earlier than the dates shown.
*Source:* Federal Reserve Bank of St. Louis

Growth of the CD market can be seen in Figure 2-5, on the facing page, which graphs the increase in negotiable CDs of $100,000 or more for large weekly-reporting U.S. commercial banks.

# Bankers' Acceptances

*What are bankers' acceptances?*     Bankers' acceptances are negotiable time drafts, which represent one type of a broad class of credit in-

**FIGURE 2-5**

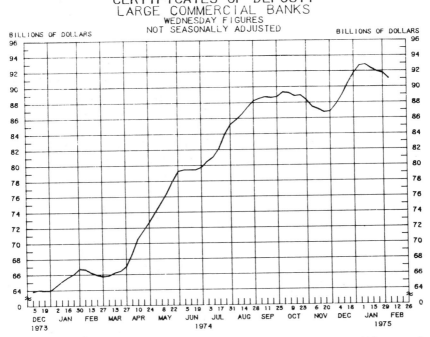

CERTIFICATES OF DEPOSIT
LARGE COMMERCIAL BANKS
WEDNESDAY FIGURES
NOT SEASONALLY ADJUSTED

Note: Negotiable time certificates of deposit issued in denominations of $100,000 or more by large weekly reporting commercial banks are indicated.

SOURCE: Federal Reserve Bank of St. Louis.

struments known as "bills of exchange." Bills of exchange are orders to pay specified amounts of money at specified times drawn on individuals, business firms, or financial institutions. When the drawee formally acknowledges his obligation to honor such a draft (usually by writing "accepted" or "I accept" with the required signature), it becomes an acceptance.

*What makes bankers' acceptances attractive money market instruments?*

Bankers' acceptances generally have a high degree of safety. They are examples of what is called in financial circles "two-name paper." The safety thus results from the fact that both the drawer, who endorses the acceptance when he sells it, and the accepting bank are obligors of the draft.

*How can one rate bankers' acceptances?*

The rating of the various bankers' acceptances is done on the basis of the reputation and financial soundness of the bank involved.

*How do banks open acceptance credits?*

Banks open acceptance credits (or accept drafts) usually under letters of credit.

*How do bankers' acceptances usually arise?*

They usually arise from letters of credit in foreign trade transactions.

*Why do banks prefer to hold acceptances drawn on other banks rather than themselves?*

While banks do hold acceptances drawn on themselves, they prefer to hold acceptances drawn on other banks because of advantages of marketability. When an acceptance is endorsed by the drawer and two banks, it is known as "three-name paper."

*Who are the main investors in "three-name paper"?*

Such bankers' acceptances are especially attractive to foreign investors. Some of them will only purchase this type.

*What is a "swap"?*

This market technique describes the practice of accepting banks which sell to dealers their acquisitions of acceptances drawn on themselves and replace them in their portfolios with acceptances drawn on other banks.

*What are the maturity periods for bankers' acceptances?*

Maturity periods usually range from 30 to 180 days, with 90 days the most common, but the maturity period can exceed 180 days.

*How do bankers' acceptances compare to U.S. Treasury bills with regard to liquidity, safety, and yields?*

Bankers' acceptances run below Treasury bills in liquidity and safety. As a result, the yields on acceptances usually run higher than on Treasury bills.

*Why is it that the market yields on bankers' acceptances do not give a true picture of the costs to the borrower?*

The reason for this is that accepting banks charge fees for this service. Traditionally, the charge has been $1\frac{1}{2}\%$ per year (or $\frac{1}{8}\%$ per month) for accepting a draft on behalf of nonbank customers with the best credit ratings. The fees rise according to how much below the highest credit rating a particular customer is rated.

*What is the actual cost to the borrower?*

The actual cost to the borrower equals the fee plus the discount on the acceptance. When a foreign bank acquires an acceptance on a U.S. bank for purposes of obtaining dollar exchange, the discount is sometimes absorbed directly and sometimes indirectly. The borrower should, however, be aware that often the discount is paid but the payment shows up in an increase in the price of the merchandise.

*Is there a secondary market for bankers' acceptances?*

Yes. Bankers' acceptances are high-grade negotiable money market instruments and can be sold in a secondary market before the maturity date of the acceptance.

*Where is the secondary market located?*

The secondary market is centered in New York City.

*Who are the main dealers in the secondary market?*

Briggs Schaedle & Co., Inc.
Discount Corporation of New York
First Boston Corporation
M&T Discount Corporation

Merrill Lynch, Pierce, Fenner &
  Smith, Inc.
Hanseatic Corporation
Salomon Brothers

*On what basis are bankers'
acceptances sold?*

Bankers' acceptances are sold on a
discount basis. The yield is quoted
on the basis of a 360-day year. As a
result, the quoted yield is less than
an investor's actual return on investment. As with U.S. Treasury bills
and commercial paper, conversion
has to be made from the 360-day
year basis to a bond-equivalent basis
(i.e., 365-day year basis).

*In what denominations are bankers'
acceptances sold to the investor?*

Bankers' acceptances are not sold in
specified denominations like other
money market securities (e.g., U.S.
Treasury bills, U.S. Treasury notes,
commercial paper and negotiable
CDs). They may vary in denomination depending upon the particular
bankers' acceptance involved. The
usual range, however, is $25,000 to
$1,000,000.

*What is the tax status of bankers'
acceptances?*

The income from bankers' acceptances is subject to Federal, state,
and local government income taxes
for U.S. citizens. *Foreign holders,
however, are usually exempt from
U.S. income taxes.*

## INFORMATION IN DEPTH

### Development of the Market

Bankers' acceptances have a long history in Europe, dating back to
premodern times. They have enjoyed great popularity in Europe, but in the
United States, they have not been so popular.

They were used quite widely before the American Civil War, but at the
time of the establishment of the Federal Reserve System, at the end of 1913,
very little acceptance financing was engaged in by American banks and
nonbanking institutions.

The Federal Reserve System set itself the task of developing a strong and viable acceptance market soon after it started operations in 1914. Throughout the period 1934 to 1955, Federal Reserve activity declined. As agent for foreign central banks, however, the Federal Reserve operated on both sides of the market.

Volume rose to $1.7 billion in 1929 and then sharply declined during the Great Depression of the 1930s and fell to $110 million in 1944. From 1934 to 1955, the Federal Reserve System provided some market support, which was strengthened during the period 1955 to 1974. Open-market operations in bankers' acceptances was centered in the Federal Reserve Bank of New York, and total volume rose to a record $16.9 billion in October 1974.

### The Investors

The largest group in the acceptance market consists of foreign banks and foreign nonbank institutions. A big incentive for foreign investors has been the fact that they are generally exempted from U.S. income taxes. The net yield is, therefore, higher for acceptances than for Treasury bills. A foreign investor, however, in order to get an accurate picture would have to consider any reciprocal tax treaties between his country and the United States which might offset this tax advantage.

The next largest group is that of the accepting banks. On November 30, 1974, out of a total of $16,553,219,000 of bankers' acceptances, accepting banks held $3,788,560,000 ($3,289,978,000 of their own bills plus $498,582,000 of the bills of others).

The Federal Reserve System holds acceptances for its own account and for foreigners. U.S. nonbank corporations have holdings, with the size of their holdings depending primarily on the actual acceptance yields compared to the yields on other money market instruments and the yields on capital market securities.

Individual American investors have generally lacked knowledge of this market and have, therefore, stayed away from it. American investors should get more involved in this market, however, because it offers yields that are comparable and sometimes higher than other money markets.

### Creation of a Banker's Acceptance

A banker's acceptance is created in connection with payment by a buyer to a seller. As it is usually created in connection with foreign trade rather than in trade within the United States, importers and exporters are usually involved. Living in different countries, they often don't know each other's credit standing. An acceptance provides the means by which an internationally known U.S. bank assumes the obligation of paying the required amount at a certain date. Most acceptances are for short-term periods (i.e., six months or less).

For example, a foreign shoe manufacturer might want to sell shoes to a U.S. importer. The U.S. importer could approach his bank for acceptance credit. If the importer's bank agrees to the financing, it would send a letter to the shoe manufacturer (or his bank) informing him that credit has been established. This is known as a "letter of credit." The shoe manufacturer is then authorized to draw a time draft on the U.S. bank. For a fee, the U.S. bank agrees to accept the draft when presented if it is accompanied by documents specified by the U.S. importer (e.g., an invoice, a bill of lading as evidence of shipment, the transfer of title to the merchandise, and insurance papers). When arrangements for the shipment have been completed, the foreign shoe manufacturer draws the time draft on the U.S. bank and delivers it to his local bank, together with the supporting documents.

The foreign shoe manufacturer can obtain the cash immediately by selling the draft to his bank. The amount received would be less than the face value of the draft because of the charges by the bank for risk, handling costs, and the advance that the bank is making for an obligation that does not become payable until a future date. The difference between the face value of the draft and the amount paid to the shoe manufacturer is known as the "discount."

Thus, the shoe manufacturer can obtain his money before the U.S. importer has paid for the shoes. The shoe manufacturer's bank then remits the discounted draft to the U.S. bank for acceptance and discount.

The U.S. bank then forwards the supporting documents to the U.S. importer so that he can take possession of the shoes when they arrive. The U.S. bank, at this point, has the option of holding the acceptance as an earning asset or selling it in the secondary market at the market rate of discount for its maturity period.

The U.S. importer has to pay the U.S. bank before maturity of the acceptance.

This is an example of what is known as the creation of a "dollar acceptance."

The advantages of using a dollar acceptance are several. The exporter receives his money promptly, avoiding any delays connected with the shipping of the merchandise. The exporter does not have to worry about foreign exchange costs and risks because his bank pays him in the currency of his country. Further, the exporter does not have to worry about the credit standing of the importer because a bank has guaranteed payment.

### Return on Investment and Money Rates

The pattern of yields on bankers' acceptances in the secondary market generally follows very closely that of the other money market instruments.

Yields on acceptances sharply declined in 1960 and 1961, gradually rose during 1962 to 1965 and sharply rose in 1966, as a result of the "tight-money" policy. Yields averaged 5.36% in 1966. After a brief decline in 1967, rates rose steadily and hit record highs in mid-1974. In the last quarter of 1974, rates were down sharply from those highs. Prime bankers' acceptances hit an average rate of 12.16% on August 23, 1974.

The average rates for prime bankers' acceptances and three-month Treasury bills at the end of 1974 are shown in Table 2-3.

**TABLE 2-3**

Prime Bankers' Acceptances Compared to U.S. Treasury Bills
(% per year)

| Date | Prime Bankers' Acceptances | Three-Month Treasury Bills |
|------|-----------------------------|----------------------------|
| Nov.  1, 1974 | 8.95 | 7.95 |
| Nov.  8, 1974 | 8.83 | 7.66 |
| Nov. 15, 1974 | 8.94 | 7.26 |
| Nov. 22, 1974 | 9.00 | 7.46 |
| Nov. 29, 1974 | 9.41 | 7.45 |
| Dec.  6, 1974 | 9.55 | 7.44 |
| Dec. 13, 1974 | 9.03 | 7.24 |
| Dec. 20, 1974 | 9.03 | 6.92 |
| Dec. 27, 1974 | 9.13 | 7.06 |

*Source:* Federal Reserve Bank of St. Louis

### Significant Developments

During November and December of 1974, the bankers' acceptance market sustained only moderate rate increases.

In the early part of November 1974, the Federal Reserve Bank of New York announced a suspension of the Federal Reserve System's practice of guaranteeing acceptance purchases on behalf of foreign official accounts. In announcing the change, the Federal Reserve Bank of New York took note of the fact that the volume of bankers' acceptances held for foreign official accounts and carrying the Federal Reserve System's guarantee had risen sharply in recent years to over $2 billion and that there was a good possibility of further large increases. Partly as a result of the suspension, small banks found that they had to pay more in comparison with the large banks than previously.

# *capital markets*

$$\rule{6cm}{0.5cm}$$

# 3

In general, investments in the capital markets are considered to be long-term. Investments which are for maturity periods of five years or more are definitely classified in the capital markets.

The primary components of the capital markets are the stock market and the bond market. In the stock market, interest centers on common stock rather than preferred stock and on capital gains rather than on dividends. In the words of a popular saying in the financial community, however, when it comes to the stock market "an investor talks long-term but thinks short-term." In the case of the bond market, an investor more usually thinks long-term and in terms of a fixed income rather than capital gains.

It should be noted that the various capital markets display more diversity than the money markets.

The chapter on capital markets which you are about to consider is broken down into two sections, "Stocks and the Stock Market" and "Bonds and the Bond Market."

In the section "Stocks and the Stock Market," you will learn what to look for in evaluating your possible investments. You will find out what the Balance Sheet and Income Statement represent, how to make a financial analysis, and how to calculate financial ratios that will give you insight into how well a company is doing, and you will learn how to judge corporate managements. You will also learn about the various stock market averages and indexes.

In the section "Bonds and the Bond Market," you will find out what a bond is, you will find out about the various types of bonds, and you will be in a position to decide whether you want to invest in bonds for the purpose of obtaining a fixed income.

# Stocks and the Stock Market

## THE BULLS vs. THE BEARS

You are a "bull" if you think that the common stock of a corporation is going to go up in value. You are a "bear" if you think that it is going to go down in value. In general, for each traded stock, there are bulls and bears. Some people expect the stock price to go up, and some expect the stock price to go down.

A "bull market" is a period during which the stock market is headed sharply upward. This is not to say that the stock of every single corporation is headed sharply upward, but rather that this is the general trend. Some stocks do go down even in a bull market. There was a strong bull market from the end of 1966 to the end of 1968.

A "bear market" is a period during which the stock market is headed sharply downward, although some stocks may buck the trend. There was a strong bear market from January 11, 1973 (when the Dow-Jones Industrial Average hit a historic high of 1051.70) to the end of 1974.

## MARKET TRENDS

Various averages and indexes (e.g., the Dow-Jones Industrial Average, Dow-Jones Transportation Average, Dow-Jones Utility Average, Dow-Jones Composite Average, Standard and Poor's Indexes, New York Stock Exchange Indexes, American Stock Exchange Price Level Index, the New York Times Averages) are helpful to the investor by indicating general market trends, and they will be dealt with in detail later in this chapter.

While the averages and indexes are helpful, the key question to ask yourself is: "How is my stock doing?" It doesn't help you to know that all the averages and indexes are going sharply up, while your stock is going sharply down.

### Ups and Downs

People usually boast about the stocks they have that went up in value, but don't usually mention the stocks they have that went down. Remember that stocks can go either way.

Find out all you can about a company before you buy the stock. What is the potential? There can also be different reasons for buying a stock. You might want to buy a stock just for the dividends, although most people usually think in terms of buying a stock for appreciation.

Something to remember is that no matter what the stock is, you are not married to it. If it doesn't perform the way you want it to after a reasonable length of time, sell it.

Stocks, to a large extent, reflect the ability of the corporate managements. Some are conservative and some are highly growth-oriented, some are operated under sound financial principles and some are "fly-by-nights." The growth of some stocks has been truly spectacular, especially if you bought the stocks when they first went public, such as AT&T, General Motors, IBM, Polaroid, Syntex, and Xerox.

All stocks, however, have their ups and downs. Don't expect them to go straight up or straight down. The one thing you can be sure of is that they will fluctuate.

## SOME BASICS

All corporations have to issue common stock. They may not want to issue any other securities, but they must issue common stock.

When you buy common stock you become an owner of the corporation. It is the riskiest of the various securities, because you are assured of nothing. You may or may not receive dividends, the stock price may go up or down and, in the event of bankruptcy, you will be the last to receive any remaining assets after the other holders of securities and the creditors have received their money (which sometimes means you end up with nothing). Yet, in spite of all this, common stock is much desired by individual investors and institutional investors alike, because common stock has the greatest potential for growth.

There is also preferred stock, another class of stock, which carries only limited ownership in the corporation (preferred stock is considered in more detail later in this chapter).

It is advisable at this point for you to get a clear view of what a corporation is. A corporation was defined very well by Chief Justice John Marshall of the U.S. Supreme Court in the Dartmouth College case of 1819, and this definition is frequently quoted even today:

A corporation is an artificial being, invisible, intangible, and existing only in contemplation of the law. Being a mere creature of law, it possesses only those properties which the charter of its creation confers upon it, either expressly or as incidental to its very existence.

The increase in the formation of corporations since the Dartmouth College case resulted particularly from the fact that there is limited liability for the investors. If you buy stock you are generally not held personally liable for the debts of the corporation (unlike other forms of business, such as a single proprietorship or a general partnership, in which you might bear full liability and your private property might be taken from you to pay the obligations of the business).

Other advantages which led to an increasing number of corporations are that larger amounts of money can be raised by corporations generally than by other forms of business, the shares of stock are transferable, there is a great deal of stability, the potential for growth is greater than for other forms of business, and there is continuous life for the corporation (theoretically, at least, the corporate life is perpetual, subject, of course, to bankruptcies or other calamities or contingencies).

## BUYING COMMON STOCK

Common stock can be bought as a hedge against inflation, for income (i.e., dividends), for speculation, or for capital gains (i.e., buying low and selling high, either short-term or long-term).

Which common stock you should buy (if any) depends upon the type of person you are. Therefore, "Know thyself."

The big question is: How much risk are you willing to take?

Security analysts (or "financial analysts," as they are also called) rate common stocks according to beta and alpha coefficients. A beta coefficient is calculated in order to evaluate the degree of risk. The higher the degree of risk involved in a stock, the higher its beta coefficient. The alpha coefficient is calculated to determine to what degree the common stock has not reacted as expected.

Regarding the particular stock which you might want to buy, you have to decide how much safety you want. Do you want to emphasize safety or growth? Do you want to speculate or do you want income (i.e., dividends)?

The type of investment should fit the type of person that you are. If you are in high school or college, your potential for higher income than you presently have is, by the law of averages, in your favor, and you can afford to take the more speculative common stock or growth-oriented stocks. If you are in graduate school or have just acquired an MBA degree, your potential is still greater. If you are a young top executive with a corporation, your potential is even greater.

On the other hand, if you are widowed or elderly and live on a fixed income, you should be extra careful and emphasize safety.

If you have no more than an average income (e.g., $10,000-$15,000 per year), then you should be cautious, emphasize safety, and don't speculate. The average investor (or "small investor") should not assume great risks.

### How to Buy Common Stock

There are various ways of buying common stock:

1. In *buying outright,* you pay the full amount for the shares of stock. For example, if the stock is selling at $20 per share and you buy 100 shares, then you pay:

   $20 per share × 100 shares = $2000

   plus commission and other fees.

2. In *buying on margin,* you do not put up the full amount for the shares of stock. You borrow money from your broker. The amount of margin is set by the Board of Governors of the Federal Reserve System. For example, if the margin is at 60%, then you have to put up 60% of the money and your broker puts up 40%. You still have the commission and fees.

3. In *dollar-cost averaging (or dollar averaging),* you buy the stock regularly in the same dollar value regardless of whether the stock goes up or down. As a result, over a period of time, your average cost for the shares will be less than your average price for the shares.

4. In *buying shares of an investment company,* you are really buying the expertise of its management, and you are seeking professional management and diversification. There are two broad types of investment companies:

   "closed-end investment companies," whose shares of stock sell like any other and are subject to supply and demand for that stock like any other stock, and

   "open-end investment companies" (or "mutual funds"), whose shares of stock are generally sold continuously at net asset value, some with a fixed charge (or "load") to buy into the fund and some without a fixed charge (or "no-load"). Hence, there are "load funds" and "no-load funds." Unlike the closed-end investment companies, the mutual funds redeem their shares upon demand.

   Payments for mutual funds can be made in different ways:

   *by contractual plan,* in which you agree to make payments on a periodic basis.

   *by voluntary plan,* in which you pay what you want when you want.

   *by regular plan,* in which you make only a single payment.

5. *New York Stock Exchange Monthly Investment Plan* ("MIP"). The MIP was started by the New York Stock Exchange on January 25, 1954, for the purpose of giving the "small investor" an opportunity to take advantage of dollar-cost averaging. MIP is best for the long-term. You can buy common

stocks listed on the New York Stock Exchange. If you want diversification, you can buy the common stock of the closed-end investment companies listed on the New York Stock Exchange.

## Placing Orders

1. Common stock orders are in round-lots of 100 shares (or multiples of 100) for stocks that trade in 100-share units. There are also stocks which have round-lots of 10 shares or multiples of 10 for stocks that trade in 10-share units.

   Odd-lots are orders for less than 100 shares for stocks that trade in 100-share units or less than 10 shares for stocks that trade in 10-share units.

   Round-lot orders should give a somewhat better price than odd-lot orders. How good a price you actually get depends a lot on your broker's bargaining ability.

   To order a round-lot, you place your order with a Registered Representative (or "Account Executive") at a brokerage firm, who fills out the order slip. The order is then relayed to the floor of the exchange (e.g., New York Stock Exchange).

   If you place an odd-lot order with your Registered Representative, your order is then relayed to a special odd-lot dealer. A fractional amount is added on to the next round-lot for the price. You might not be able to buy a round-lot because you don't have enough money. You should, however, buy in round-lots whenever possible.

   The commission and fees are added on for both the round-lot and odd-lot orders.

2. If your order is a *"day order,"* it will expire at the end of the business day on which it was made. It may be cancelled by you before the end of the business day, if you want to.

3. If your order is a *"GTC order,"* it will expire on the last business day of April or October (whichever applies), unless renewed. "GTC" originally meant "Good Till Cancelled," but now has the renewal requirement.

4. When you place a *"market order,"* you make no limitation as to price. It will simply be the best price your broker can obtain on the market.

5. In a *"limit order,"* you specify a particular price. If you place an order to buy hypothetical stock ABC at 20, it must be bought only at $20 per share (or less), but not more than $20 per share. If you place an order to sell hypothetical stock XYZ at 50, it must be sold at $50 per share (or more), but not at less than $50 per share.

6. You will place a *"stop order to buy,"* if you want to limit any possible loss or you want to protect a prof t which you may have made. For example, you can use this type of order if you sold short (i.e., you sold stock which you did not own, but borrowed the stock through your broker, with the expectation that the stock price would decline). If you sold short, hypothetical stock DEF at 80 (i.e., $80 per share) and it is now selling at 50 (i.e. $50 per share), you now have an unrealized profit of $30 per share. You can now enter a "buy stop order" at, for example, 53 (i.e., $53 per share). Thus, if the stock goes up to $53, the "buy stop order" will then be executed, and any loss will be limited.

7. You will place a *"stop order to sell"* if you want to protect an unrealized profit after a stock has gone up in price. For example, assume that you bought hypothetical stock TUV at 10 (i.e., $10 per share) and it is now selling at 90 (i.e., $90 per share). You can place a "stop sell order" at 86 (i.e., $86 per share). If the stock declines to 86, your "Stop Sell Order" will be executed, and any loss will be limited.

8. If you decide not to buy, after placing a buy order or not to sell, after placing a sell order, place a *cancellation order* as soon as possible. Time is of the essence here. You can also make changes in the price you might want to buy at or sell at, but do it fast.

### For Quotations

If you want to get quotations on the ticker tape or quote machines, be sure to find out the correct symbol. Some symbols of popular stocks are given here:

| | |
|---|---|
| American Telephone & Telegraph | T |
| DuPont | DD |
| General Electric | GE |
| General Motors | GM |
| International Business Machines | IBM |
| Merck | MRK |
| Radio Corporation of America | RCA |
| U.S. Steel | X |
| Westinghouse | WX |
| Woolworth | Z |
| Xerox | XRX |

When you look for quotes in the newspapers (e.g., *The New York Times, The Wall Street Journal,* or *The Washington Post*), all you have to know is the name of the company that you are interested in.

There are some stocks which you will not find quoted in newspapers that are traded in the Over-the-Counter market. These stocks you will find quoted in what are called the "pink sheets," which you may find in brokerage offices.

## FUNDAMENTAL ANALYSIS VERSUS TECHNICAL ANALYSIS

Fundamental analysis is practiced by those security analysts (or financial analysts) who concentrate on: the overall economy, a particular industry, or a particular company.

There are security analysts who specialize in only one industry. Some, however, specialize in several industries, and those who are called "generalists" cover any industries. The fundamental analysts try to get to know companies in a particular industry very well, to study their financial statements (e.g., balance sheets, income statements, sources and uses statements, statements of retained earnings) and to make earnings forecasts for those companies.

Those security analysts who practice technical analysis are called "technical analysts" (or "chartists"). They attempt to make forecasts on the basis of patterns in stock prices for individual companies.

You can obtain both fundamental and technical analyses from various services as well as from brokerage firms. Below are listed useful publications put out by some services. See the portion of this book entitled "Where You Can Get Information and Data on a Continuous Basis" (Appendix E) under "Stocks & Bonds" for additional sources of information.

*For Fundamental Analysis*

"Handbook of Common Stocks"
"Stock Survey"
Moody's Investors Service
99 Church Street
New York, N.Y. 10007

"Industry Surveys"
"Stock Reports"
Standard & Poor's
345 Hudson Street
New York, N.Y. 10014

"The Value Line Investment Survey"
Arnold Bernhard & Co., Inc.
5 East 44th Street
New York, N.Y. 10017

*For Technical Analysis*

"Chartcraft"
Chartcraft, Inc.
Dept. B-644
Larchmont, N.Y. 10538

"Crosscraft"
Dines Chart Corporation
18 East 41st Street
New York, N.Y. 10017

"Trendline"
Trendline
345 Hudson Street
New York, N.Y. 10014

## DOCUMENTS

One who wishes to make money by investing in stocks should understand certain basics in order to know how financially "solid" or speculative a company is. Two basic financial statements should be understood, the balance sheet and the income statement. Although there are many other financial statements, these two are fundamental.

The company's annual report can give some valuable information, and one should be sure to look carefully at the footnotes, but the annual report is essentially a publicity tool for the management of the company.

As a prospectus can give a lot of important information, one should insist on seeing the latest prospectus for a company. The document of greatest value, however, for the potential investor or present investor is the Securities and Exchange Commission's Form 10-K.

Form 10-K is an annual report filed with the Securities and Exchange Commission (SEC) pursuant to Section 13 of the Securities Exchange Act of 1934. This is the document to insist upon seeing. Some companies, however, don't like the Form 10-K to be seen, while others send them for a fee upon request or even free of charge. They are, however, available for reading in SEC libraries.

Form 10-K, prospectus, and annual report contain balance sheets and income statements. For the purpose of explaining these financial statements, they will be analyzed for a hypothetical company called "Corporation X." This will be followed by a consideration of the stock market itself.

### TABLE 3-1

CORPORATION X
December 31, 19 ____
(in millions)

*ASSETS*

*Current Assets*

| | | |
|---|---|---|
| Cash | | $  5 |
| Marketable securities | | 10 |
| Accounts receivable (minus uncollectables) | | 20 |
| Inventories | | 25 |
| | Total Current Assets | $60 |

*Fixed Assets*

| | | |
|---|---|---|
| Land | $25 | |
| Buildings | 10 | |
| Equipment | 10 | |
| (minus accumulated depreciation) | — | |
| | Net Fixed Assets | $45 |

*Other Assets* ..................................................... $ 1

| | | |
|---|---|---|
| (Goodwill, Patents, Trademarks, Copyrights) | | $ 1 |
| | Total Assets | $106 |

**TABLE 3-1** *(continued)*

---

### *LIABILITIES AND STOCKHOLDERS' EQUITY*

*Current Liabilities*

| | |
|---|---:|
| Accounts payable .................................... | $10 |
| Notes payable ....................................... | 5 |
| Federal income taxes ................................ | 6 |
| Taxes other than Federal income taxes .................. | 4 |
| Accrued salaries and wages .......................... | 5 |
| Total Current Liabilities | $30 |

*Long-term Debt*

| | |
|---|---:|
| Real estate mortgage bonds ........................... | $ 5 |
| Debentures ......................................... | $ 8 |
| Subordinated debentures ............................. | $ 2 |
| Total Long-Term Debt | $15 |

*Stockholders' Equity*

*Capital Stock*

| | |
|---|---:|
| Common stock, $1 par value, authorized, issued, and outstanding, 24,000,000 shares ............................... | $24 |
| *Capital in excess of par value of common stock* ............... | 14 |
| *Retained earnings* ....................................... | 23 |
| Total Stockholders' Equity | $61 |
| Total Liabilities and Stockholders' Equity | $106 |

---

## FINANCIAL ANALYSIS

Four broad types of analyses are used in appraising a company's financial position: liquidity analysis, debt analysis, investment-sales analysis, and profitability analysis.

### Liquidity Analysis

*Liquidity analysis* measures a company's degree of solvency. All the measurements are for determining the degree of solvency for meeting obligations coming due within one year.

*Gross working capital* refers to a company's total current assets. For Corporation X,

Gross Working Capital = $60 million.

**TABLE 3-2**

CORPORATION X
Income Statement
For Year Ended December 31, 1975*

| | |
|---|---|
| Net sales | $70 |
| *Minus:* cost of goods sold | 60 |
| Gross profit | $10 |
| *Minus:* Marketing, administrative, and research expenses | 4 |
| Gross operating income | $ 6 |
| Minus: Depreciation | 1 |
| Net operating income | $ 5 |
| Minus: Other expenses | 2 |
| Interest | |
| Contribution to employees' profit-sharing plan | |
| Profits before income taxes | $ 3 |
| Income taxes (Federal and foreign) | 1 |
| Net profits after taxes | $ 2 |
| Net earnings per share of common stock | $ 0.08 |

*In millions except for net earnings per share of common stock.

*Net working capital* is often simply referred to as *working capital.* It is what remains after "total current liabilities" is deducted from "total current assets." For Corporation X,

| | |
|---|---|
| Total Current Assets | $60 million |
| Total Current Liabilities | − 30 million |
| Net Working Capital | $30 million |

Net working capital is a particularly important figure. It tells you how easily a company can meet the costs of normal operations (e.g., meet the payroll, pay for raw materials, pay for transportation costs), expand facilities, and cope with sudden emergencies. It is far more significant than the value obtained by deducting "total liabilities" from "total assets," because the fixed assets included in "total assets" cannot be readily converted into cash if funds are suddenly necessary. A case in point is the Penn Central bankruptcy in 1970, which was clearly a problem of net working capital (or liquidity).

The *current ratio* gives a broad gauge of a company's liquidity. The higher the value of the current ratio, the greater the margin of safety the company possesses to meet short-term obligations. Each industry should be considered separately. An industry average should be obtained, and then the current ratio for the particular company one is interested in should be compared with the average. Comparison should also be made for different years to see the trend. In general, the ratio should be 2 or more, although a lower value than 2 might be justified by a particular company.

For Corporation X, the current ratio is calculated as follows:

$$\text{Current Ratio} = \frac{\text{Current Assets}}{\text{Current Liabilities}}$$

$$= \frac{\$60 \text{ million}}{\$30 \text{ million}}$$

$$= 2$$

*The acid-test* ratio gives a more accurate indication of a company's liquidity than the current ratio. The value of inventories is removed from the current assets, because it is very often difficult to convert inventories into cash. The acid-test ratio is sometimes called the "quick ratio." In general, it should be 1 or more, although a lower value than 1 might at times be justified.

For Corporation X, the acid-test ratio is calculated as follows:

$$\text{Acid-Test Ratio} = \frac{\text{Current Assets—Inventories}}{\text{Current Liabilities}}$$

$$= \frac{\$60 \text{ million--}\$25 \text{ million}}{\$30 \text{ million}}$$

$$= 1.17$$

### Debt Analysis

*Debt analysis* measures how well a company can meet its long-term obligations. It is also referred to as "leverage" analysis.

The *debt-to-equity ratio* is the ratio of debt to stockholders' equity. Stockholders' equity is sometimes referred to as "shareholders' equity," "net worth," "capital," or "proprietorship." If a company has issued preferred stock, it is advisable to include the value for preferred stock as debt, because it represents a prior claim on company assets to that of common stock. The current liabilities should definitely be included with the long-term debt. This ratio is of particular interest to banks, credit-rating services, potential bond buyers, and potential purchasers of stock because it permits one to compare the financial strength of one company with that of others in the same industry. For Corporation X,

$$\text{Debt-to-Equity Ratio} = \frac{\text{Total Debt}}{\text{Stockholders' Equity}}$$

$$= \frac{\$45 \text{ million}}{\$61 \text{ million}}$$

$$= 0.74$$

The *debt-to-assets ratio* indicates how much of the company's overall financing has been supplied by creditors rather than by the stockholders. As with the other ratios, the ratio of the company should be compared with the industry average, and it should be below the industry average rather than above it. Comparison should also be made for the same company for different years to see the trend.

For Corporation X,

$$\text{Debt-to-Assets Ratio} = \frac{\text{Total Debt}}{\text{Total Assets}}$$

$$= \frac{\$45 \text{ million}}{\$106 \text{ million}}$$

$$= 0.42$$

It is also advisable to determine the debt-to-assets ratio without including the intangible assets of a company (e.g., goodwill, patents, trademarks, copyrights) as assets. Only the tangible assets (i.e., current assets plus net fixed assets) are then considered.

For Corporation X,

$$\text{Debt-to-Tangible Assets Ratio} = \frac{\text{Total Debt}}{\text{Total Tangible Assets}}$$

$$= \frac{\$45 \text{ million}}{\$(60 + 45) \text{ million}}$$

$$= \frac{\$45 \text{ million}}{\$105 \text{ million}}$$

$$= 0.43$$

The *debt ratio* indicates the magnitude of long-term debt in the capital structure of a company. The ratio is calculated from the long-term debt and the capitalization which equals stockholders' equity plus long-term debt.

For Corporation X, the debt ratio is calculated as follows:

$$\text{Debt Ratio} = \frac{\text{Long-term Debt}}{\text{Total Capitalization}}$$

$$= \frac{\$15 \text{ million}}{\$(15 + 61) \text{ million}}$$

$$= \frac{\$15 \text{ million}}{\$76 \text{ million}}$$

$$= 0.20$$

### Investment-sales Analysis

*Investment-sales analysis* indicates the efficiency with which a company is operating. It relates the company's investment to its sales and expenses. Two measurements which are used are the inventory turnover ratio and the average collection period ratio.

The *inventory turnover ratio* measures how fast inventory is turned into actual sales. There are two ways of calculating this rate, by using the net sales figure or by using the cost of goods sold figure. For Corporation X,

$$\text{Inventory Turnover Ratio} = \frac{\text{Net Sales}}{\text{Inventories}}$$

$$= \frac{\$70 \text{ million}}{\$25 \text{ million}}$$

$$= 2.8$$

$$\text{Inventory Turnover Ratio} = \frac{\text{Cost of Goods Sold}}{\text{Inventories}}$$

$$= \frac{\$60 \text{ million}}{\$25 \text{ million}}$$

$$= 2.4$$

As both methods are used by credit-rating services, one has to know the method used, if one is to make adequate intra-industry comparisons.

The *average collection period ratio* tells how long it takes, on the average, to convert sales into cash. For Corporation X,

$$\text{Average Collection Period Ratio} = \frac{\text{Accounts Receivable} \times \text{days per year}}{\text{Credit Sales per year}}$$

$$= \frac{\$20 \text{ million} \times 365}{\$70 \text{ million}}$$

$$= 104.3 \text{ days}$$

This ratio for a particular company has to be compared with those of other companies in its industry. The values can range quite widely, depending on the industry. In general, the average collection period should be kept as low as possible. Comparison should also be for the same company for different years to see the trend.

### Profitability Analysis

Profitability analysis measures how efficiently the management is operating the company. Useful measurements are the profit margin, the return on investment, the return on assets, and the price-earnings ratio.

The *profit margin* ratio measures how profitably the company is operating in relationship to sales. It is calculated by taking the net income (excluding extraordinary charges or nonrecurring credits or charges) as a percentage of net sales.

For Corporation X,

$$\text{Profit Margin} = \frac{\text{Net Profits after Taxes}}{\text{Net Sales}}$$

$$= \frac{\$2 \text{ million}}{\$70 \text{ million}}$$

$$= 2.86\%$$

This ratio also should be compared with that of other companies in its industry. The higher the profit margin the better. Different years should be compared for the same company in order to see the trend.

The *return on investment* is also called "return on equity," "return on net worth" or "rate of return." It considers profits after taxes as a percentage of stockholders' equity. For Corporation X,

$$\text{Return on Investment} = \frac{\text{Net Profits after Taxes}}{\text{Stockholders' Equity}}$$

$$= \frac{\$2 \text{ million}}{\$61 \text{ million}}$$

$$= 3.3\%$$

The higher the return on investment, the better. As with the other ratios, however, the value for a particular company has to be compared with other companies in its industry and different years for the same company should be compared.

If a company has issued preferred stock in addition to common stock, one should determine the return strictly on the common stock equity. This can be done by deducting the preferred stock dividend from the "net profits after taxes" in the numerator and by deducting the par value of the preferred stock, if any, from the stockholders' equity in the denominator.

The *return on assets* should be determined for total assets. For Corporation X,

$$\text{Return on Assets} = \frac{\text{Net Profits after Taxes}}{\text{Total Assets}}$$

$$= \frac{\$2 \text{ million}}{\$106 \text{ million}}$$

$$= 1.9\%$$

This ratio also measures a company's earning power. A comparison of the "return on assets" (or earning power) of a particular company with other companies in its industry is especially valuable. One should also compare the trend of a company in its return on assets for several years, preferably for ten years or more.

The *price-earnings ratio* is an extremely valuable ratio for a potential investor, an officer in a company, or anyone interested in a company. In financial circles, this ratio is often called the "P/E ratio," the "P-E multiple" or just the "multiple." At a particular time, it tells by how many times the stock price exceeds the net profits after taxes that the company has earned. A "current price-earnings ratio" is determined from the latest annual net profits after taxes and the present stock price. A "future price-earnings ratio" is determined from estimates of future net profits after taxes.

If the common stock of Corporation X is selling at $2.00 per share today, then the price-earnings ratio for Corporation X is calculated as follows:

$$\text{Price-Earnings Ratio} = \frac{\text{Stock Price per Share}}{\text{Net Earnings per Share of Common Stock}}$$

$$= \frac{\text{Market Value per Share}}{\text{Net Earnings per Share of Common Stock}}$$

$$= \frac{\$2.00}{\$0.08}$$

$$= 25$$

In making the determination, one has to be sure to use the value for net profits after taxes, taken per share.

A technique often used for determining the price-earnings ratio from the stock prices taken over a one-year period is to calculate the average of the high and low stock prices of the common stock for the given period (either for a calendar year or for a fiscal year, when it differs from the calendar year) and to divide it by the net profits after taxes taken per share of common stock.

The price-earnings ratio of a company should be compared with its industry average. If it is above or below the industry average, one should find out why and in what direction it appears to be headed. Comparison should also be made for the same company for different years, in order to see what the trend is.

## MEASURING THE STOCK MARKET

Several indicators are used to indicate the movement of stock prices. Some of them are:

Dow-Jones Averages, which include the:
Dow-Jones Industrial Average
Dow-Jones Transportation Average
Dow-Jones Utility Average
Dow-Jones Composite Average

Standard and Poor's Indexes, which include the:
S&P Industrial Index
S&P Rail Index
S&P Utility Index
S&P Composite Index

New York Stock Exchange Indexes

American Stock Exchange Price Level Index

NASDAQ-OTC

New York Times Averages, which include the:
New York Times Industrial Average
New York Times Rail Average

Barron's 50-Stock Average

### Dow-Jones Averages

The Dow-Jones Averages are the best known of the stock market indicators. The Dow-Jones Industrial Average is watched especially as an indicator of stock market movement. It is the most widely disseminated on television, the radio, in the press and by other media. One reason that the Dow-Jones average is so well known is its longevity. It was initiated in 1884.

The Dow-Jones Industrial Average consists of 30 industrial companies. The Dow-Jones Transportation Average consists of 20 transportation companies. The Dow-Jones Utility Average consists of 15 utilities. The Dow-Jones Composite Average is the composite average of all 65 stocks. The Monday issue of *The Wall Street Journal,* on the next to the last page, regularly lists all the stocks in the Dow-Jones Averages.

The Dow-Jones Averages lack weighting and, as a result, the higher-priced stocks carry more weight. Thus, if a $10 stock and a $100 stock were each to advance by the same percentage, say 5% (½ point and 5 points, respectively), the effect of the higher-priced stock on the Average would be ten times greater than the effect of the lower-priced stock. A downward movement of the same percentage would be subject to the same discrepancy.

It should be further noted that because the Dow-Jones Industrial Average consists entirely of "blue chips" on the New York Stock Exchange it is not fully representative of all stocks listed on the Exchange. Computation of the Dow-Jones Industrial Average is more complicated than just taking an arithmetic average of the 30 prices of the component stocks. As stock-splits have to be accounted for, the divisor has to be reduced accordingly. This can be illustrated as follows: If three stocks are priced at $20, $40, and $60, the average price equals $40. If the $60 stock has a 2-for-1 split and its new price accordingly declines to $30, the average after the split would be $30, if an adjustment were not made for the stock-split. The divisor must be changed from 3 to 2.25, so that the Average again equals $40.

### Standard and Poor's Indexes

Standard and Poor's Indexes, like the Dow-Jones Averages, includes only a specific number of stocks. Unlike the Dow-Jones Averages, however, the S & P Indexes are weighted by the number of shares outstanding. They also include more stocks than the Dow-Jones Averages.

The S & P Indexes provide an index of 425 industrials, an index of 20 railroads, an index of 55 utilities, and a 500-company composite index, which is a total of the three subgroups.

The price per share of each component stock is multiplied by the number of shares outstanding, to obtain the total market value for each stock. The individual stock's market values are then added and expressed as an index, with the 1941-1943 average values set equal to 10. Adjustments have to be made for mergers, acquisitions, liquidations, and sales of additional stock.

The effects of a stock-split are largely eliminated by this method, because a stock-split changes only the price per share but not the market value of the total security valuation. Also, higher-priced stocks do not get undue weight. The large corporations do, however, carry greater weight. IBM gets more weight than Control Data, General Motors more weight than Chrysler, Standard Oil of New Jersey more weight than Standard Oil of Indiana.

### New York Stock Exchange Indexes

Like the S & P Indexes, the New York Stock Exchange Indexes are capitalization-weighted. The coverage, however, is more comprehensive than that of the S & P Indexes because all common stocks listed on the New York Stock Exchange are included. There are four industry indexes, the industrial index, the transportation index, the utility index, and the financial index, and a composite index.

Adjustments have to be made to eliminate capitalization changes and new listings and delistings.

The New York Stock Exchange intentionally keeps a narrow spread between the Index level and the actual average price per listed share. Thus, when the Index reaches 100, it will be "split" and brought back to a level of

50. The base value of 50 was deliberately set at that level for the base date (December 31, 1965), because this figure was close to the actual average price of a New York Stock Exchange share on that date ($53.33). A New York Stock Exchange Index of 100 is approximately equal to a Dow-Jones Industrial Average of 2,000.

The NYSE Indexes are subject to the same type of distortions as the S & P Indexes. The large corporations get more weight in the Indexes.

### American Stock Exchange Price Level Index ("Amex Index")

The Amex Index includes all common stocks (and warrants) listed on the American Stock Exchange. It makes no adjustments, however, for company capitalization. In this respect, it resembles the Dow-Jones Averages.

The Amex Index was started with a base date of April 29, 1966, and a base value equal to 16.88 (the actual average per share of all common stocks and warrants admitted to dealings on that date). A new price level is determined each day by adding up all the changes (the pluses and minuses in net prices) and dividing the total by the number of common stocks and warrants. This amount is then added to (or subtracted from) the previous day's closing Index.

If, for example, the total net changes equaled minus 90 ($-90$) and the number of issues used as a divisor totaled 1,000, then 9 cents would be deducted from the previous day's closing figure to yield the latest Price Level Index.

Adjustments are made for stock-splits and new listings and delistings.

The Amex Index is subject to the same problems as the Dow-Jones Averages. Only price changes are considered and not the relative importance of a stock's net change to its price. A 50-cent movement in a $10 stock gets the same weight as a 50-cent movement in a $100 stock.[1]

## NASDAQ-OTC

"NASDAQ-OTC" stands for the National Association of Securities Dealers Automated Quotations of the Over-the-Counter securities market. This is an electronic computerized system which was first established on February 8, 1971.

It should be noted that operation of the Over-the-Counter market differs in a definite way from the operation of the stock exchanges. The OTC is a *negotiated market,* unlike the stock exchanges, which are *auction*

[1] Karen Kidder, *Wall Street: Before the Fall* (Federal Reserve Bank of San Francisco,) *Monthly Review Supplement,* 1970), pp. 32-36.

*markets.* With the OTC market, prices have to be negotiated for the best possible terms. Negotiation used to be conducted strictly over the telephone or by telegraph, but now the NASDAQ electronic computerized quotations system has served to create a single marketplace for the widely dispersed broker-dealers trading in this market. The OTC market, however, does not have one fixed location. In contrast, the securities exchanges do have fixed geographical locations where the auctions are conducted (e.g., the New York Stock Exchange and the American Stock Exchange).

## USING AND UNDERSTANDING
## THE STOCK MARKET INDEXES AND AVERAGES

The various stock market indexes and averages are primarily valuable in indicating trends.

With regard to the matter of trends, a distinction has to be drawn between a fundamental trend and mere deviations from the fundamental trend. The fundamental trend indicates an equilibrium trend or firm movement for the overall stock market, which can be up, down, or horizontal. The fundamental trend reflects, to a large extent, economic realities and economic expectations

Some primary factors that affect the fundamental trend and the indicators used to measure those factors are the following:

1. *The corporate profit picture.* The corporate profits figure is compiled and published by the U.S. Department of Commerce. It is watched very closely. Corporate profits are given before and after taxes together with dividends and retained earnings.

2. *National income.* This figure is also compiled and published by the U.S. Department of Commerce. It measures the total earnings of the factors of production (i.e., labor and property) in producing the nation's output of goods and services. It is the sum of employee compensation, interest, rents received by persons, and business incomes. One component of this figure is corporate profits. In addition to corporate profits, another component that is watched closely is personal income. Two of the several components of personal income are "wages and salaries" and "dividends," which are also important indicators. Another item of great interest in the national income is the amount of income available for spending—called disposable personal income—which is found by deducting taxes from total personal income. Taxes in this case include personal taxes (such as income and estate taxes) and non-tax payments (such as fines), but exclude property and commodity taxes. When the amount people spend for personal

outlays is deducted from disposable personal income, an estimate of current personal savings is obtained, another important figure.

3. *Gross National Product (GNP).* GNP is probably the most widely used measure of total economic activity. It is used a lot to make forecasts of the business cycle. It measures the market value of the country's total output of final goods and services. GNP figures are compiled by the U.S. Department of Commerce and are published quarterly. The figure to be watched most is the "real" GNP (i.e., where the inflationary factor has been removed or, in other words, where correction has been made for mere price changes) as opposed to the "current" or "money" GNP, where no correction for price changes is made. Real GNP is often referred to as GNP in constant dollars. The components of GNP are:

(a) Personal Consumption Expenditures
    1. Durable goods
    2. Nondurable goods
    3. Services
(b) Gross Private Domestic Investment
    1. Fixed investment
       a. Nonresidential
         Structures
         Producers' durable equipment
       b. Residential structures
         Nonfarm
         Farm
(c) Net Exports of Goods and Services
    1. Exports
    2. Imports
(d) Government Purchases of Goods and Services
    1. Federal
       a. National defense
       b. Other
    2. State and local

4. *Consumer Price Index (CPI).* The CPI measures the changes in the prices of goods and services purchased by urban wage earners and clerical workers. It does not apply to all consumers. The index is divided into five major group indexes: food, housing, apparel and upkeep, health and recreation, and transportation. The CPI is compiled and published by the Bureau of Labor Statistics of the U.S. Department of Labor.

5. *Wholesale Price Index (WPI)*. The WPI measures price changes in the primary markets. It is also compiled and published by the Bureau of Labor Statistics of the U.S. Department of Labor.

6. *GNP Price Index*. The full name for this index is the GNP Implicit Price Deflator. It is much more comprehensive than the CPI or WPI because it includes all the goods and services that make up GNP.

7. *Unemployment rate*. There are several measures of unemployment. One measure of total unemployment is derived from a monthly survey of a sample of households. Another measure used is a weekly compilation of unemployment insurance claims. There are also other measures. The various measures are compiled by the U.S. Department of Labor.

8. *Industrial production*. The Board of Governors of the Federal Reserve System publishes an index of industrial production. Watched very closely, as components of the index, are changes in automobile production, iron, steel, textiles, paper, chemicals, appliances, and furniture. Not all industries are included in this index, so it should not be viewed as a measure of general business activity.

9. *Productivity*. Productivity is determined and published by the U.S. Department of Labor and indicates output (or production) per manhour.

10. *Monetary and financial factors*. The Board of Governors of the Federal Reserve System and the individual Federal Reserve Banks publish numerous statistics on monetary and financial developments. Some changes watched with particular interest are: Federal Reserve credit, reserves of the member banks of the Federal Reserve System, net free reserves, commercial bank credit, the monetary aggregates, and time deposits. (See the chapters entitled "Money and Interest Rates" and "Federal Reserve System and the U.S. Banking System" for a discussion of these various factors.)

11. *Interest rates*. Key factors to watch are changes by the Board of Governors of the Federal Reserve System in open-market operations, the discount rate, and the legal reserve requirements. (For further discussion see the chapters entitled "Money and Interest Rates" and "Federal Reserve System and the U.S. Banking System".)

12. *Business cycle indicators*. The National Bureau of Economic Research, Inc. (NBER), located in New York City, has developed a series of

business cycle indicators that are watched very closely. There are leading, lagging, and coincident indicators. They are used to determine turning points in business cycles (i.e., "peaks" and "troughs").

13. *Balance of Payments.* This is a record of the economic transactions of one country with the rest of the world. The overall balance of payments statement is always in balance, because double-entry bookkeeping is used. It is only certain portions of the balance of payments statement that are in deficit or surplus. One portion that is watched very closely is the balance of trade (i.e., exports compared to imports). A deficit in the balance of trade is also called an unfavorable balance of trade. It exists when imports are greater than exports. A surplus in the balance of trade is also called a favorable balance of trade. A surplus in the balance of trade exists when exports are greater than imports. The balance of payments statement is compiled and published by the U.S. Department of Commerce.

14. *Exchange rates.* Exchange rates give the values of the currencies of different countries. Comparisons are made regularly and are reported over the radio, on television, and in the press of the strength of the U.S. dollar as against other currencies.

15. *The Index of Leading Economic Indicators.* This is a composite index compiled and published by the U.S. Department of Commerce. This index is considered particularly valuable for providing an indication of future business activity and business trends.

*Note:* Sources for the fifteen items listed and discussions of the significance of their effects on the fundamental trend of the stock market can be found in the publications listed for the categories "Economic News and Analyses" and "Stocks & Bonds" in Appendix E.

This list of fifteen items is merely illustrative of some significant factors which should be followed. The list, however, should by no means be considered exhaustive. There are numerous other factors both of an economic and non-economic nature which affect the fundamental trend. These other factors are also discussed in the publications listed in Appendix E (e.g., *Barron's, Business Week, Newsweek, The Journal of Commerce, The New York Times, The Wall Street Journal, Time,* and *U.S. News & World Report*).

### Significant Developments

The movements that are deviations from the fundamental trend often result from the transactions of traders and speculators who are trying to outguess the stock market, or from irrational factors, such as the possibility of a certain political leader being deposed in a certain country or the fear of the possible outbreak of a war, or similar uncertainties that may never occur. The various stock market indexes and averages are useful in helping to spot the fundamental trend and the deviations from that trend.

With regard to the stock market indexes and averages used to gauge the performance of the stock market, it should be realized that the effects are not all one way. The stock market indexes and averages are affected by changes in business conditions, broader economic factors, and non-economic factors, but in turn the movements of these indexes and averages often affect business conditions and the other factors. The indexes and averages sometimes act as leading indicators and, therefore, rise ahead of the economy or fall ahead of the economy. There is nothing inevitable, however, about the indexes and averages being leading indicators. They can also be lagging or coincident indicators.

An important thing to remember is that if you are buying the stock of a particular company, you have to concentrate on the performance of that company, its stock, and the future expectations for that particular company. The trends indicated by the stock market indexes and averages can be helpful, but you are buying one particular stock, not all the stocks in any stock market index or average.

*Note:* In addition to the various economic indexes and economic fluctuations, the investor should be aware of the development of what is known as the "two-tier market" over the past few years. This development refers to the rise of one tier of stocks, those that are considered growth stocks by institutional investors and that are favored by them. The second tier refers to all the other stocks. The second-tier stocks are not strongly favored by institutional investors, although they may at times buy them. The favored growth stocks are looked on as representing superior quality. The favored one-tier stocks change at times. For the specific stocks one should, therefore, read the various financial publications.

Inasmuch as institutional investors have dominated stock trading to an increasing extent since World War II, institutional trading has a strong impact on the stock market indexes and the stock market.

Institutional portfolio managers possess great power, and their transactions should be watched closely for possible indications of future stock market movements. What the portfolio managers are doing or may do in the future can be followed in such publications as the *Institutional Investor, Barron's,* and *The Wall Street Journal.*

Related to the institutional trading is legislation (e.g., the Pension Reform Act of 1974) that may control how the various financial institutions may invest. Such legislation must also be watched.

One should actually follow the transactions of as many investor groups as possible in the financial press. Holdings of corporate common and preferred stock (equities) are mainly in the hands of "households" (a category that includes personal trusts and nonprofit institutions as well as individuals), insurance companies, pension funds, and foreign investors. The proportion of total net new issues acquired by each of these groups has varied substantially from year to year. It should be realized, however, that net acquisitions by the various investor groups, when taken as an aggregate, determine the ability of corporations to sell new issues.

A study by the Federal Reserve Bank of Chicago (*Business Conditions,* August 1975, pp. 3-12) shows that the household sector now holds (not to be confused with trades) 75 percent of all outstanding corporate equities. This proportion has declined quite steadily from over 90 percent in the years immediately following World War II. Meanwhile, private pension funds now hold about 10 percent of outstanding equities. Life insurance companies, state and local government retirement funds, open-end investment companies (mutual funds), non-life insurance companies, and foreigners each account for 3 percent or less.

Sales of corporate equities by the household sector (including shares of open-end investment companies) have exceeded purchases each year since 1961. Although hundreds of thousands of individuals have acquired stocks during this period, their purchases have been more than offset by sales of other individuals, trusts, and foundations. Some huge blocks of stock have been sold (frequently through underwriters) by individuals, by their estates, or by the trust funds and nonprofit institutions that they have endowed. Substantial portions of these offerings have gone into the portfolios of institutions. Purchases of investment company shares, mostly by people of moderate wealth, had been a supportive factor in the stock market for most of the postwar period, but even these investments have been liquidated on balance in the past three years.

Private pension funds have been by far the largest net purchasers of equities since World War II. Acquisitions reached a peak of $8.9 billion in 1971, almost two-thirds of the new supply that year. Private pension fund net purchases of equities have declined each year since 1971 and were only $2.3 billion in 1974.

Life insurance companies were not important purchasers of equities until the 1960s, after state laws and regulations restricting such investments were relaxed to some degree. Net purchases of equities by life insurance companies totaled about $3.5 billion in each of the three years 1971-1973, before declining to $2.2 billion in 1974.

State and local government retirement funds began to purchase equities in appreciable volume in the mid-1960s. Their purchases rose steadily to a peak of $3.9 billion in 1973. Purchases declined to $3.5 billion in 1974, but this was still the largest amount absorbed by any single category that year and equaled 70 percent of net new issues.

Non-life insurance companies (mainly fire and casualty companies) have regularly invested a significant portion of their reserves in equities. Their purchases peaked in 1972 and in 1974 sales exceeded purchases.

Purchases of equities of United States corporations by foreign investors have become a significant factor in the past seven to eight years. Such purchases have fluctuated widely, falling from $2.8 billion in 1973 to less than $0.5 billion in 1974.

For the remainder of the 1970s, it would appear that corporations will require large amounts of money to produce the necessary goods and services for the growing American population. These amounts will be inflated by outlays to promote health and safety and to preserve or improve the environment. Financial pressures will be intensified for the funding of pension plans. Uncertainties will be increased due to energy shortages and possible liabilities resulting from litigation of various kinds that has assumed a much larger role than in the past. Corporations will also have to compete with other sectors of the economy, including the Federal, state and local governments, whose needs will also be great.

These are some of the factors that investors will have to be cognizant of in gauging the stock market and its future performance.

## NEGOTIATED COMMISSION RATES

On May 1, 1975, the investment community entered a new environment, because on that date fully negotiated commission rates went into effect. The previous system of fixed commission rates for brokers has been removed by the Securities and Exchange Commission on the assumption that investors will benefit from increased competition among brokerage firms.

In the new environment, the conflict between New York Stock Exchange specialists and Third Market firms has become more pronounced.

The specialist is a member of the New York Stock Exchange who specializes in the trading of one stock or, more usually, a few stocks listed on the New York Stock Exchange. He possesses enormous power and prestige, serves as a broker for brokers on the floor of the New York Stock Exchange and, as a result of a long tradition, is able to apply a great deal of expertise to the execution of orders. A prime function of a specialist is to see to it that an orderly market is maintained in the stocks in which he specializes.

Third Market firms are brokerage firms that trade listed stocks of the New York Stock Exchange outside the New York Stock Exchange. More specifically, they engage in over-the-counter trading of New York Stock

Exchange listed stocks. Third Market firms are thus in direct competition with the New York Stock Exchange specialists.

Although New York Stock Exchange listed stocks figure as the most important in the Third Market, Third Market trading also involves securities listed on other securities exchanges. Third Market firms deal mainly with institutional investors and big money is involved, running into billions of dollars worth of securities being traded per year.

The Third Market has to be distinguished from what is known as the Second Market, that is, over-the-counter trading of stocks not listed on the New York Stock Exchange or other securities exchanges. The Second Market represents an area of much greater speculation and risk than the Third Market, because you are dealing with companies that have not met the standards of the New York Stock Exchange or some other exchange. The Second Market, however, does appear to offer increasing potential for both Third Market firms and New York Stock Exchange firms.

Another result of the new competitive environment in the investment community is that you have to pay for research services if you want them. Otherwise, you have to do most of the research on securities by yourself, and you simply use a brokerage firm to execute your orders.

It is still too early to be sure how the new system ushered in by fully negotiated commission rates will work out. The Securities and Exchange Commission is monitoring to see to it that a few large brokerage firms do not gain too much control over the securities markets and that there is no loss in liquidity. There is a danger of loss of liquidity if commission rates are forced down too far and a danger of some of the smaller brokerage firms being forced out of business or being forced to consolidate or merge with the bigger firms.

Another development to watch is the movement toward a central stock exchange for the entire country, which is related to the move toward more competition and the charge by some Third Market firms that the New York Stock Exchange is not truly the auction market it is supposed to be primarily because of the existence of the specialists.

## A CENTRAL STOCK EXCHANGE

An advisory panel of the Securities and Exchange Commission (SEC) has recommended that all the securities exchanges of the United States should be unified into one National Securities Exchange. It would be regulated by a National Market Board. The National Association of Securities Dealers (NASD) would continue to supervise the Over-the-Counter (OTC) market.

At the present time, in addition to the New York Stock Exchange, some of the other securities exchanges in the United States are the American Stock Exchange, the Boston Stock Exchange, the Detroit Stock Exchange, the Midwest Stock Exchange, the Pacific Coast Stock Exchange, and the Philadelphia-Baltimore-Washington (usually referred to as the "PBW") Stock Exchange.

## GLOSSARY OF STOCK TERMS

*Asked price:* Also called the "offering price." It is the lowest price at which a security can be sold. It is quoted per share (see "bid price").

*Asset:* Something of value which is owned or can be claimed for ownership. Different types of assets are distinguished, e.g., current assets, fixed assets, and intangible assets (see under separate types of assets for definitions).

*Bear:* Someone who expects the stock of a certain corporation to go down in value or someone who expects the stock market, in general, to go down (see "bull").

*Bid price:* The highest price at which a security can be bought. It is quoted per share (see "asked price").

*Big Board:* A term often used in financial circles to refer to the New York Stock Exchange.

*Blue Chip Stock:* The stock of a high quality corporation.

*Blue sky laws:* The laws applied in various states for the purpose of regulating the trading of securities for the protection of the public.

*Book value:* Also called "net asset value" or "tangible asset value." It is the value of a corporation's assets after all intangible assets and liabilities have been deducted. It is usually stated per share (see "asset," "current assets," "fixed assets," "intangible assets" and "liability").

*Broker:* A person who acts as an agent for another for the purpose of buying or selling securities. He receives a commission for performing this service. This term can be applied not only to an individual, but to a partnership or corporation that acts as an agent and receives a commission (see "dealer").

*Bull:* Someone who expects the stock of a certain corporation to go up in value or someone who expects the stock market, in general, to go up (see "bear").

*Capital gains:* The income, or profit, obtained by buying a security at a low price and selling it at a higher price (e.g., you buy common stock of a certain corporation at $10 per share and you sell it at $100 per share; the $90 increase in value per share represents your capital gains). There are two types of capital gains: short-term and long-term. Short-term refers to holding the security for 6 months or less, long-term over 6 months. For Federal income tax purposes, short-term capital gains get taxed at a person's regular income tax rate, while long-term capital gains get taxed at a maximum of 25% (see "capital losses").

*Capital losses:* The losses resulting from selling a security below the price at which it was bought. There are two types of capital losses: short-term and long-term. Short-term refers to holding the security for 6 months or less, long-term over 6 months (see "capital gains").

*Capital stock:* Refers to securities which represent ownership of a corporation, i.e., common stock and preferred stock.

*Capital structure:* The breakdown of a corporation's capitalization with regard to the amount of securities which it has issued, e.g., common stock, preferred stock, and bonds (see "capitalization").

*Capitalization:* The total dollar value of all the securities issued by a corporation.

*Common stock:* A security which represents ownership of a corporation. A corporation must issue common stock. It is not required to issue any other type of security, although the management of the corporation may choose to issue other securities (e.g., preferred stock, bonds, commercial paper). A common stockholder risks losing all his investment if the business should fail. He may or may not receive dividends. In case of bankruptcy, he has the last claim on the assets of the corporation and may receive nothing. Each share of common stock represents partial ownership of the corporation.

*Current assets:* Also called "liquid assets" and "quick assets." They consist of cash and assets which can ordinarily be converted into cash within one year (e.g., marketable securities, accounts receivable, and inventories).

*Current liabilities:* Debts due to be paid within one year (e.g., accounts payable, notes payable, Federal income taxes, taxes other than Federal income taxes, salaries and wages owed to employees, and dividends to be paid).

*Dealer:* Participant in a securities transaction as a principal and not as a broker (or agent). The participant can be an individual, partnership or corporation and the securities are bought or sold for his own account. A commission is not charged, as with a broker, but rather a profit is obtained, when the price charged is above the original cost to the dealer. Firms or individuals are referred to as "broker-dealers," because they can operate in both a broker-capacity and dealer-capacity at different times (see "broker").

*Depreciation:* The ordinary wearing out of a fixed asset (e.g., the wearing out of a car, a piece of equipment or a building).

*Dividend:* A payment, usually in cash, to common stockholders and preferred stockholders. It is generally paid out of profits. A specified percentage of profits is paid per share. For common stockholders, the percentage is at the discretion of the corporate management.

*Double taxation:* A tax by the U.S. government on the profits of a corporation plus a tax on the dividends to the stockholder paid out of the corporate profits.

*Equity:* Ownership of a corporation as represented by common stock and preferred stock.

*Ex-dividend date:* A specified date on which and after which the seller and not the buyer of stock has a right to receive the dividend already declared.

*FIFO:* First-In-First-Out method of inventory valuation. It assumes that the goods first bought for inventory are the first sold. In recent years, there has been a shift by many corporations from the FIFO method to the LIFO method of inventory valuation.

*Fiscal year:* Any twelve month period chosen by a corporation as its business year. It is very often the same as the calendar year, but it does not have to be the same.

*Fixed assets:* These are tangible assets which are of a permanent nature (e.g., land, buildings, and equipment).

*Growth stock:* A stock which is expected to increase in value.

*Intangible assets:* Assets for which it is difficult to set a precise value (e.g., goodwill, patents, trademarks, and copyrights).

*Liability:* Something which is owed. A corporation will usually break up its liabilities into current liabilities and long-term liabilities.

*LIFO:* Last-In-First-Out method of inventory valuation. It assumes that the goods that were bought last are the first to be sold. During an inflation (i.e., a period of rising prices), this method results in a lower profit figure and, therefore, lower taxes. During the past few years, a growing number of corporations have switched from the FIFO method to this method, in order to take advantage of the lower taxes to be paid.

*Margin requirement:* The proportion of the price that an investor must pay when he buys securities on credit. The broker (or registered representative) pays the remaining money. The amount is set by the Federal Reserve Board.

If the margin requirement is 50%, the investor puts up half the money, and the broker puts up the remainder.

If the margin requirement is 40%, the investor puts up 40% of the money, and the broker puts up the remainder. If the price of the stock declines below a certain point, established by the broker's firm or by a securities exchange, the investor will be asked to put up additional money. During the 1920s, a great deal of stock was bought on margin rather than outright, which was a contributing factor to the stock market crash of 1929.

*Market price:* Also called "market value." The latest price at which the particular stock was bought or sold.

*NASD:* National Association of Securities Dealers, Inc., which has jurisdiction over the Over-the-Counter (OTC) markets and operates under the SEC (see "SEC").

*Option:* An arrangement to buy or sell a certain security at a definite price and time. Arrangements in the options market can be highly complex and are for the sophisticated investor. Two basic arrangements are "puts" and "calls."

*The Put:* An option to sell shares of stock at a definite price which expires on a definite date.

*The Call:* An option to buy shares of stock at a definite price which expires on a definite date.

*Over-the-counter market:* Also referred to as the OTC market. This is a market for many different types of securities. The stocks of companies not listed on a securities exchanges (i.e., the New York Stock Exchange, the American Stock Exchange and the other stock exchanges) are traded in this market. This is known as the Second Market. The OTC market also involves the trading of some stocks that are listed on securities exchanges. This is known as the Third Market. The OTC market is the main market for industrial corporations that first go public with stock offerings (i.e., the new issue market). It is the market for most bank stocks and insurance company stocks. Municipal securities and U.S. government securities (i.e., U.S. Treasury bills, U.S. Treasury notes and U.S. Treasury bonds) are traded in the OTC market, as are railroad equipment trust certificates, corporate bonds, and the securities of some foreign corporations. In addition, this is the market for mutual fund shares. Unlike the securities exchanges, the OTC market has no fixed geographical location. The broker-dealers trading in this market are widely dispersed. Trading used to be conducted by negotiation by the broker-dealers strictly over the telephone and by telegraph, but now an electronic computerized quotations system is used. The National Association of Securities Dealers, Inc. (NASD) has jurisdiction over the OTC market.

*Pre-emptive right:* The right of existing stockholders to buy any new stock issued by the corporation, allowing each stockholder to maintain his proportionate ownership in the corporation. It is a legal right only if it is actually provided for in the corporate charter. The value of one right sold when attached to the stock can be computed as follows:

$$\text{Value of one right} = \frac{M - S}{R + 1}$$

M = market price of the old stock with rights attached (also called "cum-rights" or "rights-on" per share of stock)
S = subscription price per share of stock
R = number of rights necessary to buy one share of stock

*Preferred stock:* A security which represents limited ownership in a corporation. A preferred stockholder very often does not have voting rights; he receives a stated dividend, which he must receive before the common stockholder can get his dividend. The preferred stockholder can have his preferred stock with or without par value. When the preferred stock is with par value, the par value is usually $100, and the dividend is stated in terms of a percentage of the par value. If the preferred stock is without par value (called "no par value"), the dividend is stated in a specified number of dollars. There are several types of preferred stock:

*Callable Preferred Stock:* The corporation has the right to retire the preferred stock at a specified price.

*Convertible Preferred Stock:* The preferred stock can be converted into other securities (usually common stock) under specified conditions.

*Cumulative Preferred Stock:* If dividends are not paid for a certain period, the dividends accumulate and must be paid before the common stockholders can be paid any dividends.

*Noncumulative Preferred Stock:* If dividends are not paid in any period, they will not be paid in the future.

*Participating Preferred Stock:* The preferred stockholder gets his stated dividend and also "participates" or gets a portion of the profits available for the common stockholders.

*Proxy:* Authorization by the owner of a stock to have someone vote his share of stock.

*Quick assets:* Same as current assets (see *Current assets*).

*Record date:* The date on which a stockholder must have his name recorded in the corporate books in order to receive dividends, receive rights offerings, vote, or exercise any of the rights to which a stockholder is entitled. The date is set by the corporation.

*Red herring:* A preliminary prospectus, which can be used only for setting forth information about a corporation when an offering of securities is being arranged. It may not be used for the actual sale of the securities, which must be done by a prospectus.

*Retained earnings:* The amount of profits kept in a corporation after dividends have been distributed.

*Reverse stock split:* The stockholder receives a proportionate decrease in the number of shares of stock he is holding. For example, a "1-for-2 split" could be declared. The stockholder would then receive one share of stock for every two shares he originally held. It is thus the reverse of the stock split. The par value of the stock will be proportionately increased on the books of the corporation, while the number of shares decreases proportionately and the dollar value of the common stock, retained earnings, and capital surplus remains the same.

The reverse split is usually employed when the management of a corporation tries to prevent the stock price from falling further after a sharp decline. The practice often has a bad psychological effect on the image of the corporation (see "stock split").

*SEC:* Securities and Exchange Commission (established by the Securities Exchange Act of 1934).

*Selling short:* A practice engaged in when a person believes that the price of a stock will decline within a short period of time. The person will realize a profit only if the stock price does decline. He can have a loss instead of a profit if the stock price rises. A short seller usually sells stock which he does not own, but there are cases of selling a stock short where the person actually owns the stock but does not expect to deliver. He is then hedging on a possible decline in the stock price.

*Securities Act of 1933:* Legislation which requires the use of a prospectus for a sale of securities. Its purpose is to prevent fraudulent practices in the sale of securities. The legislation specifically covers the following and related areas:

1. Definitions of
   security

   person

   sale, sell, offer to sell, offer for sale

   issuer

   Commission (originally, at the time of enactment, the Commission referred to in this Act was the Federal Trade Commission. The Securities and Exchange Commission (SEC) has since taken over the stated functions. The SEC was created by the Securities Exchange Act of 1934.)

   territory

   interstate commerce

   registration statement

   write or written

   prospectus

   underwriter

   dealer

2. Exempted securities
3. Exempted transactions
4. Prohibitions relating to interstate commerce and the mails
5. Registration of securities
6. Information required in prospectus
7. Matters relating to civil liabilities
8. Unlawful representatives
9. Penalties—"Any person who willfully violates any of the provisions of this title, or the rules and regulations promulgated by the Commission under authority thereof, or any person who willfully, in a registration statement filed under this title, makes any untrue statement of a material fact or omits to state any material fact required to be stated therein or necessary to make the statements therein not misleading, *shall upon conviction be fined not more than $5,000 or imprisoned not more than five years, or both."* (Author's italics.)

*Securities Exchange Act of 1934:* Legislation that established the Securities and Exchange Commission (SEC) and gave the SEC the authority to regulate securities transactions "upon securities exchanges and over-the-counter markets." There is criminal liability. "Any person who willfully violates any provision of this title . . . *shall upon conviction be fined not more than $10,000, or imprisoned not more than two years, or both, except that when such person is an exchange, a fine not exceeding $500,000 may be imposed.*" Any issuer which fails "to file information, documents, or reports" required by this legislation "shall forfeit to the United States the sum of $100 for each and every day such failure to file shall continue."

The Securities Exchange Act of 1934 also gave the Federal Reserve Board authority over the setting of margin requirements.

*Stock dividend:* A dividend in the form of more shares of stock rather than in cash. A stock dividend is a way for a corporation to save cash and thereby to keep money in the corporation for expansion. It is usually employed by corporations oriented towards growth and towards providing appreciation in stock price for the investor than towards providing dividends to the investor who is interested in income. When a stock dividend is declared, a decline in the stock price can be expected.

The stockholder often neither gains nor loses because of the decline in stock price. The stockholders' equity is the same as before the stock dividend. The value of a stock dividend is largely psychological. More important than the stock dividend for the investor is the future earning potential of the corporation (see "stock split").

*Stock split:* The stockholder receives a proportionate increase in the number of shares of stock he is holding. For example, a "2-for-1 split" could be declared. In this case, a stockholder would end up with twice the number of shares he was holding. Thus, if the stockholder had 100 shares of common stock before the stock split, he would have 200 shares after the stock split.

The stock price, however, might be cut in half, e.g., a stock selling at $100 per share before the split might end up at half that price after the split. The value for the stockholder, therefore, remains the same.

With a stock split, the par value (if there is one) is proportionately decreased. On the books of the corporation, the number of shares increases proportionately, the dollar value of the total common stock remains the same, and retained earnings, capital surplus, and stockholders' equity remain the same.

The stockholder may neither gain nor lose, and as with a stock dividend the value to the stockholder may merely be psychological. The future earning potential of the corporation is far more important than the stock split itself.

Corporations may use a stock split as a means of bringing the price of a stock down so that more investors can buy the stock, thus giving it greater distribution. Wider distribution may be needed for the corporation to qualify for listing on a stock exchange. However, some corporations simply pursue a principle of not allowing the stock price to get up too high.

*Warrant:* A right to buy stock at specified terms (e.g., a fixed price). It is issued in order to make the sale of bonds or preferred stock more appealing. There are "detachable warrants" and "nondetachable warrants." A detachable warrant may be sold independently of the security (e.g., preferred stock or bond) with which it is connected. A nondetachable warrant cannot be sold independently of the security.

# Bonds and the Bond Market

A bond is a promissory note issued by corporations and government authorities specifying a return of principal plus interest. It is a fixed-income security like the money market instruments, but it is usually held for a longer period of time.

There are the following types of bonds:

1. Corporate bonds
2. Municipal bonds ("Tax-Exempt Bonds")
3. U.S. government bonds
4. U.S. government Agency and U.S. government-sponsored Agency bonds
5. Foreign bonds
6. World Bank bonds

## CORPORATE BONDS

New issues of corporate bonds are sold in two main markets in the United States. In the *public market,* bond issues are offered to the general public. These are referred to as "public offerings." In the *private market,* bond issues are offered to a limited number of investors. These are referred to as "private placements."

In the past few years, there has been increased interest in the private placement market.[2] The private placement market actually declined from the mid-1960s to 1970. This market markedly rose, however, from 1970 to 1972. From $4.9 billion in 1970, the volume of private placements nearly doubled to $9.5 billion in 1972. As a percentage of public offerings, private placements rose from 19% in 1970 to 52% in 1972.

A comparison of these two types of corporate bond financing is made in the two graphs comparing public and private placements in Figure 3-1.

Growth in these markets is shown in Table 3-3.

Issuers of corporate bonds can be placed into three broad categories: (1) public utilities, (2) real estate and financial firms, and (3) industrial and miscellaneous firms.

---

[2]John D. Rea and Peggy Brockschmidt, "The Relationship Between Publicly Offered and Privately Placed Corporate Bonds," Federal Reserve Bank of Kansas City, *Monthly Review* (November 1973), pp. 11-20.

**FIGURE 3-1**

Corporate Bond Financing

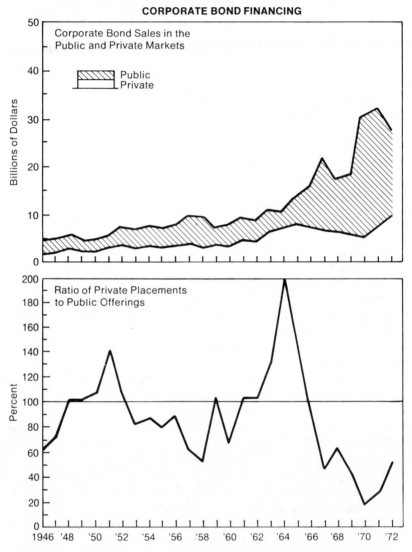

*Source:* Federal Reserve Bank of Kansas City, *Monthly Review* (November 1973), p. 11.

Most long-term debt financing by public utilities has been done in the public market. Real estate and financial financings have until recent years been concentrated in the private market. Industrial and miscellaneous financings have fluctuated between the public and private markets.

**TABLE 3-3**

Growth of Public Offerings and Private Placements

| Period | Annual Growth Rate of Public Offerings | Private Placements |
|--------|------------------|--------------------|
| 1946-51 | − 4.8% | 12.3% |
| 1952-58 | 15.1 | − 0.1 |
| 1959-65 | − 8.9 | 13.7 |
| 1966-70 | 35.4 | − 9.6 |
| 1971-72 | − 15.0 | 38.5 |

*Source:* Federal Reserve Bank of Kansas City, *Monthly Review* (November 1973), p. 12.

## Types of Corporate Bonds

*Collateral trust bonds:* One corporation places the securities of another corporation in trust and uses these securities as collateral for the issuance of bonds by the first corporation.

*Convertible bonds:* Bonds that are convertible into other securities (usually common stock).

*Coupon bonds:* Bonds issued in bearer form that have coupons for future payments of interest.

*Debenture bonds:* Bonds that are unsecured by any specific asset. They are issued against the general credit and prestige of the corporation.

*Equipment trust bonds:* Bonds that are secured by specific pieces of equipment. They are usually issued by railroads and are then generally called "railroad equipment trust certificates."

*Guaranteed bonds:* Bonds for which the payment of principal and/or interest is guaranteed by a corporation other than the issuing corporation.

*Serial bonds:* Bonds that are broken up into a series of maturity periods. In other words, the original issue bears various maturity dates rather than maturing at one time.

*Series bonds:* Bonds that are backed by the same assets but have different dates of issue (they may or may not mature at the same time).

*Sinking fund bonds:* Bonds in which there is a specific provision that a certain amount of money be set aside at regular periods (usually each year) to pay back the bonds when due.

*Income bonds:* Bonds in which the corporation only makes a definite commitment to pay the principal on a stated date. The interest will be paid only if it is earned. Interest may therefore never be paid. Some types of income bonds may accumulate unpaid interest and may have to be paid when the bonds become due. These bonds are sometimes called "adjustment bonds."

*Mortgage bonds:* Bonds secured by specific property (e.g., land or buildings). These bonds have prior claim to a corporation's assets over all other securities. There can be first, second, or third mortgages. There are "general mortgage bonds," which only have a general coverage on a corporation's property. The regular mortgage bonds have prior claim to general mortgage bonds.

### Decisions for the Investor

General Motors' record offering on March 20, 1975, of $300 million of 8-5/8% debentures due in the year 2005 and $300 million of 8.05% notes due in 1985 points up the need for the investor to think in broad terms about the capital market.

This was the largest debt offering of a U.S. manufacturer, surpassing the previous record offering of $500 million by DuPont in November 1974. The General Motors offering, however, had to compete with a $1.25 billion U.S. Treasury bond offering of 15-year maturity at an average yield of 8.31% the same day.

Investors generally preferred the Treasury bond issue to the General Motors issue because the slightly higher GM yield differential on the debentures could not overcome the greater safety and liquidity offered by the U.S. Treasury.

This direct competition of the corporate bond market with the U.S. Treasury bond market points up the need for the investor to consider the broad spectrum of bond offerings and to take into account such factors as safety, liquidity, and tax status and other considerations as well.

## MUNICIPAL BONDS

Municipal bonds are long-term securities issued by state and local governments within the United States. There are also short-term state and local government securities (e.g., municipal notes).

The long-term and short-term state and local government securities taken together are often referred to as "tax-exempts." The term "tax-exempts," however, can be easily misunderstood. These securities are definitely tax-exempt only with regard to Federal income taxes. Federal income taxes do not have to be paid on the interest income, but state and local government income taxes may have to be paid, depending on the provisions of the particular issue.

The rationale behind the exemption from Federal income taxes is that without the tax exemption the state and local governments would have to raise their income taxes or other taxes for capital improvements. The legal history, however, has been a torturous one, and criticism has especially grown in recent years of continuation of the tax exemption status.

This tax exemption provision has led to a long history of the use of state and local government securities as "tax shelters" by investors. The main investors in this market are individuals in high income tax brackets, casualty insurance companies, and commercial banks.

## Significant Developments

The area of municipal bonds and municipal notes has recently become an especially prominent financial field. This prominence has resulted from the inflation and recession simultaneously developing in the United States creating financial problems for many cities around the country.

New York City has probably been hurt the hardest. Mayor Abraham Beame has had to contend with a large budget deficit, powerful labor leaders, borough presidents, the City University of New York, the Municipal Assistance Corporation (commonly referred to as "Big MAC"), Governor Hugh Carey, and many others.

With the real danger of default on its debt securities, New York City is being watched very carefully by many concerned parties. The big New York City banks, with their large holdings of New York City municipal bonds and notes, would stand to lose a great deal by any default. Other banks in New York City and in other parts of the country, as well, would also stand to lose a great deal simply by virtue of the fact that New York City is the center of so many financial markets. A default, of course, would also hurt New York City employees, workers in private industry in many parts of the city, and New York State itself.

"Big MAC" was established by Governor Carey as an agency of New York State in June 1975 in order to help New York City get out of its financial crisis. More specifically, "Big MAC" was to help New York City refund its municipal notes (short-term debt securities) as they matured and had to be paid.

"Big MAC" can be expected to play an increasingly important role in the fiscal and monetary operation of New York City. In July 1975, "Big MAC" came out with a bond issue of $1 billion, with Morgan Guaranty Trust Company of New York and Salomon Brothers as the managers of the underwriting group. The yield range was set at 6.5% to 9.5% per year, the specific yield depending on the particular maturity period chosen. The 9.5% rate was considerably higher than the record 7.69% rate that New York City itself had to offer in 1974. Mayor Beame found it difficult to accept the sale at over 9%. The high rates of the "Big MAC" offer, however, illustrated very well the increasing difficulty in getting investors to buy New York City securities.

The case of New York City stands as a prime example of the many considerations that have to go into the purchase of municipal bonds and municipal notes. The danger of default has to be reckoned with in all cases. In addition, for any municipality, besides making the requisite financial considerations, the various organizations existing in the municipality, their particular power bases, and their goals have to be analyzed and given their due weight.

### Types of Municipal Bonds

*General obligation bonds* ("GO bonds"): Bonds issued with the "full faith and credit" of the issuing government or governmental authority. These securities have the protection, for principal and interest, of the taxing power of the governmental body involved.

*Revenue bonds:* Bonds issued without the protection of the taxing power of the governmental body. The condition here is that payment of principal and/or interest is made only if the facility involved earns the necessary revenue. Examples of projects frequently covered by "revenue bonds" are bridges, tunnels, toll roads, and airports. The Port of New York Authority has frequently used revenue bonds.

*Special tax bonds:* Bonds in which a tax is levied for special purposes, e.g., local area development programs, such as educational programs.

*Public Housing Authority bonds* ("PHA Bonds"): Bonds used to finance low-cost housing. They are considered attractive investments because they are backed by the U.S. government and generally have exemption from state and local government income taxes.

*Pollution-control bonds:* Bonds which are issued by municipal authorities together with industrial corporations which are involved in pollution control operations. For example, a $21-million new issue (dated March 1, 1975) was made by the Savannah Port Authority of 6.80% Pollution Control Revenue Bonds (on the American Cyanamid Company Project), to be due March 1, 2000.

*Industrial revenue bonds:* Bonds in which there are lease payments made by industrial corporations located on the premises being financed.

### Municipal Bonds versus Corporate Bonds

The investor or potential investor deciding whether to buy a municipal bond or a corporate bond has to take into account his income tax bracket. Remember, the municipal bond is definitely tax-exempt only with regard to Federal income taxes. It may or may not be tax-exempt with regard to state or local income taxes. The investor should check whether there is exemption from state and local income taxes for the particular municipal bond. The corporate bond is subject to all income taxes.

According to his income tax bracket, the investor can determine his choice by computing yield on municipal bonds and the yield on corporate bonds by the following formulas.

Tax Exemption Value = Income Tax Rate on Corporate Bond Yield
minus Income Tax Bracket

= 100% − Income Tax Bracket

Equivalent Corporate Bond Yield for Municipal Bond =

$$\frac{\text{Municipal Bond Yield}}{100\% - \text{Income Tax Bracket}}$$

Equivalent Municipal Yield for Corporate Bond
$$= \text{Municipal Bond Yield} \times (100\% - \text{Income Tax Bracket})$$

For example, for a person in the 25% Federal income tax bracket considering a municipal bond yield of 5%,

$$\text{Equivalent Corporate Bond Yield} = \frac{\text{Municipal Bond Yield}}{100\% - \text{Income Tax Bracket}}$$

$$= \frac{5\%}{100\% - 25\%}$$

$$= \frac{5\%}{75\%}$$

$$= 6.67\%$$

If the corporate bond is yielding less than 6.67%, it is yielding less than the tax-exempt municipal bond. If the corporate bond is yielding more than 6.67%, it is yielding more than the tax-exempt municipal bond.

For a person in the 50% Federal income tax bracket, considering the same municipal bond yield of 5%,

$$\text{Equivalent Corporate Bond Yield} = \frac{\text{Municipal Bond Yield}}{100\% - \text{Income Tax Bracket}}$$

$$= \frac{5\%}{100\% - 50\%}$$

$$= \frac{5\%}{50\%}$$

$$= 10\%$$

For a person in 60% income bracket, municipal bond yield = 5% (same as previous example),

$$\text{Equivalent Corporate Bond Yield} = \frac{\text{Municipal Bond Yield}}{100\% - \text{Income Tax Bracket}}$$

$$= \frac{5\%}{100\% - 60\%}$$

$$= \frac{5\%}{40\%}$$

$$= 12.5\%$$

For a person in the 70% Federal income tax bracket, considering the same municipal bond yield of 5%,

$$\text{Equivalent Corporate Bond Yield} = \frac{\text{Municipal Bond Yield}}{100\% - \text{Income Tax Bracket}}$$

$$= \frac{5\%}{100\% - 70\%}$$

$$= \frac{5\%}{30\%}$$

$$= 16.67\%$$

*Note:* In order to determine your Federal income tax bracket, consult the publication entitled *Federal Income Tax Forms,* which can be obtained from the Internal Revenue Service of the U.S. Department of the Treasury (phone or write to your local IRS office). You will find your Federal income tax bracket by consulting the "Tax Rate Schedules" in that publication. For example, the Federal income tax brackets in the foregoing examples were obtained from page 26 of the *1974 Federal Income Tax Forms* from the table entitled "Married Taxpayers Filing Joint Returns and Certain Widows and Widowers":

| Taxable Income | | Federal Income Tax Bracket |
|---|---|---|
| Over- | But not over- | |
| $12,000 | $16,000 | 25% |
| $44,000 | $52,000 | 50% |
| $88,000 | $100,000 | 60% |
| $200,000 | ......... | 70% |

In the foregoing calculations, the element of risk has not been considered. You should compare the risk of the particular municipal bond that you are interested in with the risk of the corporate bond.

## U.S. GOVERNMENT BONDS

U.S. Treasury bonds
U.S. Savings bonds

### The Purchase of U.S. Treasury Bonds

The following information explains how one may purchase new U.S. Treasury bonds.[3] Outstanding bonds (those issued previously) must be

[3]Federal Reserve Bank of New York, *Information Concerning the Purchase of U.S. Treasury Notes and Bonds* (April 1973.)

purchased privately or in the securities market through a commercial bank, a securities dealer, or a broker.

*Treasury bonds* are direct obligations of the United States government. The interest is payable semi-annually, either by coupon or by check. They do not earn interest after their maturity date. Treasury bonds are issued in denominations of $1,000, $5,000, $10,000, $100,000, and $1,000,000.

To purchase new bonds, one may subscribe, in person, on the days of the offering at a Federal Reserve Bank. If one cannot come in person, the subscription and payment may be mailed to the Federal Reserve Bank. The subscription must be received in the Bank no later than the time indicated in the offering notice. Late subscriptions will not be accepted.

One may pay for Treasury Bonds in either of two ways. The simplest way is to make payment for the full face value of the notes or bonds with one's subscription, in one of the following forms:

In U.S. currency (if one appears in person).

By certified personal check or by official bank check (i.e., cashier's check); the check must be payable on its face to the Federal Reserve Bank of New York (endorsed checks cannot be accepted); print your name on the check, if it is not a certified personal check, so that it can be associated with your subscription.

In maturing Government securities (only as provided in the offering circular).

The more difficult way to pay is to submit partial payment of the face value of the notes subscribed to (usually 10%, i.e., $500 for a $5,000 subscription). The partial payment must be submitted with one's subscription form on the days of the offering. Final payment must then be made on or before the issue date. Only a Federal funds check or U.S. currency will be accepted from individual subscribers on the issue date. If one fails to make final payment on or before the issue date, the subscription will be cancelled and the partial payment will either be kept or returned at the Treasury's option.

Bearer Treasury bonds are payable to anyone who has possession (the same as currency). They must be treated and safeguarded as carefully as cash. They carry interest coupons that are clipped and redeemed for cash as they mature each six months. They may be cashed through any commercial bank or through a Federal Reserve Bank.

A registered Treasury bond is registered as to principal and interest and bears the owner's name on its face. It cannot be negotiated without the owner's written assignment on the back. The signature to the assignment must be certified by an officer of a commercial bank or trust company and must bear the corporate seal (or savings bond validating stamp) of the attesting officer's bank. Interest is mailed semiannually by check from the Treasury Department.

A Treasury bond may be registered in any of the following forms:

*In one name:* John A. Doe (123-45-6789)
*In two names:* John A. Doe (123-45-6789) *or* Mrs. Mary C. Doe
            John A. Doe (123-45-6789) *and* Mrs. Mary C. Doe
            (either party's Social Security number is acceptable)
*For minors:* John R. Jones as natural guardian of Henry B. Jones, a minor
            (123-45-6789)
            William C. Smith, as custodian for John A. Smith, a minor
            (123-45-6789) under the California Uniform Gifts to Minors Act.
*Note:* Treasury securities may not be registered solely in the name of a minor.

Treasury bonds may be picked up in person at the Federal Reserve Bank, or one may request that they be sent to by registered mail, at the expense of the Treasury Department. In either case, allow several weeks for delivery.

*Note:* See Appendix C for data on U.S. Treasury bonds.

## U.S. SAVINGS BONDS

Sales of U.S. Savings Bonds have markedly increased since April 1974 when the U.S. Treasury announced that it was increasing the interest rate from 5½% to 6%. This increase is for the only two U.S. Savings Bonds presently being sold, Series E[4] bonds and Series H bonds,[5] and have served to make them much more attractive investment vehicles. Other bond issues have been issued, but they no longer qualify for interest (see Tables). Information about the various series follows.

Series A through D were sold from March 1, 1935 through April 30, 1941.
Series E has been on sale since May 1, 1941.
Series F and G were sold from May 1, 1941 through April 30, 1952.
Series H has been on sale since June 1, 1952.
Series J and K were sold from May 1, 1952 through April 30, 1957.
*Note:* See Appendix D for data on U.S. Savings Bonds.

### Series E Bonds

*Denominations and Prices.* Series E bonds are issued on a discount basis. The denominations and purchase prices are as follows.

[4]*Federal Register* (April 23, 1974), pp. 14412-14461.
[5]*Federal Register* (April 19, 1974), pp. 14062-14109.

| Denomination | Purchase Price |
|---|---|
| $25 | $18.75 |
| $50 | 37.50 |
| $75 | 56.25 |
| $100 | 75.00 |
| $200 | 150.00 |
| $500 | 375.00 |
| $1,000 | 750.00 |
| $10,000 | 7,500.00 |
| $100,000 | 75,000.00 |

The $100,000 denomination is available only for purchase by trustees of employees' savings and savings and vacation plans.

*Inscription and Issue.* At the time of issue, the issuing agent will inscribe on the face of each bond the name, Social Security number, and address of the owner and the name of the beneficiary (if any), or the name, Social Security number and address of the first-named co-owner and the name of the other co-owner.

If the bond is being purchased as a gift or award and the owner's Social Security number is not known, the purchaser's Social Security number or employer identification number must be furnished. In this event, the issuing agent will inscribe the word "GIFT" and the purchaser's number on the bond.

The agent will then enter in the upper right-hand portion of the bond the issue date and imprint the agent's dating stamp in the lower right-hand portion to show the date that the bond is actually inscribed. A Series E bond shall be valid only if an authorized issuing agent receives payment and duly inscribes, dates, and stamps it.

*Term of Series E Bonds.* A Series E bond is dated as of the first day of the month in which payment of the purchase price is received by an agent authorized to issue bonds. This date is the "issue date," and the bond will mature and be payable at the maturity value 5 years from the issue date.

The bond may not be called for redemption by the Secretary of the Treasury prior to maturity or the end of any extended period. The owner does have the option of redeeming the bond any time after two months from the issue date at fixed redemption values. The Department of the Treasury, nevertheless, may require reasonable notice of presentation for redemption prior to the maturity date or any extended maturity date.

*Investment Yield (or Interest).* The investment yield (or interest) on a Series E bond is approximately 6% per year (compounded semi-annually), if the bond is held to maturity. The yield will be less if one redeems the bond before the maturity date. For the first six months from the issue date, the bond is redeemable only at the purchase price. Its redemption value increases at the beginning of each successive half-year period.

*Regulations.* Series E bonds are subject to the regulations contained in U.S. Department of Treasury Circular No. 530, current revision. Copies may be obtained from any Federal Reserve Bank or Branch or from the Bureau of the Public Debt, Washington, D.C. 20226.

Generally, only residents of the United States, its territories and possessions, the Commonwealth of Puerto Rico, the Canal Zone, and citizens of the United States temporarily residing abroad are eligible to be named as owners of Series E bonds.

The bonds may be registered in natural persons in their own right, fiduciaries, or private and public organizations. Series E bonds may not be registered in the names of commercial banks.

The amount of Series E bonds originally issued during any one calendar year that may be held by any one person, at any one time, is limited to $10,000 (face amount). There is a special limitation for employees' savings plans of $2,000 (face amount) multiplied by the highest number of participants in any eligible employees' savings plan, at any time during the year in which the bonds are issued. Savings and vacation plans may be eligible for this special limitation.

*Purchase.* Series E bonds may be purchased over the counter, by mail order, or with savings stamps. Bonds registered in names of natural persons in their own right only can be bought at incorporated banks, trust companies, and other agencies duly qualified as issuing agents at selected U.S. post offices.

Bonds registered in the names of trustees of employees' savings plans must be bought at an agent who is an eligible trustee of an approved employees' savings plan. Prior approval must, in addition, be obtained from the Federal Reserve Bank of the agent's district. The agent may be an incorporated bank, trust company, or other agency which qualified as indicated.

Bonds registered in all authorized forms may be bought at Federal Reserve Banks and Branches and at the Department of the Treasury, Washington, D.C. 20226.

Purchases may be made by mail upon application to any Federal Reserve Bank or Branch or to the Department of the Treasury accompanied by a remittance to cover the issue price.

Any form of exchange (including personal checks) is acceptable subject to collection. Checks or other forms of exchange should be made payable to the Federal Reserve Bank or the "United States Treasury" (as the case may be). Checks payable to endorsement are not acceptable.

Any depository qualified pursuant to the provisions of U.S. Department of the Treasury Circular No. 92, current revision, will be permitted to make payment by credit for bonds applied for on behalf of its customers up to any amount for which it shall be qualified in excess of existing deposits, when notified by the Federal Reserve Bank of its district.

The sale of United States Savings Stamps was terminated effective June 30, 1970. Outstanding stamps affixed in fully or partially completed albums, however, may be used to buy Series E bonds at banks or other financial institutions authorized to issue bonds. Otherwise, the stamps may be redeemed for cash at post offices.

*Extended Terms and Improved Yields for Outstanding Series E Bonds.* Owners of Series E bonds with issue dates of May 1, 1941, through April 1, 1952, may retain their bonds for a third and final extended maturity period of 10 years.

Owners of Series E bonds with issue dates of May 1, 1952, through January 1, 1957, may retain their bonds for a second extended maturity period of 10 years.

The investment yield on all outstanding Series E bonds has been increased as follows:

For bonds in original maturity period on December 1, 1973, by approximately ½ of 1 percent per year, compounded semi-annually for the remaining period to the maturity date. The increase began with the first interest accrual period starting on or after December 1, 1973.

For bonds in extended maturity periods on December 1, 1973, by approximately ½ of 1 percent per year, compounded semi-annually, for the remaining period to the next maturity date. The increase will begin with the first interest accrual period starting on or after December 1, 1973.

For bonds entering extended maturity periods on December 1, 1973, and January 1, 1974, to approximately 6 percent per year, compounded semi-annually, for the extended maturity period.

*Payment or Redemption.* A Series E bond may be redeemed in accordance with its terms at the appropriate redemption value, but the redemption value of bonds in the denomination of $100,000 is equal to the total redemption values of ten $10,000 bonds bearing the same issue dates.

Owners of Series E bonds may obtain payment upon presentation and surrender of the bonds to a Federal Reserve Bank or Branch or to the Department of the Treasury with the requests for payment on the bonds duly executed and certified in accordance with the governing regulations.

An individual (natural person) whose name is inscribed on a Series E bond either as owner or co-owner in his own right may present such bond to any incorporated bank or trust company or other financial institution which is qualified as a paying agent under Department of the Treasury Circular No. 750, current revision. If such bond is in order for payment by the paying agent, the owner or co-owner, upon establishing his identity to the satisfaction of the agent and upon signing the request for payment and adding his home or business address, may receive payment of its current redemption value.

### Series H Bonds

*Denominations and Prices.* Series H bonds are issued at face (or par) amount and are available in denominations of $500, $1,000, $5,000, and $10,000.

*Inscription and Issue.* At the time of issue the issuing agent will inscribe on the face of each Series H bond the name, Social Security number, and address of the owner and the name of the beneficiary (if any), or the name, Social Security number, and address of the first-named coowner and the name of the other coowner.

The agent will then enter in the upper right-hand portion of the bond the issue date and imprint the agent's dating stamp in the lower right-hand portion to show the date of the bond is actually inscribed. A Series H bond shall be valid only if an authorized issuing agent receives payment and duly inscribes, dates and stamps it.

*Term of Series H Bonds.* A Series H bond is dated as of the first day of the month in which payment is received by an agent authorized to issue bonds. This date is the "issue date," and the bond will mature and be payable 10 years from the issue date.

The bond may not be called for redemption prior to maturity or the end of any extended maturity period. The bond may be redeemed at par after six months from the issue date, although the U.S. Treasury Department may require reasonable notice of presentation for redemption before the maturity date or any authorized extended maturity date.

*Investment Yield (or Interest).* The investment yield (or interest) on a Series H bond will be paid semi-annually by check drawn to the order of the registered owner or co-owners, beginning six months from the issue date.

Interest payments will be on a graduated scale, fixed to produce an investment yield of approximately 6% per year (compounded semi-annually) if the bond is held to maturity, but the yield will be less if the bond is redeemed before the maturity date.

Interest will cease at maturity or at the end of the extended maturity period or, if redeemed before the maturity date or extended maturity date, at the end of the interest period next preceding the date of redemption. *If the date of redemption falls on an interest payment date, interest will cease on that date.*

*Regulations.* Series H bonds are subject to the regulations contained in U.S. Department of Treasury Circular No. 530, current revision. Copies may be obtained from any Federal Reserve Bank or Branch or from the Bureau of the Public Debt, Washington, D.C. 20226.

Generally, only residents of the United States, its territories and possessions, the Commonwealth of Puerto Rico, the Canal Zone, and citizens of the United States residing abroad are eligible to be named as owners of Series H Bonds.

The bonds may be registered in natural persons in their own right, fiduciaries, and private and public organizations. Series H bonds may not be registered in the names of commercial banks.

The amount of Series H bonds originally issued during any one calendar year that may be held by any one person, at any one time, is limited to $10,000 (face amount). There is a special limitation for gifts to exempt organizations of under $200,000 (face amount) for bonds received as gifts by an organization which at the time of purchase is an exempt organization.

*Purchase.* Only the Federal Reserve Banks and branches and the Department of the Treasury are authorized to act as official issuing agents for the sale of Series H bonds. However, financial institutions may forward applications for purchase of the bonds. The date an issuing agent receives the application and payment will govern the issue date of the bond purchased.

The applicant for purchase of Series H bonds should furnish (1) instructions for registration of the bonds to be issued, which must be in an authorized form; (2) the appropriate Social Security or employer identification number; (3) the post office address of the owner or first-named co-owner; and (4) the address(es) for delivery of the bonds and for mailing checks in payment of interest, if other than that of the owner or first-named co-owner. The application should be forwarded to a Federal Reserve Bank or Branch, or the Department of the Treasury, Washington, D.C. 20226, accompanied by a remittance to cover the purchase price. Any form of exchange, including personal checks, will be accepted subject to collection. Checks or other forms of exchange should be drawn to the order of the Federal Reserve Bank of the "United States Treasury," as the case may be. Checks payable by endorsement are not acceptable. Any depositary qualified pursuant to Department of the Treasury Circular No. 92, current revision, will be permitted to make payment by credit for bonds applied for on behalf of its customers up to any amount for which it shall be qualified in excess of existing deposits, when so notified by the Federal Reserve Bank of its district.

*Extended terms and improved yields for outstanding Series H bonds.* Owners of Series H bonds with issue dates of June 1, 1952, through January 1, 1957, may retain their bonds for an extended maturity period of 10 years.

Owners of Series H bonds with issue dates of February 1, 1957, or thereafter, may retain their bonds for an extended maturity period of 10 years.

The investment yield on all outstanding Series H bonds is increased as follows:

For bonds in original maturity period on December 1, 1973, by approximately ½ of 1 percent per annum, compounded semi-annually, for the remaining period to the maturity date. The increase will be included in the interest checks issued on or after June 1, 1974.

For bonds in an extended or second extended maturity period on December 1, 1973, by approximately ½ of 1 percent per annum, compounded semi-annually, for the remaining period to the extended maturity date or second extended maturity date, as the case may be. The increase will be included in the interest checks on or after June 1, 1974.

For bonds entering an extended or second extended maturity period on December 1, 1973, or January 1, 1974, to 6 percent per year, compounded semi-annually, for the extended or second extended maturity period.

*Redemption.*   A Series H bond may be redeemed at par at any time after six months from the issue date. The bond must be presented and surrendered, with a duly executed request for payment, to (a) a Federal Reserve Bank or Branch, (b) the Department of the Treasury, Washington, D.C. 20226, or (c) the Bureau of the Public Debt, 536 South Clark Street, Chicago, Illinois 60605. A bond received by an agent during the calendar month preceding an interest payment date may not be redeemed until that date.

### Income Tax Status for Series E and Series H Bonds

The interest on Series E and Series H bonds, as with all U.S. government securities since March 1, 1941, is subject to Federal income tax. The interest, however, as well as the security itself, is exempt from tax by any state, municipal, or local taxing authority.[6]

The following table indicates the Federal income tax liability on Series E and Series H bonds, where the bonds are registered in co-ownership form and are cashed during the lifetimes of both co-owners.

If a taxpayer is on the accrual accounting basis for income tax purposes, the interest on Series E bonds must be reported as income each year.

If a taxpayer is on a cash accounting basis, he may choose one of two methods in accounting for the interest on his Series E bonds. He may defer reporting of interest until the year in which the bonds are disposed of or

---

[6]U.S. Savings Bonds Division, Department of the Treasury, *United States Savings Bonds: Legal Aspects* (Washington, D.C.: U.S. Government Printing Office, 1973).

**TABLE 3-4**

Income Tax Liability on Bonds Registered in Co-ownership Form

| *How Purchased* | *Who is Liable for Tax* |
|---|---|
| "A" buys bond in name of "A" and "B" as co-owners. | Interest is income to "A" as the person who contributed the purchase price. |
| "A" and "B" buy bonds in co-ownership, each contributing part of the purchase price. | Interest is income to both "A" and "B" in proportion to their contributions to the purchase price. |
| "A" and "B" receive bonds in co-ownership as a gift from "C." | Interest is income to both "A" and "B" —50% to each co-owner. |

reach final maturity (whichever comes first), or he may report the interest each year as it accrues.

If the first method is used, the taxpayer may change to the second method without permission from the Internal Revenue Service, but once the second method is chosen, he may not change the method without obtaining permission from the Internal Revenue Service (Internal Revenue Service, Washington, D.C. 20224).

Interest on Series H bonds is received semi-annually and must be reported annually for Federal income tax purposes.

*Shifting of Income Tax Liability.* A change of ownership of a Series E or Series H bond bearing a tax-deferred increment notation resulting from a reissue usually does not have the effect of shifting Federal income tax liability for the accumulated interest. A change of ownership resulting from death of the owner, however, does, in most cases shift to the new owner the income tax liability for interest already accumulated.

For example, a woman buys a Series E bond listing her nephew as co-owner (or beneficiary). She dies after several years; the nephew becomes sole and absolute owner of the bond. The death of the original owner does not result in what is called a "taxable event" for Federal income tax purposes. The income tax liability on the accumulated interest would pass, with the bond, to the nephew and would remain his, along with liability on additional accruals. However, if the person filing the final income tax return of the decedent elects to include all interest earned on the bond to the date of her death, the nephew's tax liability would apply only to the interest accruing from that date.

In another example, a father who has bought and has held a Series E bond for several years decides to make a gift of it to his son. He has it re-issued in the son's name alone or with himself or someone else as beneficiary.

Such reissue results in a "taxable event." Any accrued interest previously unreported would have to be included in the gross income of the father for the taxable year in which the reissue took place. The interest accruing thereafter would be the liability of the son for income tax purposes.

In the foregoing examples, it is assumed that all persons are on the cash reporting basis and have not elected to report their bond interest annually as it accrues.

*Rights of Survivors.* The legal representative of a decedent's estate should be aware of the rights of surviving co-owners or beneficiaries. Savings bonds registered in either co-owner or beneficiary form become the sole property of the survivor, notwithstanding any terms of a will to the contrary. However, this provision does not alter any estate or inheritance tax liability to which bonds are subject.

Savings Bonds on which there is a surviving co-owner or beneficiary do not form a part of the decedent's estate for probate purposes—but their value usually must be included in computing the gross estate for estate and inheritance tax purposes.

An estate tax return must be filed if the value of the decedent's gross estate—including savings bonds—exceeds $60,000. The tax return is due within nine months after the date of death.

*Federal Gift Tax.* A gift tax return must be filed by the donor if he makes gifts, including savings bonds, of more than $3,000 to any donee during the calendar year. There is also a $30,000 lifetime exemption, over and above the $3,000 annual exclusion of gifts to each donee; it may be used all in one year or over a lifetime, and with respect to any number of donees.

*Bond Exchange Privilege.* E Bonds, alone, or in combination with Savings Notes (Freedom Shares), may be exchanged with or without deferral of reporting of the accumulated interest for Federal income tax purposes for H Bonds. E Bonds and Shares submitted in exchange must have a current redemption value of $500 or more.

H Bonds, which are issued at face amount, pay interest semi-annually by Treasury check. Unless owners have a need for current income, they should consider the matter carefully before making an exchange, as they may find interest earnings on the Series H Bonds, particularly during the first year, less than on the securities exchanged.

H Bonds received in an exchange are not subject to the annual limitation on holdings. H Bonds may also carry a different form of registration from the E Bonds and Shares exchanged, without permission of previous co-owners or beneficiaries.

If a cash adjustment is received in an exchange, the amount received is interest income to the extent of unreported interest earned on the securities exchanged.

**FIGURE 3-2**

Form PD 2507 (Rev. 3/73)
Dept. of the Treasury
Bureau of the Public Debt

**APPLICATION FOR**   Ref. No. _____

# United States Savings Bonds—Series E

The undersigned hereby applies for United States Savings Bonds of Series E as follows:

| NUMBER OF BONDS | DENOM. (Face amount) | ISSUE PRICE (Each bond) | AMOUNT (Total cost) | SERIAL NUMBERS OF BONDS ISSUED (For use of Issuing Agent) | |
|---|---|---|---|---|---|
| | $ 25 | $ 18.75 | $ | Q | E |
| | 50 | 37.50 | | L | E |
| | 75 | 56.25 | | K | E |
| | 100 | 75.00 | | C | E |
| | 200 | 150.00 | | R | E |
| | 500 | 375.00 | | D | E |
| | 1,000 | 750.00 | | M | E |
| Total amount of purchase ▶ | | | $ | | |

**———— GIFT BOND PURCHASES ————**

IMPORTANT – If this is a GIFT BOND application, please read the instructions below and insert the appropriate number, if required, in the following box.

Social Security Account Number        Employer Identification Number

Purchaser's:  ⎵⎵⎵ – ⎵⎵ – ⎵⎵⎵⎵  **OR**  ⎵⎵ – ⎵⎵⎵⎵⎵⎵⎵

INSTRUCTIONS: If the bond is being purchased as a gift or award and the owner's social security account number is not known, the purchaser's social security account number or employer identification number must be inserted in the box provided above. In this event, the issuing agent will inscribe the word "GIFT" and the purchaser's number on the bond. (The word "GIFT" is only inscribed on the bond when the owner's social security number is not known and the purchaser's number is used to identify the bond.) This will prevent the bond from being associated with the purchaser's own holdings.

**BONDS TO BE INSCRIBED**  { See Department Circular No. 530 for authorized forms of registration. }

Name _____

**T Y P E  O R  P R I N T**

Owner's:  Social Security Account Number  ⎵⎵⎵ – ⎵⎵ – ⎵⎵⎵⎵  **OR**  Employer Identification Number  ⎵⎵ – ⎵⎵⎵⎵⎵⎵⎵

Address _____
(Number and street or rural route)

(City or town)        (State)        (ZIP Code)

The following person, if any, to be named as ☐ coowner ☐ beneficiary:

Name _____

Social Security Account Number  ⎵⎵⎵ – ⎵⎵ – ⎵⎵⎵⎵  { For record-keeping purposes, etc., furnish the co-owner's or beneficiary's number where possible; if a woman is named, either "Miss" or "Mrs.", or this number, must be shown.

Bonds will be delivered to below-named purchaser unless otherwise here instructed:

**SIGN AND DATE HERE ▶**   Date _____

Signature of Purchaser _____

Address _____
(Number and street or rural route)     (City or town)     (State)     (ZIP Code)

**METHOD OF PAYMENT ▶**  ☐ CASH, SAVINGS STAMPS, OR CHECK  ☐ DEBIT MY/OUR ACCOUNT  ☐

**FOR INSTITUTIONAL USE ONLY**

☐ Check or cash enclosed.

☐ Charge our reserve a/c.        (Name of institution)

☐ Charge our Treas. Tax & Loan a/c.

        (Authorized signature)

**———— FOR USE OF ISSUING AGENT ————**

| Application No. | Issue month | Date of issue | Bonds inscribed by | Bonds verified by |
|---|---|---|---|---|
| Date mailed/delivered | Shipping No. | | Bonds received by | |

**MEMORANDUM RECEIPT** *(For use by agent receiving applications)*  Ref. No. _____

Received, $ _____ from _____

purchase price of $ _____ (face amount) United States Savings Bonds, Series E.

Date _____        _____

☆U.S.GPO: 1973 — 506-761

## FIGURE 3-3

Form PD 3700
Dept. of the Treasury
Bureau of the Public Debt
(Rev. June 1974)

**APPLICATION FOR**

Ref. No. _____

United States Savings Bonds – Series H

To Federal Reserve Bank or Branch at _____

The undersigned hereby applies for United States Savings Bonds of Series H (issued pursuant to Treasury Department Circular No. 905, as revised and amended) as follows:

| NO. OF BONDS | DENOMINATION (Issue Price & Face Amount) | AMOUNT (Total Cost) | SERIAL NUMBERS OF BONDS ISSUED (For Use of Federal Reserve Bank) | |
|---|---|---|---|---|
| | $ 500 | $ | D | H |
| | 1,000 | | M | H |
| | 5,000 | | V | H |
| | 10,000 | | X | H |
| Total amount of purchase ▶ | $ | | | |

**NONINDIVIDUAL OWNERS**

If bonds are to be registered other than in name(s) of individual(s), please indicate the investor class group by inserting the proper code number in the following box:

| INVESTOR CODE |
|---|
| |

(See Instruction 1 for identifying code numbers.)

**BONDS TO BE INSCRIBED** { See Department Circular No. 530 for authorized forms of registration. }

Name _____

Owner's: Social Security Account Number [ ] – [ ] – [ ]   **OR**   Employer Identification Number [ ] – [ ]

Address _____
(Number and street or rural route)

_____
(City or town)    (State)    (ZIP code)

The following person, if any, to be named as ☐ coowner ☐ beneficiary:

Name _____

Social Security Account Number [ ] – [ ] – [ ]   { For record-keeping purposes, etc., furnish the co-owner's or beneficiary's number where possible; if a woman is named, either "Miss" or "Mrs.", or the number, must be shown.

Address (include ZIP code) for mailing interest checks, if other than that of owner or first-named coowner: _____

Bonds will be delivered to the purchaser named below unless otherwise here instructed:

Name _____

Address _____
(Number and street or rural route)    (City or town)    (State)    (ZIP code)

**SIGN AND DATE HERE** ▶ Signature of Purchaser _____

Address (if not given above) _____
(Number and street or rural route)    (City or town)    (State)    (ZIP code)

**METHOD OF PAYMENT** ▶ ☐ Cash or check   ☐ Debit my/our account   Date _____

**FOR INSTITUTIONAL USE ONLY**

☐ Check or cash enclosed
☐ Charge our reserve a/c
☐ Charge our Treas. Tax & Loan a/c
(Enclose Certificate of Advice)

_____
(Name of institution)

(City)    (County)    (State)

_____
(Authorized signature)

**FOR USE OF FEDERAL RESERVE BANK**

| APPLICATION NO. | ISSUE MONTH | DATE OF ISSUE | BONDS INSCRIBED BY | BONDS VERIFIED BY |
|---|---|---|---|---|
| | | | | |

| DATE MAILED/ DELIVERED | SHIPPING NO. | | BONDS RECEIVED BY | |
|---|---|---|---|---|
| | | | | |

**MEMORANDUM RECEIPT** *(For use by agent receiving applications)* Ref. No. _____

Received, $ _____ from _____

purchase price of $ _____ (Face Amount) United States Savings Bonds, Series H.

_____

Date _____    _____

*Partial Redemption.* A savings bond in a denomination larger than the smallest one of the same series may be redeemed prior to maturity in part at current redemption value. For example, consider a request for partial redemption of a $100 E Bond to the extent of a $50 (face amount) E Bond. The owner would receive a check representing the redemption value of a $50 bond having the same issue date as the $100 bond being turned in. In addition, he would receive a bond with an issue date the same as the original $100 bond and having a face value of $50.

*Lost or Mutilated Savings Bonds.* All U.S. Savings Bonds are issued in registered form. When lost, stolen, mutilated, or destroyed, they may be replaced without cost to the owner.

A record of bonds owned—with dates and series numbers—will assist in identifying the bonds as required by law before duplicates may be issued. In the case of H Bonds, Social Security or employer identification numbers should be included. There is ordinarily a six-month waiting period for lost bonds. Use Form PD 1048 to apply for relief on account of lost, stolen, or destroyed bonds.

Note: See Figures 3-2 and 3-3 for copies of application forms for Series E and H bonds.

## U.S. GOVERNMENT AGENCY AND U.S. GOVERNMENT-SPONSORED AGENCY BONDS

See the portion in this book entitled "U.S. Government Agency Securities and Related Securities" for coverage of this area.

## FOREIGN BONDS

Bonds of foreign governments and foreign corporations have to be looked at in a special light by the investor or potential investor. They should be considered fixed-income investments which are subject to especially great hazards when compared to U.S. bond issues.

A foreign government or foreign corporation can default, leaving the investor little recourse. Political considerations become significant factors in assessing these bonds. The investor has to be aware of political developments in the country and the possibility of nationalization for a particular foreign corporation.

Over the years some foreign governments and foreign corporations have been very diligent in making their payments, but, particularly with regard to foreign bonds, the investor is advised to follow the wisdom so succinctly expressed in the Latin phrase *caveat emptor!*—"Let the buyer beware."

## WORLD BANK BONDS

Unlike many foreign securities, World Bank bonds do have good backing. They are backed by the member countries of the World Bank.

The World Bank (or International Bank for Reconstruction and Development) first opened its doors for business in June 1946 as part of the United Nations. Over the years, its structure has changed so that now it is referred to as the "World Bank Group" and consists of three organizations:

The World Bank itself or the International Bank for Reconstruction and Development (IBRD).

The International Development Association (IDA).

The International Finance Corporation (IFC).

The IDA was established in 1960 and derives its funds primarily from 18 rich countries. The IFC, the smallest of the three organizations, was established in 1965.

The World Bank Group raises much of its funds from floating bond issues in various countries, especially in the United States. The money is used primarily to make loans to developing countries. The original IBRD was concerned with rebuilding the economies devastated by the Second World War, but it now concentrates upon the developing countries.

In fiscal year 1947, the World Bank granted one loan of $250 million. Its activity has grown steadily since then, with 148 loans, totaling $3.4 billion, granted in fiscal year 1973.[7]

See Table 3-9 for information and data on World Bank loans and IDA credits. Table 3-10 presents detailed information and data on some World Bank bonds, notes and other obligations (more specifically, the International Bank for Reconstruction and Development).

---

[7]John A. King, "Reorganizing the World Bank," *Finance and Development* (Washington, D.C.: International Monetary Fund and the World Bank Group, March 1974) p. 5.

**TABLE 3-5**

## World Bank loans approved during third quarter of fiscal 1975

(ended March 31, 1975)

| Country | Purpose | Amount ($ millions) |
|---------|---------|---------------------|
| Brazil (2) | Highways, railways | 285.0 |
| Colombia (3) | DFC, water supply, telecommunications | 47.5 |
| Egypt (2) | Industry, railways | 77.0 |
| Honduras | Power | 35.0 |
| Indonesia | Industry | 115.0 |
| India | Industry | 109.0 |
| Ivory Coast (3) | Cotton, sewerage, education supplement | 42.2 |
| Kenya* | Agriculture | 7.5 |
| Korea | Urbanization, DFCs, education | 197.5 |
| Romania (2) | Agricultural credit, irrigation | 100.0 |
| Sierra Leone | Highways supplement | 2.3 |
| Tunisia | Sewerage | 28.0 |
| Turkey | DFC | 65.0 |
| Zaïre | Industry | 100.0 |
| Total loans during third quarter of fiscal 1975 | | 1,211.0 |
| Total loans during first three quarters of fiscal 1975 | | 2,420.85 |

*With a $7.5 million IDA credit

## IDA credits during third quarter of fiscal 1975

(ended March 31, 1975)

| Country | Purpose | Amount ($ millions) |
|---------|---------|---------------------|
| Bangladesh (3) | Industry, population, imports | 73.0 |
| Ghana | Oil palm | 13.6 |
| India (3) | Industrial imports (2), agriculture | 245.0 |
| Jordan | Education | 6.0 |
| Kenya* | Agriculture | 7.5 |
| Malawi | Rural development | 8.5 |
| Mali (2) | Livestock, rice irrigation supplement | 15.9 |
| Senegal | Education | 15.0 |
| Western Samoa | Highways | 4.4 |
| Yemen, P. D. R. | Fisheries supplement | 1.6 |
| Zaïre | Highways | 26.0 |
| Total credits during the third quarter of fiscal 1975 | | 416.5 |
| Total credits during first three quarters of fiscal 1975 | | 971.55 |

*With a $7.5 million Bank loan

Source: International Monetary Fund and the World Bank Group, *Finance & Development* (June 1975), p. 5.

## TABLE 3-6

| Payable in UNITED STATES DOLLARS U.S. $-16- August 21, 1975 | Principal Amount Authorized | Maturity | Sinking Fund Requirements Annually on or Before Date Shown (Principal Amount) |
|---|---|---|---|
| 9% - 2 Yr. Bonds of 1974, due 1976 Dated: September 15, 1974 Interest Payable: March 15 & September 15 | $200,000,000 | September 15, 1976 | None |
| 8% Loan of 1974, due 1986/87 Dated: Tranche I: $75 million October 15, 1974 Tranche II: $75 million March 17, 1975 Interest Payable: Tranche I: April & Oct. 15 Tranche II: March & Sept.17 | $150,000,000 | Tranche I: $75,000,000 on October 15,1986 Tranche II: $75,000,000 on March 17, 1987 | None |
| 8% Loan of 1974, due 1979 Dated: December 6, 1974 Interest payable: June 1 & December 1 | $5,000,000 | December 1, 1979 | None |
| 8% - 5 Yr. Notes of 1975, due 1980 Dated: January 1, 1975 Interest Payable: January 1 & July 1 | $300,000,000 | January 1, 1980 | None |
| 8.15% - 10 Yr. Notes of 1975, due 1985 Dated: January 1, 1975 Interest Payable: January 1 & July 1 | $200,000,000 | January 1, 1985 | None |

| Payable in CANADIAN DOLLARS Can.$-2- August 21, 1975 | Principal Amount Authorized | Maturity | Sinking Fund Requirements Annually on or Before Date Shown (Principal Amount) |
|---|---|---|---|
| 7% - 25 Year Bonds of 1968, due 1993 Dated February 15, 1968 Interest Payable: February 15 & August 15 | Can$ 15,000,000 | February 15, 1993 | Sinking Fund - None Purchase Fund - Bank will use best efforts to purchase Can$ 225,000 at not more than 97.50% from 1970 to 1988 inclusive |
| 7-1/4% 8 Year Bonds of 1971, due 1979 Dated November 1, 1971 Interest Payable: May 1 & November 1 | Can$ 25,000,000 | November 1, 1979 | None |
| 7-1/4% - 8 Yr Loan of 1971, due 1976/79 Dated: December 17, 1971 Interest Payable: December 17 | Can$ 50,000,000 | Can$ 11,000,000 on Dec. 17,1976, Can$ 12,000,000 on Dec. 17,1977, Can$ 13,000,000 on Dec. 17,1978 & Can$ 14,000,000 on Dec. 17,1979 | None |

**TABLE 3-6** (continued)

| Callable as a Whole or in Part by Lot, on at Least 45 Days' Notice at any Time to Each Date Shown Unless Otherwise Specified | Fiscal or Paying Agent | Listed In | Offered |
|---|---|---|---|
| Not Callable | Federal Reserve Bank of New York | Not Listed | At 100 on August 20, 1974 to investors outside the United States by private placement |
| Not Callable | Federal Reserve Bank of New York | Not Listed | At 100 on October 14, 1974 by private placement to the Imperial Government of Iran |
| Not Callable | Payment of principal & interest to be made directly by Bank to Trinidad & Tobago at Federal Reserve Bank of N.Y. | Not Listed | At 100 on December 5, 1974 by private placement to the government of Trinidad & Tobago |
| Not Callable | Federal Reserve Bank of New York | New York | At 100.284% on December 11, 1974 by an underwriting group headed by Salomon Brothers, The First Boston Corporation and Morgan Stanley & Co. Incorporated |
| Not Callable | Federal Reserve Bank of New York | New York | At 100 on December 11, 1974 by an underwriting group headed by Salomon Brothers, The First Boston Corporation and Morgan Stanley & Co. Incorporated |

| Callable as a Whole or in Part by Lot, on at Least 45 Days' Notice at any Time to Each Date Shown Unless Otherwise Specified | Fiscal or Paying Agent | Listed In | Offered |
|---|---|---|---|
| On and after February 15, 1990 at 100. | Bank of Canada | Not Listed | At 97.50 on January 29, 1968 by an underwriting group headed by Dominion Securities Corporation Limited, A.E. Ames & Co. Limited and Wood Gundy Securities Limited. |
| Not callable | Bank of Canada | Not Listed | At 99.75 on October 14, 1971 by an underwriting group headed by A.E. Ames & Co. Limited, Wood Gundy Limited and Dominion Securities Corporation Limited |
| On not less than 90 days notice on December 17, 1974, or on any December 17 thereafter in amounts not to exceed 50% of the original principal amount in any one year. | Bank of Montreal | Not Listed | On December 17, 1971 by private placement with the Bank of Montreal. |

TABLE 3-6 (*Continued*)

| Payable in<br>DEUTSCHE MARKS<br>*DM-9-*<br>*August 21, 1975* | Principal<br>Amount<br>Authorized | Maturity | Sinking Fund Requirements<br>Annually on<br>or<br>Before Date Shown<br>(Principal Amount) |
|---|---|---|---|
| 6-7/8% Note of 1972,<br>due 1976<br>Dated: February 1, 1972<br>Interest Payable:<br>February 1 and August 1 | DM 157,500,000 | August 1, 1976 | None |
| 6-3/4% - 15 Yr Bonds of 1972,<br>due 1987<br>Dated: March 1, 1972<br>Interest Payable:<br>March 1 | DM 250,000,000 | DM 25,000,000<br>each<br>March 1, 1978-87 | None |
| 6-1/4% - 5 Yr Notes of 1972,<br>due 1977<br>Dated: March 1, 1972<br>Interest Payable:<br>March 1 | DM 150,000,000 | March 1, 1977 | None |
| 6-1/2% - 10 Yr Bonds of 1972,<br>due 1982<br>Dated: July 1, 1972<br>Interest Payable:<br>July 1 | DM 250,000,000 | July 1, 1982 | None |
| 6.50% Loan of 1972, due 1974<br>Dated: July 3, 1972<br>Interest Payable:<br>July 3 | DM 25,000,000 | July 3, 1974 | None |
| 7-1/8% Note of 1972,<br>due 1976<br>Dated: August 1, 1972<br>Interest Payable:<br>February 1 & August 1 | DM 92,500,000 | August 1, 1976 | None |
| 7-1/8% Note of 1972,<br>due 1977<br>Dated: August 1, 1972<br>Interest Payable:<br>February 1 & August 1 | DM 127,500,000 | February 1, 1977 | None |

| Payable in<br>FRENCH FRANCS<br>*FF-1-*<br>*August 21, 1975* | Principal<br>Amount<br>Authorized | Maturity | Sinking Fund Requirements<br>Annually on<br>or<br>Before Date Shown<br>(Principal Amount) |
|---|---|---|---|
| 7-1/4% - 15 Year Bonds of<br>1972, due 1987<br>Dated: June 15, 1972<br>Interest Payable:<br>June 15 | F 150,000,000 | F 7,500,000 on June 15<br>in each of the years<br>1977-80<br>F 15,000,000 on June 15<br>in each of the years<br>1981-86<br>F 30,000,000 on<br>June 15, 1987; Bank has<br>option to double each<br>annual installment at<br>par. Installments may<br>be anticipated by<br>purchases in the<br>market | None |

**TABLE 3-6** (*Continued*)

| Callable | Fiscal or Paying Agent | Listed In | Offered |
|---|---|---|---|
| Not callable | Deutsche Bundesbank | Not Listed | At 100 on February 1, 1972 by private placement to Deutsche Bundesbank to refinance Notes maturing February 1, 1972. |
| Callable at par on or after March 1, 1978 on any repayment date. | All syndicate members | Berlin Bremen Dusseldorf Frankfort Hamburg Hanover Munchen Stuttgart | At 100 on February 25, 1972 by an underwriting group headed by the Deutsche Bank A.G. and the Dresdner Bank A.G. |
| Not callable | All syndicate members | Not Listed | At 100 on February 25, 1972 by an underwriting group headed by the Deutsche Bank A.G. and the Dresdner Bank A.G. |
| Not callable | All syndicate members | Berlin Bremen Dusseldorf Frankfort Hamburg Hanover Munchen Stuttgart | At 99-1/2 on July 3, 1972 by an underwriting group headed by the Deutsche Bank A.G. and the Dresdner Bank A.G. |
| Not callable | Deutsche Bundesbank | Not Listed | On July 3, 1972 by private placement to Deutsche Girozentral. Deutsche Kommunalbank. |
| Not callable | Deutsche Bundesbank | Not Listed | At 100 on August 1, 1972 by private placement to Deutsche Bundesbank to refinance Notes maturing August 1, 1972. |
| Not callable | Deutsche Bundesbank | Not Listed | At 100 on August 1, 1972 by private placement to Deutsche Bundesbank to refinance Notes maturing August 1, 1972 |

| Callable as a Whole or in Part by Lot, on at Least 45 Days' Notice | Fiscal or Paying Agent | Listed In | Offered |
|---|---|---|---|
| On June 15, 1975 at par plus premium of 1.50% and on any June 15 thereafter at declining premiums | Banque de Paris et des Pays Bas, Luxembourg | Luxembourg | At 99.75% on June 9, 1972 by an underwriting group headed by M.M. Lazard Freres & Cie. |

**TABLE 3-6** (*Continued*)

| Payable in ITALIAN LIRE Lit.-1- *August 21, 1975* | Principal Amount Authorized | Maturity | Sinking Fund Requirements Annually on or Before Date Shown (Principal Amount) |
|---|---|---|---|
| 5% - 15 Year Bonds of 1961, due 1976 Dated July 1, 1961 Interest Payable January 1 & July 1 | Lit 15,000,000,000 | July 1, 1976 | None |
| 7% - 15 Year Bonds of 1972, due August 1, 1987 Dated August 1,1972 Interest Payable February 1 & August 1 | Lit 25,000,000,000 | Lit 1,500,000,000 on 8/1/78, Lit 2,250,000,000 on 8/1/79-81, Lit 2,500,000,000 on 8/1/82-83, Lit 2,750,000,000 on 8/1/84, Lit 3,000,000,000 on 8/1/85-87 | None |
| 7-1/4% - 15 Year Notes of 1973, due August 1, 1988 Dated: August 1, 1973 Interest Payable: February 1 & August 1 | Lit 20,000,000,000 | Lit 500,000,000 on 8/1/78 Lit 1,000,000,000 on 8/1/79 Lit 1,500,000,000 each August 1, 1980 through 1983 Lit 2,500,000,000 each August 1, 1984 through 1988 | None |

| Payable in JAPANESE YEN ¥-2- *August 21, 1975* | Principal Amount Authorized | Maturity | Sinking Fund Requirements Annually on or Before Date Shown (Principal Amount) |
|---|---|---|---|
| 7.24% Serial Obligations of 1971 (Sept. Issue) due 1975-1976 Dated: September 29, 1971 Interest Payable: March 29 & September 29 | ¥ 6,000,000,000 | ¥ 2,000,000,000 semi-annually Sept. 29,1975 to Sept. 29, 1976 | None |
| 7-1/2% Japanese Yen Bonds of 1971-Second Series Dated: October 20,1971 Interest Payable: April 20 & October 20 | ¥ 12,000,000,000 | October 20, 1981 | ¥ 1,200,000,000 on each October 20,1977 - 1980 ¥ 7,200,000,000 on Oct.20,1981 |
| 7.40% Japanese Yen Bonds of 1972 - Third Series Dated: February 18,1972 Interest Payable: February 18 & August 18 | ¥ 15,000,000,000 | February 18,1982 | ¥ 1,500,000,000 on each February 18,1978-1981 ¥ 9,000,000,000 on Feb. 18,1982 |

**TABLE 3-6** *(Continued)*

| Callable | Fiscal or Paying Agent | Listed In | Offered |
|---|---|---|---|
| At 100 on or after July 1,1966 (a) in full on 3 months notice; (b) in part (not less than Lit 1 billion) by lot on 45 days' notice. | All syndicate members | Rome Milan | At 100 on July 3, 1961 by a syndicate of Italian banks, headed by Banca d'Italia. |
| In whole or in part on August 1, 1976 @ 101½ and on any August 1 thereafter at prices declining by 1/8 of 1% | All syndicate members | Rome Milan | At 98-1/2 on July 13,1972 by a syndicate of Italian banks, headed by Banca Commerciale Italiana. |
| On any maturity date commencing August 1,1979 at 101% of par for Notes redeemed more than three years before their maturity and at par in every other case. | Payments of Principal and Interest to be paid directly to Ufficio Italiano dei Cambi (in case of transfers Banca d'Italia will act as paying agent for the notes transferred.) | Not Listed | At par on August 1, 1973 by private placement to Ufficio Italiano dei Cambi. |

| Callable | Fiscal or Paying Agent | Listed In | Offered |
|---|---|---|---|
| Not callable | The Bank of Japan | Not Listed | At 100 on September 27,1971 by private placement to The Bank of Japan |
| In whole or in part by lot on at least 60 days' notice on any interest payment date on or after Oct. 20, 1977 October 20,1978 @ 102 April 20, 1979 - October 20, 1980 @ 101 Thereafter @ 100 Callable for sinking fund at 100. | The Industrial Bank of Japan, Limited | Tokyo Osaka | At 99.50 on September 28, through October 15, 1971, by an underwriting group headed by The Nikko Securities Co., Ltd. |
| In whole or in part by lot on at least 60 days' notice on any interest payment date in the years: 1978-1979 @ 102 1980 @ 101 Thereafter @ 100 Callable for sinking fund at 100. | The Industrial Bank of Japan, Limited | Tokyo Osaka | At 99.50 on January 31, 1972 through February 14,1972 by an underwriting group headed by The Daiwa Securities Co.,Ltd. |

**TABLE 3-6** (*Continued*)

| Payable in KUWAITI DINARS *KD-1-* *August 21, 1975* | Principal Amount Authorized | Maturity | Sinking Fund Requirements Annually on or Before Date Shown (Principal Amount) |
|---|---|---|---|
| 6-1/2% - 20 Year Bonds of 1968, due 1988 Dated September 15, 1968 Interest Payable: March 15 & September 15 | KD 15,000,000 | September 15, 1988 | September 15, 1978-87 KD 750,000 |
| 7-1/2% 10 Year Bonds of 1971, due 1981 Dated November 1, 1971 Interest Payable: May 1 & November 1 | KD 30,000,000 | Serially, KD 3,333,000 each Nov. 1 1973-1980; KD 3,336,000 on Nov. 1,1981 | None |
| 6-3/4% 10 Year Bonds of 1972, due 1982 Dated: April 1, 1972 Interest Payable: April 1 & Ocotber 1 | KD 20,000,000 | Serially, KD 2,500,000 each April 1 1975-1982 | None |
| 7% 19 Year Bonds of 1972, due 1991 Dated: August 15, 1972 Interest Payable: February 15 & August 15 KD 5 million drawn on August 16, 1972 KD 5 million drawn on November 15, 1972 KD 5 million drawn on February 14, 1973 | KD 15,000,000 | Serially, KD 1,000,000 each Aug. 15 1977-1991 | None |
| 7% 19 Year Bonds of 1973, due 1992 Dated: March 1, 1973 Interest Payable: March 1 & September 1 KD 12.5 million drawn on March 1, 1973 KD 12.5 million drawn on August 31,1973 | KD 25,000,000 | Serially, KD 1,666,000 each March 1, 1978-1991 KD 1,676,000 March 1,1992 | None |

| Payable in LEBANESE POUNDS *LL-1-* *August 21, 1975* | Principal Amount Authorized | Maturity | Sinking Fund Requirements Annually on or Before Date Shown (Principal Amount) |
|---|---|---|---|
| 6-7/8% - 5Yr Bonds of 1973, due 1978 Dated: January 22, 1973 Interest Payable: January 22 | LL 75,000,000 | January 22, 1978 | None |

146

**TABLE 3-6** *(Continued)*

| Callable as a Whole or in Part by Lot, on at Least 30 Days' Notice at any Time to Each Date Shown Unless Otherwise Specified | Fiscal or Paying Agent | Listed In | Offered |
|---|---|---|---|
| On and after September 15,1973 to<br>  September 15, 1978    104<br>  September 15, 1983    102<br>Thereafter                100<br>Partial redemption of Bonds will be credited in the inverse order. | Kuwait Invest-ment Company (S.A.K.) | Not Listed | At 99% on August 14, 1968 by Kuwait Investment Company (S.A.K) |
| Not Callable | Kuwait Invest-ment Company (S.A.K.) | Not Listed | At 100% on October 27, 1971 by Kuwait Investment Company (SAK) |
| Not Callable | Kuwait Invest-ment Company (S.A.K.) | Not Listed | At 99.75% on April 5, 1972 by Kuwait Investment Company (SAK) |
| As a whole on and after<br>Aug. 15,1982 to Aug. 14,1985  102<br>Aug. 15,1985 to Aug. 14,1988  101<br>Aug. 15,1988 and thereafer   100 | Kuwait Invest-ment Company (S.A.K.) | Not Listed | At 99.50% on August 15, 1972 by Kuwait Investment Company (SAK) |
| As a whole on and after<br>Mar. 1,1983 to Feb. 28,1986  102<br>Mar. 1,1986 to Feb. 28,1989  101<br>Mar. 1,1989 and thereafter   100 | Kuwait Invest-ment Company (S.A.K.) | Not Listed | At 99% on February 10, 1973 by Kuwait Investment Company (SAK). |

| Callable | Fiscal or Paying Agent | Listed In | Offered |
|---|---|---|---|
| Not callable | Banque du Liban | Not Listed | At 100 on January 18, 1973 by private placement to a syndicate of Lebanese banks, represented by Mr. Joseph T. Geagea. |

## TABLE 3-6 *(Continued)*

| Payable in NETHERLANDS GUILDERS F.-2- August 21, 1975 | Principal Amount Authorized | Maturity | Sinking Fund Requirements Annually on or Before Date Shown (Principal Amount) |
|---|---|---|---|
| 8-1/4% - 15 Year Bonds of 1971, due 1982/1986 Dated January 1, 1971 Interest Payable: January 1 | f. 60,000,000 | f. 12,000,000 each Jan. 1, 1982-1986 | None |
| 7-3/4% - 5 Year Notes of 1971, due 1976 Dated January 2, 1971 Interest Payable: January 2 | f. 60,000,000 | January 2, 1976 | None |
| 8% - 7 Year Loan of 1971, due 1976/78 Dated October 15, 1971 Interest Payable: October 15 | f. 60,000,000 | f. 12,000,000 each Oct. 15, 1976-1978 to Algemene Bank Nederland N.V. and f. 8,000,000 each Oct. 15, 1976-1978 to Amsterdam-Rotterdam Bank N.V. | None |
| 6-7/8% - 12 Yr Loan of 1972, due 1980/85 Dated: January 15, 1973 Interest Payable: January 15 | f. 200,000,000 | f. 16,600,000 each Jan.15,1980-84 and f. 17,000,000 on Jan.15, 1985 to Algemene Bank Nederland N.V. f. 12,500,000 each Jan.15,1980-85 to Amsterdam-Rotterdam Bank N.V. f. 4,150,000 each Jan.15, 1980-84 and f.4,250,000 on Jan.15,1985 to Bank Mees & Hope N.V. | None |

| Payable in POUNDS STERLING £-1- August 21, 1975 | Principal Amount Authorized | Maturity | Sinking Fund Requirements Annually on or Before Date Shown (Principal Amount) |
|---|---|---|---|
| 3-1/2% - 20 Year Stock of 1951, due 1971 Issued June 1, 1951 Interest Payable: June 15 & December 15 | £ 5,000,000 | June 15, 1971 | £ 166,700 annually beginning year ending June 15,1957 to be applied to purchase stock in market at or under par, or to redeem stock at par. |
| 3-1/2% - 20 Year Stock of 1954, due 1974 Issued July 29, 1954 Interest Payable: April 15 & October 15 | £ 5,000,000 | October 15, 1974 | £ 166,700 annually beginning year ending October 15, 1960, to be applied to purchase stock in market at or under par, or to redeem stock at par. |
| 5% - 23 Year Stock of 1959, due 1982 Issued December 21, 1959 Interest Payable: February 15 & August 15 | £ 10,000,000 | August 15, 1982 | £ 278,000 annually beginning year ending August 15, 1965, to be applied to purchase stock in market at or under par, or to redeem stock at par. |
| 8% Stock of 1971, due 1976 Issued: August 13, 1971 Interest Payable: January 31 & July 31 | £ 10,000,000 | July 31, 1976 | None |

TABLE 3-6 *(Continued)*

| Callable as a Whole or in Part by Lot, on at Least 60 Days' Notice at any Time to Each Date Shown Unless Otherwise Specified | Fiscal or Paying Agent | Listed In | Offered |
|---|---|---|---|
| Not Callable | Algemene Bank Nederland N.V. | Amsterdam | At 99 on December 3, 1970 by an underwriting group headed by Algemene Bank Nederland N.V. |
| Not Callable | Algemene Bank Nederland N.V. | Not listed | At 99.25 on December 7, 1970 by an underwriting group headed by Algemene Bank Nederland N.V. |
| Not Callable | Payments of Principal and Interest to be paid directly by Bank to Algemene Bank Nederland N.V. and Amsterdam-Rotterdam Bank N.V. | Not Listed | On October 5, 1971 by private placement to Algemene Bank Nederland N.V. and Amsterdam-Rotterdam Bank N.V. |
| Not Callable | Payments of Principal and Interest to be paid directly by Bank to Algemene Bank Nederland N.V., Amsterdam-Rotterdam Bank N.V. and Bank Mees & Hope N.V. | Not Listed | On October 26, 1972 by private placement to Algemene Bank Nederland N.V., Amsterdam-Rotterdam Bank N.V. and Bank Mees & Hope N.V. |

| Callable | Fiscal or Paying Agent | Listed In | Offered |
|---|---|---|---|
| At 100 on or after June 15, 1966. In whole or in part by lot on 3 months' notice. | Baring Brothers & Co. Limited | London | At 97 on May 21, 1951 by an underwriting group headed by Baring Brothers & Co., Limited. |
| At 100 on or after October 15, 1969. In whole or in part by lot on 3 months' notice. | Baring Brothers & Co., Limited | London | At 98 on July 16, 1954 by an underwriting group headed by Baring Brothers & Co., Limited. |
| At 100 on or after August 15, 1977. In whole or in part by lot on 3 months' notice. | Baring Brothers & Co., Limited | London | At 96-1/2 on December 11, 1959 by an underwriting group headed by Baring Brothers & Co., Limited. |
| Not callable. However, the Bank may at any time purchase Stock at a price not to exceed 110 per cent inclusive of expenses and accrued interest. | Baring Brothers & Co. Limited | London | At 100 on August 9, 1971 by an underwriting group headed by Baring Brothers & Co. Limited. |

## TABLE 3-6 *(Continued)*

| Payable in<br>SAUDI ARABIAN RIYALS<br>*SRL-1$_S$*<br>*August 21, 1975* | Principal<br>Amount<br>Authorized | Maturity | Sinking Fund Requirements<br>Annually on<br>or<br>Before Date Shown<br>(Principal Amount) |
|---|---|---|---|
| 8% - 10 year Bonds of 1974,<br>due 1984<br>Dated: July 1, 1974<br>Two equal payments of SRL:<br>250 million each on August<br>1, 1974 and September 1,<br>1974.<br>Commission payable:<br>semi-annually | SRL$_S$500,000,000 | July 1, 1984 | None |

| Payable in<br>SWISS FRANCS<br>*SwF-5-*<br>*August 21, 1975* | Principal<br>Amount<br>Authorized | Maturity | Sinking Fund Requirements<br>Annually on<br>or<br>Before Date Shown<br>(Principal Amount) |
|---|---|---|---|
| 6-3/8% - Notes of 1973,<br>due 1979<br>Dated: July 31, 1973<br>Interest Payable:<br>July 31 | SwF 150,000,000 | July 31, 1979 | None |
| 6-1/2% - Notes of 1973,<br>due 1980<br>Dated: July 31, 1973<br>Interest Payable:<br>July 31 | SwF 150,000,000 | July 31, 1980 | None |
| 6-1/2% - Notes of 1973,<br>due 1981<br>Dated: July 31, 1973<br>Interest Payable:<br>July 31 | SwF 150,000,000 | July 31, 1981 | None |
| 7% - 15 Year Bonds of 1974,<br>due 1989<br>Dated: February 1, 1974<br>Interest Payable:<br>February 1 | SwF 100,000,000 | February 1, 1989 | Sinking Fund - None<br>In each of the year 1985 to 1988<br>Bank to repurchase SwF20,000,000<br>in the market to the extent this<br>can be done at or below par<br>during the 60 days preceding<br>coupon date, but on a non-cumula-<br>tive basis and subject to the<br>right to credit against the<br>annual quotas bonds purchased<br>otherwise. |
| 8-1/4% - Notes of 1975, due<br>198<br>Dated: July 1, 1975<br>Interest Payable: July 1 | SwF 300,000,000 | July 1, 1982 | None |

150

**TABLE 3-6** *(Continued)*

| Callable | Fiscal or Paying Agent | Listed In | Offered |
|---|---|---|---|
| The Bank has the right to redeem in advance of maturity $SRL_s$ 100 million principal amount of the Bonds per annum on July 1 of each of the years 1979 through 1983. This right is non-cumulative and cannot be carried from one year to another. | Saudi Arabian Monetary Agency. | Not Listed | At 100% plus accrued commission on June 20, 1974 by private placement to the Saudi Arabian Monetary Agency (SAMA). |

| Callable as a whole on at Least 3 Months' Notice or in Part by lot on at Least 45 Days' Notice on Any Interest Date Unless Otherwise Specified | Fiscal or Paying Agent | Listed In | Offered |
|---|---|---|---|
| In its entirety, at Bank's option, at 101% of par on 7/31/76, at 100-3/4% on 7/31/77, and at 100-1/2% on 7/31/78. | All syndicate members | Not Listed | On June 27, 1973 at par, by private placement with the Swiss Credit Bank, the Union Bank of Switzerland and the Swiss Bank Corporation. |
| In its entirety, at Bank's option, at 101-1/4% of par on 7/31/76, at 101% on 7/31/77, at 100-3/4% on 7/31/78, and at 100-1/2% on 7/31/79. | All syndicate members | Not Listed | On June 27, 1973 at par, by private placement with the Swiss Credit Bank, the Union Bank of Switzerland and the Swiss Bank Corporation. |
| In its entirety, at Bank's option, at 101-1/2% of par on 7/31/76, at 101-1/4% on 7/31/77, at 101% on 7/31/78, at 100-3/4% on 7/31/79, and at 100-1/2% on 7/31/80 | All syndicate members | Not Listed | On June 27, 1973 at 99.50%, by private placement with the Swiss Credit Bank, the Union Bank of Switzerland and the Swiss Bank Corporation. |
| At par on and after February 1, 1984 in its entirety on at least 3 months' notice | All syndicate members | Basle Zurich Geneva Berne Lausanne | At 100 on January 18, 1974 to January 24, 1974 by an underwriting group headed by Swiss Credit Bank. |
| In its entirety, at Bank's option, at 101-1/4% of par on 7/1/78, at 101% on 7/1/79, at 100-3/4% on 7/1/80, at 100-1/2% on 7/1/81. | All syndicate members | Not Listed | on June 11, 1975 at par, by private placement with the Swiss Bank Corporation, the Union Bank of Switzerland and the Swiss Credit Bank. |

## TABLE 3-6 *(Continued)*

| Payable in UNITED ARAB EMIRATES DIRHAMS *UAED-1- August 21, 1975* | Principal Amount Authorized | Maturity | Sinking Fund Requirements Annually on or Before Date Shown (Principal Amount) |
|---|---|---|---|
| 8% - 15 Year Bonds of 1974, due 1980/89 <br> Dated: May 15, 1974 <br> Proceeds of issue paid in 6 weekly payments of UAED 50 million each from May 15, 1974 to June 19, 1974 <br> Interest payable: <br> Semi-annually | UAED300,000,000 | Ten equal annual instalments of UAED 30,000,000 on May 15, in each of the years 1980 through 1989. | None |

| Payable in VENEZUELAN BOLIVARES *Bs-1- August 21, 1975* | Principal Amount Authorized | Maturity | Sinking Fund Requirements Annually on or Before Date Shown (Principal Amount) |
|---|---|---|---|
| 7% - 13 Year Bonds of 1974, due 1977/87 <br> Dated: March 1, 1974 <br> Interest Payable: <br> September 1 & March 1 | Bs 100,000,000 | Bs 5,000,000 each September 1 and March 1 beginning September 1, 1977 and ending March 1, 1987. | None |
| 8% - 15 Year Loan of 1974, due 1979/89 <br> Dated: <br> Loan payment in six tranches as follows: <br> Bs 50 million on Aug.15,1974 <br> Bs 50 million on Sept.16,1974 <br> Bs 50 million on Oct. 1,1974 <br> Bs100 million on Oct.15, 1974 <br> Bs100 million on Nov. 4,1974 <br> Bs 80 million on Nov.18,1974 <br><br> Interest payable: <br> February 15 & August 15 | Bs 430,000,000 | Bs 30.1 million each August 15, 1979/88; Bs 129 million August 15, 1989. | None |

**TABLE 3-6** *(Continued)*

| Callable | Fiscal or Paying Agent | Listed In | Offered |
|---|---|---|---|
| The Bank has the right to redeem in advance of maturity Bonds in the principal amount of UAED 30,000,000 per annum on May 15 of each of the years 1984 through 1986. This right is non-cumulative and cannot be carried from one year to another. | United Arab Emirates Currency Board | Not Listed | At 100% on May 15, 1974 by private placement to the government of Abu Dhabi. |

| Callable and Other Terms | Fiscal or Paying Agent | Listed In | Offered |
|---|---|---|---|
| Not Callable | Banco Central de Venezuela | Not Listed | At 97% on March 11, 1974 by a group of banks headed by Banco de Venezuela. |
| Prepayment:After August 15, 1979, in whole or in part in multiples of Bs 5 million on any interest payment date on at least 90 days' notice, to be applied in inverse order of maturity. | Banco Central de Venezuela | Not Listed | At 100 on August 14, 1974 by private placement to the Fondo de Inversiones de Venezuela (Fondo). |

*Source:* Securities Division, Treasurer's Department, International Bank for Reconstruction and Development, *Description of Bonds, Notes, and Other Obligations* (August 21, 1975).

## GLOSSARY OF BOND TERMS

*Arbitrage:* when the holder of a convertible bond, which is usually convertible into common stock, can make a riskless profit when there is a difference in the market prices of the bond and the stock. The holder has to buy the convertible bond, convert it into the stock, and sell the stock short. The price discrepancy has to be wide enough to permit a profit after all commissions, fees, taxes, and any other expenses are considered.

> *For example,* consider a convertible bond selling at $1000. The bond is convertible into 100 shares of common stock, selling at $1500 (100 shares at $15 per share = $1500).
>
> | | |
> |---|---:|
> | Bond converted into common stock | $1500 |
> | Bond price | 1000 |
> | Profit before commission, fees, taxes, and other expenses | $500 |

*Bearer Bond:* A bond in which the owner's name is not recorded or indicated on the bond. The person bearing (or possessing) the bond will be paid the interest upon presentation of the bond's coupon to the authority paying the interest.

*Callable Bond:* a type of bond in which it is specified that the bond may be redeemed before the maturity date. The conditions are specified in the indenture.

*Coupon rate:* the annual rate of interest which the issuer agrees to pay the bond buyer. This is called the "nominal interest rate" or "stated interest rate."

*Current yield:* the percentage amount of the annual interest received on the price of the bond.

*Discount:* the difference between the bond's par value and a price below par value:

> *For example:*
>
> | | |
> |---|---|
> | Par value = 100 = | $1,000 |
> | Bond is selling at 90 = | 900 |
> | Discount = | 100 |

*Indenture:* the contract which states the terms and conditions of the bond issue.

*Par value:* the face value of a bond. It is quoted as "100." The par value of most bonds is $1,000 (or 100% = $1,000). The par value is the amount of money that the issuer of the bond agrees to pay on the maturity date.

*Premium:* the difference between the bond's par value and a price above par value.

> *For example:*
>
> | | |
> |---|---|
> | Par value = 100 = | $1,000 |
> | Bond price at 110 = | $1,100 |
> | Premium = | $100 |

*Registered Bond:* a bond which is registered (or recorded) in the name of the owner for payment of principal and/or interest.

*Yield to maturity:* the annual return (in percentage terms) on a bond, when the annual interest rate, price, and remaining time to maturity are taken into account.

## Computation of Bond Yields

*Current yield* for a bond selling at a premium:

A 6% bond is bought at 120. The original cost of the bond ("par value") was 100 or $1,000.

The annual interest on the bond is 6% of $1,000 or $60.

The current price, 120% of par value (or face value), is $1200.

$$\text{Current Yield} = \frac{\text{Annual Interest on Bond}}{\text{Current Price of Bond}}$$

$$= \frac{\$60}{\$1200}$$

$$= 5\%$$

Current yield for a bond selling at a discount:

A 6% bond is bought at 90. The original cost of the bond ("par value") was 100, or $1,000.

The annual interest on the bond is 6% of $1,000 or $60. The current price, 90% of par value (or face value), is $900.

$$\text{Current Yield} = \frac{\text{Annual Interest on Bond}}{\text{Current Price of Bond}}$$

$$= \frac{\$60}{\$900}$$

$$= 6.67\%$$

*Yield to Maturity*

The "yield to maturity" varies depending upon whether the bond was bought at a premium or a discount.

Consult bond-yield tables, found in bond books, to determine the "yield to maturity." The following are some excellent bond books:

Financial Publishing Company,
*Investors Bond Values Table*
(Second Edition; Boston, Mass.:   Financial Publishing Co., 1972).
Two volumes.

White, Weld & Co., *Bond Yield Tables*
(Boston, Mass.: Financial Publishing Co., July 1965)

# money and interest rates

![separator bar]

# 4

As newspaper reports often refer to various measurements of the money supply (or money stock), the investor should know what these measurements (known as "monetary aggregates") refer to and how they are determined. We will deal first with some basics about money, monetary policy, and fiscal policy and then with the monetary aggregates.

In very primitive times there was no money. If a person wanted to obtain something that someone else had, he had to exchange his product or service for someone else's product or service. This was the *barter system*.

This system is still used at times in the modern world, but it is awkward. For example, how many chickens would you exchange for a jet plane? a rocket to the moon? or vitamin pills? Money developed as a medium of exchange, so that the time otherwise necessary for finding someone to trade with could be used more productively.

At first, many different types of commodities (e.g., salt, tea, cattle, grain) were used as money. Eventually, metals were substituted for these commodities, especially gold and silver. These metals were used to measure value, and they could be saved (or stored).

There are three basic functions of money. It is used as

a medium of exchange
a measure of value
a store of value

From these basic functions, four other uses are derived:

a standard of deferred payment
a basis for bank credit
a store of purchasing power
a way of holding one's wealth

What is money? Money is any asset (i.e., something of value) that people are willing to accept as payment for goods and services. A simple test is to ask:

Can you buy the groceries with it?
Can you pay the rent with it?
Can you buy clothing with it?
Can you pay the dentist with it?

Basic types of modern money are coins, paper money (or currency), and checkbook money (also called demand deposits). Most of the money in the United States is checkbook money.

## The Price of Borrowed Money

People usually think in terms of what money will buy. It has value because it can be exchanged now or at some future time for what one needs or desires.

Money, however, can be bargained for by people who want to use it in the same manner as any other commodity. Commercial banks and other financial institutions which have money can lend it for a fee. The price, cost, or fee for using the money is called the *interest rate.*

The interest rate is determined by the amount that the lenders charge (subject to restrictions required by law) and the amount that the borrower is willing to pay.

The interest rate fluctuates. When borrower demand is higher and lender supplies of money are low, the interest rate rises. When borrower demand is low and lender supplies of money are high, the interest rate falls.

Control over the supply of money is, therefore, a critical factor in determining the interest rate and in determining the economic development of a country.

Sometimes a lender does not want to wait until the maturity date of the loan to get his money. Instead, he might sell the debt to someone else who has money to lend. This is done in the *money and capital markets.*

A lender ordinarily exchanges his money for a promise by the borrower to repay called an *evidence of debt.* A simple promise to pay is an I.O.U. In more formal business transactions, promises to pay are U.S. Treasury bills, U.S. Treasury notes, negotiable certificates of deposit, bankers' acceptances, promissory notes, mortgages, corporate bonds, municipal bonds, U.S. Treasury bonds and other securities.

A person, a business, a financial institution or a government can buy or sell many evidences of debt in the money and capital markets.

## ECONOMIC POLICY

Economic policy is decided upon by the government policymakers of a country and determines the economic development (or lack of development) for a country and also the economic system of the country.

Basic goals of modern economic policy are:

Price stability
High employment
Economic growth (i.e., the production of more and better goods and services)

Two prime components of economic policy are *monetary policy and fiscal policy.* As one reads a great deal about them in newspapers and other periodicals, it is good to know just what they refer to. They both directly affect the money and capital markets.

Monetary policy consists of the decisions which affect the money supply, the interest rate, credit terms and related areas. The power to set monetary policy centers in the central bank of a country (in the United States, the Federal Reserve System).

Fiscal policy consists of the decisions that affect how much money the government spends, how the government acquires the money, what tax system the government will use, whether it should issue more securities, raise taxes or lower taxes, and what kind of budget should be drawn up. The power to set fiscal policy centers in the Chief of State of a country and its legislature. In the United States, the President of the United States and his Cabinet members and advisers, together with Congress, set national fiscal policy. Other fiscal authorities, in the United States are the governors, state legislatures, mayors, and city councils.

### Keynesians versus Monetarists

Considerable debate has developed regarding such matters as how the money and capital markets should be dealt with, as well as how monetary policy and fiscal policy should be employed.

In financial circles and in newspapers, magazine articles, and books, much heat has been generated over the differences between the Keynesians and monetarists regarding these matters. What is all the furor about? We will find out without getting involved in the many technical points which have been debated.

*Keynesians.* The name Keynesian is derived from that of the economist John Maynard Keynes (1883-1946), whose main economic views were presented in his book *The General Theory of Employment, Interest, and Money* (1936). The Keynesians emphasize the use of fiscal policy and believe that monetary policy should also be employed. The interest rate is viewed by them as of great consequence, and many of them believe that monetary aggregates are also important.

Keynesians are sometimes referred to as "fiscalists" or "liberal economists." A major leader of the Keynesians is Professor Paul A. Samuelson of the Massachusetts Institute of Technology (MIT), Nobel Prizewinner in Economics in 1970.

*Monetarists.* Monetarists place emphasis on monetary policy, especially the growth in the money supply and do not believe that fiscal policy is very important for economic growth. In general, they believe that the money supply should be increased on the basis of a rule (preferably 3% to 5% per year); that the power of discretion over this growth should be removed from the monetary authorities; and that the monetary aggregates are of critical importance, while the interest rates are not very significant. They also believe that the Federal government should stay out of economic activity as much as possible.

While accepting some of the contributions of John Maynard Keynes, they look particularly to Adam Smith (1723-1790), whose main work was *The Wealth of Nations* (1776).

The monetarists are sometimes referred to as "conservative economists." Their main leader is Professor Milton Friedman of the University of Chicago.

The monetarists place prime emphasis on the money supply itself, while the Keynesians place their emphasis not so much on the money supply itself as how the money supply is used. While the monetarists seek to keep the government out of economic matters as much as possible (i.e., a laissez-faire policy), the Keynesians believe in government intervention in the economic process and favor the use of wage-price controls when they find such controls necessary. Monetarists generally oppose the use of wage-price controls.

Monetarists look upon control of the growth of the money supply as the key factor in a country's economic development. Keynesians believe that the monetarist view is oversimplistic and that in addition to the money supply other highly complex factors have to be taken into account (e.g., the labor market, the production of goods and services, and the advance of technology).

## The Monetary Aggregates

Over the years, increasing emphasis has been placed on the importance of monetary aggregates in setting monetary policy. Both monetarists and

Keynesians consider the aggregates important, although the monetarists have long placed greater significance on them than the Keynesians. The point of determining these aggregates is to be able to gauge the size and direction of change of the money supply (or money stock) and therefore to efficiently employ monetary policy.

Keynesians, in general, look upon the effect of a change in the money stock as passing through the entire range of *financial assets,* moving through the money markets, and eventually reaching the capital markets. As the change proceeds from the money markets to the capital markets, the force of the change and its predictability diminishes. Thus, the Federal Reserve Board's policy operating through the Federal funds rate to bring down the short-term money market rates, at the end of 1974 and in early 1975, is then viewed as working its way through eventually to bring down long-term rates in the capital markets (e.g., corporate bond rates and mortgage rates).

The Keynesian view sees the effects of changes in the money stock as coming almost exclusively through changes in interest rates on financial assets brought about by monetary policies. The Keynesian view sees monetary policy as acting upon the availability of credit and the value of assets, especially the value of common stocks.

The monetarist view, in general, considers money as a very unique asset which allows it to be substituted for all assets, both financial and economic.

The Keynesians believe that people will buy financial assets (e.g., securities) when they have excess money. The monetarists see the changes in money stocks as being much broader, with purchase of these financial assets and goods (e.g., consumer durables, such as cars and appliances).

The main monetary aggregates (or measurements of the money stock) referred to in newspapers are:

$M_1$ = Coins and paper currency in the hands of the public (i.e., outside banks)
plus checking accounts (also called "demand deposits").
($M_1$ is sometimes referred to as the "U.S. official money stock, "U.S. money stock" or just simply "money stock"). (See Figure 4-2.)

$M_2$ = $M_1$ plus time deposits at commercial banks except for large-denomination negotiable certificates of deposits (CD's).

$M_3$ = $M_2$ plus deposits at savings banks (also called "mutual savings banks), savings and loan association shares, and credit union shares.

$M_4$ = $M_2$ plus large negotiable time certificates of deposits issued by large weekly reporting commercial banks.

$M_5$ = $M_3$ plus large negotiable certificates of deposits issued by large weekly reporting commercial banks.

For illustrative purposes, computation of $M_1$, $M_2$, and $M_3$ is shown in Figure 4-1. This breakdown indicates both the components and the broader definitions of money.

**FIGURE 4-1**

| | Bil. $ |
|---|---|
| The estimation begins with the **GROSS DEMAND DEPOSITS** at U. S. commercial banks, as reported by banks which are members of the Federal Reserve System, and as estimated for those which are not members. From these gross demand deposits are subtracted, | **258.0** |
| first, domestic **INTERBANK DEMAND DEPOSITS**, as reported by member banks and as estimated for non-members, and, | (−) 27 6 |
| second, **U. S. GOVERNMENT DEMAND DEPOSITS**, as shown by the records kept for the U. S. Treasury by the Federal Reserve, thereby yielding an estimate of | (−) 4.0 |
| **PRIVATE DEMAND DEPOSITS.** This estimate is further modified. . . | (=) 226.4 |
| . . . to exclude **ADJUSTED CASH ITEMS** in an attempt to eliminate double-counted demand deposits (see article), . . . | (−) 20.5 |
| . . . to exclude **FEDERAL RESERVE FLOAT** for the same reason, . . . | (−) 5.4 |
| . . . and to include **FOREIGN DEPOSITS AT THE FEDERAL RESERVE BANKS.** | (+) 0.3 |

|  | | Seas. Adj. |
|---|---|---|
| The resulting figure is the **DEMAND DEPOSIT COMPONENT OF THE MONEY STOCK.** Seasonal adjustment, which is designed to allow for "typical" August behavior in previous years, produces the "seasonally adjusted" estimate of the demand deposit component shown at the far right. To this is added . . . | (=) 200.8 | 204.2 |
| . . . the amount of **CURRENCY AND COIN** outside the Treasury, the Federal Reserve Banks, and vaults of commercial banks. This addition results in . . . | (+) 60.0 | 59.7 |
| . . . the **NARROWLY-DEFINED OR M₁ MONEY STOCK,** seasonally adjusted (right) and unadjusted (left). For a broader measure of the money stock, one can add . . . | (=) 260.7 | 263.9 |
| . . . the **TIME AND SAVINGS DEPOSITS AT COMMERCIAL BANKS** (excluding their large-denomination "negotiable" certificates of deposit) to get. . . | + 286.3 | 286.6 |
| . . . the **M₂ MONEY STOCK,** seasonally adjusted and unadjusted. For an even broader measure, one can add estimates of . . . | (=) 547.0 | 550.5 |
| . . . **DEPOSITS AT SAVINGS AND LOAN ASSOCIATIONS AND MUTUAL SAVING BANKS** to get, finally . . . | (+) 315.8 | 315.9 |
| . . . the **M₃ MONEY STOCK.** | (=) 862.8 | 866.4 |

Source: August 1973 Federal Reserve **Bulletin** (Table A-16, where possible, otherwise estimated or forced from Tables A-12, A-18). Totals may not add because of rounding.

Calculation of $M_1$, $M_2$, and $M_3$*

*The figures used are for August 1973.

*Source:* Federal Reserve Bank of Atlanta, *The Monthly Review* (November 1973), p. 180.

FIGURE 4-2

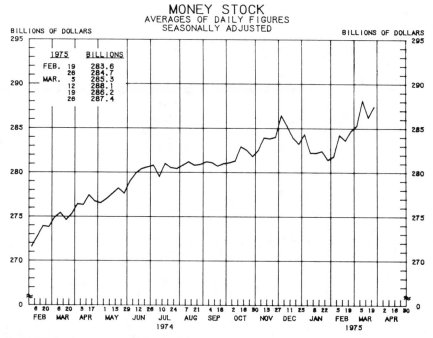

Source: Federal Reserve Bank of St. Louis.

Other monetary aggregates are:

Monetary Base = Deposits of Federal Reserve member banks at the Federal Reserve plus currency in circulation (coins and paper currency held by the public and in the vaults of commercial banks, adjusted for reserve requirement changes and shifts in deposits).

L = $M_3$ plus CD's plus deposits at the Postal Savings System plus U.S. government savings bonds plus short-term U.S. government securities.

RPDs = Federal Reserve member bank Reserves available for Private nonbank Deposits.

$M_6$ = $M_5$ plus short-term marketable U.S. government securities and savings bonds.

$M_7$ = $M_6$ plus short-term commercial paper.

Data on the monetary aggregates (or money stock measures) $M_1$, $M_2$, $M_3$, $M_4$, and $M_5$ are shown in Tables 4-1, 4-2, and 4-3. These tables indicate how the money supply of the United States is growing. A rapid increase in the money supply is inflationary.

TABLE 4-1

# FEDERAL RESERVE  statistical release

## MONEY STOCK MEASURES

APRIL 3, 1975

### IN BILLIONS OF DOLLARS

| Date | M₁ Currency Plus Demand Deposits 1/ | M₂ M₁ Plus Time Deposits at Commercial Banks Other Than Large CD's 2/ | M₃ M₂ Plus Deposits at Nonbank Thrift Institutions 3/ | M₄ M₃ Plus Large Negotiable CD's 4/ | M₅ M₃ Plus Large Negotiable CD's 5/ | M₁ Currency Plus Demand Deposits 1/ | M₂ M₁ Plus Time Deposits at Commercial Banks Other Than Large CD's 2/ | M₃ M₂ Plus Deposits at Nonbank Thrift Institutions 3/ | M₄ M₂ Plus Large Negotiable CD's 4/ | M₅ M₃ Plus Large Negotiable CD's 5/ |
|---|---|---|---|---|---|---|---|---|---|---|
| | Seasonally Adjusted | | | | | Not Seasonally Adjusted | | | | |
| 1974--FEB. | 273.1 | 580.9 | 932.5 | 649.1 | 1000.7 | 270.2 | 578.5 | 930.2 | 644.6 | 996.3 |
| MAR. | 275.2 | 585.5 | 940.0 | 653.4 | 1007.9 | 272.5 | 584.9 | 941.1 | 651.5 | 1007.7 |
| APR. | 276.6 | 589.4 | 945.9 | 663.3 | 1019.8 | 278.2 | 593.5 | 952.2 | 665.3 | 1024.0 |
| MAY | 277.6 | 591.6 | 948.8 | 670.2 | 1027.3 | 272.9 | 589.7 | 948.3 | 666.9 | 1025.5 |
| JUNE | 280.0 | 597.1 | 955.9 | 678.5 | 1037.2 | 278.2 | 596.6 | 957.4 | 676.2 | 1037.0 |
| JULY | 280.5 | 599.7 | 959.9 | 683.3 | 1043.5 | 280.1 | 599.3 | 961.2 | 682.1 | 1044.0 |
| AUG. | 280.7 | 602.2 | 963.0 | 686.0 | 1046.7 | 277.5 | 598.7 | 958.9 | 685.8 | 1046.0 |
| SEPT. | 281.1 | 603.8 | 965.5 | 688.7 | 1050.3 | 279.4 | 600.7 | 961.2 | 689.4 | 1049.9 |
| OCT. | 282.2 | 608.1 | 971.2 | 694.3 | 1057.4 | 281.7 | 606.3 | 968.0 | 695.1 | 1056.7 |
| NOV. | 283.8 | 613.0 | 978.3 | 698.5 | 1063.8 | 285.3 | 611.1 | 974.2 | 698.2 | 1061.2 |
| DEC. | 284.3 | 614.3 | 982.5 | 704.6 | 1072.8 | 292.2 | 619.4 | 985.8 | 709.8 | 1076.3 |
| 1975--JAN. | 282.2 | 616.0 | 987.5 | 708.9 | 1080.4 | 289.3 | 621.9 | 992.9 | 714.0 | 1085.0 |
| FEB. | 283.8 | 621.0 | 996.0 | 713.2 | 1088.2 | 280.8 | 618.5 | 993.3 | 707.9 | 1082.8 |
| WEEK ENDING: | | | | | | | | | | |
| FEB. 5 | 281.8 | 616.8 | | 709.7 | | 282.0 | 616.5 | | 707.4 | |
| 12 | 284.2 | 621.2 | | 714.1 | | 281.8 | 619.0 | | 709.1 | |
| 19 | 283.6 | 621.0 | | 713.3 | | 281.1 | 619.1 | | 708.3 | |
| 26 | R 284.7 | 623.4 | | 714.7 | | 278.0 | 617.7 | | 705.9 | |
| MAR. 5 | 285.3 | 624.0 | | 714.2 | | 283.3 | 623.6 | | 711.4 | |
| 12 | 288.1 | R 628.0 | | 717.2 | | 285.4 | 627.4 | | 715.4 | |
| 19 P | R 286.2 | 627.0 | | 716.7 | | 284.1 | 627.0 | | 715.2 | |
| 26 P | 287.4 | 628.2 | | 718.5 | | R 282.4 | 625.8 | | 714.3 | |

1/ INCLUDES (1) DEMAND DEPOSITS AT ALL COMMERCIAL BANKS OTHER THAN THOSE DUE TO DOMESTIC COMMERCIAL BANKS AND THE U.S.GOVERNMENT, LESS CASH ITEMS IN THE PROCESS OF COLLECTION AND F.R.FLOAT; (2) FOREIGN DEMAND BALANCES AT F.R.BANKS; AND (3) CURRENCY OUTSIDE THE TREASURY, F.R.BANKS AND VAULTS OF ALL COMMERCIAL BANKS.
2/ INCLUDES, IN ADDITION TO CURRENCY AND DEMAND DEPOSITS, SAVINGS DEPOSITS, TIME DEPOSITS OPEN ACCOUNT, AND TIME CERTIFICATES OF DEPOSITS OTHER THAN NEGOTIABLE TIME CERTIFICATES OF DEPOSIT ISSUED IN DENOMINATIONS OF $100,000 OR MORE BY LARGE WEEKLY REPORTING COMMERCIAL BANKS.
3/ INCLUDES M2, PLUS THE AVERAGE OF THE BEGINNING AND END OF MONTH DEPOSITS OF MUTUAL SAVINGS BANK, SAVINGS AND LOAN SHARES, AND CREDIT UNION SHARES.
4/ INCLUDES M3, PLUS NEGOTIABLE TIME CERTIFICATES OF DEPOSIT ISSUED IN DENOMINATIONS OF $100,000 OR MORE.
5/ INCLUDES M3, PLUS NEGOTIABLE TIME CERTIFICATES OF DEPOSIT ISSUED IN DENOMINATIONS OF $100,000 OR MORE.
P - PRELIMINARY; R - REVISED

TABLE 4-2

## COMPONENTS OF MONEY STOCK MEASURES AND RELATED ITEMS

### SEASONALLY ADJUSTED, IN BILLIONS OF DOLLARS

| Date | Currency | Demand Deposits | Time and Savings Deposits CD's 1/ | Time and Savings Deposits Other | Time and Savings Deposits Total | Nonbank Thrift Institutions 2/ |
|---|---|---|---|---|---|---|
| 1974--FEB. | 62.7 | 210.4 | 68.2 | 307.8 | 376.0 | 351.7 |
| MAR. | 63.3 | 211.9 | 68.0 | 310.3 | 378.3 | 354.5 |
| APR. | 63.9 | 212.8 | 73.9 | 312.7 | 386.7 | 356.5 |
| MAY | 64.3 | 213.3 | 78.5 | 314.0 | 392.5 | 357.1 |
| JUNE | 64.6 | 215.4 | 81.3 | 317.1 | 398.4 | 358.8 |
| JULY | 64.8 | 215.7 | 83.6 | 319.2 | 402.8 | 360.2 |
| AUG. | 65.5 | 215.3 | 83.8 | 321.5 | 405.2 | 360.7 |
| SEPT. | 65.9 | 215.3 | 84.8 | 322.7 | 407.5 | 361.6 |
| OCT. | 66.5 | 215.7 | 86.2 | 325.9 | 412.1 | 363.1 |
| NOV. | 67.3 | 216.5 | 85.5 | 329.2 | 414.7 | 365.3 |
| DEC. | 67.8 | 216.6 | 90.3 | 330.0 | 420.3 | 368.3 |
| 1975--JAN. | 68.1 | 214.1 | 92.9 | 333.8 | 426.7 | 371.5 |
| FEB. | 68.6 | 215.1 | 92.2 | 337.2 | 429.4 | 375.0 |
| WEEK ENDING: | | | | | | |
| 1975--FEB. 5 | 68.2 | 213.6 | 93.0 | 335.0 | 427.9 | .0 |
| 12 | 68.6 | 215.6 | 92.9 | 337.1 | 430.0 | .0 |
| 19 | 68.8 | 214.8 | 92.3 | 337.4 | 429.7 | .0 |
| 26 | 68.8 | 215.9 | 91.3 | 338.7 | 430.0 | .0 |
| MAR. 5 | 68.9 | 216.4 | 90.2 | 338.7 | 428.9 | .0 |
| 12 | 69.4 | 218.7 | 89.3 | 339.8 | 429.1 | .0 |
| 19 P | 69.3 | 216.9 | R 89.6 | 340.8 | 430.4 | .0 |
| 26 P | 69.4 | 218.0 | 90.3 | 340.8 | 431.1 | .0 |

1/ INCLUDES NEGOTIABLE TIME CERTIFICATES OF DEPOSIT ISSUED IN DENOMINATIONS OF $100,000 OR MORE BY LARGE WEEKLY REPORTING COMMERCIAL BANKS.
2/ AVERAGE OF BEGINNING AND END OF MONTH DEPOSITS AT MUTUAL SAVINGS BANKS, SAVINGS AND LOAN SHARES, AND CREDIT UNION SHARES.
P - PRELIMINARY; R - REVISED

TABLE 4-3

## COMPONENTS OF MONEY STOCK MEASURES AND RELATED ITEMS
### NOT SEASONALLY ADJUSTED, IN BILLIONS OF DOLLARS

| Date | Currency | Demand Deposits | | | Time and Savings Deposit | | | Nonbank Thrift Institutions[4] | U.S. Gov't. Demand[5] |
| | | Total[1] | Member | Domestic Nonmember[2] | CD's[3] | Other | Total | | |
|---|---|---|---|---|---|---|---|---|---|
| 1974--FEB. | 61.9 | 208.3 | 151.1 | 54.6 | 66.1 | 308.3 | 374.4 | 351.7 | 6.6 |
| MAR. | 62.7 | 209.8 | 152.3 | 54.7 | 66.7 | 312.4 | 379.1 | 356.2 | 6.4 |
| APR. | 63.5 | 214.7 | 155.8 | 56.2 | 71.8 | 315.3 | 387.1 | 358.7 | 6.0 |
| MAY | 64.1 | 208.8 | 151.3 | 54.8 | 77.2 | 316.7 | 393.9 | 358.7 | 7.6 |
| JUNE | 64.8 | 213.5 | 153.6 | 56.1 | 79.6 | 318.3 | 397.9 | 360.8 | 6.1 |
| JULY | 65.3 | 214.8 | 154.4 | 56.6 | 82.8 | 319.2 | 402.0 | 361.9 | 5.4 |
| AUG. | 65.7 | 211.9 | 152.3 | 56.3 | 87.1 | 321.1 | 408.2 | 360.3 | 4.0 |
| SEPT. | 65.8 | 213.6 | 153.3 | 57.0 | 88.7 | 321.3 | 410.1 | 360.5 | 5.5 |
| OCT. | 66.4 | 215.3 | 154.4 | 57.7 | 88.8 | 324.6 | 413.3 | 361.7 | 3.7 |
| NOV. | 67.8 | 217.5 | 155.9 | 58.4 | 87.1 | 325.8 | 412.9 | 363.0 | 3.3 |
| DEC. | 68.9 | 223.3 | 160.3 | 59.7 | 90.5 | 327.2 | 417.6 | 366.5 | 4.8 |
| 1975--JAN. | 67.7 | 221.6 | 158.7 | 59.7 | 92.1 | 332.7 | 424.7 | 371.0 | 4.0 |
| FEB. | 67.8 | 213.0 | 152.2 | 57.6 | 89.4 | 337.8 | 427.1 | 375.0 | 3.3 |
| WEEK ENDING: | | | | | | | | | |
| 1975--FEB. 5 | 67.4 | 214.7 | 153.8 | 57.7 | 90.8 | 334.5 | 425.3 | .0 | 4.3 |
| 12 | 68.2 | 213.7 | 152.6 | 57.9 | 90.1 | 337.2 | 427.3 | .0 | 3.0 |
| 19 | 68.0 | 213.1 | 152.1 | 57.8 | 89.2 | 338.0 | 427.2 | .0 | 3.1 |
| 26 | 67.3 | 210.7 | 150.6 | 57.0 | 88.1 | 339.8 | 427.9 | .0 | 3.4 |
| MAR. 5 | 68.2 | 215.1 | 154.1 | 57.9 | 87.8 | 340.3 | 428.1 | .0 | 2.7 |
| 12 | 69.1 | 216.3 | 154.4 | 58.8 | 87.9 | 342.0 | R 430.0 | .0 | 2.8 |
| 19 P | 68.8 | 215.4 | R 153.8 | 58.3 | 88.2 | 342.9 | 431.1 | .0 | 4.4 |
| 26 P | 68.5 | 213.8 | 153.0 | 57.6 | 88.6 | 343.4 | 432.0 | .0 | 4.4 |

1/ TOTAL DEPOSITS INCLUDE, IN ADDITION TO THE MEMBER AND DOMESTIC NONMEMBER DEPOSITS SHOWN, DEPOSITS DUE TO FOREIGN AND INTERNATIONAL INSTITUTIONS AT F.R.BANKS AND M1 TYPE BALANCES AT AGENCIES AND BRANCHES OF FOREIGN BANKS.
2/ BASED ON MOST RECENT CALL REPORT SINGLE-DAY OBSERVATIONS.
3/ INCLUDES NEGOTIABLE TIME CERTIFICATES OF DEPOSIT ISSUED IN DENOMINATIONS OF $100,000 OR MORE BY LARGE WEEKLY REPORTING COMMERCIAL BANKS.
4/ AVERAGE OF BEGINNING AND END OF MONTH DEPOSITS AT MUTUAL SAVINGS BANKS, SAVINGS AND LOAN SHARES, AND CREDIT UNION SHARES.
5/ U.S.GOVERNMENT DEMAND DEPOSITS AT ALL COMMERCIAL BANKS.
P - PRELIMINARY; R - REVISED

You can use the foregoing material for reference on monetary aggregates when reading articles dealing with the money stocks.

See Figure 4-3 for a diagram of the flow of currency in the United States.

## COMPUTATION OF INTEREST RATES

You should be aware of the fact that the interest charge which you might be quoted for a loan or other purpose is not enough information. How the stated interest rate is used can significantly change the amount of interest that you actually pay in dollars and cents. Find out the method used to calculate *your* interest charges.

The importance of this principle is clearly illustrated in the following examples taken from a publication of the Federal Reserve Bank of Chicago.[8]

These examples will make it possible for you to compute the actual interest charges. They will also serve to show you what interest calculation

[8]Anne Marie LaPorte, "ABCs of figuring interest," Federal Reserve Bank of Chicago *Business Conditions* (September 1973), pp. 3-11.

**FIGURE 4-3**

From the U.S. Treasury . . .  Through the Federal Reserve Bank . . .  To the Public and Back

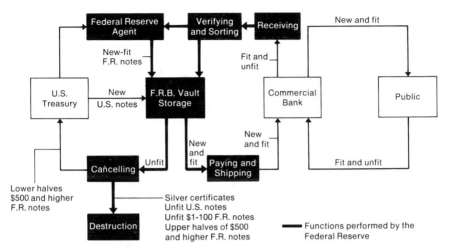

*Source:* Federal Reserve Bank of Atlanta, *Fundamental Facts About United States Money* (March 1972).

methods are used, what interest you are actually being charged on a loan, or whether you are receiving the amount of interest to which you are entitled on your savings account.

For maximum benefit, it is suggested that you take pencil and paper when reading these examples and do all the calculations as they are presented in the examples.

Among the things that you should look for in these examples are answers to the following questions:

1. How can I make the interest calculations on my own?
2. What is the "nominal rate of interest"?
3. What effect does the frequency of payments on my loan have on my actual interest charges? For example, what are the differences if I pay back semi-annually as opposed to quarterly or monthly?
4. What is meant by the "effective annual rate of interest"?
5. What are the mechanics of having a loan on the declining balance method? the add-on method? the bank discount method? Which method is best?
6. How does the frequency of payments affect the effective rate of interest of the add-on method?
7. How does compound interest affect the amount of interest that I receive?
8. How does the number of days used for a year affect how much interest I pay on a loan? What is the "365-360 method"?
9. What is the effect on the interest I am paid on my savings account if I deal

with a savings institution that pays interest for "grace periods"? Does it work to my advantage or against me?

10. What is the "Rule of 78"? What is its importance with regard to the interest that I might pay on a loan?

11. How does the amount of interest that I have to pay under the Rule of 78 compare with what I would have to pay under the declining balance method?

12. What are mortgage points?

13. How do mortgage points affect the interest that I actually pay when I buy a house (i.e., my effective rate of interest)?

14. What is a compensating balance?

15. How does a compensating balance affect the interest that I actually pay (i.e., my effective rate of interest)?

# THE ABCs OF CALCULATING INTEREST RATES

## Interest Calculations

Interest represents the price borrowers pay to lenders for credit over specified periods of time. The amount of interest paid depends on a number of factors: the dollar amount lent or borrowed, the length of time involved in the transaction, the stated (or nominal) annual rate of interest, the repayment schedule, and the method used to calculate interest.

If, for example, an individual deposits $1,000 for one year in a bank paying 5 percent interest on savings, then at the end of the year the depositor may receive interest of $50, or he may receive some other amount, depending on the way interest is calculated. Alternatively, an individual who borrows $1,000 for one year at 5 percent and repays the loan in one payment at the end of a year, may pay $50 in interest, or he may pay some other amount, again depending on the calculation method used.

## Simple Interest

The various methods used to calculate interest are basically variations of the simple interest calculation method.

The basic concept underlying simple interest is that interest is paid only on the original amount borrowed for the length of time the borrower has use of the credit. The amount borrowed is referred to as the principal. In the simple interest calculation, interest is computed only on that portion of the original principal still owed.

*Example 1:* Suppose $1,000 is borrowed at 5 percent and repaid in one payment at the end of one year. Using the simple interest calculation, the interest amount would be 5 percent of $1,000 for one year or $50 since the borrower had use of $1,000 for the entire year.

When more than one payment is made on a simple interest loan, the method of computing interest is referred to as "interest on the declining balance." Since the borrower only pays interest on that amount of original principal which has not yet been repaid, interest paid will be smaller the more frequent the payments. At the same time, of course, the amount of credit the borrower has at his disposal is also smaller.

*Example 2:* Using simple interest on the declining balance to compute interest charges, a loan repaid on two payments—one at the end of the first half-year and another at the end of the second half-year—would accumulate total interest charges of $37.50. The first payment would be $500 plus $25 (5 percent of $1,000 for one-half year), or $525; the second payment would be $500 plus $12.50 (5 percent of $500 for one-half year), or $512.50. The total amount paid would be $525 plus $512.50, or $1,037.50. Interest equals the difference between the amount repaid and the amount borrowed, or $37.50. If four quarterly payments of $250 plus interest were made, the interest amount would be $31.25; if 12 monthly payments of $83.33 plus interest were made, the interest amount would be $27.08.

*Example 3:* When interest on the declining balance method is applied to a loan that is to be repaid in two equal payments, payments of $518.83 would be made at the end of the first half-year and at the end of the second half-year. Interest due at the end of the first half-year remains $25; therefore, with the first payment the balance is reduced by $493.83 ($518.83 less $25), leaving the borrower $506.17 to use during the second half-year. The interest for the second half-year is 5 percent of $506.17 for one-half year, or $12.66. The final $518.83 payment, then, covers interest of $12.66 plus the outstanding balance of $506.17. Total interest paid is $25 plus $12.66, or $37.66, slightly more than in Example 2.

This equal payment variation is commonly used with mortgage payment schedules. Each payment over the duration of the loan is split into two parts. Part one is the interest due at the time the payment is made, and part two—the remainder—is applied to the balance or amount still owed. In addition to mortgage lenders, credit unions typically use the simple interest/declining balance calculation method for computing interest on loans. Consumer installment loans are normally set up on this method and in recent months a number of banks have also begun offering personal loans using this method.

## Other Calculation Methods

Add-on interest, bank discount, and compound interest calculation methods differ from the simple interest method as to when, how, and on what balance interest is paid. The "effective annual rate," or the annual percentage rate, for these methods is that annual rate of interest which when used in the simple interest rate formula equals the amount of interest payable in these other calculation methods. For the declining balance method, the effective annual rate of interest is the stated or nominal annual rate of interest. For the methods to be described below, the effective annual rate of interest differs from the nominal rate.

*Add-on interest.* When the add-on interest method is used, interest is calculated on the full amount of the original principal. The interest amount is immediately added to the original principal and payments are determined by dividing principal plus interest by the number of payments to be made. When only one payment is involved, this method produces the same effective interest rate as the simple interest method. When two or more payments are to be made, however, use of the add-on interest method results in an effective rate of interest that is greater than the nominal rate. True, the interest amount is calculated by applying the nominal rate to the total amount borrowed, but the borrower does not have use of the total amount for the entire time period if two or more payments are made.

*Example 4:* Consider, again, the two-payment loan in Example 3. Using the add-on interest method, interest of $50 (5 percent of $1,000 for one year) is added to the $1,000 borrowed, giving $1,050 to be repaid; half (or $525) at the end of the first half-year and the other half at the end of the second half-year.

Recall that in Example 3, where the declining balance method was used, an effective rate of 5 percent meant two equal payments of $518.83 were to be made. Now with the add-on interest method each payment is $525. The effective rate of this 5 percent add-on rate loan, then, is greater than 5 percent. In fact, the corresponding effective rate is 6.631 percent. This rate takes into account the fact that the borrower does not have use of $1,000 for the entire year, but rather use of $1,000 for the first half-year, and, excluding the interest payment, use of $508.15 for the second half-year.

To see that a one-year, two equal payment, 5 percent add-on rate loan is equivalent to a one-year, two equal payment, 6.631 percent declining balance loan, consider the following. When the first $525 payment is made, $33.15 in interest is due (6.631 percent of $1,000 for one-half year). Deducting the $33.15 from $525 leaves $491.85 to be applied to the outstanding balance of $1,000. The second $525 payment covers $16.85 in interest (6.631 percent of $508.15 for one-half year) and the $508.15 balance due.

In this particular example, using the add-on interest method means that no matter how many payments are to be made, the interest will always be $50. As the number of payments increases, the borrower has use of less and less credit over the year. For example, if four quarterly payments of $262.50 are made, the borrower has the use of $1,000 during the first quarter, around $750 during the second quarter, around $500 around the third quarter, and around $250 during the fourth and final quarter. Therefore, as the number of payments increases, the effective rate of interest also increases. For instance, in the current example, if four quarterly payments are made, the effective rate of interest would be 7.922 percent; if 12 monthly payments are made, the effective interest rate would be 9.105 percent. The add-on interest method is commonly used by finance companies and some banks in determining interest on consumer loans.

*Bank discount.* When the bank discount rate calculation method is used interest is calculated on the amount to be paid back and the borrower receives the difference between the amount to be paid back and the interest amount. In Example 1, a 5 percent $1,000 loan is to be paid back at the end of one year. Using the bank discount rate method two approaches are possible.

*Example 5:* The first approach would be to deduct the interest amount of $50 from the $1,000, leaving the borrower with $950 to use over the year. At the end of the year he pays $1,000. The interest amount of $50 is the same as in Example 1. The borrower in Example 1, however, had the use of $1,000 over the year. Thus, the effective rate of interest using the bank discount rate method is greater than that for the simple interest rate calculation. The effective rate of interest here would be 5.263 percent—i.e., $50 ÷ $950—compared to 5 percent in Example 1.

*Example 6:* The second approach would be to determine the amount that would have to be paid back so that once the interest amount was deducted, the borrower would have the use of $1,000 over the year. This amount is $1,052.63 and this becomes the face value of the note on which interest is calculated. The interest amount (5 percent of $1,052.63 for one year) is $52.63, and this is deducted leaving the borrower with $1,000 to use over the year. The effective rate of interest, again, is 5.263 percent. The bank discount method is commonly used with short-term business loans. Generally there are no intermediate payments and the duration of the loan is one year or less.

*Compound interest.* When the compound interest calculation is used, interest is calculated on the original principal plus all interest accrued to that point in time. Since interest is paid on interest as well as on the amount borrowed, the effective interest rate is greater than the nominal interest rate. The compound interest rate method is often used by banks and savings institutions in determining interest they pay on savings deposits "loaned" to the institutions by the depositors.

*Example 7:* Suppose $1,000 is deposited in a bank that pays a 5 percent nominal annual rate of interest, compounded semi-annually (i.e., twice a year). At the end of the first half-year, $25 in interest (5 percent of $1,000 for one-half year) is payable. At the end of the year, the interest amount is calculated on the $1,000 plus the $25 in interest already paid, so that the second interest payment is $25.63 (5 percent of $1,025 for one-half year). The interest amount payable for the year, then, is $25 plus $25.63, or $50.63. The effective rate of interest is 5.063 percent which is greater then the nominal 5 percent rate.

The more often interest is compounded within a particular time period, the greater will be the effective rate of interest. In a year, a 5 percent nominal annual rate of interest compounded four times (quarterly) results in an effective annual rate of 5.0945 percent; compounded 12 times (monthly), 5.1162 percent; and compounded 365 times (daily), 5.1267 percent. When the interval of time between compoundings approaches zero (even shorter than a second), then the method is known as continuous compounding. Five percent continuously compounded for one year will result in an effective annual rate of 5.1271.

## How Long is a Year?

In the above examples, a year is assumed to be 365 days long. Historically, in order to simplify interest calculations, financial institutions have often used 12 30-day months, yielding a 360-day year. If a 360-day year is assumed in the calculation and the amount borrowed is actually used by the borrower for one full year (365 or 366 days), then interest is paid for an additional 5/360 or 6/360 of a "year." For any given nominal rate of interest, the effective rate of interest will be greater when a 360-day year is used in the interest rate calculation than when a 365-day year is used. This has come to be known as the 365-360 method.

*Example 8:* Suppose $1,000 is deposited in a bank paying a 5 percent nominal annual rate of interest, compounded daily. As pointed out earlier, the effective annual rate of interest for one year, based on a 365-day year, is 5.1267 percent. The interest payable on the 365th day would be $51.27. Daily compounding means that each day the daily rate of 0.0137 percent (5 percent divided by 365 days) was paid on the $1,000 deposit plus all interest payable up to that day. Now suppose a 360-day year is used in the calculation. The daily rate paid becomes 0.0139 percent (5 percent divided by 360 days) so that on the 365th day the interest amount payable would be $52. The effective annual rate of interest, based on a 360-day year, would be 5.1997 percent.

*Example 9:* Supose that a $1,000 note is discounted at 5 percent and payable in 365 days. This is the situation discussed in Example 5 where, based on a 365-day year, the effective rate of interest was seen to be 5.263 percent. If the bank discount rate calculation assumes a 360-day year, then the length of time is computed to be 365/360 or 1 1/72 years instead of one year, the interest deducted (the discount) equals $50.69 instead of $50, and the effective annual rate of interest is 5.267 percent.

## When Repayment is Early

In the above examples, it was assumed that periodic loan payments were always made exactly when due. Often, however, a loan may be completely repaid before it is due. When the declining balance method for calculating interest is used, the borrower is not penalized for prepayment since interest is paid only on the balance outstanding for the length of time that amount is owed. When the add-on interest calculation is used, however, prepayment implies that the lender obtains some interest which is unearned. The borrower then is actually paying an even higher effective rate since he does not use the funds for the length of time of the original loan contract.

Some loan contracts make provisions for an interest rebate if the loan is prepaid. One of the common methods used in determining the amount of the interest rebate is referred to as the "Rule of 78." Application of the Rule of 78 yields the percentage of the total interest amount that is to be returned to the borrower in the event of prepayment. The percentage figure is arrived at by dividing the sum of the integer numbers (digits) from one to the number of payments remaining by the sum of the digits from one to the total number of payments specified in the original loan contract. For example, if a five-month loan is paid off by the end of the second month (i.e., there are three payments remaining), the percentage of the interest that the lender would rebate is $1 + 2 + 3 = 6 \div 1 + 2 + 3 + 4 + 5 = 15$, or 40 percent. The name derives from the fact that 78 is the sum of the digits from one to 12 and, therefore, is the denominator in calculating interest rebate percentages for all 12-period loans.

Application of the Rule of 78 results in the borrower paying somewhat more interest than he would have paid with a comparable declining balance loan. How much more depends on the effective rate of interest charged and the total number of payments specified in the original loan contract. The higher the effective rate of interest charged and the greater the specified total number of payments, the greater the amount of interest figures under the Rule of 78 exceeds that under the declining balance method.

The difference between the Rule of 78 interest and the declining balance interest also varies depending upon when the prepayment occurs. This difference over the term of the loan tends to increase up to about the one-third point of the term and then decrease after this point. For example, with a 12-month term, the difference with prepayment occurring in the second month would be greater than the difference that would occur with prepayment in the first month; the third-month difference would be greater than the second-month difference; the fourth month (being the one-third point) would be greater than both the third-month difference and the fifth-month difference. After the fifth month, each succeeding month's difference would be less than the previous month's difference.

*Example 10:* Suppose that there are two $1,000 loans that are to be repaid over 12 months. Interest on the first loan is calculated using a 5 percent add-on method which results in equal payments of $87.50 due at the end of each month ($1,000 plus $50 interest divided by 12 months). The effective annual rate of interest for this loan is 9.105 percent. Any interest rebate due because of prepayment is to be determined by the Rule of 78.

Interest on the second loan is calculated using a declining balance method where the annual rate of interest is the effective annual rate of interest from the first loan, or 9.105 percent. Equal payments of $87.50 are also due at the end of each month for the second loan.

Suppose that repayment on both loans occurs after one-sixth of the term of the loan has passed, i.e., at the end of the second month, with the regular first month's payment being made for both loans. The interest paid on the first loan will be $14.74, while the interest paid on the second loan will be $14.57, a difference of 17 cents. If the prepayment occurs at the one-third point, i.e., at the end of the fourth month (regular payments having been made at the end of the first, second, and third months), interest of $26.92 is paid on the first loan and interest of $26.69 on the second loan, a difference of 23 cents. If the prepayment occurs later, say at the three-fourths point, i.e., at the end of the nine month (regular payments having been made at the end of the first through eighth months), $46.16 in interest is paid on the first loan and $46.07 in interest paid on the second loan, a difference of but 9 cents.

## Bonus Interest

Savings institutions are permitted to pay interest from the first calendar day of the month on deposits received by the tenth calendar day of the month, and also on deposits withdrawn during the last three business days of a month ending a regular quarterly or semi-annual interest period. If a savings institution chooses to do this, then it is paying for the use of the depositor's money for some period of time during which the savings institution does not have the use of the money. The effective rate of interest is, therefore, greater than it would be otherwise.

*Example 11:* Suppose that on January 10, $1,000 is deposited in a bank paying 5 percent interest compounded daily based on a 365-day year and that funds deposited by the 10th of any month earn interest from the 1st of that month. On the following December 31, 355 days after the deposit is made, interest for 365 days is payable on the deposit, or $51.27. The bank, however, had the use of the funds for only 355 days. The effective rate of interest, or that rate which when compounded daily for 355 days would yield the interest amount $51.27, is 5.1408 percent.

Although savings institutions choosing to pay interest for these grace periods are prohibited from advertising an effective yield which takes this into account, depositors should be aware of the effect such practice has on the price paid for the use of their money.

## Charges Other than Interest

In addition to the interest which must be paid, loan agreements often will include other provisions which must be satisfied. Two of these provisions are mortgage points and required (compensating) deposit balances.

*Mortgage points.*   Mortgage lenders will sometimes require the borrower to pay a charge in addition to the interest. This extra charge is calculated as a certain percentage of the mortgage amount and is referred to as mortgage points. For example, if 2 points are charged on a $10,000 mortgage, then 2 percent of $10,000 or $200, must be paid in addition to the stated interest. The borrower, therefore, is paying a higher price than if points were not charged— i.e., the effective rate of interest is increased. In order to determine what the effective rate of interest is when points are charged, it is necessary to deduct the dollar amount resulting from the point calculation from the mortgage amount and add it to the interest amount to be paid. The borrower is viewed as having the mortgage amount less the point charge amount rather than the entire mortgage amount.

*Example 12:*   Suppose that 2 points are charged on a 20-year, $10,000 mortgage where the rate of interest (declining balance calculation) is 7 percent. The payments are to be $77.53 per month. Once the borrower pays the $200 point charge, he starts out with $9,800 to use. With payments of $77.53 a month over 20 years, the result of the 2 point charge is an effective rate of 7.262 percent.

The longer the time period of the mortgage, the lower will be the effective rate of interest when points are charged because the point charge is spread out over more payments. In the above example, if the mortgage had been for 30 years instead of 20 years, the effective rate of interest would have been 7.201 percent.

*Required (compensating) deposit balances.*   A bank may require that a borrower maintain a certain percentage of the loan amount on deposit as a condition for obtaining the loan. The borrower, then, does not have the use of the entire loan amount but rather the use of the loan amount less the amount that must be kept on deposit. The effective rate of interest is greater than it would be if no compensating deposit balance were required.

*Example 13:*   Suppose that $1,000 is borrowed at 5 percent from a bank to be paid back at the end of one year. Suppose, further, that the lending bank requires that 10 percent of the loan amount be kept on deposit. The borrower, therefore, has the use of only $900 ($1,000 less 10 percent) on which he pays an interest amount of $50 (5 percent of $1,000 for one year). The effective rate of interest is, therefore, 5.556 percent as opposed to 5 percent when no compensating balance is required.

# *Federal Reserve System and the U.S. banking system*

# 5

The Federal Reserve System is the central bank of the United States. It affects the value of the money in one's pocket, in savings accounts, and in other forms.

The Federal Reserve System does the following jobs:

Operates as the country's money manager.
Serves as a bank for banks.
Functions as the Federal government's bank.
Supervises its member banks.

It has the following broad functions:

To foster a flow of credit and money to facilitate orderly economic growth.
To stabilize the dollar.
To achieve a long-run balance in the U.S. international payments.

The broad purpose of the Federal Reserve System is to provide an efficient monetary mechanism that permits utilization of the country's resources, a steady growth in the standard of living, and a continual improvement in the quality of life.

See the Federal Reserve Map of the United States (Figure 5-1).

FIGURE 5-1

# FEDERAL RESERVE MAP OF THE UNITED STATES

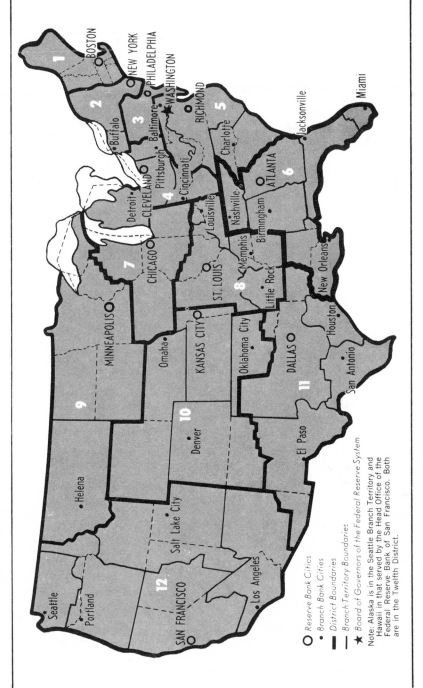

O  *Reserve Bank Cities*

•  *Branch Bank Cities*

▮  *District Boundaries*

▬  *Branch Territory Boundaries*

★  *Board of Governors of the Federal Reserve System*

Note: Alaska is in the Seattle Branch Territory and
Hawaii in that served by the Head Office of the
Federal Reserve Bank of San Francisco. Both
are in the Twelfth District.

*Source:* Federal Reserve Bank of Atlanta and Federal Reserve Bank of Minneapolis.

On December 23, 1913, President Woodrow Wilson signed the Federal Reserve Act which established the Federal Reserve System. He expressed his economic view in his first Inaugural Address as follows: "We shall deal with our economic system as it is and as it may be modified, not as it might be if we had a clean sheet of paper to write upon, and step by step we shall make it what it should be." This approach of modification has been well illustrated in the case of the Federal Reserve System.

## STRUCTURE

The Federal Reserve System (often referred to as "the Fed," "the System," and the "Federal Reserve" consists of:

The Board of Governors (often referred to as the "Federal Reserve Board")
The Federal Open Market Committee (FOMC)
The Federal Advisory Council
The Federal Reserve Banks and their Branches
The member banks

See Figure 5-2 for the organizational set-up of the Federal Reserve System.

*Board of Governors of the Federal Reserve System.* The Board of Governors, a governmental agency located in Washington, D.C., consists of 7 persons appointed for 14-year terms by the President of the United States with the advice and consent of the Senate. It has supervision over the operations of the Federal Reserve System.

The Board, in general, is responsible for formulating national credit policies and for supervising their execution.

More specifically, it does the following:

Issues regulations interpreting the laws which apply to the Reserve Bank operations.
Represents the entire System in relations with the Federal government.
Exercises special supervision over the foreign contacts and international operations of the Reserve Banks.
Has full authority over reserve requirements (as a percentage of deposits), within limits set by Congress.
Establishes maximum rates of interest that member banks may pay on time deposits.
Reviews and determines discount rates established by the Reserve Banks.
Directs the System's activities in bank examinations.
Coordinates its economic research and publications.

**FIGURE 5-2**

**THE FEDERAL RESERVE SYSTEM: ORGANIZATION**

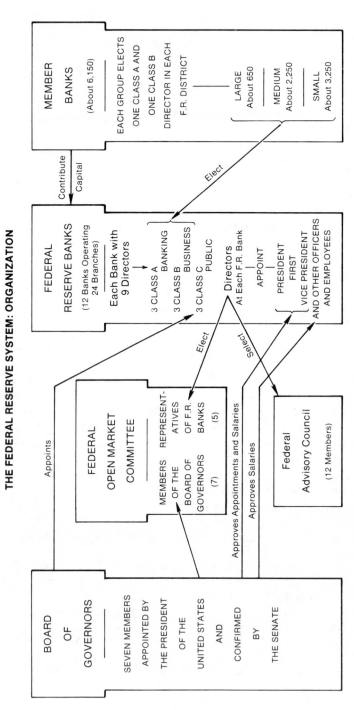

*Source:* Board of Governors of the Federal Reserve System, *The Federal Reserve System: Purposes and Functions,* Fifth Edition (November 1967), p. 23.

Must grant its approval for appointment of the president and first vice president of each Reserve Bank (after they have been elected by the Board of Directors of the Bank).

Appoints 3 of the 9 directors of each Federal Reserve Bank (including the chairman and deputy chairman).

*Federal Open Market Committee.*   The Federal Open Market Committee (FOMC) consists of 12 persons (7 members of the Board of Governors and 5 of the Federal Reserve Bank presidents). It is engaged in the buying and selling of securities in the open market. It conducts open market transactions for a single System Account by the Federal Reserve Bank of New York on behalf of all Reserve Banks.

The open market transactions are supervised by a Manager of the System Account, who is an officer of the Federal Reserve Bank of New York.

When the FOMC buys securities, it creates reserves and puts them into the banking system. When it sells securities, it removes reserves from the banking system and extinguishes them.

*Federal Advisory Council.*   The Federal Advisory Council consists of 12 citizens, each elected by the Board of Directors of a Federal Reserve Bank (usually from among bankers of its district). It meets at least four times a year to confer with the Board of Governors and makes advisory recommendations on Federal Reserve matters.

*Federal Reserve Banks and Their Branches.*   Federal Reserve Banks are corporations chartered by Congress to operate in the public interest. There are 12 regional banks.

Unlike central banks in most other countries, the Federal Reserve System is highly decentralized. Each Reserve Bank sets its own discount rate (subject to review by the Board of Governors), and the capital stock of a Reserve Bank is owned by the member banks in its district.

Reserve banks hold the bulk of the cash reserves of their member banks. They also provide checking accounts to the U.S. Treasury, issue currency (Federal Reserve Notes), collect checks, supervise and examine member banks, handle issuance and redemption of U.S. government securities, and otherwise act as fiscal agents for the Federal government. (See Table 5-1 for Federal Reserve banks, branches and offices.)

*Member Banks.*   Of the aproximately 14,000 commercial banks in the United States, less than half of them are members of the Federal Reserve System. The member banks, however, represent the largest banks and the majority of the country's deposits.

All national banks (i.e., nationally chartered banks) and most of the large state-chartered banks, as well as some small ones, are members.

TABLE 5-1

# Federal Reserve Banks, Branches, and Offices

| FEDERAL RESERVE BANK, branch, *or facility*   Zip | Chairman Deputy Chairman | President First Vice President | Vice President in charge of branch |
|---|---|---|---|
| BOSTON* ............ 02106 | Louis W. Cabot Robert M. Solow | Frank E. Morris James A. McIntosh | |
| NEW YORK* ........ 10045 Buffalo ............. 14240 | Roswell L. Gilpatric Frank R. Milliken Donald Nesbitt | Alfred Hayes Richard A. Debs | Ronald B. Gray |
| PHILADELPHIA ...... 19105 | John R. Coleman Edward J. Dwyer | David P. Eastburn Mark H. Willes | |
| CLEVELAND* ....... 44101 Cincinnati .......... 45201 Pittsburgh .......... 15230 | Horace A. Shepard Robert E. Kirby Phillip R. Shriver G. Jackson Tankersley | Willis J. Winn Walter H. MacDonald | Robert E. Showalter Robert D. Duggan |
| RICHMOND* .......... 23261 Baltimore ........... 21203 Charlotte ........... 28201 *Culpeper Communications Center* ........... 22701 | Robert W. Lawson, Jr. E. Craig Wall, Sr. James A. Harlow Charles W. DeBell | Robert P. Black George C. Rankin | Jimmie R. Monhollon Stuart P. Fishburne J. Gordon Dickerson, Jr. |
| ATLANTA ........... 30303 Birmingham ........ 35202 Jacksonville ........ 32203 Nashville ........... 37203 New Orleans ....... 70161 *Miami Office* ........ 33152 | H. G. Pattillo Clifford M. Kirtland, Jr. Frank P. Samford, Jr. James E. Lyons John C. Tune Floyd W. Lewis | Monroe Kimbrel Kyle K. Fossum | Hiram J. Honea Edward C. Rainey Jeffrey J. Wells George C. Guynn W. M. Davis |
| CHICAGO* .......... 60690 Detroit .............. 48231 | Peter B. Clark Robert H. Strotz W. M. Defoe | Robert P. Mayo Daniel M. Doyle | William C. Conrad |
| ST. LOUIS .......... 63166 Little Rock ......... 72203 Louisville .......... 40201 Memphis ........... 38101 | Edward J. Schnuck Sam Cooper Vacancy James H. Davis Jeanne L. Holley | Darryl R. Francis Eugene A. Leonard | John F. Breen Donald L. Henry L. Terry Britt |
| MINNEAPOLIS ....... 55480 Helena .............. 59601 | Bruce B. Dayton James P. McFarland William A. Cordingley | Bruce K. MacLaury Clement A. Van Nice | Howard L. Knous |
| KANSAS CITY ....... 64198 Denver ............. 80217 Oklahoma City ...... 73125 Omaha ............. 68102 | Robert T. Person Harold W. Andersen Maurice B. Mitchell James G. Harlow, Jr. Durward B. Varner | George H. Clay John T. Boysen | J. David Hamilton William G. Evans Robert D. Hamilton |
| DALLAS ............. 75222 El Paso ............. 79999 Houston ............ 77001 San Antonio ........ 78295 | John Lawrence Charles T. Beaird Herbert M. Schwartz Thomas J. Barlow Pete J. Morales, Jr. | Ernest T. Baughman T. W. Plant | Fredric W. Reed James L. Cauthen Carl H. Moore |
| SAN FRANCISCO ....94120 Los Angeles ........ 90051 Portland ............ 97208 Salt Lake City ...... 84110 Seattle ............. 98124 | O. Meredith Wilson Joseph F. Alibrandi Joseph R. Vaughan Loran L. Stewart Sam Bennion Malcolm T. Stamper | John J. Balles John B. Williams | Gerald R. Kelly William M. Brown A. Grant Holman Paul W. Cavan |

The member banks elect six of the nine directors on the policy-making board of their Federal Reserve Bank. Only three of these six directors can be bankers; the other three must be actively engaged in commerce, industry, or agriculture in the District and may not be officers, directors, or employees of any bank.

The third group of three directors is appointed by the Board of Governors. These directors may not be bankers, nor may they hold stock in any bank. All nine directors represent the public.

Member banks must subscribe to the capital of their Federal Reserve Bank an amount equal to 6% of their own capital and surplus. Only half of this sum is actually paid in; the other half is subject to call.

Member banks must comply with reserve requirements, with regulations governing branch banking, check collection, and other banking matters.

Privileges of member banks include:

Borrowing from the Federal Reserve Bank.
Using Federal Reserve facilities for collecting checks.
Settling balances.
Transferring funds to other cities.
Obtaining currency as needed.
Receiving a dividend of 6% per year on Federal Reserve Bank stock.

**FIGURE 5-3**

As the Federal Reserve buys securities . . . it creates reserve dollars for the banking system.

The only way the Federal Reserve Banks can prevent a decline in Government security prices is to stand ready to buy all the bonds at a support price. But the reserve dollars created in those purchases make possible a multiple growth in checkbook money.

*Source:* Federal Reserve Bank of New York, *Money: Master or Servant?* (Sixth Edition, 1971).

### Membership and Political Insulation

All national banks and many state banks are members of the Fed. When the Fed was first established, it was decided that it should be insulated from political influence. This insulation has been fairly well preserved over its history, although numerous attempts have been made by Congress and various Presidents of the United States to curtail its independent action. Such attempts are still being made.

One big reason that the Fed can afford to be independent is that it pays its own way. Unlike traditional Federal agencies, the Fed receives no money appropriations from Congress. Federal Reserve Banks generate their own income from the interest that they charge on loans to member banks and the interest income on U.S. government securities bought and sold by the Federal Reserve System to influence the volume of bank reserves in the country.

When a conflict exists between serving the country's best interests and making income, the Fed is supposed to decide in favor of the country's best interests. In addition, Federal Reserve Banks transfer to the U.S. Treasury any earnings in excess of expenses.

## THE MONETARY TOOLS

The Federal Reserve System's monetary tools, by which it enforces monetary policy, include:

Open market operations.
Changing the discount rate.
Changing the legal reserve requirement.
Moral suasion.
Setting the margin requirements.
Setting the maximum interest rate that member banks can pay on time deposits.

The tool of open market operations is used most frequently. On a day-to-day basis, it involves the buying and selling of securities (e.g., U.S. Treasury bills and U.S. Treasury bonds) by the Fed.

Changing the discount rate is the second most frequently used tool. This is the interest rate which the Federal Reserve Banks charge the member banks for loans (it used to be called the "Rediscount Rate").

Changing the legal reserve requirement is a tool which the Fed tries not to employ very much, because it has powerful economic effects. It determines the amount that a commercial bank has to keep on reserve to back up its checking accounts.

**FIGURE 5-4**

Whenever the Federal Reserve Banks increase their loans or investments, they also increase bank reserves an equal amount.

*Source:* Federal Reserve Bank of New York, *Money: Master or Servant?* (Sixth Edition, 1971).

**FIGURE 5-5**

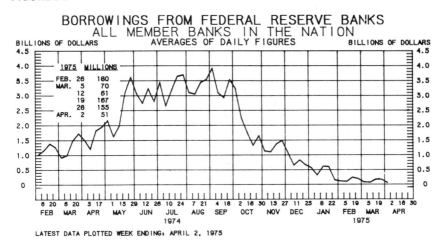

LATEST DATA PLOTTED WEEK ENDING: APRIL 2, 1975

*Source:* Federal Reserve Bank of St. Louis.

Moral suasion is an intangible type of monetary control which Federal Reserve authorities, especially the Chairman of the Board of Governors, can exercise to get executives at commercial banks to comply with the desires of the Fed. It is a kind of "arm-twisting" that has proven very effective at times.

**FIGURE 5-6**

If reserve requirements average 20%, our reserve dollar can support five deposit dollars; if reserve requirements average 10%, our reserve dollar can support ten deposit dollars.

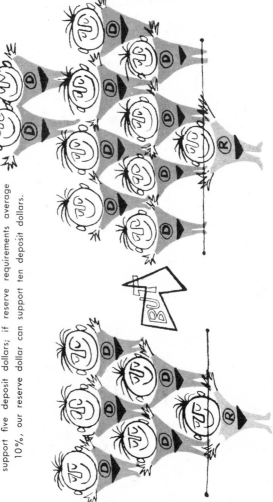

*Source:* Federal Reserve Bank of New York, *Money: Master or Servant?* (Sixth Edition, 1971).

Setting the margin requirements is another tool. Since 1933 the Fed has been directed by law to restrain the undue use of bank credit for speculation in securities, real estate, or commodities. With the Securities Exchange Act of 1934, the Fed was specifically authorized to curb the excessive use of credit for buying or carrying securities by setting limitations on the amount that brokers and dealers in securities, banks, and others may lend on securities. The margin requirement is the minimum amount that a person must pay if he wants to buy corporate stock (e.g., if the margin requirement is 60%, a person must pay 60% of the amount for buying stock and borrow the other 40% from a broker). (See Table 5-2).

Congress has only at times authorized the Board of Governors of the Fed to specifically control credit in the mortgage and consumer markets (e.g., downpayments on houses and installment payments).

The Board of Governors can also set the maximum interest rate that member banks can pay on time and savings deposits, under Regulation Q. Regulation Q affects certificates of deposit, as well as other time deposits. (See Table 5-3 and Figures 5-8, 5-9, and 5-10 on pp. 184-189.)

## *Monetary Policies*

The Fed can pursue:

1. "Easy-Money" Policy against a recession.
2. "Tight-Money" Policy against inflation.

1. Under an easy-money policy:
   (a) The Fed can buy securities (e.g., U.S. Treasury bills).
   (b) The Fed can lower the discount rate.
   (c) The Fed can lower the legal reserve requirements.

2. Under tight-money policy:
   (a) The Fed can sell securities (e.g., U.S. Treasury bills).
   (b) The Fed can raise the discount rate.
   (c) The Fed can raise the legal reserve requirement.

In an easy money policy, the goal of the Federal Reserve is to combat a recession by causing interest rates to decline (e.g., the interest rate charged by banks for loans). By causing interest rates to decline, the Federal Reserve is seeking to get business firms to take out loans, so that they will expand productive capacity and create jobs. This expansion, it is expected, will then cause an increase in national income (or GNP, i.e., Gross National Product).

# TABLE 5-2

## MARGIN REQUIREMENTS
(Per cent of market value)

| Period | | For credit extended under Regulations T (brokers and dealers), U (banks), and G (others than brokers, dealers, or banks) | | | | | | |
| --- | --- | --- | --- | --- | --- | --- | --- | --- |
| Beginning date | Ending date | On margin stocks | | | On convertible bonds | | | On short sales (T) |
| | | T | U | G | T | U | G | |
| 1937—Nov. 1 | 1945—Feb. 4 | | 40 | | | | | 50 |
| 1945—Feb. 5 | July 4 | | 50 | | | | | 50 |
| July 5 | 1946—Jan. 20 | | 75 | | | | | 75 |
| 1946—Jan. 21 | 1947—Jan. 31 | | 100 | | | | | 100 |
| 1947—Feb. 1 | 1949—Mar. 29 | | 75 | | | | | 75 |
| 1949—Mar. 30 | 1951—Jan. 16 | | 50 | | | | | 50 |
| 1951—Jan. 17 | 1953—Feb. 19 | | 75 | | | | | 75 |
| 1953—Feb. 20 | 1955—Jan. 3 | | 50 | | | | | 50 |
| 1955—Jan. 4 | Apr. 22 | | 60 | | | | | 60 |
| Apr. 23 | 1958—Jan. 15 | | 70 | | | | | 70 |
| 1958—Jan. 16 | Aug. 4 | | 50 | | | | | 50 |
| Aug. 5 | Oct. 15 | | 70 | | | | | 70 |
| Oct. 16 | 1960—July 27 | | 90 | | | | | 90 |
| 1960—July 28 | 1962—July 9 | | 70 | | | | | 70 |
| 1962—July 10 | 1963—Nov. 5 | | 50 | | | | | 50 |
| 1963—Nov. 6 | 1968—Mar. 10 | | 70 | | | | | 70 |
| 1968—Mar. 11 | June 7 | | 70 | | | 50 | | 70 |
| June 8 | 1970—May 5 | | 80 | | | 60 | | 80 |
| 1970—May 6 | 1971—Dec. 3 | | 65 | | | 50 | | 65 |
| 1971—Dec. 4 | 1972—Nov. 22 | | 55 | | | 50 | | 55 |
| 1972—Nov. 24 | 1974—Jan. 2 | | 65 | | | 50 | | 65 |
| Effective Jan. 3, 1974 | | | 50 | | | 50 | | 50 |

NOTE.—Regulations G, T, and U, prescribed in accordance with the Securities Exchange Act of 1934, limit the amount of credit to purchase and carry margin stocks that may be extended on securities as collateral by prescribing a maximum loan value, which is a specified percentage of the market value of the collateral at the time the credit is extended; margin requirements are the difference between the market value (100 per cent) and the maximum loan value. The term margin stocks is defined in the corresponding regulation.

Regulation G and special margin requirements for bonds convertible into stocks were adopted by the Board of Governors effective Mar. 11, 1968.

Source: Federal Reserve Bulletin.

## TABLE 5-3 MAXIMUM INTEREST RATES PAYABLE ON TIME AND SAVINGS DEPOSITS

(Per cent per annum)

**Rates July 20, 1966—June 30, 1973**

| Type and size of deposit | Effective date: July 20, 1966 | Sept. 26, 1966 | Apr. 19, 1968 | Jan. 21, 1970 |
|---|---|---|---|---|
| Savings deposits | 4 | 4 | 4 | 4½ |
| Other time deposits:1 | | | | |
| Multiple maturity:2 | | | | |
| 30–89 days | 4 | 4 | 4 | 4½ |
| 90 days to 1 year | | | | 5 |
| 1–2 years | 5 | 5 | 5 | 5½ |
| 2 years or more | | | | 5¾ |
| Single-maturity: | | | | |
| Less than $100,000: | | | | |
| 30 days to 1 year | | | | 5 |
| 1–2 years | 5½ | 5 | 5 | 5½ |
| 2 years or more | | | | 5¾ |
| $100,000 or more: | | | | |
| 30–59 days | | | 5½ | (3) |
| 60–89 days | | | 5¾ | (3) |
| 90–179 days | 5½ | 5½ | 6 | (3) |
| 180 days to 1 year | | | 6¼ | (3) |
| 1 year or more | | | 6¼ | (3) |

**Rates beginning July 1, 1973**

| Type and size of deposit | Effective date: July 1, 1973 | Nov. 1, 1973 | Nov. 27, 1974 | Dec. 23, 1974 |
|---|---|---|---|---|
| Savings deposits | 5 | 5 | 5 | 5 |
| Other time deposits (multiple- and single-maturity):1, 2 | | | | |
| Less than $100,000: | | | | |
| 30–89 days | 5 | 5 | 5 | 5 |
| 90 days to 1 year | 5½ | 5½ | 5½ | 5½ |
| 1–2½ years | 6 | 6 | 6 | 6 |
| 2½ years or more | 6½ | 6½ | 6½ | 6½ |
| Minimum denomination of $1,000: | | | | |
| 4–6 years | (4) | 7¼ | 7¼ | 7¼ |
| 6 years or more | | | | 7½ |
| Governmental units | (5) | (5) | 7½ | 7¾ |
| $100,000 or more | (3) | (3) | (3) | (3) |

1 For exceptions with respect to certain foreign time deposits, see BULLETIN for Feb. 1968, p. 167.

2 Multiple-maturity time deposits include deposits that are automatically renewable at maturity without action by the depositor and deposits that are payable after written notice of withdrawal.

3 Maximum rates on all single-maturity time deposits in denominations of $100,000 or more have been suspended. Rates that were effective Jan. 21, 1970, and the dates when they were suspended are:

| | | |
|---|---|---|
| 30–59 days | 6¼ per cent | June 24, 1970 |
| 60–89 days | 6½ per cent | |
| 90–179 days | 6¾ per cent | May 16, 1973 |
| 180 days to 1 year | 7 per cent | |
| 1 year or more | 7½ per cent | |

Rates on multiple-maturity time deposits in denominations of $100,000 or more were suspended July 16, 1973, when the distinction between single- and multiple-maturity deposits was eliminated.

4 Between July 1 and Oct. 31, 1973, there was no ceiling for certificates maturing in 4 years or more with minimum denominations of $1,000. The amount of such certificates that a bank could issue was limited to 5 per cent of its total time and savings deposits. Sales in excess of that amount were subject to the 6½ per cent ceiling that applies to time deposits maturing in 2½ years or more.

Effective Nov. 1, 1973, a ceiling rate of 7¼ per cent was imposed on certificates maturing in 4 years or more with minimum denominations of $1,000. There is no limitation on the amount of these certificates that banks may issue.

5 Prior to Nov. 27, 1974, no distinction was made between the time deposits of governmental units and of other holders, insofar as Regulation Q ceilings on rates payable were concerned. Effective Nov. 27, 1974, governmental units were permitted to hold savings deposits and could receive interest rates on time deposits with denominations under $100,000 irrespective of maturity, as high as the maximum rate permitted on such deposits at any Federally insured depositary institution.

NOTE.— Maximum rates that may be paid by member banks are established by the Board of Governors under provisions of Regulation Q; however, a member bank may not pay a rate in excess of the maximum rate payable by State banks or trust companies on like deposits under the laws of the State in which the member bank is located. Beginning Feb. 1, 1936, maximum rates that may be paid by nonmember insured commercial banks, as established by the FDIC, have been the same as those in effect for member banks.

For previous changes, see earlier issues of the BULLETIN.

*Source: Federal Reserve Bulletin,* (January 1975, p. A-10.)

**FIGURE 5-7**

## THE FEDERAL RESERVE SYSTEM: RELATION TO INSTRUMENTS OF CREDIT POLICY

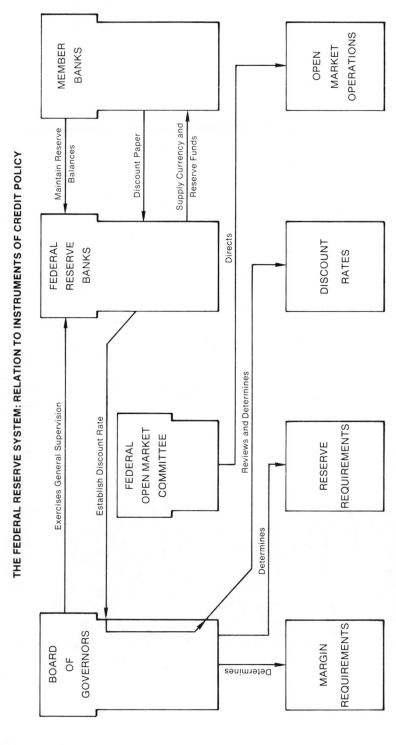

*Source*: Board of Governors of the Federal Reserve System, *The Federal Reserve System: Purposes and Functions*, Fifth Edition (November 1967), p. 227.

**FIGURE 5-8**

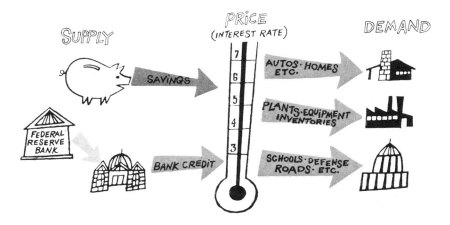

In our economy, the "credit market" is where
lenders and borrowers meet.

*Source:* Federal Reserve Bank of New York, *Money: Master or Servant?* (Sixth Edition, 1971).

**FIGURE 5-9**

The bank gives us its credit (promise to pay anybody) in exchange for
our credit (promise to pay the bank). The bank's credit is so widely and
readily acceptable that it is a form of money in our economy.

*Source:* Federal Reserve Bank of New York, *Money: Master or Servant?* (Sixth Edition, 1971).

**FIGURE 5-10**

When the price of money (the interest rate) goes up, some people refuse to borrow, and some people decide to save more of their incomes.

*Source:* Federal Reserve Bank of New York, *Money: Master or Servant?* (Sixth Edition, 1971).

**FIGURE 5-11**

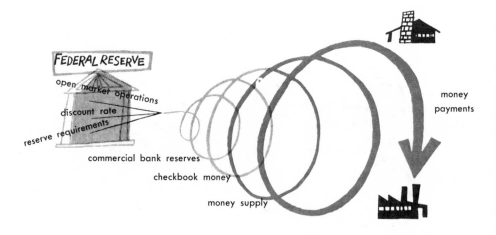

The Federal Reserve's tools work on the economy indirectly.

*Source:* Federal Reserve Bank of New York, *Money: Master or Servant?* (Sixth Edition, 1971).

The process described in the previous paragraph, however, is by no means automatic due to an uncertain link. That uncertain link is that even if the interest rate declines, there is no assurance that business firms will take out more loans. The executives at the various firms take out loans at their own discretion. They cannot be forced to take out loans even if the Federal Reserve wants them to and even if the Fed believes that it is in the best interest of the country for them to do so.

In a tight money policy, the goal of the Federal Reserve is to combat an inflation by causing interest rates to rise, in order to cut down on the size and number of loans taken out by business firms. By means of this policy, the Fed seeks to reduce expansion by business firms. Here, too, there is an uncertain link, because business firms can continue to expand, for example, through the use of retained earnings and the sale of securities that they own.

With an easy money policy, the decline in interest rates is also expected to increase consumer loans as a means of combating a recession, whereas a tight money policy, by raising interest rates, is expected to cut down on consumer loans as an additional means of combating an inflation.

Numerous difficulties arise in the conduct of the monetary policy when there is an inflation and recession at the same time, such as the United States has recently been experiencing. To combat this type of situation, the Federal Reserve can fluctuate back and forth from an easy money policy to a tight money policy, which is what the Fed has been doing. Such a course of action is, however, highly hazardous and not really satisfactory.

It is also necessary to recognize that there are different types of inflations, which further serve to compound the difficulties not only for the Federal Reserve but for Congress and the Executive Branch of government. Thus, in a demand-pull inflation, which occurs when too much money is chasing too few goods, a tight money policy can be quite effective.

In a cost-push inflation, however, a tight money policy and monetary policy, in general, are rendered very ineffective. A cost-push inflation exists when monopolistic elements in the economy cause prices to rise. There are two types: a profit-push type and a wage-push type. In a profit-push type, employers, especially large corporations, raise the prices of their goods to get higher profits and then the labor unions demand higher wages, which they get, thus causing a spiral as prices are raised again and wages are raised again in a continuing process. In a wage-push type, the labor unions get higher wages and then the employers raise the prices of their goods, justifying the rise in prices on the basis of the higher wages that they have to pay, also setting off a spiral of rising prices. The monopolistic elements in this type of inflation are the power bases represented by the large corporations and the labor unions.

Owing to the existence of a cost-push inflation, wage-price controls had to be imposed in the United States on August 15, 1971. A 90-day freeze was placed on all wages and prices (with the exception of prices on raw agricultural commodities). Gradually, the wage-price controls were phased out.

Other types of inflations that are also recognized and that render monetary policy very ineffective are the commodity-type and structural-type.

The commodity-type occurs when the price of a particular commodity is raised. A case in point is the raising of the price of oil by the oil cartel OPEC (the Organization of Petroleum Exporting Countries).

The structural-type is where psychological and institutional changes take place in an economy that become embedded in the very structure of the society. Those who hold that such an inflation exists in the United States point to such changes as growing fragmentation of the American society into numerous competing factions, each seeking to increase its relative share of income; changes in the age-sex composition of the labor force, with more young workers and women entering the labor force; growing pressure by workers, in general, for higher wages; and a shift toward service industries.

The Keynesians accept the existence of these various types of inflations and call for government intervention, when necessary, to deal with them through the use of fiscal and monetary policies and wage-price controls. The monetarists hold that an inflation is primarily a monetary phenomenon that can be controlled by proper monetary policy, particularly regulation of the money supply. Monetarists accept that there is a demand-pull type of inflation but do not accept that a cost-push type can exist and that the other types bring in non-economic factors.

A group known as the institutional economists accept that the different types of inflations do indeed exist, but they place great emphasis on the structural-type, which they believe presently exists in the United States to a high degree. Thus, whereas the Keynesians favor wage-price controls and government intervention when necessary and the monetarists oppose wage-price controls and want any government intervention to be kept at a bare minimum, the institutional economists believe that more radical solutions are necessary to control the present inflation and especially the inflation plus recession than those proposed by the Keynesians and monetarists. Rather than merely having government intervention, the institutionalists call for a broad range of government planning. Some notable institutional economists are John Kenneth Galbraith and Gunnar Myrdal, Nobel Prize-winner in Economics in 1974.

## The Prime Rate

The prime rate is the rate which commercial banks charge their most credit-worthy (or "prime") customers when they borrow money. Other

**FIGURE 5-12**

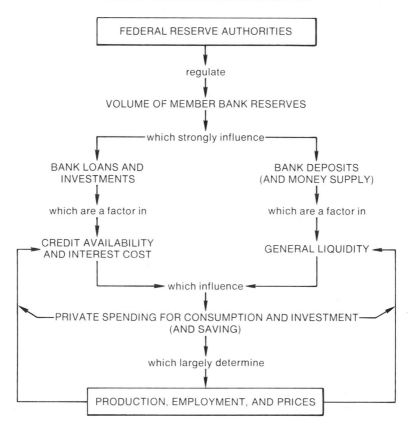

FLOW OF FEDERAL RESERVE INFLUENCE

*Source:* Board of Governors of the Federal Reserve System, *The Federal Reserve System: Purposes and Functions,* Fifth Edition (November 1967), p. 129.

borrowers are charged rates above the prime rate. Bank loan rates are arranged separately with each customer and depend upon many factors (e.g., compensating balances, additional lines of credit). However, the Federal Reserve can exert pressure on the movement of the prime rate, as was especially seen in late 1974 and early 1975.

The prime rate was formally established by the banking community for the first time in the 1930s as a "floor rate" to prevent competition from driving rates too low (i.e., below the administrative and servicing costs associated with bank loans).

During the Great Depression, business activity came to a virtual standstill, and the demand for business loans was negligible. With banks flush with reserves and lending capacity, interest rates were forced to extremely low levels. Fearing that some banks might be willing to make loans at or below cost for the short term, many banks felt that a uniform minimum lending rate would be appropriate.

Thus, the prime rate emerged at 1 ½ % and stayed there until 1947.

After 1947, the prime rate was changed more frequently, especially during the 1950s and the second half of the 1960s. The prime rate, however, usually lagged behind credit market and economic conditions. It, for example, did not move the way the U.S. Treasury bill rate did (i.e., responding on a day-to-day basis in response to changes in supply and demand conditions).[9]

As a result, in the fall of 1971, a few large commercial banks adopted a floating prime rate in order to make bank loan rates more responsive to the cost of attracting additional funds and remove the loan rates from the political arena. This was done after a testing period by three large New York banks, after credit conditions had eased in the second half of 1970 and 1971. In October 1971, First National City Bank of New York, the country's second largest commercial bank, adopted a floating prime rate.

The floating prime rate, in general, was tied to the commercial paper rate, although the CD rate has also been used.

Banks on the floating prime rate use a definite formula, but they have not always gone along with the calculated prime rate for various reasons. A case in point took place in April 1975 when First National City Bank, the second largest bank in the United States, changed its own prime rate formula in order not to bring down its prime rate to 7%. As a result, it kept its prime rate at 7 ¼ %.

First National City Bank felt obliged to do this because its main banking competitors had prime rates at 7 ½ %.

## U.S. BANKING SYSTEM

In a rigorous sense, the banking system consists only of commercial banks. There are about 14,000 commercial banks in the United States.

Commercial banks are organized to make a profit, just like other business enterprises. They differ from other business and financial enterprises by virtue of the fact that they are permitted by law to operate checking accounts (also referred to as "demand deposits"). By means of checking accounts, commercial banks, operating as a system, can create money. This ability to create money on the part of commercial banks represents great economic power.

[9]Philip H. Davidson, "Floating the Prime Rate," Federal Reserve Bank of Richmond, *Monthly Review* (August 1972), pp. 10-14.

The largest component, by far, of the U.S. money stock is checking accounts. The remainder consists of paper currency and coins in the hands of the public. The U.S. money stock is what is usually referred to as the money supply of the United States.

Two commercial banking systems operate within the United States, the national banks and the state banks.

Three Federal agencies actively and directly engage in supervision over commercial banks: The Office of Comptroller of the Currency, the Federal Deposit Insurance Corporation (FDIC), and the Federal Reserve System.

The Office of the Comptroller of the Currency is a bureau of the U.S. Treasury Department established in 1863. It has charter and supervisory authority with respect to the national banks.

The Federal Reserve System, just discussed in this chapter, has supervisory authority with respect to all its members and all bank holding companies. In practice, it confines its field examinations to state-member banks and whenever practicable, it makes such examinations jointly with state supervisory authorities.

The Federal Deposit Insurance Corporation, established in 1933, has supervisory authority in connection with its responsibility to insure deposits of banks that are members of the Federal Reserve System and other banks that voluntarily become insured by the FDIC (and savings banks also called "mutual savings banks"). In practice, the FDIC generally examines those insured banks that are not subject to examination by another Federal supervisory agency. The FDIC is primarily concerned with insuring deposits (up to a maximum of $40,000), but it also seeks to prevent bank failures.

## Bank Holding Companies

The past few years have seen an increase in the number of bank holding companies and their domination of the U.S. banking system. There has been a substantial increase in the number of financially related fields that bank holding companies have moved into. In addition, the bank holding companies have moved into nonbank activities.

During 1974, a reduction in bank holding company activity took place as a result of a definite policy of the Board of Governors of the Federal Reserve System. The Board of Governors has the responsibility of regulating the bank holding companies and has to determine which nonbank activities are "closely related to banking" as specified in Section 4 (c) (8) of the 1970 Amendments to the Bank Holding Company Act.

As 1973 opened, the Board had approved 16 general classes of nonbank activities as being permissible for bank holding companies, had denied seven specific activities, and was still weighing the merits of five activities.

In late 1973 and early 1974, three of the "pending" activities were added to the permissible list (see Figure 5-13).[10]

## International Banking

By the end of 1973, approximately 140 U.S. banks had established themselves in 150 foreign countries by means of branches or subsidiaries. Meanwhile, by the end of 1973, 168 foreign banks from 38 countries had penetrated the U.S. market. Total assets in the United States of foreign banking organizations exceeded $50 billion by the middle of 1974.[11]

As a result of the expansion of U.S. banks into foreign countries and foreign banks into the United States, the Board of Governors of the Federal Reserve System created the steering Committee on International Banking Regulation in February 1973.

The Board of Governors is the main U.S. agency involved in regulating the international operations of U.S. banking organizations. The Board's statutory authority comes from

Section 25 of the Federal Reserve Act as amended in 1916, 1962 and 1966.

Section 25 (a) of the Federal Reserve Act (added in 1919 and also known as the "Edge Act")

The Bank Holding Company Act of 1956 as amended in 1970

(See Figure 5-14 for the organizational structure of U.S. banks and their affiliates overseas.)

[10]Harvey Rosenblum, "Bank holding company review 1973/74—Part 1," Federal Reserve Bank of Chicago, *Business Conditions* (February 1975), pp. 3-10.

[11]Allen Frankel, "International banking," Federal Reserve Bank of Chicago, *Business Conditions* (October 1974), pp. 3-11.

**FIGURE 5-13**

### Activities APPROVED by the Board

1. Dealer in bankers' acceptances
2. Mortgage company
3. Finance company
4. Credit card company
5. Factoring company
6. Operating an industrial bank
7. Servicing loans
8. Trust company
9. Adviser to real estate investment trusts and other investment companies
10. General economic information and advice
11. Portfolio investment advice
12. Full pay-out leasing of personal property
13. Full pay-out leasing of real property
14. Community welfare investments
15. Bookkeeping and data processing services
16. Insurance agent or broker in connection with credit extensions
17. Underwriting credit life and credit accident and health insurance
18. Courier service
19. Management consulting to nonaffiliated banks
20. Sale of travelers checks
21. Bullion broker

### Activities DENIED by the Board

1. Equity funding (combined sale of mutual funds and insurance)
2. Underwriting general life insurance
3. Real estate brokerage
4. Land development
5. Real estate syndication
6. General management consulting
7. Property management

### Activities UNDER CONSIDERATION by the Board

1. Armored car services
2. Mortgage guarantee insurance
3. Savings and loan associations
4. Travel agencies
5. Underwriting and dealing in U.S. Government and certain municipal securities

*Source:* Federal Reserve Bank of Chicago, *Business Conditions* (February 1975).

**FIGURE 5-14**

**ORGANIZATIONAL STRUCTURE OF U.S. BANKS AND THEIR AFFILIATES OVERSEAS**

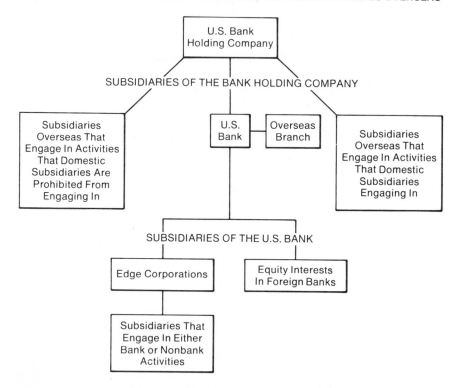

*Source:* Federal Reserve Bank of Chicago, *Business Conditions* (October 1974).

# the federal funds market

A

If you are interested in buying stocks, bonds, money market instruments, gold or silver, then the Federal funds market is of great importance to you. The Federal funds market is also of great importance to you if you want to buy a car, buy a home, buy land, if you want to take out a loan, or if you are simply concerned about just how far you will be able to stretch your dollar at the local supermarket.

It is unfortunate, however, that most people do not know about the Federal funds market and, especially, the Federal funds rate.

Federal funds are excess reserves which one commercial bank has available to lend to another commercial bank. Member banks of the Federal Reserve System (e.g., Bank of America, First National City Bank, Chase Manhattan, Manufacturers Hanover Trust, Morgan Guaranty Trust Company, and many other large commercial banks) are required to maintain deposits (reserves) at Federal Reserve Banks. They have to maintain the legal reserve requirement.

The small rural commercial banks usually have excess reserves, while the big city commercial banks usually need additional reserves to have the required amount. The big city banks, therefore, often borrow reserves from the small rural banks. This gives rise to the important Federal funds rate, i.e., the interest rate charged for these excess reserves.

It is the Federal funds rate that you should watch very carefully, by reading various newspapers (e.g., *The New York Times, The Wall Street Journal,* and *The Washington Post*).

The movement of the Federal funds rate will give you an indication of which way other interest rates can be expected to move. For example, if the Federal funds rate is moving sharply downward, the other money market rates can be expected to move sharply downward and to also bring down bond rates, mortgage rates, personal loan rates, and other rates. Such a decline in interest rates can then be expected to cause the stock market to rise (but not every single stock!). A sharp rise in the Federal funds rate can be expected to have the reverse effect.

Don't expect the changes in rates to happen immediately. You should realize that there is nothing preordained about the effects. What the Federal funds rate does give you, however, is a guideline, one more relevant than the highly publicized "prime rate."

Being aware of the Federal funds rate also gives you insight into monetary policy, which is set by the Federal Reserve System. Monetary policy affects you directly in your pocketbook and wallet. It affects the value of your dollar.

The Federal Reserve System, for example, exerted strong pressure to bring down the Federal funds rate in the second half of 1974 and into early 1975, in order to prevent the recession from becoming worse. In the first quarter of 1975, the stock market rose.

This appendix should give you an understanding of the highly important Federal funds market and Federal funds rate. The basic definitions in the question-and-answer section are followed by an in-depth discussion of these topics.

## THE FEDERAL FUNDS MARKET

*Why is the Federal funds market important?*

The Federal funds market is important because it lies at the very heart of the money market and the commercial banking system. It gives rise to the Federal funds rate, which is a highly sensitive indicator for the overall money market, monetary policy, and the overall economy. Federal funds are, in fact, often referred to as "high-powered money."

*What are Federal funds?*

The original definition of the term "Federal funds" referred strictly to funds maintained on deposit by member banks of the Federal Reserve System at Federal Reserve Banks. Over the years, however, its meaning has changed, as is explained in the following pages.

*What economic functions does the Federal funds rate serve?*

It adds precision to monetary policy and provides increased efficiency to the commercial banking system for borrowers and depositors.

*How does the Federal funds rate react to monetary policies?*

It generally moves to the low end of the money market rates during periods of "easy-money" policies and generally moves to the high end of money market rates during periods of "tight-money" policies.

*What are the basic types of Federal funds transactions?*

There are three basic types of Federal funds transactions:

1. "Straight" transactions, in which there is a purchase and sale of Federal funds on an unsecured overnight basis between commercial banks.
2. Secured transactions, in which the borrower (or buyer) of Federal funds provides collateral for the loan.
3. Repurchase agreements, in which the borrowing (or buying) bank obtains the Federal funds by selling securities to the lending bank and repays the loan on the following day by repurchasing the securities, usually at the same price plus interest at a rate stated in a contract (some repurchase agreements are made for more than one business day).

*On what does the Federal funds rate depend?*

The Federal funds rate depends on supply and demand in the marketplace.

*Why does the Federal funds rate generally fluctuate more widely than other money market rates?*

The Federal funds rate generally fluctuates more widely than other money market rates because, as a result of the legal reserve requirment set by the Federal Reserve System for its member banks, the reserve requirements must be met on a daily average basis over the statement week. The period runs from Thursday to Wednesday. The legal reserves are cash funds, which do not earn money for the bank. Banks hold on to excess reserves during the first part of the reserve period and release them to the market o.ily when it is made obvious that they are not necessary. As a result, the Federal funds rate generally breaks sharply on Wednesday as the banks close out their reserve settlement period. During periods when a "tight-money" policy is pursued by the Federal Reserve System, banks tend to hold on even longer to excess reserve than during periods of an "easy-money" policy.

(See the rest of this chapter, and Chapter 5 on the Federal Reserve System and the U.S. Banking System for additional explanation of this highly important area.)

## INFORMATION IN DEPTH

### Background

The Federal funds market was initiated in New York City in 1921. It developed as a response to the growth of the regulatory network of the Federal Reserve System. The Federal Reserve Act of 1913, establishing the Federal Reserve System, had stipulated that member banks of the Federal Reserve System would have to maintain reserve requirements and required member banks to keep account balances at the Federal Reserve Banks in order to meet the reserve requirements, at least partially.

The initial trading in Federal funds by New York City banks rapidly led to such trading by large banks throughout the United States. Fed by the climate of the "Roaring Twenties" and its frenetic period of investment, the Federal funds market grew in size and importance. U.S. government securities dealers began to participate in the Federal funds market.

After the stock market crash of 1929, however, trading in Federal funds sharply declined and remained low during the Great Depression of the 1930s as the banks built up large excess reserves. The Federal funds market continued at a low level during the Second World War, as the Federal Reserve System helped finance the war by standing ready to buy U.S. government securities at fixed prices. Commercial banks during the 1940s, in general, had a strong preference for making reserve adjustments by trading in U.S. government securities rather than Federal funds. Government securities were preferred because the Federal Reserve System held to practices which eliminated the risks of market losses.

Starting with 1951, significant activity in the Federal funds market began once again. Nevertheless, the estimated average daily volume in 1955 was still less than $2 billion. In the 1960s, however, the net volume of funds purchased daily increased more than five-fold. As the Federal funds market took on added significance in the commercial banks' mobilization of financial resources for economic activity, volume in Federal funds transactions continued to grow. From a volume of less than $17 billion at the end of 1970, purchases of Federal funds by commercial banks more than tripled by the end of 1973, reaching over $50 billion.

## Terminology

Although a sale of Federal funds is clearly in the nature of a loan, the terms "purchase" (or "buy") and "sell" are often used instead of the terms "borrow" and "lend." Usage of the terms "purchase" and "sell" stems from the pracice in the early days of the market for the borrowing bank to pay for funds at the time of the borrowing with a check that would be sent to a clearinghouse and paid to the lender on the next day. This arrangement for immediate payment gave the transaction the character of a purchase and sale.

In 1963, this terminology of "purchase" and "sale" was given official recognition when the Comptroller of the Currency, in a controversial ruling, declared that a Federal funds transaction does not create an obligation subject to bank borrowing and lending limits and should be considered a purchase and sale of funds.

## Bank Reserves

Reserves held by member banks at the Federal Banks are deposit balances (or working balances) through which various transactions, such as the clearing of checks, are channeled. When a bank has a greater value of checks written on its deposits than the value of checks deposited with it (written on other banks), it draws on its reserve account in order to pay the difference.

The Federal Reserve System requires member banks to maintain a specified amount of reserves for each weekly reporting period. This period runs from Thursday to Wednesday, and the amount of reserves is called the "legal reserve requirement." The legal reserve requirement equals a specific percentage of checking deposits, and the percentage is set by the Federal Reserve. It is by this means that the monetary authorities at the Federal Reserve apply one of their very important monetary tools for controlling the money supply of their member banks and to a large extent the national banking system.

A member bank which holds reserves that barely meet the legal reserve requirement is in danger of falling below the required reserve limit if there is an unexpected deposit outflow.

## The Changing Meaning of Federal Funds and the Federal Funds Market

The term "Federal funds" originally referred strictly to Federal Reserve Bank funds (i.e., Federal Reserve member bank deposits at Federal Reserve Banks).

Thus, Federal funds are often referred to as "high-powered money," because checks written against member bank deposits are accepted by member banks for immediate payment. A recipient of a Federal funds check can go to a commercial bank and obtain his money immediately. This differs from a regular check or any check drawn on a commercial bank which requires clearing, which can take one day or more. As a result, a person with a check drawn on a commercial bank may not get immediate payment, and a loss of interest of a day or more can be expected.

During the past few years, however, another type of market has developed which is also referred to as a "Federal funds market." In this market, the emphasis is strictly on "immediately available funds." Member bank deposits at Federal Reserve banks are not involved. A nonmember bank of the Federal Reserve System can, for example, lend money to a correspondent bank with which it has an account, and these funds are immediately available to the borrowing bank from the lender's correspondent account. An individual or a corporation can also lend immediately available funds to a bank where it has funds on deposit by purchasing short-term U.S. government or U.S. government agency securities under a repurchase agreement. In these cases, the money is immediately available to the borrower because the money is already on deposit in the lender's account at the borrowing bank.

The original type of Federal funds and the newer type of "immediately available funds" are both referred to more and more as "Federal funds."

Instructions to national banks and state banks, which are members of the Federal Reserve System, direct these banks, in filling out the "Report of Condition," to include both types as "Federal funds." Both types trade at, or close to, the same rate of interest.

## Management of Reserves

A member bank running a deficiency of reserves has several courses of action open to it in order to rectify that deficiency. It can:

Sell assets (e.g., U.S. Treasury bills).
Borrow reserves at the Federal Reserve System's "discount window."
Use the Federal funds market to borrow (or purchase) the necessary amount.

In deciding upon its course of action, a bank has to consider the expense of each alternative.

Thus, the selling of assets can often be quite expensive. Whatever the particular asset involved, this is generally an awkward method for meeting day-to-day changes.

Borrowing reserves from the Federal Reserve System's "discount window" can often be undesirable because it subjects the member bank (only member banks can use the discount window) to greater scrutiny by the Federal Reserve administrators. The Federal Reserve frowns upon excessive use of the discount window.

The "Federal funds market" is an interbank loan market based on the fact that the outflow of deposits and reserves is generally matched by an equal inflow of deposits and reserves at some other bank. The change in the reserve positions can, therefore, be eliminated to some extent for both banks. The mechanism of the Federal funds market, as a result, permits the banking system to operate with lower excess reserves, which, in turn, provides the possibility of the depositor getting a higher interest rate or the borrower paying a lower interest charge.

## Market Patterns

The Federal funds market has developed a definite weekly pattern in its rate structure, because of the relationship of the rate structure to the periods in the bank's settlement week. Thus, the settlement week runs from Thursday to Wednesday. A weekly average has to be maintained. Studies show that in the early part of the settlement week, the Federal funds rate tends to be fairly stable and slightly above the weekly average. In the latter part of the settlement week (Tuesday and Wednesday), however, the Federal funds rate becomes more volatile and on the average declines from the higher levels in the early part of the settlement week, as can be seen in the accompanying graph in Figure A-1.

FIGURE A-1

# The federal funds rate tends to be higher early in the week, declining as the week progresses.

### daily rate as percent of weekly average

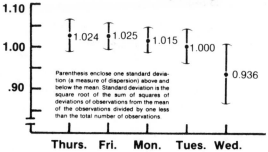

Parenthesis enclose one standard deviation (a measure of dispersion) above and below the mean. Standard deviation is the square root of the sum of squares of deviations of observations from the mean of the observations divided by one less than the total number of observations.

Data from Federal Reserve Bank of New York, Daily Effective Federal Funds Rate, September 21, 1968-September 11, 1971.

*Source:* Federal Reserve Bank of Chicago, *Business Conditions* (November 1974), p. 5.

Shifts in the Federal funds rate then serve to exert pressure on the other rates in the money markets.

*Market Structure.* The broad structure of the Federal funds market is for the small banks, in general, to be net sellers and the large banks to be net buyers, as can be seen in Table A-1.

TABLE A-1

Large banks tend to be net buyers of federal funds, while small banks are net sellers

| Seventh Federal Reserve District Banks | Average total deposits:[1] 1973 | Average net purchases of federal[2] funds: 1973 |
|---|---|---|
| | *(millions)* | *(millions)* |
| 8 money market banks | 3539.89 | 249.15 |
| 45 other weekly reporting banks | 433.57 | 12.86 |
| 880 other district member banks | 32.26 | 1.08 |

[1]Data from June 1973 and December 1973 call reports.
[2]Data from Federal Reserve Bank of Chicago for 1973.
*Source:* Federal Reserve Bank of Chicago, *Business Conditions* (November 1974), p. 6.

*Federal Funds Rate and Other Rates.* Figure A-2 shows a comparison of the Federal funds rate, the three-month Treasury bill market yield, and the discount rate (i.e., the rate which the Federal Reserve charges its member banks).

**FIGURE A-2**

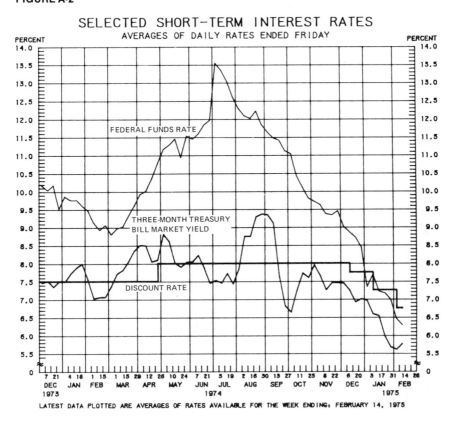

SELECTED SHORT—TERM INTEREST RATES

AVERAGES OF DAILY RATES ENDED FRIDAY

LATEST DATA PLOTTED ARE AVERAGES OF RATES AVAILABLE FOR THE WEEK ENDING: FEBRUARY 14, 1975

*Source:* Federal Reserve Bank of St. Louis.

## Operations of the Federal Funds Market

In order to add depth to an understanding of the Federal funds market, the following detailed study of the Eleventh Federal Reserve District is presented (from Federal Reserve Bank of Dallas, *Business Review,* January 1975, pp. 2-5):

Expansion of the Federal funds market in the Eleventh District has been rapid in terms of both the number of banks participating in the market and the average size of transactions. Where at the end of 1970, fewer than half of the banks in the District sold Federal funds, at the end of 1973, almost 80 percent were selling funds. And while the average amount sold was only $2.2 million at the end of 1970, the average was $3.3 million by the end of 1973.

Despite gains by nonmembers in recent years, fewer nonmember banks participate in the Federal funds market than member banks of comparable size. Moreover, nonmember banks that do participate sell smaller amounts, on average, than member banks.

**TABLE A-2**

**COMMERCIAL BANKS IN THE FEDERAL FUNDS MARKET**

Eleventh Federal Reserve District

(End-of-year figures)

| Bank deposit size (Million dollars) | Total number of District banks | | Percent of banks | | | |
|---|---|---|---|---|---|---|
| | | | Selling Federal funds | | Buying Federal funds | |
| | 1970 | 1973 | 1970 | 1973 | 1970 | 1973 |
| **Member banks** | | | | | | |
| $500 or more ... | 6 | 9 | 83.3% | 100.0% | 100.0% | 100.0% |
| $100 to $499 .... | 33 | 40 | 90.9 | 90.0 | 90.9 | 95.0 |
| $50 to $99 ..... | 28 | 41 | 75.0 | 75.6 | 53.6 | 61.0 |
| $10 to $49 ..... | 241 | 334 | 64.7 | 82.3 | 7.5 | 11.7 |
| Less than $10 ... | 326 | 218 | 54.9 | 80.7 | 2.5 | 4.1 |
| All sizes ..... | 634 | 642 | 61.7 | 82.1 | 12.1 | 18.7 |
| **Nonmember banks** | | | | | | |
| $500 or more ... | 0 | 0 | — | — | — | — |
| $100 to $499 .... | 1 | 8 | 100.0 | 75.0 | .0 | 75.0 |
| $50 to $99 ..... | 17 | 29 | 70.6 | 69.0 | 5.9 | 20.7 |
| $10 to $49 ..... | 217 | 332 | 51.6 | 76.5 | 2.3 | 10.2 |
| Less than $10 ... | 464 | 410 | 38.6 | 74.1 | 1.7 | 3.9 |
| All sizes ..... | 699 | 779 | 43.5 | 75.0 | 2.0 | 8.0 |
| **All banks** | | | | | | |
| $500 or more ... | 6 | 9 | 83.3 | 100.0 | 100.0 | 100.0 |
| $100 to $499 .... | 34 | 48 | 91.2 | 87.5 | 88.2 | 91.7 |
| $50 to $99 ..... | 45 | 70 | 73.3 | 72.8 | 35.5 | 44.3 |
| $10 to $49 ..... | ʹ458 | 666 | 58.5 | 79.4 | 5.0 | 11.0 |
| Less than $10 ... | 790 | 628 | 45.3 | 76.4 | 2.0 | 4.0 |
| All sizes ..... | 1,333 | 1,421 | 46.7% | 78.2% | 6.1% | 12.8% |

*Source:* Federal Deposit Insurance Corporation and Federal Reserve Bank of Dallas.

Only member banks, of course, maintain balances of immediately available funds at Federal Reserve banks—balances that can be transferred directly to the account of any other member bank in the nation. Nonmember bank participation, however, is limited to banks at which they have correspondent balances.

*Small-bank participation.*    The sharp rise in the Federal funds rate in recent years is partly responsible for the rapid growth in sales. Transactions that were not worthwhile at 4 or 5 percent in 1971 and 1972 became profitable when the rate paid on Federal funds rose sharply higher—to a level as high as 10 percent in 1973.

The higher yields on Federal funds sales were especially important in increasing the participation of small banks. Until recent years, transactions of less than $1 million were rare. And as long as transactions were large, most small banks were excluded from the market.

The rise in interest rates, however, made smaller transactions profitable, allowing small banks to participate. With more attractive yields and the development of convenient trading arrangements between correspondent banks, transactions of less than $100,000 became so commonplace that even the smallest banks sell funds.

As a result, the proportion of banks with less than $10 million in deposits that sell Federal funds has increased markedly—rising from 55 percent in 1970 to more than 80 percent in 1973. During that time, the proportion of participating banks with $10 million to $50 million in deposits increased from 65 percent to 82 percent.

Once participation became feasible, small banks became an important source of funds in the market. Since loans and deposits of small banks, particularly in agricultural areas, are subject to strong seasonal pressures, small banks hold a large part of their assets in readily marketable form.

As small transactions in Federal funds became feasible, small banks were able to substitute Federal funds sales for some of the other assets they had been holding as secondary reserves. By the end of 1973, banks with less than $50 million in deposits held only 27 percent of their assets in cash, deposits at other banks, and Government agency securities, compared with 32 percent at the end of 1970.

*Large-bank domination.* Large banks still dominate the Federal funds market in the Eleventh District. And their influence is growing, despite increased participation by small banks.

At the end of 1970, six banks in the District held deposits of more than $500 million. Together, they accounted for about 37 percent of the Federal funds sold in the District and more than 75 percent of the funds purchased.

By the end of 1973, there were nine banks that size. But even though these banks held only a fourth of the total deposits in the District, they accounted for almost two-thirds of the Federal funds sales and four-fifths of the purchases in the District.

*Participation by others.* In late 1969 and early 1970, a growing number of banks began making participation in the Federal funds market available to business corporations. To limit this practice, the Board of Governors of the Federal Reserve System expanded the definition of deposits to include most short-term borrowings by member banks.

To ascertain dollar amounts of reserve requirements and administer the ceilings on rate banks could pay on specified types of liabilities, the Board redefined deposits in 1970 to include "a member bank's liability on any promissory note, acknowledgment of advance, due bill, or similar obligation (written or oral) that is issued or undertaken by a member bank principally as a means of obtaining funds to be used in its banking business."

This amendment to Federal Reserve regulations would have effectively ended the Federal funds market by subjecting all short-term borrowing to reserve requirements and interest rate ceilings. But important exceptions to this reclassification allowed wide participation in the market to continue.

TABLE A-3

## SALES OF FEDERAL FUNDS BY COMMERCIAL BANKS

Eleventh Federal Reserve District

(End-of-year figures. Million dollars)

| Bank deposit size (Million dollars) | Total sales | | | | Average sales | | | |
|---|---|---|---|---|---|---|---|---|
| | 1970 | 1971 | 1972 | 1973 | 1970 | 1971 | 1972 | 1973 |
| **Member banks** | | | | | | | | |
| $500 or more | $551 | $966 | $1,050 | $1,366 | $110.1 | $120.7 | $131.3 | $151.8 |
| $100 to $499 | 325 | 331 | 476 | 699 | 10.8 | 10.6 | 15.3 | 19.4 |
| $50 to $99 | 65 | 93 | 143 | 183 | 3.1 | 4.0 | 4.3 | 5.9 |
| $10 to $49 | 214 | 260 | 368 | 513 | 1.4 | 1.4 | 1.6 | 1.9 |
| Less than $10 | 98 | 92 | 104 | 141 | .5 | .6 | .6 | .8 |
| All sizes | 1,252 | 1,742 | 2,141 | 2,902 | 3.2 | 4.2 | 4.4 | 5.5 |
| **Nonmember banks** | | | | | | | | |
| $500 or more | 0 | 0 | 0 | 0 | — | — | — | — |
| $100 to $499 | 5 | 32 | 42 | 86 | 5.0 | 10.5 | 7.0 | 14.4 |
| $50 to $99 | 43 | 47 | 60 | 104 | 3.6 | 4.2 | 3.8 | 5.2 |
| $10 to $49 | 134 | 209 | 255 | 406 | 1.2 | 1.3 | 1.4 | 1.6 |
| Less than $10 | 70 | 100 | 129 | 191 | .4 | .5 | .5 | .6 |
| All sizes | 251 | 388 | 486 | 786 | .8 | 1.0 | 1.1 | 1.3 |
| **All banks** | | | | | | | | |
| $500 or more | 551 | 966 | 1,050 | 1,366 | 110.1 | 120.7 | 131.3 | 151.8 |
| $100 to $499 | 330 | 362 | 518 | 785 | 10.6 | 10.7 | 13.9 | 18.7 |
| $50 to $99 | 108 | 140 | 203 | 287 | 3.3 | 4.1 | 4.1 | 5.6 |
| $10 to $49 | 347 | 469 | 623 | 919 | 1.3 | 1.4 | 1.5 | 1.7 |
| Less than $10 | 168 | 193 | 233 | 332 | .5 | .5 | .5 | .7 |
| All sizes | $1,503 | $2,130 | $2,627 | $3,689 | $2.2 | $2.7 | $2.8 | $3.3 |

NOTE: Details may not add to totals because of rounding.

*Source:* Federal Deposit Insurance Corporation and Federal Reserve Bank of Dallas.

**TABLE A-4**

## PURCHASES OF FEDERAL FUNDS BY COMMERCIAL BANKS

Eleventh Federal Reserve District

(End-of-year figures. Million dollars)

| Bank deposit size (Million dollars) | Total purchases | | | | Average purchases | | | |
|---|---|---|---|---|---|---|---|---|
| | 1970 | 1971 | 1972 | 1973 | 1970 | 1971 | 1972 | 1973 |
| **Member banks** | | | | | | | | |
| $500 or more | $989 | $1,453 | $2,001 | $2,778 | $164.8 | $181.6 | $250.0 | $308.7 |
| $100 to $499 | 276 | 316 | 433 | 581 | 9.2 | 9.6 | 12.7 | 15.3 |
| $50 to $99 | 19 | 25 | 46 | 52 | 1.2 | 1.6 | 2.4 | 2.1 |
| $10 to $49 | 12 | 13 | 31 | 35 | .7 | .5 | 1.0 | .9 |
| Less than $10 | 2 | 1 | 1 | 2 | .3 | .2 | .3 | .2 |
| All sizes | 1,298 | 1,808 | 2,512 | 3,449 | 16.9 | 20.8 | 25.9 | 28.7 |
| **Nonmember banks** | | | | | | | | |
| $500 or more | 0 | 0 | 0 | 0 | — | — | — | — |
| $100 to $499 | 0 | 5 | 8 | 33 | — | 2.7 | 2.8 | 5.5 |
| $50 to $99 | 6 | 4 | 13 | 23 | 6.4 | 1.1 | 3.3 | 3.9 |
| $10 to $49 | 2 | 17 | 13 | 25 | .5 | .8 | .6 | .7 |
| Less than $10 | 3 | 2 | 5 | 5 | .4 | .2 | .4 | .3 |
| All sizes | 12 | 28 | 40 | 86 | .9 | .8 | 1.0 | 1.4 |
| **All banks** | | | | | | | | |
| $500 or more | 989 | 1,453 | 2,001 | 2,778 | 164.8 | 181.6 | 250.1 | 308.7 |
| $100 to $499 | 276 | 321 | 442 | 614 | 9.2 | 9.2 | 11.9 | 13.9 |
| $50 to $99 | 25 | 29 | 59 | 75 | 1.6 | 1.5 | 2.5 | 2.4 |
| $10 to $49 | 14 | 29 | 44 | 60 | .6 | .7 | .8 | .8 |
| Less than $10 | 6 | 3 | 6 | 7 | .4 | .2 | .4 | .3 |
| All sizes | $1,310 | $1,836 | $2,551 | $3,535 | $14.4 | $14.9 | $18.6 | $19.4 |

NOTE: Details may not add to totals because of rounding.

*Source:* Federal Deposit Insurance Corporation and Federal Reserve Bank of Dallas.

One exception kept the market open for borrowing and lending between "banks"—broadly defined to include not only commercial banks (member and nonmember) but also savings banks, savings and loan associations, cooperative banks, foreign banks, and certain bank subsidiaries.

Another exception allowed banks to borrow through the use of repurchase agreements involving "direct obligations of, or obligations that are fully guaranteed as to principal and interest by, the United States or any agency thereof that the bank is obligated to repurchase." This exclusion of repurchase agreements on Government and agency securities kept the Federal funds market available to nonbank investors.

While sources other than commercial banks probably supply only a small part of the Federal funds sold to banks in the Eleventh District, participation by nonbank investors is more extensive in major financial centers. This is especially true in New York, where many large corporations with the resources and expertise needed to participate in the market maintain their national offices and do most of their banking.

At the end of 1973, commercial banks in the United States reported net borrowing of almost $16 billion through Federal funds purchases and sales of securities under repurchase agreements. Thus, almost a third of the total Federal funds volume of $51.2 billion originated at sources other than commercial banks.

*Redistribution of reserves.*    The Federal funds market facilitates the distribution of reserves among banks, contributing to the efficient allocation of bank credit. This mobilization of reserves is particularly important in Texas, which, like other unit-banking states, is characterized by a large number of small banks. Texas has over 1,400 banks. Of these, more than 90 percent have less than $50 million in deposits and almost half have deposits less than $10 million.

There are, of course, practical limits to the lending capacity of small banks. But there are also legal restrictions on the lending of most banks. National banks are not allowed to lend any one borrower an amount that is more than 10 percent of the bank's capital stock plus its unimpaired surplus.

Because of capacity and legal limitations, even large banks in the Eleventh District have indicated they cannot meet all the banking needs of their largest corporate customers. The Federal funds market provides one mechanism for large banks in financial centers across the country to gain access to the resources of a large number of small banks. And as funds sold in the market earn competitive rates of interest, the market, in effect, gives the small banks a share of the income earned from the eventual use to which these funds are put.

Net purchases and sales of participating banks give an indication of the impact of the market on the final distribution of funds. Net purchases in the Eleventh District are highly concentrated. At the end of 1973, more than 180 banks purchased Federal funds but only half of them purchased more than they sold. And the five largest banks accounted for 87 percent of the net purchases.

Conversely, net sales were widely dispersed. Nearly 1,100 banks in the District were net sellers. Most of them were small. About 1,000 banks with deposits less than $50 million accounted for two-thirds of the net sales by banks in the District.

# the Eurodollar market
# and the
# Eurocurrency market

# B

If you are interested in buying gold or silver as an investment, what goes on in the Eurodollar market and the broader Eurocurrency market should be of concern to you. If you are interested in alternative forms of investment (e.g., U.S. Treasury bills, U.S. Treasury notes, certificates of deposit, commercial paper, bankers' acceptances, U.S. government agency securities, U.S. government-sponsored agency securities, stocks, and bonds), developments in the Eurodollar market and overall Eurocurrency market should again be of concern to you.

Developments in these markets can have profound effects on interest rates, on inflationary trends, and on recessionary trends. Such effects should be of great concern to you if you are considering investing in gold, silver, money market instruments, stocks, bonds, or other investment vehicles. Such effects should, in fact, be of great concern to you not only as an investor, but as a consumer, employee, and employer.

Actual trading in the Eurodollar market and the overall Eurocurrency market is appealing because of the generally higher yields it offers, as compared to other interest-bearing securities and savings accounts. The emphasis is on yield and not on liquidity. Trading is for the highly sophisticated investor and for those with great wealth. The usual trading unit is one million units of a currency (e.g., one million U.S. dollars).

The financial press regularly reports on developments in these markets, and building up an understanding of these markets will give you a new perspective on money matters, whether or not you actually engage in trading. Such understanding will broaden your scope on the significance of money and add precision to your comprehension of monetary policy and economic developments.

The Eurodollar market is part of a broader market known as the Eurocurrency market, but it is the Eurodollar market that has become particularly important for investors, borrowers, and lenders on a truly international level. The Eurodollar market has special significance for the multinational banks, multinational corporations (MNCs), holders of petrodollars (especially the Arab oil countries), and other holders of great wealth.

The overall Eurocurrency market has grown enormously since its inception, as has the Eurodollar market. From less than $1 billion at the end of the 1950s, the overall Eurocurrency market grew to an estimated net size of approximately $220 billion at the end of 1974. It is extremely difficult to know just how large the markets really are because most transactions are conducted privately over the telephone or by cable. The Bank for International Settlements (BIS) makes estimates of the size of the market.

The Eurocurrency market lies in both the money and capital markets. Thus, the Eurodollar short-term market is referred to as the "Eurodollar money market," while the Eurodollar capital market (i.e., medium-term and long-term) is referred to as the "Eurobond market."

## WHAT ARE EURODOLLARS?

Eurodollars are deposits denominated in U.S. dollars which are placed with commercial banks outside the United States, including deposits at foreign branches of U.S. commercial banks.[12]

> U.S. citizens transfer their dollar deposits (i.e., demand deposits or checking account balances) in U.S. banks to foreign banks.
>
> Foreign holders of U.S. dollar-deposits at U.S. banks transfer their deposits to foreign banks.
>
> Foreigners, receiving payments drawn on accounts at U.S. banks, deposit the dollars in banks in their countries.
>
> Holders of convertible currencies (e.g., West German marks) exchange them for U.S. dollars and deposit them in a foreign bank.

### Early Practice

The Eurodollar market is only part of the broader Eurocurrency market. There are many foreign-currency-denominated deposits loaned and

---

[12]Federal Reserve Bank of Chicago, *Business Conditions* (June 1969), p. 9.

borrowed by banks and corporations throughout the world. Actually, the currency of any country can become a Eurocurrency if it is freely convertible into the world's major currencies.

Thus, there are deposits denominated in British pound sterling (Eurosterling), West German marks (Euromarks), Belgian francs (Eurofrancs Belgian), French francs (Eurofrancs French), Swiss francs (Eurofrancs Swiss), Japanese yens (Euroyens), and others. They are held and traded by banks outside the countries in which they are national currencies.

The method of operating goes far back in the history of international trade. In the 1920s, deposits denominated in British pounds were common when the British pound was the major currency in international transactions.

The modern type of Eurodollar market, however, did not develop until after the Second World War.

One story regarding the origin of the modern Eurodollar market and its very name has it that many Eastern European countries in the early 1950s decided to transfer their dollar accounts from New York City to the European Continent, in order to avoid attachments and in order to establish lines of dollar credit outside the United States.

A major supplier of dollar deposits to European banks in the early 1950s was the State Bank of the U.S.S.R., which used its Paris affiliate, "Banque Commerciale pour l'Europe du Nord, S.A." whose international cable code was "EUROBANK." The cable code "EUROBANK" also became associated with the dollars of the Eastern European countries and, as a result, the dollars on deposit outside of the United States were given the name "EURODOLLARS."[13,14]

Banks that handled Eurodollars and other Eurocurrencies became known as "Eurobanks." These Eurobanks, however, were not located just in Europe but in many parts of the world.

In 1958, the Eurodollar market greatly expanded as many countries lifted exchange controls. London became the center of the Eurodollar market and overall Eurocurrency market, and many more Eurobanks were formed. Eurodollar market centers developed in Paris, Zürich, Basel, Geneva, Brussels, Amsterdam, Frankfurt, Rome, Vienna, Beirut, Singapore, Nassau (in the Bahamas), and other places. The London banks, however, became the first banks to take advantage of the Eurodollar market and built upon their expertise. As a result, London is still the center of the market.

A dollar shortage developed after the Second World War, as the U.S. dollar became more and more necessary for international transactions.

---

[13]Federal Reserve Bank of Chicago, *Business Conditions* (June 1969), p. 2.
[14]Federal Reserve Bank of Cleveland, *Money Market Instruments* (August 1970), p. 93.

After 1958, however, the shortage clearly changed to a dollar glut (i.e., a surplus of U.S. dollars).

It was the dollar shortage which had laid the basis for the Eurodollar market by encouraging the use of U.S. dollars outside of the United States. The "dollar glut" only served to add to the growth of the Eurodollar market. Thus, foreign residents and financial institutions found that the best place for them to utilize their dollar holdings for financial earning assets was in the U.S. money and capital markets. Still further adding to the value of the U.S. dollar was the fact that it was designated by the International Monetary Fund (IMF) as the "intervention currency." In other words, it became the key international currency when the IMF was first established in 1946.

As a result, under the rules of the IMF, foreign currencies were to be supported in relation to the U.S. dollar. This led to the majority of official business in the foreign exchange market being conducted in terms of the U.S. dollar. Significant moves away from the dollar were the decisions of Iran, Saudi Arabia, Kuwait, and Qatar, in early 1975, to cut the ties of their currencies to the U.S. dollar and, instead, to tie their currencies to SDRs (Special Drawing Rights on the IMF).[15] The Eurodollar market has, in fact, to a large extent, served as the banking system for these countries and the other members of the OPEC (Organization of Petroleum Exporting Countries) cartel.

### Control Over the Eurodollar Market

The Eurodollar market is an international market, and there is no effective supra-national control over its operations.

The market operates primarily on the basis of supply and demand. It responds to actual commercial, economic, and international conditions. Transactions are conducted mainly over the telephone and by cable. Some intervention has at times been exercised by the Federal Reserve System, other central banks, and the Bank for International Settlements (BIS), but it is essentially an unregulated market. In sharp contrast, the U.S. money market is highly regulated.

### Risks

The generally higher returns possible in the Eurodollar market have made it more attractive than the U.S. money markets. However, there are risks. In the financial press, the quoted Eurodollar interest rates are normally deposit rates. The spread of the deposit and loan rates is set at the discretion of the Eurobanks subject to supply and demand conditions. It is by means of this spread that the Eurobanks profit from Eurodollar transactions.

---

[15]Federal Reserve Bank of Chicago, *International Letter* (March 21, 1975).

Eurodollar non-bank and interbank loans are generally unsecured. It is the borrower's reputation which mainly determines the loan rate.

Original Eurodollar deposits and funds secured by interbank deposits are generally of shorter duration than Eurodollar loans.

Eurobanks are subject to the risks of imbalances in the currencies in which their foreign assets and liabilities are denominated. Thus, a Eurobank may have more liabilities than assets denominated in U.S. dollars and, therefore, may be exposed to potential losses if exchange rates move adversely. There is the danger that Eurobanks can overextend themselves by borrowing short and lending long. In addition, there is the danger of Eurobanks making disproportionately large commitments to individual countries or in individual currencies. Eurobanks should, therefore, hedge their foreign exchange commitments to avoid exchange market risks.

Eurobanks have no lender of last resort within the Eurodollar market. The Eurodollar market and the overall Eurocurrency markets are international markets and there is no supranational central bank. Eurobanks, therefore, do not have a governmental agency, such as the Federal Reserve System for U.S. banks, to turn to in case of trouble. A central bank may attempt to aid a commercial bank in its country operating as a Eurobank, but the central bank is limited because its top priorities go to its domestic considerations. The risk involved here, however, is reduced because central banks do have agreements to maintain orderly foreign exchange markets.

### The Eurobond Market

The Eurocurrency market was originally a short-term market (overnight to 1 year maturities). Medium-term financing with 3-to-7-year maturity periods has now become quite important. It has been the fastest-growing area of the Eurocurrency market but it has also become a big problem area. It has developed into a market of international instability with great dangers of defaults. Dangers lurk for Eurobankers, Eurobanks, many developing countries, and some developed countries. The World Bank has complained against the granting of loans without considering the credit-worthiness of the borrowers carefully.

The borrowers in the medium-term Eurocurrency market may be developing countries, as well as developed countries (such as the United Kingdom, Italy, and Denmark) and corporations.

In the long-term Eurobond market maturity periods run 7 years and over.

## GROWTH OF THE EUROCURRENCY MARKET

Two important developments led to the growth of the Eurocurrency market (especially the Eurodollar market). The first was the Interest

Equalization Tax, which was passed in the United States in 1964. Imposition of this tax raised the cost of obtaining capital for borrowers in foreign countries. They therefore had to seek money outside the United States. This tax was removed in early 1974.

The second was the placing of restrictions on direct foreign investment by U.S. corporations. They were voluntary in 1965 and were made mandatory in 1968. The U.S. corporations, as a result, had to obtain funds outside the United States. The purpose was to reduce the U.S. balance-of-payments deficit. The mandatory controls were removed in early 1974.

### Significant Developments

From August 1974 through January 1975, the overall Eurocurrency market suffered from the erosion of confidence that afflicted international banking following the failure of banks in several countries over the previous 12-month period.

The resultant nervousness in the market was reflected in new cuts in credit lines to many Eurocurrency market participants. Small and even medium-sized banks and banks in countries under balance-of-payment pressure remained subject to tight credit ceilings. Strains in the Eurocurrency market subsided, however, with the result that differentials between the rates charged to different classes of banks narrowed and almost disappeared early in 1975.

The improved market tone owed a great deal to an announcement by the Bank for International Settlements (BIS) on September 10, 1974, that the central bank governors meeting at Basel, after a discussion of the problems of a "lender of last resort" in the Eurocurrency market, had concluded that means are available for the provision of temporary liquidity and will be used if and when necessary. A further optimistic note was struck when a consortium of banks responded to support the Bank of England's request for firm commitments from shareholders to support the banks' operations if they ran into problems at any time.

Particularly reassuring was an official statement that the "Federal Reserve is prepared, as a lender of last resort, to advance sufficient funds, suitably collateralized, to assure the continued operation of any solvent and soundly managed member bank that may be experiencing temporary liquidity difficulties associated with the abrupt withdrawal of petrodollar . . . deposits."[16]

After a fairly steep decline in outstanding deposits in the summer of 1974, the Eurocurrency market resumed its expansion in the final quarter of 1974, although at a reduced rate. Its continued growth greatly benefited from renewed placements of sizable OPEC deposits, which brought the

---

[16]Federal Reserve Bulletin (March 1975), p. 148.

total for 1974 to an estimated $23 billion, or 40% of OPEC (i.e., the oil cartel Organization of Petroleum Exporting Countries) surpluses.

The Eurocurrency market remained the major receptacle for those funds that the oil-producing countries were unable to spend for goods and services and did not employ for grants-in-aid and loans to oil-importing countries.

During the summer and fall of 1974, the Eurocurrency market also benefited from sizable advances by U.S. banks to their branches (notably those located in the Bahamas), which then passed on these funds to a variety of bank and nonbank borrowers.

As OPEC and other major supplier countries added further to their Eurocurrency holdings, overall liquidity in the market improved, but the market continued to suffer from a maldistribution of liquidity. The very large banks in the market had ample funds at their disposal, often more than they desired in view of their capital and surplus positions. While the very large banks grew in strength and importance, however, the role of some of the medium-sized and smaller banks became stationary or diminished. A few banks unable to comand the relatively attractive rates offered to their bigger competitors actually scaled down their operations.

It was the medium-term loan market that was most seriously affected by the strains in international banking. In the summer and fall of 1974, the rate of increase in the volume of medium-term loans slowed down considerably, as many syndicate participants no longer were able to secure funds at competitive interest rates. Consequently, the syndication of balance-of-payments and project loans carrying very distant repayment schedules diminished significantly.

Reduced competition permitted lenders to widen the spreads of rates on loans over the rates they paid for funding these loans and to tighten other terms and conditions, including the shortening of average maturities for medium-term loans funded with short-term funds on a floating-rate basis. As money market conditions in many parts of the world became easier, spreads between loan and deposit rates again narrowed.

Interest rates in the market, after having risen to virtually unprecedented levels, fell in September and October 1974 in response to sharp across-the-board declines in U.S. money market rates. The downtrend in Eurodollar rates stalled toward the end of November 1974, as the decline in U.S. domestic rates slowed and as year-end positioning prompted some bidding for dollar funds.

Early in 1975, rates resumed their precipitous fall in response to actual and expected declines in U.S. prime rates and other interest rates. By the end of January 1975, three-month rates had declined below 8%, almost one-half of the peak levels reached in the summer of 1974.

Developments concerning reserve requirements in Eurodollar borrowing have been very important, because they involve how much money definitely cannot be used for loans or investments. Effective April 10, 1975, reserve requirements on Eurodollar borrowings by U.S. banks and foreign banking institutions operating in the United States were reduced from 8% to 4% by the Board of Governors of the Federal Reserve System.

A reserve requirement had originally been imposed in 1969 to discourage the borrowing of Eurodollars, which reached $14.6 billion by late July 1969. Initially set at 10% against borrowings above an amount outstanding in May 1969, the requirement was raised to 20% in November 1970 and was reduced to 8% in May 1973.

When the Federal Reserve Board announced the reduction to 4%, it explained that this will bring the Eurodollar reserve requirement into better alignment with reserve requirements on such other sources of bank funds as U.S. domestic time and savings deposits. In addition, it is expected that U.S. bank borrowing of dollars held on deposit abroad will help reduce the supply of dollars held abroad. This it is hoped will help strengthen the position of the U.S. dollar in foreign exchange markets.[17]

See Figure B-1 for selected Eurodollar and U.S. money market rates.

**FIGURE B-1**

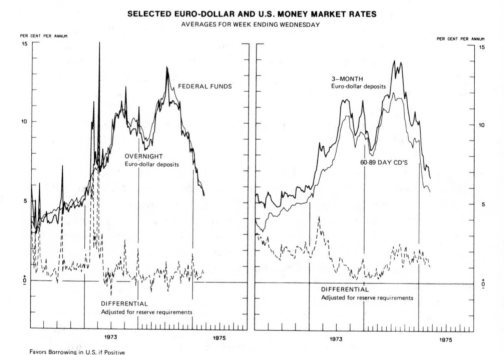

SELECTED EURO-DOLLAR AND U.S. MONEY MARKET RATES
AVERAGES FOR WEEK ENDING WEDNESDAY

*Source:* Board of Governors of the Federal Reserve System.

[17]Federal Reserve Bank of Chicago, *International Letter* (April 11, 1975).

# ownership of securities issued by the U.S. government, U.S. government agencies, and related agencies

C

**TABLE 10**

# —— TREASURY SURVEY OF OWNERSHIP, MARCH 31, 1975 ——

The monthly Treasury Survey of Ownership covers securities issued by the United States Government, Federal agencies, Federally-sponsored agencies, and the District of Columbia. The banks and insurance companies included in the Survey currently account for about 80 percent of all such securities held by these institutions. The similar proportion for corporations and for savings and loan associations is 50 percent, and for State and local governments, 40 percent. Data were first published for banks and insurance companies in the May 1941 Treasury Bulletin, for corporations and savings and loan associations in the September 1960 Bulletin, and for State and local governments in the February 1962 Bulletin.

Holdings by commercial banks distributed according to Federal Reserve member bank classes and nonmember banks are published for June 30 and December 31. Holdings by corporate pension trust funds are published quarterly, first appearing in the March 1954 Bulletin.

# Summary of Federal Securities

(Par values - in millions of dollars)

| Classification | Total amount outstanding 1/ | U.S. Government accounts and Federal Reserve banks | Total private investors | Held by private investors covered in Treasury Survey | | | | | | | | | Memorandum: held by corporate pension trust funds 4/ |
|---|---|---|---|---|---|---|---|---|---|---|---|---|---|
| | | | | 5,564 commercial banks 2/ | 475 mutual savings banks 2/ | Insurance companies 289 Life | 444 fire, casualty, and marine | 486 savings and loan associations | 461 corporations | State and local government 315 general funds | 188 pension and retirement funds | All other private investors 3/ | 557,701 |
| **Public debt issues:** | | | | | | | | | | | | | |
| Interest-bearing public debt securities: | | | | | | | | | | | | | |
| marketable 5/ | 299,989 | 102,259 | 197,730 | 48,840 | 1,751 | 2,539 | 2,580 | 1,969 | 4,911 | 7,058 | 1,131 | 126,951 | 2,817 |
| Nonmarketable 5/ | 208,592 | 117,620 | 90,972 | - | - | - | - | - | - | - | - | 90,972 | - |
| Total interest-bearing public debt securities | 508,581 | 219,879 | 288,702 | 48,840 | 1,751 | 2,539 | 2,580 | 1,969 | 4,911 | 7,058 | 1,131 | 217,923 | 2,817 |
| Matured debt and debt bearing no interest | 1,079 | - | 1,079 | - | - | - | - | - | - | - | - | 1,079 | - |
| Total public debt securities | 509,660 | 219,879 | 289,781 | 48,840 | 1,751 | 2,539 | 2,580 | 1,969 | 4,911 | 7,058 | 1,131 | 219,002 | 2,817 |
| **Government agency issues:** | | | | | | | | | | | | | |
| Regular issues 6/ | 5,043 | 215 | 4,828 | 1,041 | 226 | 109 | 43 | 166 | 231 | 118 | 255 | 2,639 | 96 |
| Participation certificates 6/ | 4,530 | 1,722 | 2,808 | 444 | 162 | 45 | 187 | 67 | 57 | 156 | 764 | 926 | 114 |
| Total Govt. agency securities covered in Treasury Survey | 9,573 | 1,937 | 7,636 | 1,485 | 388 | 154 | 230 | 233 | 288 | 274 | 1,019 | 3,565 | 210 |
| Nonsurveyed Govt. agency securities | 1,322 | 163 | 1,159 | | | | | | | | | | |
| Total Govt. agency securities 7/ | 10,895 | 2,100 | 8,795 | | | | | | | | | | |
| Total Federal securities | 520,555 | 221,979 | 298,576 | | | | | | | | | | |

*Source: Treasury Bulletin (May 1975)*

# TREASURY SURVEY OF OWNERSHIP, MARCH 31, 1975

## Interest-Bearing Marketable Public Debt Securities by Type and Maturity Distribution

(Par values - in millions of dollars)

| Classification | Total amount outstanding 1/ | U.S. Government accounts and Federal Reserve banks | Held by investors covered in Treasury Survey | | | | | | | | | Held by all other investors 3/ | Memorandum: Held by 57,701 corporate pension trust funds 4/ |
| | | | 5,564 commercial banks 2/ | 475 mutual savings banks 2/ | Insurance companies | | 486 savings and loan associations | 461 corporations | State and local governments | | | |
| | | | | | 289 life | 444 fire, casualty, and marine | | | 315 general funds | 188 pension and retirement funds | | |
| **By type security:** | | | | | | | | | | | | |
| Issued by U.S. Government: | | | | | | | | | | | | |
| Treasury bills............ | 123,972 | 36,598 | 6,976 | 152 | 132 | 273 | 240 | 2,011 | 3,882 | 197 | 73,512 | 1,290 |
| Treasury notes........... | 141,915 | 51,855 | 39,661 | 1,148 | 332 | 1,586 | 1,394 | 2,768 | 2,032 | 148 | 40,991 | 1,091 |
| Treasury bonds........... | 34,103 | 13,805 | 2,202 | 452 | 2,075 | 721 | 335 | 132 | 1,144 | 786 | 12,450 | 436 |
| Total................ | 299,989 | 102,259 | 48,840 | 1,751 | 2,539 | 2,580 | 1,969 | 4,911 | 7,058 | 1,131 | 126,952 | 2,817 |
| **By maturity distribution:** | | | | | | | | | | | | |
| Call classes (due or first becoming callable): | | | | | | | | | | | | |
| Within 1 year............ | 159,243 | 50,047 | 16,301 | 396 | 205 | 589 | 522 | 2,781 | 4,634 | 308 | 83,461 | 1,473 |
| 1 to 5 years............. | 91,815 | 29,440 | 26,574 | 759 | 617 | 1,067 | 1,021 | 1,813 | 1,574 | 157 | 28,793 | 614 |
| 5 to 10 years............ | 27,802 | 14,201 | 5,055 | 268 | 512 | 518 | 252 | 255 | 322 | 82 | 6,335 | 230 |
| 10 to 15 years........... | 12,918 | 5,467 | 551 | 145 | 935 | 269 | 140 | 13 | 336 | 332 | 4,731 | 218 |
| 15 to 20 years........... | 5,370 | 2,263 | 326 | 118 | 84 | 116 | 21 | 48 | 103 | 230 | 2,062 | 270 |
| 20 years and over........ | 2,841 | 841 | 34 | 65 | 186 | 21 | 14 | - | 88 | 22 | 1,571 | 12 |
| Total................ | 299,989 | 102,259 | 48,840 | 1,751 | 2,539 | 2,580 | 1,969 | 4,911 | 7,058 | 1,131 | 126,952 | 2,817 |
| Maturity classes (final maturity): | | | | | | | | | | | | |
| Within 1 year............ | 158,046 | 49,538 | 16,217 | 385 | 165 | 555 | 511 | 2,777 | 4,569 | 224 | 83,105 | 1,465 |
| 1 to 5 years............. | 90,362 | 29,158 | 26,503 | 743 | 333 | 1,024 | 995 | 1,805 | 1,477 | 113 | 28,209 | 584 |
| 5 to 10 years............ | 29,255 | 14,483 | 5,126 | 284 | 796 | 561 | 278 | 264 | 419 | 126 | 6,918 | 383 |
| 10 to 15 years........... | 7,025 | 2,747 | 327 | 114 | 762 | 137 | 83 | 7 | 217 | 181 | 2,452 | 47 |
| 15 to 20 years........... | 8,452 | 3,562 | 397 | 82 | 256 | 180 | 83 | 16 | 243 | 277 | 3,354 | 64 |
| 20 years and over........ | 6,850 | 2,770 | 272 | 143 | 226 | 122 | 19 | 41 | 133 | 210 | 2,914 | 274 |
| Total................ | 299,989 | 102,259 | 48,840 | 1,751 | 2,539 | 2,580 | 1,969 | 4,911 | 7,058 | 1,131 | 126,952 | 2,817 |

# Interest-Bearing Marketable Public Debt Securities by Issue

Par values - in millions of dollars

| Issue | Total amount outstanding [1] | Held by investors covered in Treasury Survey | | | | | | | | | Held by all other investors [3] | Memorandum: Held by 57,701 corporate pension trust funds [4] |
|---|---|---|---|---|---|---|---|---|---|---|---|---|
| | | U.S. Government accounts and Federal Reserve banks | 5,564 commercial banks [2] | 475 mutual savings banks [2] | Insurance companies | | 486 savings and loan associations | 461 corporations | State and local governments | | | |
| | | | | | 289 life | 444 fire, casualty, and marine | | | 315 general funds | 188 pension and retirement funds | | |
| **Treasury Bills:** | | | | | | | | | | | | |
| Regular weekly and annual maturing: | | | | | | | | | | | | |
| Apr. 1975 | 20,320 | 6,773 | 544 | 18 | 12 | 43 | 32 | 164 | 756 | 51 | 11,926 | 233 |
| May 1975 | 25,618 | 8,504 | 555 | 12 | 9 | 49 | 6 | 91 | 898 | 82 | 15,411 | 295 |
| June 1975 | 23,828 | 7,024 | 2,137 | 21 | 28 | 68 | 41 | 227 | 917 | 45 | 13,320 | 333 |
| July 1975 | 14,820 | 4,055 | 328 | 15 | 12 | 17 | 27 | 544 | 351 | 2 | 9,469 | 75 |
| Aug. 1975 | 11,798 | 2,918 | 442 | 44 | 40 | 24 | 48 | 240 | 326 | 2 | 7,675 | 96 |
| Sept. 1975 | 11,908 | 3,015 | 1,381 | 14 | 7 | 18 | 62 | 288 | 180 | 3 | 6,941 | 76 |
| Oct. 1975 | 2,003 | 688 | 148 | 11 | 2 | 5 | 2 | * | 71 | 1 | 1,077 | 39 |
| Nov. 1975 | 2,032 | 698 | 236 | 1 | 1 | 11 | 2 | 1 | 106 | 2 | 944 | 36 |
| Dec. 1975 | 2,001 | 778 | 67 | 6 | * | 2 | * | 38 | 48 | - | 1,062 | 28 |
| Jan. 1975 | 2,001 | 808 | 127 | 2 | - | * | 10 | 78 | 12 | - | 963 | 17 |
| Feb. 1975 | 2,103 | 593 | 410 | 1 | - | 1 | 2 | 76 | 14 | * | 1,004 | 23 |
| Mar. 1975 | 2,102 | 722 | 533 | 8 | - | 2 | 8 | 26 | 4 | - | 800 | 9 |
| Tax anticipation: | | | | | | | | | | | | |
| Apr. 1975 | 2,251 | 15 | 28 | 1 | 20 | 33 | * | 89 | 113 | 9 | 1,943 | 21 |
| June 1975 | 1,256 | 7 | 40 | - | * | 1 | * | 147 | 86 | * | 975 | 10 |
| Total Treasury Bills | 123,972 | 36,598 | 6,976 | 152 | 132 | 273 | 240 | 2,011 | 3,882 | 197 | 73,512 | 1,290 |

*Source: Treasury Bulletin* (May 1975)

# TREASURY SURVEY OF OWNERSHIP, MARCH 31, 1975

## Interest-Bearing Marketable Public Debt Securities by Issue—Continued

(Par values - in millions of dollars)

| Issue | | | Total amount outstanding 1/ | Held by investors covered in Treasury Survey | | | | | | | | | Held by all other investors 2/ | Memorandum: Held by 57,701 corporate pension trust funds 4/ |
|---|---|---|---|---|---|---|---|---|---|---|---|---|---|---|
| | | | | U.S. Government accounts and Federal Reserve banks | 5,564 commercial banks 2/ | 475 mutual savings banks 2/ | Insurance companies | | 486 savings and loan associations | 461 corporations | State and local governments | | | |
| | | | | | | | 289 life | 444 fire, casualty, and marine | | | 315 general funds | 188 pension and retirement funds | | |
| **Treasury notes:** | | | | | | | | | | | | | | |
| 5-7/8 | May | 1975-F | 1,776 | 128 | 1,050 | 32 | * | 3 | 18 | 106 | 122 | * | 316 | 10 |
| 8 | May | 1975-B | 6,760 | 4,550 | 624 | 21 | 9 | 48 | 27 | 41 | 122 | 19 | 1,300 | 25 |
| 5-7/8 | Aug | 1975-C | 7,679 | 2,823 | 2,349 | 52 | 16 | 57 | 87 | 214 | 158 | 4 | 1,919 | 46 |
| 8-3/8 | Sept | 1975-G | 2,042 | 64 | 676 | 19 | 1 | 18 | 5 | 90 | 46 | - | 1,125 | 14 |
| 7 | Nov | 1975-D | 3,115 | 748 | 950 | 20 | 1 | 35 | 20 | 12 | 70 | 1 | 1,256 | 19 |
| 7 | Dec | 1975-H | 1,731 | 231 | 740 | 12 | * | 25 | 10 | 73 | 46 | * | 594 | 8 |
| 5-7/8 | Feb | 1976-F | 4,945 | 1,401 | 1,705 | 43 | 2 | 74 | 78 | 187 | 85 | 1 | 1,369 | 21 |
| 6-1/4 | Feb | 1976-A | 3,739 | 2,873 | 314 | 7 | 3 | 15 | 13 | 6 | 28 | 1 | 478 | 9 |
| 8 | Mar | 1976-H | 2,288 | 122 | 834 | 27 | 3 | 8 | 12 | 37 | 10 | 2 | 1,235 | 24 |
| 5-3/4 | May | 1976-E | 2,802 | 585 | 1,109 | 22 | 3 | 51 | 34 | 63 | 47 | 1 | 887 | 14 |
| 6 | May | 1976. | 1,580 | - | 830 | 13 | 1 | 1 | 17 | 67 | 4 | * | 662 | 7 |
| 6-1/2 | May | 1976-I | 2,697 | 820 | 595 | 30 | 3 | 48 | 2 | 10 | 57 | 3 | 1,114 | 9 |
| 8-3/4 | June | 1976. | 1,662 | 696 | 773 | 26 | 3 | 6 | 38 | 70 | 66 | 3 | 1,059 | 19 |
| 5-7/8 | Aug | 1976. | 2,703 | 37 | 771 | 17 | 1 | 6 | 24 | 144 | 33 | - | 613 | 15 |
| 6-1/2 | Aug | 1976-G | 3,883 | 1,858 | 1,034 | 30 | 2 | 38 | 10 | 99 | 56 | * | 744 | 24 |
| 7-1/2 | Aug | 1976-C | 4,194 | 1,665 | 905 | 33 | * | 56 | 17 | 7 | 36 | 6 | 1,473 | 35 |
| 8.25 | Sept | 1976-J | 2,023 | 303 | 1,051 | 11 | * | 18 | 41 | 80 | 29 | 2 | 511 | 15 |
| 6-1/4 | Nov | 1976-D | 2,325 | 311 | 1,626 | 24 | 3 | 51 | 10 | 195 | 95 | * | 1,943 | 58 |
| 7-1/4 | Dec | 1976-K | 2,282 | 214 | 1,125 | 13 | 39 | 16 | 68 | 153 | 53 | * | 698 | 30 |
| 6 | Feb | 1977. | 1,665 | 87 | 644 | 16 | - | 6 | 17 | 46 | 4 | - | 792 | 14 |
| 8 | Feb | 1977-A | 5,163 | 3,065 | 657 | 40 | 2 | 33 | 23 | 11 | 53 | 3 | 1,283 | 11 |
| 6-1/2 | Mar | 1977-C | 2,564 | 269 | 1,070 | 20 | 1 | 19 | 26 | 15 | 18 | - | 1,130 | 29 |
| 6-7/8 | May | 1977. | 2,565 | 549 | 1,039 | 18 | * | 67 | 4 | 131 | 98 | 1 | 627 | 16 |
| 9 | May | 1977-D | 5,329 | 2,964 | 686 | 18 | 9 | 13 | | 38 | 45 | * | 1,559 | |

| Coupon | Issue | Month | | | | | | | | | | | | |
|---|---|---|---|---|---|---|---|---|---|---|---|---|---|---|
| 7-3/4 | 1977-B | Aug. | 4,918 | 1,636 | 1,356 | 46 | 4 | 61 | 21 | 76 | 104 | 14 | 1,600 | 25 |
| 7-3/4 | 1977-E | Nov. | 3,630 | 1,168 | 1,235 | 33 | 5 | 20 | 22 | 168 | 38 | 1 | 939 | 15 |
| 6-1/4 | 1978-A | Feb. | 8,389 | 3,384 | 1,940 | 85 | 35 | 98 | 173 | 42 | 104 | 25 | 2,502 | 48 |
| 7-1/8 | 1978-D | May | 3,960 | 844 | 1,908 | 31 | 3 | 36 | 30 | 112 | 28 | 8 | 910 | 67 |
| 8-3/4 | 1978-C | Aug. | 2,462 | 618 | 729 | 24 | 2 | 37 | 6 | 23 | 15 | 2 | 1,007 | 23 |
| 6 | 1978-B | Nov. | 8,207 | 3,602 | 1,842 | 56 | 34 | 75 | 186 | 14 | 165 | 5 | 2,228 | 22 |
| 7-7/8 | 1979-D | May | 2,269 | 316 | 1,272 | 51 | 3 | 37 | 29 | 19 | 12 | 4 | 525 | 25 |
| 6-1/4 | 1979-A | Aug. | 4,559 | 1,759 | 951 | 34 | 19 | 42 | 35 | 31 | 46 | 7 | 1,635 | 11 |
| 6-5/8 | 1979-B | Nov. | 1,604 | 1,124 | 201 | 5 | 1 | 26 | 3 | 6 | 17 | * | 222 | 6 |
| 7 | 1979-C | Nov. | 2,241 | 422 | 957 | 11 | 4 | 61 | 39 | 152 | 12 | 1 | 582 | 20 |
| 6-7/8 | 1980-A | May | 7,265 | 5,546 | 735 | 54 | 8 | 76 | 77 | 23 | 46 | 7 | 696 | 32 |
| 9 | 1980-B | Aug. | 4,296 | 2,573 | 641 | 25 | * | 65 | 2 | 21 | 26 | 4 | 937 | 28 |
| **7** | **1981-A** | **Feb.** | 1,842 | 484 | 806 | 2 | 26 | 50 | 28 | 14 | 11 | 7 | 420 | 10 |
| 7-3/8 | 1981-C | Feb. | 2,168 | 562 | 569 | 37 | 33 | 84 | 43 | 34 | 4 | * | 784 | 128 |
| 7-3/4 | 1981-B | Nov. | 4,477 | 1,453 | 1,344 | 86 | 37 | 93 | 42 | 125 | 20 | 18 | 1,270 | 133 |
| Exchange Series | | | 120 | - | 19 | | 17 | 14 | 3 | 16 | 2 | 6 | 47 | 12 |
| **Total Treasury notes** | | | 141,915 | 51,855 | 39,661 | 1,148 | 332 | 1,586 | 1,394 | 2,768 | 2,032 | 148 | 40,991 | 1,091 |
| **Treasury bonds:** | | | | | | | | | | | | | | |
| 4-1/4 | 1975-85 | May | 1,196 | 508 | 84 | 11 | 40 | 34 | 11 | 3 | 65 | 84 | 356 | 8 |
| 3-1/4 | 1978-83 | June | 1,453 | 282 | 71 | 16 | 283 | 43 | 25 | 9 | 97 | 44 | 584 | 10 |
| 4 | 1980 | Feb. | 2,568 | 862 | 177 | 34 | 139 | 89 | 64 | 20 | 239 | 26 | 919 | 19 |
| 3-1/2 | 1980 | Nov. | 1,894 | 749 | 101 | 20 | 371 | 56 | 41 | * | 110 | 36 | 404 | 9 |
| 7 | 1981 | Aug. | 807 | 407 | 106 | 3 | 2 | 5 | - | * | 5 | 1 | 277 | 3 |
| 6-3/8 | 1982 | Feb. | 2,702 | 1,049 | 536 | 27 | 18 | 62 | 13 | 12 | 24 | 9 | 952 | 6 |
| 6-3/8 | 1884 | Aug. | 2,353 | 1,377 | 218 | 13 | 16 | 27 | 7 | 22 | 77 | - | 594 | 4 |
| 3-1/4 | 1985 | May | 909 | 224 | 41 | 11 | 188 | 26 | 48 | * | 13 | 1 | 345 | 3 |
| 6-1/8 | 1986 | Nov. | 1,216 | 884 | 88 | 8 | 9 | 5 | 1 | 3 | 10 | 13 | 203 | 4 |
| 4-1/4 | 1987-92 | Aug. | 3,580 | 1,435 | 85 | 34 | 129 | 118 | 30 | 4 | 135 | 5 | 1,460 | 34 |
| 4 | 1988-93 | Feb. | 224 | 70 | 3 | 4 | 29 | 3 | 8 | - | 7 | 150 | 95 | 5 |
| 7-1/2 | 1988-93 | Aug. | 1,914 | 1,174 | 214 | 2 | 10 | 14 | 9 | 5 | 22 | 5 | 424 | 13 |
| 4-1/8 | 1989-94 | May | 1,372 | 550 | 5 | 3 | 45 | 31 | 20 | 1 | 20 | 40 | 656 | 5 |
| 3-1/2 | 1990 | Feb. | 3,703 | 1,130 | 112 | 84 | 525 | 72 | 23 | 1 | 128 | 41 | 1,549 | 32 |
| 6-3/4 | 1993 | Feb. | 627 | 200 | 77 | 31 | 20 | 5 | 10 | 7 | 16 | 79 | 241 | 4 |
| 7 | 1993-98 | May | 692 | 294 | 149 | 2 | 7 | 3 | 3 | 12 | 13 | 20 | 187 | 15 |
| 8-1/2 | 1994-99 | May | 2,414 | 1,361 | 42 | 26 | 11 | 20 | - | 28 | 29 | 23 | 766 | 170 |
| 3 | 1995 | Feb. | 735 | 134 | 11 | 9 | 23 | 10 | 6 | * | 42 | 133 | 478 | 4 |
| 7-7/8 | 1995-2000 | Feb. | 902 | 275 | 47 | 50 | 23 | 78 | 3 | * | 4 | 22 | 390 | 77 |
| 3-1/2 | 1998 | Nov. | 2,841 | 841 | 34 | 65 | 186 | 21 | 14 | * | 88 | 32 | 1,571 | 12 |
| **Total Treasury bonds** | | | 34,103 | 13,805 | 2,202 | 452 | 2,075 | 721 | 335 | 132 | 1,144 | 786 | 12,450 | 436 |
| **Total marketable public debt securities** | | | 299,989 | 102,259 | 48,840 | 1,751 | **2,539** | 2,580 | 1,969 | 4,911 | 7,058 | 1,131 | 126,952 | 2,817 |

*Source: Treasury Bulletin (May 1975)*

# TREASURY SURVEY OF OWNERSHIP, MARCH 31, 1975

## Securities Issued by Government Agencies

(Par values - in millions of dollars)

T-13

| Type | Total amount outstanding 1/ 8/ | Held by investors covered in Treasury Survey | | | | | | | | | Held by all other investors 3/ | Memorandum: Held by 57,701 corporate pension trust funds 4/ |
|---|---|---|---|---|---|---|---|---|---|---|---|---|
| | | U.S. Government accounts and Federal Reserve banks | 5,564 commercial banks 2/ | 475 mutual savings banks 2/ | Insurance companies | | 486 savings and loan associations | 461 corporations | State and local governments | | | |
| | | | | | 289 life | 444 fire, casualty and marine | | | 315 general funds | 188 pension and retirement funds | | |
| **Export-Import Bank:** | | | | | | | | | | | | |
| 5.70 Dec. 1975 | 300 | 24 | 105 | 7 | 8 | * | 27 | - | 24 | - | 105 | * |
| 6-1/4 Aug. 1977 | 400 | 7 | 124 | 12 | - | 1 | 55 | 9 | 16 | 1 | 176 | 1 |
| 6.45 Feb. 1978 | 300 | 22 | 139 | 8 | - | 2 | 6 | 45 | 8 | - | 70 | * |
| 8.35 Aug. 1978 | 300 | - | 130 | 1 | - | - | - | 89 | 1 | * | 79 | 35 |
| 7.30 Nov. 1978 | 300 | 12 | 171 | 1 | * | 9 | 1 | 26 | 5 | * | 76 | 1 |
| 7 Mar. 1979 | 400 | 27 | 124 | 10 | * | 5 | 13 | 32 | 18 | * | 171 | 1 |
| 6.60 May 1979 | 200 | 30 | 70 | 6 | * | * | 3 | 5 | 22 | - | 63 | * |
| Issues to State & Local Govts (Mtg. Backed Bonds) 8/ | 143 | - | - | - | - | - | - | - | 143 | - | - | - |
| Participation certificates | 250 | 14 | 78 | 12 | 4 | 12 | 1 | - | 22 | 72 | 36 | 4 |
| Total | 2,593 | 134 | 941 | 56 | 13 | 29 | 106 | 206 | 259 | 73 | 777 | 42 |
| **Federal Housing Administration:** (Debentures) | 468 | 70 | 36 | 27 | 64 | 4 | 17 | - | 1 | 56 | 194 | - |
| **Government National Mortgage Association:** Participation certificates | 4,280 | 1,708 | 366 | 150 | 41 | 175 | 67 | 57 | 134 | 692 | 890 | 110 |

| | 250 | 25 | 13 | 18 | 5 | 1 | 1 | 2 | — | 20 | 166 | 8 |
|---|---|---|---|---|---|---|---|---|---|---|---|---|
| **Postal Service:** | | | | | | | | | | | | |
| 6-7/8  Feb.  1982-97 | 250 | 25 | 13 | 18 | 5 | 1 | 1 | 2 | — | 20 | 166 | 8 |
| **Tennessee Valley Authority:** | | | | | | | | | | | | |
| **Bonds:** | | | | | | | | | | | | |
| 8-3/4  June  1975 | 50 | — | 3 | 2 | — | 8 | * | — | 2 | — | 34 | * |
| 7-1/4  July  1976 | 100 | — | 15 | 5 | * | 2 | * | — | 1 | — | 77 | 1 |
| 8.10  Apr.  1979 | 100 | — | 9 | 2 | — | 3 | * | — | — | — | 84 | 3 |
| 4.40  Nov.  1985 | 50 | — | * | 1 | 5 | 1 | * | — | 1 | 20 | 15 | 1 |
| 4-5/8  July  1986 | 50 | — | * | * | 3 | 1 | 6 | — | 2 | 27 | 18 | 2 |
| 4-1/2  Feb.  1987 | 45 | — | * | * | 3 | * | * | — | * | 26 | 12 | * |
| 5.70  May  1992 | 70 | — | * | 2 | 1 | 1 | 1 | — | 3 | 25 | 37 | 1 |
| 6-3/8  Nov.  1992 | 60 | — | * | 2 | * | * | * | — | 3 | 11 | 45 | 1 |
| 8-1/4  Oct.  1994 | 100 | — | 1 | 4 | 1 | 2 | 2 | — | — | 13 | 80 | 1 |
| 9  Mar.  1995 | 100 | — | 1 | 8 | 1 | 1 | 1 | — | 1 | 3 | 87 | 1 |
| 9-1/4  June  1995 | 50 | — | * | 2 | * | — | * | — | * | 5 | 43 | * |
| 7.30  Oct.  1996 | 150 | — | 4 | 15 | 1 | 1 | — | 2 | * | 1 | 127 | 3 |
| 7  Jan.  1997 | 150 | — | 6 | 17 | 1 | 1 | * | 2 | — | 5 | 112 | 3 |
| 7.35  May  1997 | 150 | — | 4 | 16 | 1 | 9 | 2 | * | 5 | 5 | 112 | 1 |
| 7.35  July  1997 | 150 | — | 3 | 17 | 2 | 9 | 1 | 2 | 1 | 2 | 109 | 1 |
| 7.40  Oct.  1997 | 150 | — | 3 | 18 | 5 | 2 | 4 | 1 | 3 | 9 | 109 | 7 |
| 7.35  Jan.  1998 | 100 | — | 3 | 16 | 3 | 4 | 2 | 3 | — | 1 | 73 | — |
| 7.35  Apr.  1998 | 150 | — | 16 | 6 | * | — | 1 | — | — | 5 | 117 | 6 |
| 7-3/4  July  1998 | 150 | — | 22 | 1 | 2 | — | 2 | 10 | * | 18 | 103 | 18 |
| 7.70  Oct.  1998 | 100 | — | 34 | — | 1 | 1 | 1 | 1 | — | * | 55 | * |
| 8.05  Jan.  1999 | 100 | — | 4 | 1 | 1 | — | 1 | 1 | * | 1 | 90 | 1 |
| **Total** | 2,125 | 0 | 130 | 137 | 32 | 21 | 43 | 23 | 23 | 178 | 1,538 | 51 |
| **Total Government agency securities covered by survey** | 9,716 | 1,937 | 1,486 | 388 | 154 | 230 | 234 | 287 | 317 | 1,019 | 3,565 | 211 |

*Source: Treasury Bulletin* (May 1975)

227

# TREASURY SURVEY OF OWNERSHIP, MARCH 31, 1975
## - Securities Issued by Government-Sponsored Agencies and the District of Columbia

(Par values - in millions of dollars)

| Issue | Total amount outstanding | Held by investors covered in Treasury Survey | | | | | | | | | | Held by all other investors 2/ | Memorandum: Held by 57,701 corporate pension trust funds 4/ |
|---|---|---|---|---|---|---|---|---|---|---|---|---|---|
| | | U.S. Government accounts and Federal Reserve banks | 5,564 commercial banks 2/ | 475 mutual savings banks 2/ | Insurance companies | | 486 savings and loan associations | 461 corporations | State and local governments | | | |
| | | | | | 289 life | 444 fire, casualty and marine | | | 315 general funds | 188 pension and retirement funds | | |
| **Banks for Cooperatives:** | | | | | | | | | | | | |
| **Debentures:** | | | | | | | | | | | | |
| 9.55% 1975 Apr. | 447 9/ | 4 | 29 | * | 1 | 1 | 3 | 5 | 93 | - | 341 | 38 |
| 8.55 1975 May | 683 9/ | 34 | 74 | 8 | 1 | 1 | 10 | 14 | 112 | * | 429 | 40 |
| 8.05 1975 June | 542 9/ | 17 | 83 | 8 | 1 | * | 5 | 7 | 76 | 1 | 345 | 21 |
| 7.40 1975 July | 485 9/ | 3 | 56 | 3 | - | - | 7 | 21 | 64 | 3 | 330 | 3 |
| 7.05 1975 Aug. | 484 9/ | 7 | 72 | 7 | 1 | - | 7 | 2 | 38 | - | 351 | 2 |
| 5.05 1975 Sept. | 392 9/ | 8 | 73 | 5 | 1 | * | 7 | 2 | 46 | - | 251 | 1 |
| 7.70 1977 Apr. | 200 | - | 93 | * | - | - | 1 | 15 | 1 | - | 90 | 1 |
| 8 1979 Oct. | 201 | - | 82 | 8 | - | 2 | 8 | 11 | 8 | - | 81 | 3 |
| Total | 3,463 9/ | 74 | 563 | 38 | 3 | 4 | 48 | 76 | 437 | 4 | 2,217 | 108 |
| **Farmers Home Administration:** | | | | | | | | | | | | |
| **Insured notes:** | | | | | | | | | | | | |
| 6-5/8 1976 Aug. | 150 | - | 83 | 10 | 1 | * | 1 | - | 3 | 4 | 47 | 1 |
| 6.35 1977 Mar. | 400 | 14 | 122 | 22 | 1 | 4 | 18 | - | 10 | - | 209 | 1 |
| 6.45 1977 June | 300 | 10 | 129 | 20 | 1 | 1 | 8 | - | 20 | - | 111 | 3 |
| 6-7/8 1977 Aug. | 400 | 16 | 174 | 33 | - | 1 | 8 | 33 | 17 | - | 126 | 6 |
| 6.55 1977 Dec. | 403 | 9 | 145 | 41 | 3 | 1 | 2 | - | 11 | - | 187 | 2 |
| 7.20 1978 Mar. | 300 | 9 | 100 | 20 | 4 | 1 | 5 | - | 11 | 1 | 160 | 10 |
| 7-1/4 1978 May | 301 | 30 | 112 | 4 | 2 | 1 | 5 | - | 8 | 1 | 142 | 3 |
| 7.35 1978 July | 301 | - | 112 | 9 | * | * | 1 | - | 5 | 4 | 155 | 3 |
| 7.30 1978-CBO Dec. | 300 | - | 166 | 1 | - | * | 2 | 12 | 17 | - | 114 | 4 |
| 8.90 1980 Jan. | 150 | - | 18 | 2 | 1 | 6 | 1 | - | 23 | 28 | 71 | 9 |
| 7 1980 Nov. | 300 | 9 | 136 | 22 | 1 | 6 | 43 | - | 29 | 12 | 44 | 1 |
| 8.40 1981 Mar. | 200 | 10 | 62 | 10 | 2 | 6 | 26 | - | 3 | 9 | 71 | 6 |
| 7-7/8 1981 June | 250 | 12 | 62 | 34 | 2 | 3 | 20 | 2 | 8 | 9 | 95 | 2 |
| 7.10 1982 Jan. | 350 | 16 | 78 | 37 | 5 | 2 | 9 | - | 17 | 4 | 180 | 5 |
| 8-5/8 1985 July | 300 | 43 | 18 | 17 | 5 | 4 | 10 | - | 63 | 34 | 106 | 4 |
| 7-1/2 1986 Aug. | 150 | - | 8 | 15 | 1 | - | 2 | - | 5 | 46 | 72 | * |
| 7-1/8 1987 Dec. | 201 | 3 | 27 | 31 | 1 | 1 | 14 | - | 6 | 46 | 73 | 1 |
| 7-1/2 1988 Mar. | 201 | 3 | 1 | 25 | 2 | 1 | 17 | - | 1 | 72 | 78 | 1 |
| 7-1/2 1988 May | 200 | 10 | 16 | 6 | 3 | - | 49 | - | 3 | 54 | 59 | 5 |
| 7-3/4 1988-CBO Dec. | 200 | 38 | 47 | * | * | * | 3 | - | 1 | 1 | 110 | 2 |

Federal Home Loan Banks

| | 9 | 200 | 32 | 27 | 9 | 5 | 2 | 8 | — | 19 | 25 | 73 | 7 |
|---|---|---|---|---|---|---|---|---|---|---|---|---|---|
| **Total** | | 5,558 | 263 | 1,646 | 367 | 45 | 42 | 246 | 47 | 271 | 348 | 2,283 | 95 |
| **Apr. 1989-CBO** | | 334 | — | 26 | 6 | 1 | 2 | 2 | 9 | 91 | 3 | 194 | 29 |
| **Federal Home Loan Banks:** | | | | | | | | | | | | | |
| Discount notes | | 300 | 23 | 60 | 7 | * | 4 | 13 | 12 | 23 | 1 | 157 | 10 |
| **Bonds:** | | | | | | | | | | | | | |
| 6.80 — 1975 May | | 700 | 47 | 164 | 19 | * | 1 | 31 | 52 | 57 | 1 | 329 | 8 |
| 7.15 — 1975 May | | 265 | — | 46 | 13 | — | * | 20 | — | 4 | — | 181 | 9 |
| 8.05 — 1975 May | | 400 | 47 | 89 | 7 | 1 | 1 | 15 | 28 | 7 | — | 204 | 21 |
| 7.15 — 1975 Aug. | | 500 | 21 | 111 | 11 | * | 2 | 16 | 42 | 34 | — | 262 | 3 |
| 7-7/8 — 1975 Aug. | | 300 | 47 | 42 | 15 | — | * | 15 | — | 4 | — | 177 | 27 |
| 7.95 — 1975 Aug. | | 350 | 14 | 74 | 21 | * | 3 | 44 | 7 | 5 | 1 | 180 | 4 |
| 6-1/2 — 1975 Nov. | | 600 | 29 | 169 | 9 | 1 | 1 | 41 | 28 | 46 | 1 | 276 | 4 |
| 7.05 — 1975 Nov. | | 700 | 11 | 125 | 11 | 1 | 1 | 34 | 2 | 105 | 3 | 406 | 19 |
| 9.10 — 1975 Nov. | | 300 | 16 | 78 | 7 | * | * | 29 | — | — | * | 169 | 7 |
| 7-3/8 — 1976 Feb. | | 400 | 9 | 59 | 15 | * | * | 14 | 40 | 39 | 1 | 223 | 12 |
| 8.70 — 1976 Feb. | | 300 | * | 67 | 5 | — | 6 | 3 | — | 3 | * | 216 | 2 |
| 8.75 — 1976 Feb. | | 600 | 8 | 91 | 4 | — | 1 | 18 | 10 | 101 | * | 366 | 2 |
| 9.2 — 1976 May | | 600 | 29 | 176 | 13 | — | 1 | 28 | 47 | 62 | * | 243 | 12 |
| 7.20 — 1976 May | | 300 | 9 | 96 | 8 | 1 | — | 14 | 23 | 11 | — | 139 | 3 |
| 7.45 — 1976 Aug. | | 500 | 10 | 160 | 15 | — | * | 17 | 22 | 25 | 1 | 248 | 3 |
| 7.80 — 1976 Aug. | | 700 | 24 | 140 | 6 | — | 2 | 10 | 53 | 47 | 1 | 416 | 8 |
| 8.60 — 1976 Nov. | | 600 | 17 | 151 | 11 | — | * | 20 | 63 | 34 | 1 | 304 | 14 |
| 9.55 — 1976 Nov. | | 500 | 45 | 93 | 5 | 1 | * | 18 | 3 | 25 | * | 308 | 12 |
| 7.20 — 1977 Feb. | | 500 | 20 | 218 | 10 | 1 | 4 | 16 | 57 | 5 | 2 | 168 | 21 |
| 8.05 — 1977 Feb. | | 200 | 25 | 156 | 13 | — | 1 | 14 | 23 | 18 | 3 | 250 | 9 |
| 6.95 — 1977 May | | 500 | 2 | 44 | 13 | * | 2 | 21 | 18 | 1 | — | 108 | 8 |
| 8.70 — 1977 May | | 300 | 17 | 112 | 23 | 1 | 2 | 16 | 21 | 26 | — | 287 | 3 |
| 7.15 — 1977 Aug. | | 600 | 21 | 88 | 8 | — | 1 | 20 | 17 | 6 | — | 143 | 15 |
| 8.80 — 1977 Aug. | | 300 | 77 | 169 | 34 | 1 | 6 | 12 | 10 | 19 | — | 263 | 11 |
| 6.75 — 1977 Nov. | | 300 | 3 | 82 | 3 | — | 1 | 11 | 36 | 1 | 3 | 160 | 20 |
| 7.45 — 1977 Nov. | | 700 | 11 | 115 | 8 | 1 | * | 24 | 18 | 18 | 1 | 118 | 6 |
| 9-3/8 — 1978 Feb. | | 400 | 32 | 180 | 15 | 1 | * | 9 | 10 | 45 | 1 | 387 | 2 |
| 7.60 — 1978 May | | 500 | 2 | 223 | 12 | — | 7 | 27 | 5 | 13 | 5 | 129 | 32 |
| 9.10 — 1978 Nov. | | 497 | 24 | 170 | 17 | — | 3 | 11 | 31 | 10 | — | 211 | 8 |
| 8.65 — 1979 Feb. | | 596 | 33 | 110 | 9 | 1 | 8 | 34 | 10 | 14 | 8 | 301 | 6 |
| 9.45 — 1979 Feb. | | 596 | 70 | 126 | 17 | 1 | 11 | 20 | 38 | 14 | * | 283 | 6 |
| 8.65 — 1979 May | | 500 | 31 | 162 | 8 | — | 23 | 33 | 8 | 19 | 4 | 324 | 31 |
| 8.75 — 1979 May | | 400 | 24 | 160 | 22 | 1 | 20 | 15 | 14 | 7 | * | 220 | 27 |
| 9.50 — 1979 Aug. | | 491 | 49 | 63 | 8 | — | — | 7 | 1 | 17 | * | 232 | 20 |
| 7.50 — 1979 Nov. | | 500 | 28 | 69 | 10 | 1 | 5 | 41 | 1 | 33 | * | 328 | 25 |
| 8.15 — 1979 Nov. | | 500 | — | 131 | 18 | 1 | 12 | 22 | — | 10 | 10 | 282 | 39 |
| 7.05 — 1980 Feb. | | 300 | 35 | 143 | 12 | 1 | 3 | 12 | 7 | 9 | 3 | 265 | 31 |
| 7.75 — 1980 Feb. | | 350 | 46 | 109 | 4 | * | 1 | 14 | 4 | 12 | 13 | 113 | 21 |
| 7.80 — 1980 Oct. | | 200 | 42 | 44 | 9 | * | 2 | 7 | 2 | 2 | 4 | 224 | 31 |
| 6.60 — 1981 Nov. | | 200 | 14 | 39 | 19 | — | 3 | 2 | — | 2 | 1 | 114 | 2 |
| 8.65 — 1981 Nov. | | 400 | 8 | 54 | 7 | * | 2 | 4 | 2 | 9 | 1 | 124 | 7 |
| | | | 50 | 73 | 28 | 1 | 19 | | 4 | | 3 | 202 | 46 |

Footnotes at end of table.

# TREASURY SURVEY OF OWNERSHIP, MARCH 31, 1975

## - Securities Issued by Government-Sponsored Agencies and the District of Columbia—Continued

(Par values - in millions of dollars)

| Issue | Total amount outstanding | U.S. Government accounts and Federal Reserve banks | 5,564 commercial banks 2/ | 475 mutual savings banks 2/ | 289 life | 444 fire, casualty, and marine | 486 savings and loan associations | 461 corporations | 315 general funds | 188 pension and retirement funds | Held by all other investors 3/ | Memorandum: Held by 57,701 corporate pension trust funds 4/ |
|---|---|---|---|---|---|---|---|---|---|---|---|---|
| **Federal Home Loan Banks (Continued):** | | | | | | | | | | | | |
| **Bonds:** | | | | | | | | | | | | |
| 7.30 May 1983 | 184 | 14 | 37 | 9 | * | 1 | 1 | - | 2 | 2 | 119 | 11 |
| 7-3/8 Nov. 1983 | 300 | 29 | 63 | 6 | 1 | 1 | 5 | 8 | 11 | 3 | 174 | 19 |
| 7-3/8 Nov. 1983-93 | 400 | 80 | 128 | 5 | 1 | 1 | 27 | 4 | 4 | 7 | 144 | 4 |
| 8.75 May 1984 | 300 | 52 | 30 | 5 | 1 | 1 | * | 2 | 7 | - | 202 | 27 |
| **FHLMC Mtg. Backed Bonds: 10/** | | | | | | | | | | | | |
| 7.05 Aug. 1976 | 400 | 26 | 160 | 4 | - | 1 | 8 | - | 2 | - | 199 | 3 |
| 6.15 Feb. 1977 | 350 | 17 | 87 | 9 | 2 | 2 | 43 | 11 | 10 | - | 168 | - |
| 8.60 Nov. 1976-95 | 140 | - | 4 | 12 | 2 | - | 5 | - | - | 6 | 113 | 1 |
| 7.75 Aug. 1977-96 | 150 | - | 6 | 13 | 10 | * | 6 | - | - | 18 | 97 | 7 |
| 7.15 May 1982-97 | 150 | - | 4 | 12 | 1 | 2 | 2 | 2 | 3 | 21 | 104 | 6 |
| **FHLMC Mtg. Backed Certificates:** | | | | | | | | | | | | |
| 8.20 Mar. 2005 | 300 | - | 44 | 10 | - | 1 | 6 | 1 | 5 | 6 | 228 | 26 |
| Issues to State and local govts 8/10/ | 361 | | | | | | | | 361 | | - | - |
| **Total** | 22,615 | 1,287 | 5,418 | 620 | 35 | 172 | 901 | 803 | 1,449 | 146 | 11,783 | 741 |
| **Federal Intermediate Credit Banks: 9/** | | | | | | | | | | | | |
| **Debentures:** | | | | | | | | | | | | |
| 9-1/4 Apr. 1975 | 834 | 2 | 137 | 13 | * | 2 | 3 | 2 | 47 | 1 | 627 | 23 |
| 9.45 May 1975 | 806 | 9 | 76 | 4 | - | 4 | 9 | 8 | 46 | - | 650 | 38 |
| 9.80 June 1975 | 734 | 14 | 79 | 16 | * | 6 | 5 | 5 | 30 | - | 580 | 10 |
| 5.70 July 1975 | 302 | 12 | 104 | 11 | - | - | 23 | 13 | 16 | - | 124 | 4 |
| 9.60 July 1975 | 786 | 32 | 72 | 6 | 1 | 1 | - | 19 | 84 | - | 564 | 34 |
| 8.45 Aug. 1975 | 765 | 19 | 71 | 6 | - | 2 | 10 | 7 | 77 | * | 573 | 30 |
| 8.05 Sept. 1975 | 780 | 27 | 193 | 14 | 1 | 2 | 8 | 11 | 48 | * | 478 | 15 |
| 7.35 Oct. 1975 | 468 | 6 | 80 | 10 | - | 1 | 6 | 5 | 54 | - | 306 | 2 |
| 7.05 Nov. 1975 | 769 | 30 | 127 | 12 | - | 1 | 8 | 10 | 21 | - | 561 | 4 |
| 6.15 Dec. 1975 | 926 | 39 | 152 | 8 | 2 | 1 | 11 | 3 | 20 | - | 691 | 3 |
| 6.65 Jan. 1976 | 267 | - | 70 | 8 | - | 3 | 16 | 2 | 11 | - | 157 | 2 |
| 7.10 Jan. 1977 | 236 | - | 69 | 2 | - | 1 | 15 | 29 | 5 | 1 | 115 | 1 |
| 8.70 Apr. 1977 | 321 | 10 | 91 | 9 | - | 3 | 5 | 23 | 5 | - | 115 | 18 |
| 7.10 Jan. 1978 | 406 | 45 | 166 | 11 | 1 | 14 | 20 | 33 | 6 | 1 | 174 | 3 |
| 7.40 Jan. 1979 | 410 | 7 | 156 | 6 | - | 2 | 23 | 6 | 20 | - | 190 | 11 |
| **Total** | 8,810 | 251 | 1,643 | 135 | 4 | 39 | 170 | 177 | 489 | 3 | 5,900 | 195 |

Federal Land Banks:
Bonds:

| Issue | Amount | | | | | | | | | | | |
|---|---|---|---|---|---|---|---|---|---|---|---|---|
| 4-1/8 Feb. 1973–78 | 148 | – | 34 | 5 | 4 | 2 | 5 | 20 | 1 | 1 | 75 | 3 |
| 4-3/8 Apr. 1975 | 200 | 2 | 25 | 6 | 1 | 2 | 3 | 8 | 37 | 2 | 113 | 5 |
| 7.65 Apr. 1975 | 300 | * | 60 | 5 | * | 1 | 5 | 8 | 27 | 1 | 193 | 8 |
| 5.70 July 1975 | 425 | * | 116 | 13 | 1 | 3 | 45 | 37 | 11 | – | 198 | 2 |
| 8.30 July 1975 | 300 | 1 | 58 | 5 | – | * | 8 | 1 | 4 | * | 224 | 2 |
| 7.20 Oct. 1975 | 300 | 7 | 52 | 10 | 2 | 1 | 7 | 1 | 6 | * | 215 | 4 |
| 7.40 Oct. 1975 | 362 | 4 | 117 | 7 | * | * | 5 | 19 | 10 | – | 200 | 5 |
| 6.25 Jan. 1976 | 300 | 32 | 75 | 15 | 2 | 7 | 18 | 15 | 1 | 1 | 135 | 2 |
| 9.20 Jan. 1976 | 651 | 5 | 86 | 5 | * | 1 | 2 | 47 | 62 | 2 | 442 | 9 |
| 5 Feb. 1976 | 123 | – | 13 | 4 | 1 | 3 | 3 | 9 | 4 | 2 | 84 | 5 |
| 6-1/4 Apr. 1976 | 373 | 15 | 103 | 9 | 3 | 1 | 26 | 17 | 11 | – | 189 | 3 |
| 8-1/4 Apr. 1976 | 400 | * | 91 | 12 | * | 2 | 15 | 10 | 9 | 2 | 257 | 3 |
| 5-3/8 July 1976 | 150 | – | 12 | 4 | * | 4 | 2 | * | 6 | 6 | 114 | 5 |
| 7.05 July 1976 | 360 | 26 | 85 | 15 | * | 1 | 22 | 16 | 29 | * | 173 | 6 |
| 7.15 Oct. 1976 | 450 | 36 | 134 | 14 | * | 1 | 17 | 20 | 5 | 2 | 220 | 5 |
| 8-1/4 Apr. 1977 | 565 | 42 | 130 | 17 | * | 1 | 15 | 5 | 9 | 3 | 347 | 9 |
| 7-1/2 July 1977 | 550 | 38 | 155 | 8 | * | 10 | 23 | 10 | 54 | 5 | 240 | 7 |
| 6.35 Oct. 1977 | 300 | 29 | 103 | 13 | * | 3 | 10 | – | 12 | – | 134 | 2 |
| 8.70 Jan. 1978 | 546 | 20 | 108 | 2 | * | 1 | 10 | 4 | 5 | 1 | 384 | 25 |
| 5-1/8 Apr. 1978 | 150 | – | 17 | 20 | 1 | 6 | 2 | 7 | 13 | 5 | 96 | 3 |
| 7.60 Apr. 1978 | 269 | 3 | 245 | 8 | 2 | * | 18 | 31 | 9 | 2 | 386 | 16 |
| 6.40 July 1978 | 714 | 2 | 90 | 2 | 1 | 10 | 6 | 20 | 2 | * | 130 | 2 |
| 9.15 July 1978 | 350 | – | 67 | 3 | – | 8 | 2 | 20 | 7 | 4 | 251 | 17 |
| 7.35 Oct. 1978 | 550 | 10 | 212 | 12 | – | 1 | 31 | 71 | 16 | 4 | 203 | 5 |
| 5 Jan. 1979 | 514 | 17 | 51 | 7 | – | 2 | 12 | 20 | 19 | 1 | 365 | 3 |
| 7.10 Jan. 1979 | 300 | 10 | 105 | 18 | 6 | 1 | 35 | 5 | 17 | 1 | 123 | 2 |
| 6.85 Apr. 1979 | 235 | 36 | 47 | 14 | * | 2 | 2 | 15 | 6 | 1 | 135 | 5 |
| 7.15 July 1979 | 389 | 43 | 136 | 28 | * | 1 | 9 | 14 | 27 | 2 | 163 | 7 |
| 6.80 Oct. 1979 | 400 | 3 | 144 | 12 | * | 4 | 3 | 5 | 8 | 4 | 155 | 4 |
| 6.70 Jan. 1980 | 300 | 3 | 100 | 2 | 1 | 2 | 4 | 10 | 10 | 3 | 158 | 5 |
| 7-1/2 July 1980 | 250 | 77 | 74 | 8 | 2 | 6 | 2 | 10 | 3 | * | 147 | 12 |
| 8.70 July 1980 | 400 | 5 | 85 | 14 | * | 6 | 3 | 3 | 8 | 6 | 204 | 41 |
| 6.70 Apr. 1981 | 224 | 15 | 45 | 10 | – | * | 6 | * | 9 | – | 142 | 6 |
| 9.10 Apr. 1981 | 265 | 82 | 26 | 11 | – | 11 | * | 9 | 3 | 1 | 200 | 35 |
| 7.80 Jan. 1982 | 400 | – | 45 | 24 | – | 4 | 2 | – | 5 | – | 238 | 68 |
| 6.90 Apr. 1982 | 200 | 47 | 31 | 4 | 1 | * | 3 | – | 1 | 1 | 134 | 6 |
| 7.30 Oct. 1982 | 239 | 31 | 32 | 4 | 1 | * | 1 | – | 3 | 1 | 150 | 9 |
| 7.30 Oct. 1983 | 300 | | 58 | | 1 | 5 | 1 | 25 | 8 | 1 | 167 | 7 |
| **Total** | **13,252** | **656** | **3,168** | **376** | **31** | **122** | **379** | **500** | **475** | **59** | **7,485** | **365** |

Federal National Mortgage Association:
Discount Notes ..................  2,835  |  –  |  207  |  15  |  *  |  2  |  18  |  108  |  739  |  11  |  1,735  |  79

Debentures:

| Issue | Amount | | | | | | | | | | | |
|---|---|---|---|---|---|---|---|---|---|---|---|---|
| 5-1/4 June 1975 | 500 | 37 | 119 | 8 | 1 | 3 | 74 | 52 | 4 | 1 | 201 | 5 |
| 6.80 Sept. 1975 | 650 | 67 | 154 | 14 | 1 | 5 | 50 | 21 | 6 | 1 | 331 | 14 |
| 7.50 Sept. 1975 | 350 | 37 | 59 | 17 | * | 2 | 29 | 34 | 9 | * | 162 | 4 |
| 5.70 Dec. 1975 | 500 | 29 | 132 | 13 | 1 | 2 | 51 | 43 | 9 | * | 219 | 3 |
| 8.25 Dec. 1975 | 300 | 13 | 87 | 5 | * | 1 | 5 | 16 | 5 | – | 168 | 3 |

Footnotes at end of table.

# TREASURY SURVEY OF OWNERSHIP, MARCH 31, 1975

## - Securities Issued by Government-Sponsored Agencies and the District of Columbia—Continued

(Par values – in millions of dollars)

| Issue | Total amount outstanding | U.S. Government accounts and Federal Reserve banks | 5,564 commercial banks 2/ | 475 mutual savings banks 2/ | 289 life | 444 fire, casualty, and marine | 486 savings and loan associations | 461 corporations | 315 general funds | 188 pension and retirement funds | Held by all other investors 3/ | Memorandum: Held by 57,701 corporate pension trust funds 4/ |
|---|---|---|---|---|---|---|---|---|---|---|---|---|
| **Federal National Mortgage Association (Continued):** | | | | | | | | | | | | |
| **Debentures:** | | | | | | | | | | | | |
| 5.65 Mar. 1976...... | 500 | 45 | 120 | 10 | 1 | 6 | 78 | 13 | 9 | * | 218 | 4 |
| 7-1/8 Mar. 1976...... | 400 | 16 | 147 | 9 | - | 1 | 17 | 22 | 3 | - | 185 | 6 |
| 5.85 June 1976...... | 450 | 38 | 116 | 9 | 2 | 3 | 68 | 33 | 5 | - | 175 | 2 |
| 6.70 June 1976...... | 250 | - | 41 | 12 | * | 1 | 28 | 7 | 3 | - | 158 | 2 |
| 10 June 1976...... | 700 | 37 | 131 | 14 | 1 | 2 | 25 | 24 | 77 | * | 391 | 24 |
| 5.85 Sept. 1976...... | 500 | 41 | 141 | 23 | * | 1 | 51 | 33 | 3 | * | 206 | 1 |
| 6-1/8 Sept. 1976...... | 300 | 29 | 82 | 14 | - | * | 29 | 1 | 3 | * | 142 | 2 |
| 7.50 Sept. 1976...... | 500 | 1 | 59 | 7 | - | 1 | 6 | 5 | 3 | * | 119 | 3 |
| 6.25 Dec. 1976...... | 500 | 21 | 151 | 12 | 2 | * | 60 | 6 | 8 | - | 238 | 5 |
| 7.45 Dec. 1976...... | 300 | 30 | 54 | 18 | 1 | * | 10 | .8 | 11 | 2 | 175 | 11 |
| 8.45 Dec. 1976...... | 600 | 65 | 113 | 8 | 7 | 2 | 14 | 41 | 12 | 6 | 343 | 8 |
| 4-1/2 Feb. 1977...... | 198 | - | 15 | 6 | - | 4 | 15 | 6 | 6 | - | 134 | 4 |
| 6.30 Mar. 1977...... | 500 | 36 | 127 | 23 | * | 5 | 56 | 5 | 8 | - | 240 | 2 |
| 7.05 Mar. 1977...... | 400 | 17 | 115 | 8 | * | 1 | 38 | 13 | 33 | - | 175 | 2 |
| 6.50 June 1977...... | 150 | - | 54 | 8 | - | * | 10 | - | 1 | - | 77 | 4 |
| 6-3/8 June 1977...... | 250 | 6 | 69 | 11 | - | 1 | 16 | 1 | 1 | - | 147 | * |
| 7.20 June 1977...... | 500 | 52 | 175 | 7 | * | 13 | 27 | 31 | 18 | * | 190 | 10 |
| 6-7/8 Sept. 1977...... | 300 | 39 | 68 | 9 | - | * | 18 | 1 | 1 | - | 150 | 6 |
| 7.85 Sept. 1977...... | 400 | 66 | 106 | 8 | - | * | 16 | 18 | 14 | * | 171 | 18 |
| 7-1/4 Dec. 1977...... | 500 | 34 | 173 | 9 | * | * | 32 | 29 | 20 | 4 | 200 | 10 |
| 7.55 Dec. 1977...... | 500 | 44 | 189 | 14 | - | 2 | 27 | 53 | 31 | - | 141 | 3 |
| 6.70 Mar. 1978...... | 350 | 23 | 106 | 3 | - | 1 | 20 | 13 | 2 | 3 | 182 | 7 |
| 8.45 Mar. 1978...... | 650 | 130 | 188 | 14 | 1 | 3 | 24 | 27 | 6 | 1 | 255 | 18 |
| 7.15 June 1978...... | 600 | 66 | 191 | 14 | 1 | 2 | 38 | 7 | 41 | | 239 | 16 |

| Rate | Month | Year | | | | | | | | | | | | |
|---|---|---|---|---|---|---|---|---|---|---|---|---|---|---|
| 7.15 | Sept. | 1978 | 550 | 43 | 194 | 15 | 1 | 1 | 77 | - | 40 | - | 179 | 10 |
| 6.75 | Dec. | 1978 | 300 | 45 | 108 | 17 | * | 7 | 7 | 2 | 2 | 2 | 110 | 5 |
| 8.95 | Dec. | 1978 | 450 | 10 | 44 | 7 | 1 | 7 | 6 | 11 | 3 | * | 367 | 28 |
| 7.25 | Mar. | 1979 | 500 | 40 | 214 | 11 | 4 | * | 30 | 26 | 10 | - | 162 | 7 |
| 7.85 | June | 1979 | 300 | 60 | 89 | 5 | 1 | 3 | 4 | 10 | 7 | 1 | 125 | 12 |
| 9.80 | June | 1979 | 600 | 50 | 165 | 3 | 4 | 1 | 11 | 2 | 42 | - | 320 | 37 |
| 6.40 | Sept. | 1979 | 300 | 16 | 103 | 20 | 1 | 3 | 17 | 12 | 6 | - | 124 | 2 |
| 7.80 | Sept. | 1979 | 700 | 55 | 222 | 13 | 1 | 1 | 40 | 22 | 9 | - | 337 | 21 |
| 6.55 | Dec. | 1979 | 250 | 34 | 112 | 32 | 1 | * | 13 | * | 5 | 2 | 150 | 5 |
| 6-7/8 | Dec. | 1979 | 350 | 15 | 65 | 24 | 1 | 3 | 6 | - | 1 | * | 131 | 6 |
| 7.25 | Mar. | 1980 | 750 | 60 | 151 | 26 | - | 6 | 122 | 2 | 7 | 2 | 378 | 20 |
| 8.50 | Mar. | 1980 | 600 | 70 | 63 | 5 | - | 4 | 1 | 6 | 3 | * | 449 | 25 |
| 7.50 | June | 1980 | 400 | 58 | 186 | 4 | 1 | 1 | 4 | 21 | 4 | 2 | 121 | 9 |
| 6.60 | Sept. | 1980 | 300 | 42 | 114 | 22 | 1 | 1 | 3 | 1 | 6 | 2 | 107 | 7 |
| 7.05 | Dec. | 1980 | 350 | 12 | 63 | 8 | * | 3 | 4 | - | 2 | 8 | 256 | 12 |
| 7-1/4 | Mar. | 1981 | 250 | 23 | 42 | 13 | * | 1 | 8 | 3 | 1 | 2 | 152 | 6 |
| 7-1/4 | June | 1981 | 250 | 31 | 45 | 19 | * | 1 | 7 | 5 | 2 | 1 | 139 | 6 |
| 9.70 | Sept. | 1981 | 300 | 55 | 46 | 2 | - | 6 | 2 | 21 | 67 | * | 101 | 40 |
| 7.30 | Sept. | 1981 | 250 | 32 | 88 | 7 | * | 2 | 5 | - | 2 | 3 | 115 | 3 |
| 8-7/8 | Dec. | 1981 | 300 | 19 | 26 | 2 | 1 | * | - | 1 | 1 | 1 | 238 | 44 |
| 6.65 | Mar. | 1982 | 250 | 15 | 44 | 31 | - | 2 | 13 | 2 | 1 | - | 142 | 9 |
| 6.80 | June | 1982 | 200 | 14 | 55 | 12 | 3 | 1 | 3 | 1 | 13 | * | 97 | 3 |
| 7.35 | Sept. | 1982 | 300 | 60 | 142 | 6 | - | 2 | 4 | - | 1 | - | 88 | 7 |
| 6.75 | Dec. | 1982 | 300 | 21 | 34 | 10 | 6 | 2 | * | 3 | 3 | 1 | 115 | 3 |
| 7.30 | June | 1983 | 300 | 54 | 80 | 4 | - | 2 | 7 | 10 | 1 | - | 141 | 15 |
| 6.75 | June | 1983 | 250 | 50 | 38 | 31 | 3 | 1 | 2 | 4 | 2 | 1 | 115 | 3 |
| 6-1/4 | Sept. | 1983 | 200 | 17 | 42 | 16 | 1 | * | 9 | 4 | 5 | 1 | 105 | 1 |
| 6.75 | Sept. | 1984 | 300 | 48 | 20 | 5 | 4 | 8 | 11 | 1 | 1 | 4 | 207 | 38 |
| 7.95 | June | 1984 | 250 | 40 | 19 | 17 | - | 2 | 1 | 27 | 4 | * | 161 | 5 |
| 6.90 | Dec. | 1984 | 500 | 43 | 49 | 10 | 1 | 8 | 9 | 1 | 2 | 8 | 333 | 31 |
| 7 | Mar. | 1985 | 200 | 40 | 13 | 30 | 2 | 3 | 15 | - | 2 | 8 | 91 | 4 |
| 7.65 | Mar. | 1992 | 200 | 31 | 18 | 9 | 1 | 1 | 11 | - | 5 | 24 | 110 | 6 |
| 7.10 | June | 1992 | 200 | 23 | 10 | 16 | 10 | 1 | 8 | - | 1 | 14 | 114 | 9 |
| | Dec. | 1982-97 | | | | | | | | | | | | |
| **Capital Debentures:** | | | | | | | | | | | | | | |
| 8 | Apr. | 1975 | 200 | - | 28 | 8 | - | 1 | 10 | 2 | 22 | - | 130 | 7 |
| 4-3/8 | Oct. | 1996 | 248 | - | 3 | 3 | 2 | 8 | 8 | 12 | - | 2 | 210 | 69 |
| 7.40 | Oct. | 1982-97 | 250 | 38 | 30 | 58 | 5 | 1 | 11 | - | 3 | 22 | 83 | 7 |
| **Mtg. Backed Bonds:** | | | | | | | | | | | | | | |
| 8-3/8 | June | 1975 | 250 | 6 | 24 | 4 | * | * | 5 | 3 | 13 | 8 | 187 | 17 |
| 8-5/8 | Oct. | 1980-90 | 200 | 40 | 9 | 17 | 1 | 4 | 5 | * | 7 | 15 | 102 | 3 |
| Issues to State and local govts. 8/ | | | 551 | - | - | - | - | - | - | - | - | - | - | - |
| **Total** | | | 28,232 | 2,327 | 6,289 | 883 | 75 | 157 | 1,450 | 874 | 1,960 | 158 | 14,059 | 797 |
| **District of Columbia:** | | | 20 | | | | | | | | | | | |
| 4.20 | Dec. | 1970-79 | 20 | - | * | 3 | * | 1 | 5 | - | - | 2 | 8 | - |

Footnotes at end of table.

T-17

# TREASURY SURVEY OF OWNERSHIP, MARCH 31, 1975

## Footnotes to Treasury Survey of Ownership Tables

1/ Securities issued by the Treasury and Government agencies that are classified as debt under the new unified budget concept.

2/ Includes trust departments.

3/ Included with all other investors are those banks, insurance companies, savings and loan associations, corporations, and State and local government funds not reporting in the Treasury Survey. Also included are certain Government deposit accounts and Government-sponsored agencies.

4/ Consists of corporate pension trust funds and profit-sharing plans which involve retirement benefits. The data are compiled from quarterly reports by bank trustees who report total number of funds administered and Public Debt and Agency Securities held. It is estimated that these funds account for approximately 90 percent of Federal Securities held by all corporate pension trust funds. Since the data are not available each month, the regular monthly Survey includes holdings by these funds under "Held by all other private

investors." The quarterly data are presented as supplemental information in a memorandum column accompanying the Survey for each reporting date, beginning with December 31, 1953.

5/ Data on holdings of nonmarketable public debt were no longer collected beginning with July 1974 Treasury Survey of Ownership.

6/ Includes Export-Import Bank and Government National Mortgage Association participation certificates.

7/ Includes matured securities outstanding on which interest has ceased.

8/ Direct Placements with State and Local Governments with various interest rates and maturity dates.

9/ Includes securities issued for use as collateral for short-term borrowings.

10/ Obligation of the Federal Home Loan Mortgage Corporation. The capital stock of the Federal Home Loan Mortgage Corporation is held by the twelve Federal Home Loan Banks.

* Less than $500,000.

# MARKET QUOTATIONS ON TREASURY SECURITIES, APRIL 30, 1975

Current market quotations shown here are over-the-counter closing bid quotations in the New York market for the last trading day of the month, as reported to the Treasury by the Federal Reserve Bank of New York. The securities listed include all regularly quoted public marketable securities issued by the United States Treasury. Securities issued by Federal agencies and guaranteed by the United States Government are excluded.

## Treasury Bills

| Amount outstanding (millions) | | Issue date | | Maturity date | Bank discount | |
|---|---|---|---|---|---|---|
| 13-week | 26-week | 13-week | 26-week | | Bid | Change from last month |
| $2,702 | $2,100 | 2/6/75 | 11/7/74 | 5/8/75 | 5.41% | -.06% |
| 2,701 | 2,104 | 2/13/75 | 11/14/74 | 5/15/75 | 5.28 | -.18 |
| 2,704 | 2,105 | 2/20/75 | 11/21/74 | 5/22/75 | 5.30 | -.18 |
| 2,702 | 2,102 | 2/27/75 | 11/29/74 | 5/29/75 | 5.30 | -.18 |
| 2,702 | 2,104 | 3/6/75 | 12/5/74 | 6/5/75 | 5.36 | -.21 |
| 2,602 | 2,102 | 3/13/75 | 12/12/74 | 6/12/75 | 5.35 | -.21 |
| 2,504 | 2,001 | 3/20/75 | 12/19/74 | 6/19/75 | 5.35 | -.25 |
| 2,502 | 2,004 | 3/27/75 | 12/26/74 | 6/26/75 | 5.38 | -.15 |
| 2,705 | 2,119 | 4/3/75 | 1/2/75 | 7/3/75 | 5.44 | -.20 |
| 2,701 | 2,304 | 4/10/75 | 1/9/75 | 7/10/75 | 5.46 | -.20 |
| 2,698 | 2,205 | 4/17/75 | 1/16/75 | 7/17/75 | 5.48 | -.18 |
| 2,702 | 2,202 | 4/24/75 | 1/23/75 | 7/24/75 | 5.50 | -.18 |
| | 2,301 | | 1/30/75 | 7/31/75 | 5.50 | -.19 |
| | 2,401 | | 2/6/75 | 8/7/75 | 5.63 | -.08 |
| | 2,499 | | 2/13/75 | 8/14/75 | 5.64 | -.09 |
| | 2,503 | | 2/20/75 | 8/21/75 | 5.70 | -.05 |
| | 2,550 | | 2/27/75 | 8/28/75 | 5.78 | +.03 |
| | 2,501 | | 3/6/75 | 9/4/75 | 5.86 | +.11 |
| | 2,502 | | 3/13/75 | 9/11/75 | 5.87 | +.11 |
| | 2,502 | | 3/20/75 | 9/18/75 | 5.90 | +.15 |
| | 2,601 | | 3/27/75 | 9/25/75 | 5.91 | +.15 |
| | 2,700 | | 4/3/75 | 10/2/75 | 5.95 | - |
| | 2,801 | | 4/10/75 | 10/9/75 | 5.97 | - |
| | 2,709 | | 4/17/75 | 10/16/75 | 5.97 | - |
| | 2,701 | | 4/24/75 | 10/23/75 | 5.98 | - |
| | 2,700 | | 5/1/75 | 10/30/75 | 5.91 | - |

| Amount outstanding (millions) | Issue date | Maturity date | Bank discount | |
|---|---|---|---|---|
| 52-week | 52-week | | Bid | Change from last month |
| $1,802 | 5/7/74 | 5/6/75 | 5.48% | +.09% |
| 1,802 | 6/4/74 | 6/3/75 | 5.31 | -.21 |
| 1,802 | 7/2/74 | 7/1/75 | 5.42 | -.20 |
| 1,806 | 7/30/74 | 7/29/75 | 5.52 | -.17 |
| 1,803 | 8/27/74 | 8/26/75 | 5.73 | -.02 |
| 1,803 | 9/24/74 | 9/23/75 | 5.91 | +.21 |
| 2,003 | 10/22/74 | 10/21/75 | 5.97 | +.20 |
| 2,002 | 11/19/74 | 11/18/75 | 6.04 | +.26 |
| 2,001 | 12/17/74 | 12/16/75 | 6.11 | +.31 |
| 2,001 | 1/14/75 | 1/13/76 | 6.28 | +.36 |
| 2,103 | 2/11/75 | 2/10/76 | 6.38 | +.45 |
| 2,102 | 3/11/75 | 3/9/76 | 6.40 | +.51 |
| 2,205 | 4/8/75 | 4/6/76 | 6.33 | - |
| Special issue | | | | |
| $1,501 | 11/4/74 | 6/19/75 | 5.35% | -.25% |
| 2,003 | 9/4/75 | 6/30/75 | 5.38 | -.22 |
| 1,586 | 4/14/75 | 1/31/76 | 6.26 | - |

Federal Financing Bank bills and tax anticipation bills

| Amount outstanding (millions) | Issue date | Maturity date | Bank discount | |
|---|---|---|---|---|
| | | | Bid | Change from last month |
| $1,256 TAB | 12/5/74 | 6/17/75 | 5.35% | -.23% |

# T-18 *(Continued)*

## Treasury Notes

(Price decimals are 32d's)

| Amount outstanding (millions) | | Description | Price Bid | Price Change from last month | Yield To maturity | Yield Change from last month | Issue date | High Price | High Date | Low Price | Low Date |
|---|---|---|---|---|---|---|---|---|---|---|---|
| $6,760 | 6% | 5/15/75-B | 99.31 | .00 | 6.68% | +.56% | 5/15/68 | 105.22 | 3/22/71 | 90.00 | 5/18/71 |
| 1,776 | 5-7/8 | 5/15/75-F | 99.31 | +.01 | 6.57 | +.30 | 4/3/72 | 101.07 | 5/30/72 | 95.16 | 8/7/73 |
| 7,679 | 5-7/8 | 8/15/75-C | 99.30 | .00 | 6.02 | +.02 | 2/15/71 | 105.00 | 3/22/71 | 95.01 | 8/7/73 |
| 2,042 | 8-3/8 | 9/30/75-G | 100.27 | -.08 | 6.23 | +.14 | 9/4/73 | 102.26 | 12/17/73 | 98.04 | 8/23/74 |
| 3,115 | 7 | 11/15/75-D | 100.09 | -.08 | 6.45 | +.34 | 8/15/71 | 106.09 | 1/14/72 | 96.27 | 8/23/74 |
| 1,731 | 7 | 12/31/75-H | 100.10 | -.08 | 6.51 | +.29 | 11/15/73 | 101.00 | 2/18/75 | 96.19 | 8/23/74 |
| 3,739 | 6-1/4 | 2/15/76-A | 99.19 | -.11 | 6.78 | +.46 | 2/15/69 | 106.24 | 3/22/71 | 91.20 | 1/30/70 |
| 4,945 | 5-7/8 | 2/15/76-F | 99.10 | -.09 | 6.78 | +.42 | 8/15/72 | 100.03 | 2/5/75 | 94.04 | 8/7/73 |
| 2,288 | 8 | 3/31/76-H | 100.31 | -.19 | 6.88 | +.53 | 4/9/74 | 102.12 | 2/5/75 | 98.00 | 8/23/74 |
| 2,697 | 6-1/2 | 5/15/76-H | 99.21 | -.13 | 6.84 | +.40 | 5/15/69 | 107.24 | 3/22/71 | 92.16 | 1/30/70 |
| 2,802 | 5-3/4 | 5/15/76-E | 98.26 | -.13 | 6.95 | +.47 | 2/15/72 | 101.00 | 2/17/72 | 93.12 | 8/26/73 |
| 1,580 | 6 | 5/31/76-M | 99.02 | -.13 | 6.90 | +.45 | 3/25/75 | 99.31 | 3/14/75 | 98.27 | 4/28/75 |
| 2,703 | 8-3/4 | 6/30/76-I | 101.28 | -.23 | 7.04 | +.49 | 5/15/74 | 103.18 | 2/5/75 | 99.02 | 8/23/74 |
| 4,194 | 7-1/2 | 8/15/76-G | 100.15 | -.22 | 7.11 | +.50 | 10/1/69 | 111.08 | 3/22/71 | 97.04 | 8/26/74 |
| 3,883 | 6-1/2 | 8/15/76-G | 99.06 | -.22 | 7.16 | +.57 | 2/15/73 | 100.24 | 2/19/75 | 95.04 | 8/26/74 |
| 1,662 | 5-7/8 | 8/31/76-L | 98.10 | -.23 | 7.23 | +.62 | 3/3/75 | 99.26 | 2/21/75 | 99.01 | 3/31/75 |
| 2,023 | 8-1/4 | 9/30/76-J | 101.12 | -.26 | 7.20 | +.52 | 9/30/74 | 103.08 | 2/20/75 | 99.24 | 10/2/74 |
| 4,325 | 6-1/4 | 11/15/76-D | 98.14 | -.29 | 7.34 | +.65 | 9/8/71 | 103.27 | 12/28/71 | 94.02 | 8/23/73 |
| 1,507 | 7-1/8 | 11/30/76-N | 99.21 | — | 7.34 | — | 4/8/75 | 99.29+ | 4/1/75 | 99.13 | 4/22/75 |
| 2,282 | 7-1/4 | 12/31/76-K | 99.25 | -1.01 | 7.39 | +.64 | 12/31/74 | 102.00 | 2/19/75 | 99.17 | 4/21/75 |
| 5,163 | 8 | 2/15/77-A | 100.28 | -1.07 | 7.46 | +.67 | 2/15/70 | 114.08 | 3/22/71 | 98.08 | 8/23/74 |
| 1,665 | 6-1/2 | 2/28/77-F | 97.11 | -1.06 | 7.58 | +.75 | 3/3/75 | 99.26 | 2/21/75 | 97.03 | 4/7/75 |
| 2,576 | 6-1/4 | 3/31/77-G | 98.01 | -1.13 | 7.62 | +.81 | 3/31/75 | 99.27 | 3/20/75 | 97.26 | 4/22/75 |
| 1,570 | 7-3/8 | 4/30/77-H | 99.23 | — | 7.53 | — | 4/30/75 | 100.02 | 4/16/75 | 99.15 | 4/22/75 |
| 2,565 | 6-7/8 | 5/15/77-C | 98.18 | -1.12 | 7.65 | +.74 | 2/15/74 | 101.13 | 2/21/75 | 94.29 | 8/26/74 |
| 5,329 | 9 | 5/15/77-D | 102.16 | -1.23 | 7.65 | +.82 | 8/15/74 | 105.19 | 2/21/75 | 99.31 | 8/23/74 |
| 4,918 | 7-3/4 | 8/15/77-B | 100.08 | -1.16 | 7.62 | +.69 | 8/15/70 | 114.00 | 3/22/71 | 97.04 | 8/26/74 |
| 3,630 | 7-3/4 | 11/15/77-E | 100.04 | -1.22 | 7.69 | +.71 | 11/15/71 | 103.19 | 2/21/75 | 99.30 | 4/28/75 |
| 8,389 | 6-1/4 | 2/15/78-A | 96.06 | -1.23 | 7.79 | +.72 | 2/15/71 | 106.20 | 3/22/71 | 92.06 | 8/23/74 |
| 2,462 | 8-3/4 | 8/15/78-C | 102.16 | -2.03 | 7.87 | +.68 | 5/15/74 | 106.10 | 2/5/75 | 99.24 | 8/23/74 |
| 3,960 | 7-1/8 | 5/15/78-D | 97.30 | -2.00 | 7.90 | +.75 | 2/18/75 | 101.28 | 2/19/75 | 97.24 | 4/28/75 |
| 8,207 | 6 | 11/15/78-B | 94.11 | -1.29 | 7.86 | +.66 | 11/15/71 | 101.08 | 1/14/72 | 90.10 | 8/23/74 |
| 2,269 | 7-7/8 | 5/15/79-D | 99.18 | -2.08 | 8.00 | +.64 | 11/6/74 | 104.01 | 2/21/75 | 99.10 | 4/21/75 |
| 4,559 | 6-1/4 | 8/15/79-A | 94.08 | -2.04 | 7.85 | +.62 | 8/15/72 | 100.20 | 11/25/72 | 90.04 | 8/23/74 |
| 1,604 | 6-5/8 | 11/15/79-B | 95.08 | -2.08 | 7.89 | +.61 | 2/15/73 | 100.06 | 4/9/73 | 91.02 | 8/23/74 |
| 2,241 | 7 | 11/15/79-C | 96.16 | -2.09 | 7.93 | +.61 | 11/15/73 | 101.10 | 12/20/73 | 92.16 | 8/23/74 |

Footnotes at end of Table

# MARKET QUOTATIONS ON TREASURY SECURITIES, APRIL 30, 1975

## - Treasury Notes—Continued

(Price decimals are 32d's)

| Amount outstanding (millions) | | Description | Price | | Yield | | Issue date | Price range since first traded 1/ | | | |
|---|---|---|---|---|---|---|---|---|---|---|---|
| | | | | | | | | High | | Low | |
| | | | Bid | Change from last month | To maturity | Change from last month | | Price | Date | Price | Date |
| $7,265 | 6-7/8% | 5/15/80-A | 95.12 | -2.08 | 8.00% | +.56% | 5/15/73 | 100.22 | 10/9/73 | 91.16 | 8/23/74 |
| 4,296 | 9 | 8/15/80-B | 103.26 | -2.17 | 8.10 | +.55 | 8/15/74 | 108.18 | 2/19/75 | 100.21 | 8/23/74 |
| 1,842 | 7 | 2/15/81-A | 94.26 | -2.11 | 8.14 | +.53 | 2/15/74 | 100.26 | 2/14/74 | 91.14 | 8/23/74 |
| 2,168 | 7-3/8 | 2/15/81-C | 96.14 | -2.06 | 8.15 | +.48 | 2/18/75 | 101.13 | 2/19/75 | 96.06 | 4/28/75 |
| 4,477 | 7-3/4 | 11/15/81-B | 97.25 | -2.11 | 8.19 | +.46 | 11/15/74 | 103.05 | 12/18/74 | 97.18 | 4/28/75 |
| 30 | 1-1/2 | 10/1/75-EO | 96.14 | +.04 | 10.44 | +1.18 | 10/1/70 | 96.14 | 4/30/75 | 76.16 | 10/30/70 |
| 27 | 1-1/2 | 4/1/76-EA | 94.06 | -.02 | 8.21 | +.61 | 4/1/71 | 94.08 | 3/31/75 | 80.02 | 6/30/71 |
| 11 | 1-1/2 | 10/1/76-EO | 91.30 | .00 | 7.61 | +.33 | 10/1/71 | 99.12 | 2/28/75 | 80.26 | 10/29/73 |
| 5 | 1-1/2 | 4/1/77-EA | 88.18 | -.26 | 8.06 | +.07 | 4/1/72 | 89.12 | 3/31/75 | 80.02 | 4/28/72 |
| 17 | 1-1/2 | 10/1/77-EO | 86.18 | -.14 | 7.70 | +.45 | 10/1/72 | 87.02 | 3/31/75 | 80.16 | 10/31/72 |
| 15 | 1-1/2 | 4/1/78-EA | 84.00 | -.24 | 7.73 | +.48 | 4/1/73 | 84.24 | 3/31/75 | 79.16 | 9/30/74 |
| 3 | 1-1/2 | 10/1/78-EO | 81.24 | -.28 | 7.67 | +.46 | 10/1/73 | 82.20 | 3/31/75 | 77.20 | 9/30/74 |
| 2 | 1-1/2 | 4/1/79-EA | 79.04 | -1.00 | 7.79 | +.46 | 4/1/74 | 80.04 | 3/31/75 | 75.12 | 9/30/74 |
| 1 | 1-1/2 | 10/1/79-EO | 77.04 | -.16 | 7.70 | +.25 | 10/1/74 | 77.20 | 3/31/75 | 73.04 | 10/31/74 |
| .5 | 1-1/2 | 4/1/80-EA | 74.10 | - | 7.91 | - | 4/1/75 | 74.10 | 4/30/75 | 74.10 | 4/30/75 |

# Treasury Bonds

(Price decimals are 32d's)

| Amount outstanding (millions) | Description | | Price Bid | Price Change from last month | Yield To first call or maturity 2/ | Yield Change from last month | Issue date | Price range since first traded 1/ High Price | High Date | Low Price | Low Date |
|---|---|---|---|---|---|---|---|---|---|---|---|
| $1,196 | 4-1/4% | 5/15/75-85 | 78.28 | -1.02 | 7.24% | +.19% | 4/5/60 | 105.28 | 5/5/61 | 66.30 | 5/26/70 |
| 1,452 | 3-1/4 | 6/15/78-83 | 76.16 | -.26 | 7.10 | +.18 | 5/1/53 | 111.28 | 8/4/54 | 62.02 | 5/26/70 |
| 2,568 | 4 | 2/15/80 | 85.00 | -1.28 | 7.81 | +.56 | 1/23/59 | 103.18 | 5/12/61 | 71.04 | 12/29/69 |
| 1,893 | 3-1/2 | 11/15/80 | 82.04 | -1.12 | 7.50 | +.39 | 10/3/60 | 97.24 | 5/12/61 | 66.24 | 5/24/70 |
| 807 | 7 | 8/15/81 | 96.14 | -1.20 | 7.72 | +.33 | 8/15/71 | 110.02 | 11/15/71 | 93.16 | 9/18/74 |
| 2,702 | 6-3/8 | 2/15/82 | 92.06 | -2.10 | 7.88 | +.47 | 2/15/72 | 101.14 | 3/9/72 | 86.16 | 8/28/74 |
| 2,353 | 6-3/8 | 8/15/84 | 92.04 | -2.22 | 7.57 | +.42 | 8/15/72 | 99.24 | 11/15/72 | 87.12 | 8/27/74 |
| 907 | 3-1/4 | 5/15/85 2/ | 75.24 | -.28 | 6.59 | +.16 | 6/3/58 | 101.04 | 6/11/58 | 61.08 | 5/26/70 |
| 1,216 | 6-1/8 | 11/15/86 3/ | 90.10 | -1.12 | 7.38 | +.19 | 11/15/71 | 100.20 | 11/5/71 | 87.16 | 8/27/74 |
| 3,688 | 3-1/2 | 2/15/90 3/ | 75.20 | -1.02 | 6.01 | +.13 | 2/14/58 | 106.26 | 4/21/58 | 59.20 | 5/26/70 |
| 1,247 | 8-1/4 | 5/15/90 3/ | 98.22 | -1.12 | 8.40 | +.16 | 4/7/75 | 100.02 | 3/31/75 | 98.12 | 4/29/75 |
| 3,572 | 4-1/2 | 8/15/87-92 3/ | 76.24 | -.30 | 6.51 | +.11 | 8/15/62 | 104.10 | 12/26/62 | 63.00 | 5/26/70 |
| 223 | 4 | 2/15/88-93 3/ | 76.02 | -1.04 | 6.24 | +.11 | 1/17/63 | 100.11 | 1/16/63 | 62.18 | 5/26/70 |
| 627 | 6-3/4 | 2/15/93 3/ | 86.30 | -1.14 | 8.15 | +.17 | 1/10/73 | 99.22 | 1/4/73 | 82.18 | 8/26/74 |
| 1,914 | 7-1/2 | 8/15/88-93 3/ | 93.12 | -1.08 | 8.20 | +.13 | 8/15/73 | 104.14 | 9/28/73 | 89.16 | 8/26/74 |
| 1,367 | 4-1/4 | 5/15/89-94 3/ | 76.10 | -1.06 | 6.27 | +.13 | 4/18/63 | 100.26 | 8/28/63 | 61.26 | 8/26/74 |
| 730 | 3 | 2/15/95 3/ | 75.20 | -1.00 | 4.94 | +.10 | 2/15/55 | 101.12 | 6/18/55 | 59.20 | 5/26/70 |
| 692 | 7 | 5/15/93-98 3/ | 86.16 | -2.26 | 8.32 | +.30 | 5/15/73 | 99.22 | 9/28/73 | 84.04 | 8/26/74 |
| 2,826 | 3-1/2 | 11/15/98 3/ | 75.18 | -1.02 | 5.33 | +.09 | 10/3/60 | 95.14 | 5/12/61 | 59.20 | 5/26/70 |
| 2,414 | 8-1/2 | 5/15/94-99 3/ | 99.18 | -2.18 | 8.54 | +.24 | 5/15/74 | 106.18 | 2/21/75 | 97.02 | 8/26/74 |
| 902 | 7-7/8 | 2/15/95-00 3/ | 93.24 | -2.14 | 8.45 | +.23 | 2/18/75 | 100.30 | 2/21/75 | 93.14 | 4/28/75 |

1/ Beginning April 1953, prices are closing bid quotations in the over-the-counter market. Prices for prior dates are the mean of closing bid and ask quotations. "When issued" prices are included in the history beginning October 1941. Dates of highs and lows in case of recurrences are the latest dates.

2/ On callable issues market convention treats the yields to the yields to earliest call date as more significant when an issue is selling above par, and to maturity when it is selling at par or below.

3/ Included in the average yield of long-term taxable Treasury bonds as shown under "Average yields of Long-Term Bonds."

# FEDERAL DEBT

## - Interest-Bearing Securities Issued by Government Agencies

(In millions of dollars)

| End of fiscal year or month | Total amount outstanding 1/ | Defense Department — Family housing and homeowners assistance | Housing and Urban Development Department — Federal Housing Administration | Housing and Urban Development Department — Government National Mortgage Association | Housing and Urban Development Department — Federal National Mortgage Assoc. 2/ Secondary market operations | Export-Import Bank of the United States | Other independent agencies — Farm Credit Administration — Banks for cooperatives 3/ | Other independent agencies — Farm Credit Administration — Federal intermediate credit banks 3/ | Other independent agencies — Federal Home Loan Bank Board |
|---|---|---|---|---|---|---|---|---|---|
| 1966 | 13,377 | 2,112 | 441 | 2,110 | 3,269 | 1,385 | 881 | 2,893 | * |
| 1967 | 18,445 | 2,036 | 492 | 4,830 | 4,079 | 2,164 | 1,072 | 3,363 | * |
| 1968 | 24,399 | 1,951 | 548 | 7,900 | 5,887 | 2,571 | 1,230 | 3,779 | 6 |
| 1969 | 14,249 | 1,863 | 577 | 8,600 | - | 2,472 | - | - | 6 |
| 1970 | 12,510 | 1,775 | 517 | 7,320 | - | 1,893 | - | - | 6 |
| 1971 | 12,163 | 1,683 | 487 | 6,005 | - | 2,625 | - | - | 6 |
| 1972 | 10,894 | 1,588 | 454 | 4,920 | - | 1,819 | - | - | 5 |
| 1973 | 11,109 | 1,484 | 412 | 4,480 | - | 2,221 | - | - | 5 |
| 1974 | 12,012 | 1,382 | 408 | 4,370 | - | 2,894 | - | - | 10 |
| 1973-Dec | 11,587 | 1,439 | 415 | 4,390 | - | 2,646 | - | - | 9 |
| 1974-Mar | 11,978r | 1,418r | 409 | 4,390 | - | 3,043 | - | - | 10 |
| Apr | 12,012 | 1,407 | 412 | 4,370 | - | 3,043 | - | - | 10 |
| May | 11,984 | 1,398 | 410 | 4,370 | - | 2,897 | - | - | 10 |
| June | 12,012 | 1,382 | 408 | 4,370 | - | 2,894 | - | - | 10 |
| July | 11,895 | 1,386 | 403 | 4,335 | - | 2,893 | - | - | 10 |
| Aug | 11,831 | 1,370 | 405 | 4,335 | - | 2,893 | - | - | 10 |
| Sept | 11,664 | 1,358 | 411 | 4,335 | - | 2,893 | - | - | 10 |
| Oct | 11,422 | 1,343 | 414 | 4,335 | - | 2,893 | - | - | 10 |
| Nov | 11,404 | 1,334 | 434 | 4,305 | - | 2,893 | - | - | 10 |
| Dec | 11,367 | 1,326 | 440 | 4,280 | - | 2,893 | - | - | 10 |
| 1975-Jan | 11,343 | 1,331 | 461 | 4,280 | - | 2,893 | - | - | - |
| Feb | 11,037 | 1,324 | 462 | 4,280 | - | 2,593 | - | - | - |
| Mar | 11,042 | 1,316 | 475 | 4,280 | - | 2,593 | - | - | - |

|  | Other independent agencies - Continued | | | Memorandum - Interest-bearing securities of non-Government agencies 4/ | | | | | |
|---|---|---|---|---|---|---|---|---|---|
| End of fiscal year or month | Postal Service | Tennessee Valley Authority | Other | Banks for cooperatives 3/ | Federal home loan banks 5/ | Federal intermediate credit banks 3/ | Federal land banks | Federal National Mortgage Association 2/ 6/ | District of Columbia Stadium Fund |
| 1966 | - | 285 | * | - | 6,310 | - | 4,106 | - | 20 |
| 1967 | - | 417 | 3 | - | 4,588 | - | 4,612 | - | 20 |
| 1968 | - | 525 | 3 | - | 4,702 | - | 5,319 | - | 20 |
| 1969 | - | 728 | 3 | 1,411 | 5,524 | 4,240 | 5,720 | 8,076 | 20 |
| 1970 | - | 996 | 3 | 1,529 | 9,914 | 4,942 | 6,192 | 13,165 | 20 |
| 1971 | - | 1,355 | 3 | 1,790 | 7,923 | 5,705 | 6,652 | 14,996 | 20 |
| 1972 | 250 | 1,855 | 3 | 1,805 | 7,848 | 6,188 | 7,393 | 18,560 | 20 |
| 1973 | 250 | 2,255 | 3 | 2,338 | 12,149 | 6,673 | 9,058 | 21,087 | 20 |
| 1974 | 250 | 2,696 | 3 | 2,475 | 18,622 | 7,995 | 11,067 | 25,232 | 20 |
| 1973-Dec | 250 | 2,435 | 3 | 2,695 | 17,146 | 6,932 | 10,062 | 23,002 | **20** |
| 1974-Mar | 250 | 2,455 | 3 | 2,902 | 15,689 | 7,263 | 10,506 | 23,517 | 20 |
| Apr | 250 | 2,517 | 3 | 2,836 | 15,685 | 7,514 | 11,067 | 24,029 | 20 |
| May | 250 | 2,646 | 3 | 2,700 | 16,838 | 7,708 | 11,067 | 24,317 | 20 |
| June | 250 | 2,696 | 3 | 2,475 | 18,622 | 7,995 | 11,067 | 25,232 | 20 |
| July | 250 | 2,615 | 2 | 2,503 | 19,480 | 8,356 | 12,006 | 25,878 | 20 |
| Aug | 250 | 2,565 | 2 | 2,648 | 20,118 | 8,518 | 12,007 | 26,640 | 20 |
| Sept | 250 | 2,405 | 2 | 2,861 | 22,213 | 8,655 | 12,007 | 27,312 | 20 |
| Oct | 250 | 2,175 | 2 | 2,833 | 23,647 | 8,647 | 12,653 | 27,543 | 20 |
| Nov | 250 | 2,175 | 2 | 3,323 | 23,068 | **8,609** | 12,653 | 28,033 | 20 |
| Dec | 250 | 2,175 | 2 | 3,589 | 23,441 | 8,589 | 12,653 | 28,167 | 20 |
| 1975-Jan | 250 | 2,125 | 2 | 3,682 | 23,337 | 8,606 | 13,247 | 28,029r | 20 |
| Feb | 250 | 2,125 | 2 | 3,620 | 22,677 | 8,670 | 13,247 | 27,730 | 20 |
| Mar | 250 | 2,125 | 2 | **3,463** | **22,615** | **8,810** | **13,252** | **28,232** | 20 |

Source: Bureau of Government Financial Operations and Monthly Statement of Receipts and Outlays of the U.S. Government.

1/ Includes unredeemed matured securities outstanding on which interest has ceased.

2/ Effective September 30, 1968, Federal National Mortgage Association was converted to private ownership pursuant to provisions of the Housing and Urban Development Act of 1968 (P.L. 90-448).

3/ Effective December 31, 1968, banks for cooperatives and Federal intermediate credit banks were converted to private ownership pursuant to provisions of Public Law 90-582, October 17, 1968.

4/ For details of securities outstanding, see Table TSO-5.

5/ Includes Federal Home Loan Mortgage Corporation mortgage backed bonds beginning November 1970.

6/ Includes mortgage backed bonds beginning June 1970.

* Less than $500,000.

r Revised.

# FEDERAL DEBT

## - Participation Certificates

(In millions of dollars - face amounts)

| Fiscal year or month | Agriculture Department Commodity Credit Corporation | | | Export-Import Bank of the United States | | | Total | | | Participation certificates issued by GNMA acting as trustee | | | | | |
|---|---|---|---|---|---|---|---|---|---|---|---|---|---|---|---|
| | | | | | | | | | | Farmers Home Administration 1/ | | | Health, Education, and Welfare Department 2/ | | |
| | Sales | Retire-ments | Out-standing | Sales | Retire-ments | Out-standing | Sales | Retire-ments | Out-standing | Sales | Retire-ments | Out-standing | Sales | Retire-ments | Out-standing |
| 1966............. | - | - | - | 761 | 398 | 1,385 | 1,840 | 30 | 2,110 | 600 | - | - | 100 | - | 100 |
| 1967............. | - | - | - | 1,411 2/ | 650 2/ | 2,146 | 2,900 | 180 | 4,830 | 525 | - | 600 | 100 | - | 200 |
| 1968............. | - | - | - | 570 | 533 | 2,183 | 3,250 | 180 | 7,900 | 225 | 184 | 1,125 | 15 | 3 | 212 |
| 1969............. | - | - | - | - | 369 | 1,814 | - | 630 | 8,600 | - | 401 | 1,166 | - | 3 | 209 |
| 1970............. | 2,181 | - | - | - | 321 | 1,493 | - | 1,280 | 7,320 | - | 80 | 765 | - | 2 | 207 |
| 1971............. | - | 2,181 | - | - | 268 | 1,226 | - | 1,315 | 6,005 | - | 168 | 685 | - | 6 | 201 |
| 1972............. | - | - | - | - | 608 | 618 | - | 1,085 | 4,920 | - | 24 | 517 | - | 2 | 199 |
| 1973............. | - | - | - | - | 42 | 576 | - | 440 | 4,480 | - | - | 493 | - | - | 199 |
| 1974............. | - | - | - | - | 327 | 249 | - | 110 | 4,370 | - | - | 493 | - | - | 199 |
| 1973-Dec......... | - | - | - | - | 173 | 401 | - | 25 | 4,390 | - | - | 493 | - | - | 199 |
| 1974-Mar......... | - | - | - | - | - | 399 | - | - | 4,390 | - | - | 493 | - | - | 199 |
| Apr......... | - | - | - | - | 150 | 399 | - | 20 | 4,370 | - | - | 493 | - | - | 199 |
| May......... | - | - | - | - | - | 249 | - | - | 4,370 | - | - | 493 | - | - | 199 |
| June........ | - | - | - | - | - | 249 | - | - | 4,370 | - | - | 493 | - | - | 199 |
| July........ | - | - | - | - | - | 249 | - | 30 | 4,340 | - | - | 493 | - | - | 199 |
| Aug......... | - | - | - | - | - | 249 | - | - | 4,340 | - | - | 493 | - | - | 199 |
| Sept........ | - | - | - | - | - | 249 | - | - | 4,340 | - | - | 493 | - | - | 199 |
| Oct......... | - | - | - | - | - | 249 | - | - | 4,340 | - | - | 493 | - | - | 199 |
| Nov......... | - | - | - | - | - | 249 | - | 30 | 4,311 | - | - | 493 | - | - | 199 |
| Dec......... | - | - | - | - | - | 249 | - | 25 | 4,286 | - | - | 492 | - | - | 198 |
| 1975-Jan......... | - | - | - | - | - | 249 | - | - | 4,286 | - | - | 492 | - | - | 198 |
| Feb......... | - | - | - | - | - | 249 | - | - | 4,286 | - | - | 492 | - | - | 198 |
| Mar......... | - | - | - | - | - | 249 | - | - | 4,286 | - | - | 492 | - | - | 198 |

**T-21 (Continued)**

Participation certificates issued by GNMA acting as trustee – Continued

| Fiscal year or month | Housing and Urban Development Department | | | | | | Small Business Administration 6/ | | | Veterans Administration 7/ | | | (Memorandum) Commodity Credit Corp. (net certificates of interest authorized under Charter Act) 8/ | | |
|---|---|---|---|---|---|---|---|---|---|---|---|---|---|---|---|
| | Office of Secretary 4/ | | | Government National Mortgage Association 5/ | | | | | | | | | | | |
| | Sales | Retirements | Outstanding | Sales | Retirements | Outstanding | Sales | Retirements | Outstanding | Sales | Retirements | Outstanding | Sales | Retirements | Outstanding |
| 1966.......... | – | – | – | 605 | 20 | 785 | 350 | – | 350 | 885 | 10 | 975 | 436 | – | 855 |
| 1967.......... | 680 | – | 680 | 740 | 50 | 1,475 | 520 | 70 | 800 | 260 | 60 | 1,175 | 167 | – | 1,021 |
| 1968.......... | 1,140 | – | 1,820 | 465 | 50 | 1,891 | 430 | 70 | 1,160 | 590 | 60 | 1,704 | – | 99 | 923 |
| 1969.......... | 640 | 27 | 2,433 | 140 | 134 | 1,897 | 50 | 203 | 1,007 | 260 | 79 | 1,885 | 667 | – | 1,590 |
| 1970.......... | – | 324 | 2,109 | – | 190 | 1,707 | – | 225 | 782 | – | 136 | 1,749 | – | – | – |
| 1971.......... | – | 963 | 1,146 | – | 81 | 1,626 | – | 91 | 691 | – | 99 | 1,650 | – | – | – |
| 1972.......... | – | 405 | 741 | – | 193 | 1,433 | – | 206 | 485 | – | 107 | 1,543 | – | – | – |
| 1973.......... | – | 34 | 707 | – | 95 | 1,338 | – | 41 | 444 | – | 243 | 1,300 | – | – | – |
| 1974.......... | – | – | 707 | – | 65 | 1,273 | – | – | 444 | – | 45 | 1,255 | – | – | – |
| 1973–Dec...... | – | – | 707 | – | 15 | 1,286 | – | – | 444 | – | 10 | 1,262 | – | – | – |
| 1974–Mar...... | – | – | 707 | – | – | 1,286 | – | – | 444 | – | – | 1,262 | – | – | – |
| Apr........... | – | – | 707 | – | 13 | 1,273 | – | – | 444 | – | 7 | 1,255 | – | – | – |
| May........... | – | – | 707 | – | – | 1,273 | – | – | 444 | – | – | 1,255 | – | – | – |
| June.......... | – | – | 707 | – | – | 1,273 | – | – | 444 | – | – | 1,255 | – | – | – |
| July.......... | – | – | 707 | – | 30 | 1,243 | – | – | 444 | – | – | 1,255 | – | – | – |
| Aug........... | – | – | 707 | – | – | 1,243 | – | – | 444 | – | – | 1,255 | – | – | – |
| Sept.......... | – | – | 707 | – | – | 1,243 | – | – | 444 | – | – | 1,255 | – | – | – |
| Oct........... | – | – | 707 | – | – | 1,243 | – | – | 444 | – | – | 1,255 | – | – | – |
| Nov........... | – | – | 707 | – | 19 | 1,224 | – | – | 444 | – | 11 | 1,244 | – | – | – |
| Dec........... | – | – | 707 | – | 16 | 1,208 | – | – | 444 | – | 10 | 1,234 | – | – | – |
| 1975–Jan...... | – | – | 707 | – | – | 1,208 | – | – | 444 | – | – | 1,234 | – | – | – |
| Feb........... | – | – | 707 | – | – | 1,208 | – | – | 444 | – | – | 1,234 | – | – | – |
| Mar........... | – | – | 707 | – | – | 1,208 | – | – | 444 | – | – | 1,234 | – | – | – |

Source: Bureau of Government Financial Operations.
1/ Includes the Direct Loan program through September 1972, the Agricultural Credit Insurance fund beginning October 1972, and the Rural Housing Loan programs.
2/ Includes Construction of Higher Education Facilities, Health Professions Education Fund, and Nurse Training Fund, beginning April 1968.
3/ Includes $107 million refunding transaction.
4/ Includes College Housing, Elderly Housing, and Public Facility programs.
5/ Includes Special Assistance, and Management and Liquidating programs.
6/ Includes programs for Disaster Loans, and Business Loans and Investments.
7/ Includes Direct Loan and Loan Guaranty programs.
8/ In the case of Commodity Credit Corporation, participation certificates are called "certificates of interest" and are not included in the Participation Sales Act of 1966. Amounts shown as sales and retirements represent the net excess transactions for the period. On July 1, 1969, the amount outstanding was reclassified as agency securities.

*Source: Treasury Bulletin (May 1975)*

# U.S. savings bonds

# D

# UNITED STATES SAVINGS BONDS

Series E and Series H are the only savings bonds currently sold. Series E has been on sale since May 1, 1941, and Series H has been on sale since June 1, 1952. Series A – D were sold from March 1, 1935 through April 30, 1941. Series F and G were sold from May 1, 1941 through April 30, 1952. Series J and K were sold from May 1, 1952 through April 30, 1957. Details of the principal changes in issues, interest yields, maturities, and other terms appear in the Treasury Bulletins of April 1951, May 1952, May 1957, October and December 1959, May and October 1961, June 1968, and September 1970; and the Annual Report of the Secretary of the Treasury for fiscal years 1966 through 1974.

## Sales and Redemptions by Series, Cumulative through April 30, 1975

(In millions of dollars)

| Series | Sales 1/ | Accrued discount | Sales plus accrued discount | Redemptions 1/ | Amount outstanding | |
|---|---|---|---|---|---|---|
| | | | | | Interest-bearing debt | Matured non-interest-bearing debt |
| Series A-D 2/.............. | 3,949 | 1,054 | 5,003 | 4,999 | - | 4 |
| Series E and H............ | 178,151 | 42,795 | 220,946 | 156,216 | 64,730 | - |
| Series F and G............ | 28,396 | 1,125 | 29,521 | 29,502 | - | 19 |
| Series J and K............ | 3,556 | 198 | 3,754 | 3,749 | - | 5 |
| Total A-K................. | 214,051 | 45,172 | 259,224 | 194,466 | 64,730 | 28 |

## Table SB-2. - Sales and Redemptions by Periods, All Series Combined

(In millions of dollars)

| Period | Sales 1/ | Accrued discount | Sales plus accrued discount | Redemptions 1/ Total | Sales Price 2/ | Accrued discount 2/ | Interest-bearing debt | Matured non-interest-bearing debt |
|---|---|---|---|---|---|---|---|---|
| Fiscal years: | | | | | | | | |
| 1935-64............ | 156,519 | 22,727 | 179,246 | 129,807 | 117,782 | 12,025 | 49,299 | 139 |
| 1965............... | 4,543 | 1,517 | 6,060 | 5,346 | 4,488 | 858 | 50,043 | 110 |
| 1966............... | 4,650 | 1,554 | 6,204 | 5,724 | 4,792 | 932 | 50,537 | 95 |
| 1967............... | 4,965 | 1,626 | 6,592 | 5,922 | 4,971 | 951 | 51,213 | 88 |
| 1968............... | 4,739 | 1,735 | 6,473 | 5,982 | 4,978 | 1,003 | 51,712 | 82 |
| 1969............... | 4,550 | 1,789 | 6,338 | 6,339 | 5,237 | 1,102 | 51,711 | 82 |
| 1970............... | 4,449 | 1,841 | 6,291 | 6,748 | 5,508 | 1,240 | 51,281 | 55 |
| 1971............... | 5,082 | 2,056 | 7,138 | 5,425 | 4,342 | 1,083 | 53,003 | 46 |
| 1972............... | 5,940 | 2,310 | 8,245 | 5,338 | 4,306 | 1,032 | 55,921 | 39 |
| 1973............... | 6,514 | 2,564 | 9,078 | 5,586 | 4,494 | 1,092 | 59,418 | 34 |
| 1974............... | 6,429 | 2,749 | 9,178 | 6,681 | 5,366 | 1,314 | 61,921 | 29 |
| Calendar years: | | | | | | | | |
| 1935-64............ | 158,715 | 23,481 | 182,196 | 132,304 | 119,876 | 12,428 | 49,734 | 158 |
| 1965............... | 4,486 | 1,527 | 6,013 | 5,441 | 4,552 | 889 | 50,324 | 141 |
| 1966............... | 4,860 | 1,591 | 6,451 | 5,793 | 5,043 | 957 | 50,752 | 164 |
| 1967............... | 4,898 | 1,686 | 6,584 | 5,793 | 5,842 | 951 | 51,581 | 126 |
| 1968............... | 4,696 | 1,759 | 6,455 | 6,133 | 5,094 | 1,040 | 51,917 | 112 |
| 1969............... | 4,393 | 1,832 | 6,224 | 6,639 | 5,457 | 1,182 | 51,549 | 64 |
| 1970............... | 4,665 | 1,909 | 6,574 | 6,295 | 5,072 | 1,223 | 51,842 | 50 |
| 1971............... | 5,477 | 2,192 | 7,669 | 5,244 | 4,224 | 1,021 | 54,275 | 42 |
| 1972............... | 6,236 | 2,426 | 8,662 | 5,365 | 4,322 | 1,043 | 57,579 | 37 |
| 1973............... | 6,270 | 2,673 | 8,943 | 6,211 | 4,945 | 1,266 | 60,317 | 31 |
| 1974............... | 6,862 | 2,994 | 9,856 | 6,829 | 5,476 | 1,354 | 63,349 | 26 |
| Months: | | | | | | | | |
| 1974-Apr........... | 589 | 235 | 824 | 541 | 432 | 109 | 61,381 | 30 |
| May............... | 583 | 214 | 797 | 520 | 414 | 106 | 61,658 | 30 |
| June.............. | 636 | 242 | 878 | 616 | 496 | 119 | 61,921 | 29 |
| July.............. | 541 | 312 | 853 | 592 | 474 | 117 | 62,183 | 29 |
| Aug............... | 574 | 247 | 821 | 666 | 533 | 132 | 62,339 | 28 |
| Sept.............. | 509 | 259 | 768 | 574 | 458 | 116 | 62,533 | 28 |
| Oct............... | 558 | 265 | 822 | 543 | 436 | 107 | 62,811 | 28 |
| Nov............... | 550 | 242 | 792 | 461 | 367 | 94 | 63,144 | 29 |
| Dec............... | 447 | 279 | 726 | 523 | 425 | 98 | 63,349 | 28 |
| 1975-Jan........... | 745 | 298 | 1,043 | 666 | 534 | 132 | 63,725 | 26 |
| Feb............... | 592 | 256 | 848 | 536 | 410 | 126 | 64,036 | 28 |
| Mar............... | 554 | 267 | 821 | 486 | 378 | 108 | 64,371 | 28 |
| Apr............... | 602 | 280 | 882 | 523 | 410 | 113 | 64,730 | 28 |

Footnotes at end of Table

# UNITED STATES SAVINGS BONDS

## Sales and Redemptions by Periods, Series E through K

(In millions of dollars)

| Period | Sales 1/ | Accrued discount | Sales plus accrued discount | Redemptions 1/ | | | Amount outstanding | |
|---|---|---|---|---|---|---|---|---|
| | | | | Total | Sales price 2/ | Accrued discount 2/ | Interest-bearing debt | Matured non-interest-bearing debt |
| | | | | Series E and H combined | | | | |
| **Fiscal years:** | | | | | | | | |
| 1941-64 | 120,619 | 20,389 | 141,008 | 93,271 | 83,359 | 9,912 | 47,737 | - |
| 1965 | 4,543 | 1,502 | 6,045 | 4,987 | 4,154 | 833 | 48,795 | - |
| 1966 | 4,650 | 1,542 | 6,192 | 5,305 | 4,408 | 897 | 49,682 | - |
| 1967 | 4,965 | 1,619 | 6,584 | 5,449 | 4,536 | 913 | 50,817 | - |
| 1968 | 4,739 | 1,731 | 6,470 | 5,715 | 4,739 | 976 | 51,572 | - |
| 1969 | 4,550 | 1,788 | 6,337 | 6,198 | 5,112 | 1,086 | 51,711 | - |
| 1970 | 4,449 | 1,841 | 6,291 | 6,721 | 5,484 | 1,237 | 51,281 | - |
| 1971 | 5,082 | 2,056 | 7,138 | 5,416 | 4,334 | 1,082 | 53,003 | - |
| 1972 | 5,939 | 2,310 | 8,249 | 5,331 | 4,294 | 1,037 | 55,921 | - |
| 1973 | 6,514 | 2,564 | 9,078 | 5,581 | 4,490 | 1,091 | 59,418 | - |
| 1974 | 6,429 | 2,749 | 9,178 | 6,675 | 5,361 | 1,314 | 61,921 | - |
| **Calendar years:** | | | | | | | | |
| 1941-64 | 122,815 | 21,136 | 143,951 | 95,585 | 85,306 | 10,279 | 48,366 | - |
| 1965 | 4,486 | 1,514 | 6,000 | 5,117 | 4,254 | 863 | 49,249 | - |
| 1966 | 4,860 | 1,580 | 6,440 | 5,477 | 4,561 | 916 | 50,212 | - |
| 1967 | 4,898 | 1,680 | 6,578 | 5,439 | 4,519 | 919 | 51,352 | - |
| 1968 | 4,696 | 1,757 | 6,452 | 5,915 | 4,898 | 1,017 | 51,890 | - |
| 1969 | 4,393 | 1,832 | 6,224 | 6,565 | 5,391 | 1,173 | 51,549 | - |
| 1970 | 4,665 | 1,909 | 6,574 | 6,281 | 5,060 | 1,221 | 51,842 | - |
| 1971 | 5,477 | 2,192 | 7,669 | 5,237 | 4,217 | 1,020 | 54,275 | - |
| 1972 | 6,236 | 2,426 | 8,662 | 5,359 | 4,311 | 1,049 | 57,579 | - |
| 1973 | 6,270 | 2,673 | 8,943 | 6,206 | 4,972 | 1,234 | 60,317 | - |
| 1974 | 6,862 | 2,994 | 9,856 | 6,824 | 5,471 | 1,353 | 63,349 | - |
| **Months:** | | | | | | | | |
| 1974-Apr | 589 | 235 | 824 | 541 | 432 | 109 | 61,381 | - |
| May | 583 | 214 | 797 | 519 | 414 | 106 | 61,658 | - |
| June | 636 | 242 | 878 | 615 | 496 | 119 | 61,921 | - |
| July | 541 | 312 | 853 | 591 | 474 | 117 | 62,183 | - |
| Aug | 574 | 247 | 821 | 666 | 533 | 132 | 62,339 | - |
| Sept | 509 | 259 | 768 | 574 | 458 | 116 | 62,533 | - |
| Oct | 558 | 265 | 822 | 544 | 437 | 107 | 62,811 | - |

| | | | Series F, G, J, and K combined [4] | | | | | |
|---|---|---|---|---|---|---|---|---|
| Nov................. | 550 | 242 | 792 | 460 | 366 | 94 | 63,144 | -- |
| Dec................. | 447 | 279 | 726 | 521 | 423 | 98 | 63,349 | -- |
| 1975-Jan........... | 745 | 298 | 1,043 | 666 | 534 | 132 | 63,725 | -- |
| Feb................ | 592 | 256 | 848 | 537 | 412 | 126 | 64,036 | -- |
| Mar................ | 554 | 267 | 821 | 486 | 378 | 108 | 64,371 | -- |
| Apr................ | 602 | 280 | 882 | 523 | 410 | 113 | 64,730 | -- |
| **Fiscal years:** | | | | | | | | |
| 1941-64............ | 31,951 | 1,284 | 33,235 | 31,736 [5][6][7][8] | 30,373 | 1,172 | 1,563 | 127 |
| 1965............... | -- | 15 | 15 | 358 [9] | 333 | 24 | 1,248 | 99 |
| 1966............... | -- | 12 | 12 | 418 [9] | 384 | 35 | 856 | 86 |
| 1967............... | -- | 8 | 8 | 472 | 434 | 38 | 397 | 80 |
| 1968............... | -- | 4 | 4 | 266 | 239 | 27 | 140 | 75 |
| 1969............... | -- | 1 | 1 | 140 | 124 | 16 | -- | 76 |
| 1970............... | -- | -- | -- | 27 | 24 | 3 | -- | 49 |
| 1971............... | -- | -- | -- | 8 | 7 | 1 | -- | 41 |
| 1972............... | -- | -- | -- | 6 | 5 | 1 | -- | 34 |
| 1973............... | -- | -- | -- | 5 | 4 | 1 | -- | 30 |
| 1974............... | -- | -- | -- | 5 | 4 | 1 | -- | 25 |
| **Calendar years:** | | | | | | | | |
| 1941-64............ | 31,951 | 1,291 | 33,242 | 31,727 [5][6][7][8] | 30,544 | 1,184 | 1,368 | 147 |
| 1965............... | -- | 14 | 14 | 323 [9] | 297 | 26 | 1,075 | 131 |
| 1966............... | -- | 10 | 10 | 522 | 481 | 40 | 540 | 155 |
| 1967............... | -- | 6 | 6 | 353 | 322 | 32 | 229 | 118 |
| 1968............... | -- | 2 | 2 | 218 | 195 | 23 | 27 | 105 |
| 1969............... | -- | * | * | 74 | 65 | 9 | -- | 58 |
| 1970............... | -- | -- | -- | 13 | 11 | 2 | -- | 44 |
| 1971............... | -- | -- | -- | 7 | 6 | 1 | -- | 37 |
| 1972............... | -- | -- | -- | 5 | 5 | 1 | -- | 32 |
| 1973............... | -- | -- | -- | 5 | 4 | 1 | -- | 27 |
| 1974............... | -- | -- | -- | 5 | 4 | 1 | -- | 22 |
| **Months:** | | | | | | | | |
| 1974-Apr........... | -- | -- | -- | * | * | * | -- | 26 |
| May................ | -- | -- | -- | * | * | * | -- | 25 |
| June............... | -- | -- | -- | 1 | 1 | * | -- | 25 |
| July............... | -- | -- | -- | * | * | * | -- | 25 |
| Aug................ | -- | -- | -- | 1 | 1 | * | -- | 24 |
| Sept............... | * | -- | * | -1 | -1 | * | -- | 25 |
| Oct................ | * | -- | * | -1 | -1 | -- | -- | 25 |
| Nov................ | * | -- | * | 1 | 1 | * | -- | 24 |
| Dec................ | -- | -- | -- | 2 | 2 | * | -- | 22 |
| 1975-Jan........... | -- | -- | -- | * | * | * | -- | 22 |
| Feb................ | -- | -- | -- | -1 | -1 | * | -- | 24 |
| Mar................ | -- | -- | -- | * | * | * | -- | 24 |
| Apr................ | -- | -- | -- | * | * | * | * | 24 |

Footnotes at end of Table

# UNITED STATES SAVINGS BONDS

## Sales and Redemptions by Periods, Series E through K—Continued

(In millions of dollars)

| Period | Sales 1/ | Accrued discount | Sales plus accrued discount | Redemptions 1/ Total | Redemptions Sales price 2/ | Redemptions Accrued discount 3/ | Exchange of E bonds for H bonds | Amount outstanding (interest-bearing debt) |
|---|---|---|---|---|---|---|---|---|
| **Series E** | | | | | | | | |
| **Fiscal years:** | | | | | | | | |
| 1941-64............ | 111,750 | 20,389 | 132,139 | 90,943 | 81,031 | 9,912 | 1,006 | 40,190 |
| 1965............... | 4,112 | 1,502 | 5,614 | 4,538 | 3,705 | 833 | 188 | 41,078 |
| 1966............... | 4,246 | 1,542 | 5,787 | 4,801 | 3,904 | 897 | 212 | 41,853 |
| 1967............... | 4,599 | 1,619 | 6,217 | 4,895 | 3,982 | 913 | 216 | 42,999 |
| 1968............... | 4,466 | 1,731 | 6,196 | 5,154 | 4,178 | 976 | 196 | 43,805 |
| 1969............... | 4,343 | 1,788 | 6,131 | 5,548 | 4,462 | 1,086 | 184 | 44,205 |
| 1970............... | 4,289 | 1,841 | 6,130 | 5,959 | 4,722 | 1,237 | 210 | 44,167 |
| 1971............... | 4,870 | 2,056 | 6,926 | 4,959 | 3,877 | 1,082 | 231 | 45,902 |
| 1972............... | 5,650 | 2,310 | 7,960 | 4,972 | 3,932 | 1,037 | 292 | 48,598 |
| 1973............... | 6,190 | 2,564 | 8,755 | 5,209 | 4,118 | 1,091 | 338 | 51,806 |
| 1974............... | 6,145 | 2,749 | 8,894 | 6,156 | 4,842 | 1,314 | 310 | 54,234 |
| **Calendar years:** | | | | | | | | |
| 1941-64............ | 113,734 | 21,136 | 134,870 | 93,036 | 82,756 | 10,280 | 1,095 | 40,739 |
| 1965............... | 4,092 | 1,514 | 5,606 | 4,650 | 3,787 | 863 | 190 | 41,504 |
| 1966............... | 4,450 | 1,580 | 6,031 | 4,913 | 3,997 | 916 | 224 | 42,398 |
| 1967............... | 4,574 | 1,680 | 6,255 | 4,941 | 4,022 | 919 | 207 | 43,504 |
| 1968............... | 4,452 | 1,757 | 6,209 | 5,300 | 4,283 | 1,017 | 191 | 44,222 |
| 1969............... | 4,221 | 1,832 | 6,052 | 5,835 | 4,661 | 1,173 | 180 | 44,299 |
| 1970............... | 4,503 | 1,909 | 6,412 | 5,626 | 4,405 | 1,221 | 228 | 44,818 |
| 1971............... | 5,218 | 2,192 | 7,411 | 4,871 | 3,851 | 1,020 | 249 | 47,108 |
| 1972............... | 5,922 | 2,426 | 8,348 | 5,007 | 3,958 | 1,049 | 329 | 50,120 |
| 1973............... | 5,988 | 2,673 | 8,661 | 5,740 | 4,507 | 1,234 | 319 | 52,723 |
| 1974............... | 6,524 | 2,994 | 9,518 | 6,318 | 4,965 | 1,353 | 310 | 55,613 |
| **Months:** | | | | | | | | |
| 1974—Apr.......... | 564 | 235 | 799 | 500 | 392 | 109 | 27 | 53,710 |
| May.............. | 559 | 214 | 773 | 480 | 375 | 106 | 24 | 53,979 |
| June............. | 608 | 242 | 850 | 569 | 449 | 119 | 26 | 54,234 |
| July............. | 516 | 312 | 828 | 546 | 428 | 117 | 27 | 54,490 |
| Aug.............. | 538 | 247 | 785 | 615 | 483 | 132 | 24 | 54,636 |
| Sept............. | 491 | 259 | 750 | 526 | 411 | 116 | 22 | 54,837 |
| Oct.............. | 515 | 265 | 780 | 500 | 392 | 107 | 26 | 55,091 |

| | | | | | | | | |
|---|---|---|---|---|---|---|---|---|
| Nov........... | 524 | 242 | 766 | 424 | 331 | 94 | 20 | 55,412 |
| Dec........... | 433 | 279 | 712 | 491 | 393 | 98 | 21 | 55,613 |
| 1975—Jan...... | 708 | 298 | 1,007 | 628 | 496 | 131 | 32 | 55,961 |
| Feb........... | 563 | 256 | 819 | 503 | 377 | 126 | 24 | 56,253 |
| Mar........... | **525** | 267 | 792 | 450 | 342 | 108 | 29 | 56,566 |
| Apr........... | 577 | 280 | 857 | 490 | 377 | 113 | 29 | 56,904 |

Series H

| | | | | | | | | |
|---|---|---|---|---|---|---|---|---|
| **Fiscal years:** | | | | | | | | |
| 1952–64....... | 8,869 | – | 8,869 | 2,329 | 2,329 | – | 1,006 | 7,546 |
| 1965.......... | 431 | – | 431 | 449 | 449 | – | 188 | 7,716 |
| 1966.......... | 404 | – | 404 | 504 | 504 | – | 212 | 7,829 |
| 1967.......... | 367 | – | 367 | 553 | 553 | – | 216 | 7,858 |
| 1968.......... | 273 | – | 273 | 561 | 561 | – | 196 | 7,766 |
| 1969.......... | 207 | – | 207 | 650 | 650 | – | 184 | 7,506 |
| 1970.......... | 160 | – | 160 | 762 | 762 | – | 210 | 7,114 |
| 1971.......... | 212 | – | 212 | 457 | 457 | – | 231 | 7,101 |
| 1972.......... | 289 | – | 289 | 359 | 359 | – | 292 | 7,323 |
| 1973.......... | 322 | – | 322 | 372 | 372 | – | 338 | 7,612 |
| 1974.......... | 284 | – | 284 | 519 | 519 | – | 310 | 7,686 |
| **Calendar years:** | | | | | | | | |
| 1952–64....... | 9,081 | – | 9,081 | 2,549 | 2,549 | – | 1,095 | 7,627 |
| 1965.......... | 394 | – | 394 | 467 | 467 | – | 190 | 7,744 |
| 1966.......... | 410 | – | 410 | 564 | 564 | – | 224 | 7,815 |
| 1967.......... | 324 | – | 324 | 497 | 497 | – | 207 | 7,848 |
| 1968.......... | 244 | – | 244 | 615 | 615 | – | 191 | 7,668 |
| 1969.......... | 172 | – | 172 | 730 | 730 | – | 180 | 7,290 |
| 1970.......... | 162 | – | 162 | 655 | 655 | – | 228 | 7,025 |
| 1971.......... | 259 | – | 259 | 366 | 366 | – | 249 | 7,167 |
| 1972.......... | 314 | – | 314 | 353 | 353 | – | 329 | 7,458 |
| 1973.......... | 282 | – | 282 | 465 | 465 | – | 319 | 7,594 |
| 1974.......... | 338 | – | 338 | 506 | 506 | – | 310 | 7,736 |
| **Months:** | | | | | | | | |
| 1974—Apr...... | 25 | – | 25 | 40 | 40 | – | 27 | 7,670 |
| May........... | 23 | – | 23 | 39 | 39 | – | 24 | 7,679 |
| June.......... | 28 | – | 28 | 46 | 46 | – | 26 | 7,686 |
| July.......... | 25 | – | 25 | 46 | 46 | – | 27 | 7,692 |
| Aug........... | 36 | – | 36 | 50 | 50 | – | 24 | 7,703 |
| Sept.......... | 18 | – | 18 | 47 | 47 | – | 22 | 7,696 |
| Oct........... | 42 | – | 42 | 44 | 44 | – | 26 | 7,720 |
| Nov........... | 27 | – | 27 | 35 | 35 | – | 20 | 7,732 |
| Dec........... | 14 | – | 14 | 30 | 30 | – | 21 | 7,736 |
| 1975—Jan...... | 35 | – | 35 | 38 | 38 | – | 32 | 7,765 |
| Feb........... | 29 | – | 29 | 35 | 35 | – | 24 | 7,783 |
| Mar........... | 29 | – | 29 | 36 | 36 | – | 29 | 7,805 |
| Apr........... | 25 | – | 25 | 33 | 33 | – | 29 | 7,826 |

Footnotes at end of Table

# UNITED STATES SAVINGS BONDS

## Redemptions of Matured and Unmatured Savings Bonds

(In millions of dollars)

| Period | Total | Matured | | | Unmatured | | | Unclassified 10/ |
|---|---|---|---|---|---|---|---|---|
| | | Total | Series E and H | Other | Total | Series E and H | Other | |
| **Fiscal years:** | | | | | | | | |
| 1951-58 | 55,981 | 22,167 | 10,975 | 11,190 | 33,322 | 25,119 | 8,203 | 492 |
| 1959 | 7,249 | 3,621 | 1,996 | 1,625 | 3,778 | 3,235 | 543 | -150 |
| 1960 | 8,557 | 4,126 | 2,304 | 1,822 6/ | 4,641 | 3,285 | 1,356 | -210 |
| 1961 | 5,819 | 2,673 | 1,733 | 940 7/ | 3,358 | 3,075 | 283 | -212 |
| 1962 | 5,716 | 2,593 | 1,668 | 925 8/ | 3,070 | 2,875 | 196 | 53 |
| 1963 | 5,273 | 2,250 | 1,593 | 657 9/ | 2,951 | 2,812 | 139 | 73 |
| 1964 | 5,164 | 2,057 | 1,754 | 304 | 3,088 | 2,948 | 140 | 19 |
| 1965 | 5,346 | 2,184 | 1,938 | 246 | 3,284 | 3,165 | 118 | -121 |
| 1966 | 5,724 | 2,253 | 1,973 | 280 | 3,300 | 3,196 | 104 | 172 |
| 1967 | 5,922 | 2,471 | 2,059 | 412 | 3,351 | 3,273 | 79 | 99 |
| 1968 | 5,982 | 2,548 | 2,289 | 260 | 3,401 | 3,376 | 25 | 33 |
| 1969 | 6,339 | 2,560 | 2,417 | 143 | 3,566 | 3,560 | 6 | 213 |
| 1970 | 6,748 | 2,792 | 2,762 | 29 | 3,842 | 3,842 | - | 115 |
| 1971 | 5,425 | 2,490 | 2,481 | 9 | 3,660 | 3,660 | - | -725 |
| 1972 | 5,338 | 2,043 | 2,036 | 7 | 3,317 | 3,317 | - | -23 |
| 1973 | 5,586 | 2,126 | 2,121 | 5 | 3,393 | 3,393 | - | 67 |
| 1974 | 6,681 | 2,729 | 2,724 | 5 | 3,847 | 3,847 | - | 104 |
| **Calendar years:** | | | | | | | | |
| 1951-58 | 56,300 | 23,301 | 11,763 | 11,539 | 32,408 | 24,568 | 7,840 | 590 |
| 1959 | 8,772 | 4,701 | 2,433 | 2,268 6/ | 4,520 | 3,445 | 1,075 | -449 |
| 1960 | 6,732 | 3,033 | 1,944 | 1,089 7/ | 3,938 | 3,114 | 825 | -239 |
| 1961 | 5,595 | 2,555 | 1,633 | 922 7/8/ | 3,100 | 2,899 | 201 | -60 |
| 1962 | 5,602 | 2,387 | 1,656 | 730 8/9/ | 3,002 | 2,827 | 175 | 213 |
| 1963 | 5,021 | 2,043 | 1,617 | 426 9/ | 3,031 | 2,905 | 125 | -52 |
| 1964 | 5,252 | 2,171 | 1,889 | 282 | 3,157 | 3,026 | 131 | -76 |
| 1965 | 5,441 | 2,148 | 1,932 | 216 | 3,287 | 3,176 | 111 | 6 |
| 1966 | 6,000 | 2,472 | 2,080 | 391 | 3,384 | 3,277 | 107 | 144 |
| 1967 | 5,793 | 2,386 | 2,041 | 345 | 3,413 | 3,370 | 44 | -7 |
| 1968 | 6,133 | 2,652 | 2,443 | 209 | 3,455 | 3,441 | 13 | 26 |
| 1969 | 6,639 | 2,686 | 2,601 | 84 | 3,726 | 3,724 | 2 | 228 |

| | | | | | | | | |
|---|---|---|---|---|---|---|---|---|
| 1970 ............. | 6,295 | 2,841 | 2,827 | 15 | 3,885 | 3,885 | – | -431 |
| 1971 ............. | 5,244 | 2,022 | 2,014 | 8 | 3,305 | 3,305 | – | -83 |
| 1972 ............. | 5,365 | 2,053 | 2,047 | 6 | 3,337 | 3,337 | – | -24 |
| 1973 ............. | 6,210 | 2,508 | 2,505 | 3 | 3,578 | 3,578 | – | 123 |
| 1974 ............. | 6,833 | 2,627 | 2,622 | 5 | 3,789 | 3,789 | – | 417 |
| **Months:** | | | | | | | | |
| 1974-Apr ......... | 541 | 241 | 241 | * | 342 | 342 | – | -43 |
| May .............. | 519 | 220 | 220 | * | 314 | 314 | – | -14 |
| June ............. | 616 | 213 | 212 | 1 | 314 | 314 | – | 88 |
| July ............. | 592 | 187 | 187 | – | 233 | 233 | – | 170 |
| Aug .............. | 666 | 246 | 245 | 1 | 382 | 382 | – | 38 |
| Sept ............. | 574 | 180 | 181 | * | 272 | 272 | – | 121 |
| Oct .............. | 543 | 237 | 238 | -1 | 313 | 313 | – | -7 |
| Nov .............. | 461 | 223 | 222 | * | 381 | 381 | – | -143 |
| Dec .............. | 523 | 149 | 149 | * | 210 | 210 | – | 164 |
| 1975-Jan ......... | 666 | 213 | 213 | * | 351 | 351 | – | 102 |
| Feb .............. | 536 | 202 | 203 | -1 | 305 | **305** | – | 29 |
| Mar .............. | 436 | 245 | 244 | * | 333 | 333 | – | -91 |
| Apr .............. | 523 | 265 | 265 | * | 431 | 431 | – | -173 |

Source: Monthly Statement of the Public Debt of the U.S.; Office of Market Analysis, United States Savings Bonds Division.

Note: In these tables sales of Series A-F and J bonds are included at issue price, and redemptions and amounts outstanding at current redemption value. Series G,H, and K are included at face value throughout. Matured bonds which have been redeemed are included in redemptions. Matured J and K bonds outstanding are included in the interest-bearing debt until all bonds of the annual series have matured, and are then transferred to matured debt on which interest has ceased.

1/ Sales and redemption figures include exchanges of minor amounts of (1) matured Series E bonds for Series G and K bonds from May 1951 through April 1957; (2) Series F and J bonds for Series H bonds beginning January 1960; and (3) U.S. savings notes for Series H bonds beginning January 1972; however, they exclude exchanges of Series E bonds for Series H bonds, which are reported in Table SB-3.

2/ Details by series on a cumulative basis and by periods for Series A-D combined will be found in the February 1952 and previous issues of the Treasury Bulletin.

3/ Because there is a normal lag in classifying redemptions, the distribution of redemption between sales price and accrued discount has been estimated. Beginning with the Treasury Bulletin of March 1961 the

method of distributing redemptions between sales price and accrued discount has been changed to reflect the distribution shown in final reports of classified redemption. All periods shown have been revised on this basis.

4/ Series F and G sales were discontinued April 30, 1952, and Series J and K sales were discontinued April 30, 1957. Sales figures after April 30, 1957, represent adjustments.

5/ Includes exchanges of Series 1941 F and G savings bonds for 3-1/4% marketable bonds of 1978-83.

6/ Includes exchanges of Series 1948 F and G bonds for 4-3/4% marketable notes of 1964.

7/ Includes exchanges of Series 1949 F and G bonds for 4% marketable bonds of 1969.

8/ Includes exchanges of Series 1960 F and G bonds for 3-7/8% marketable bonds of 1968.

9/ Includes exchanges of Series 1951 and 1952 F and G bonds for 3-7/8% marketable bonds of 1971 and 4% marketable bonds of 1980.

10/ Represents changes in the amounts of redemptions not yet classified between matured and unmatured issues.

* Less than $500,000.

*Source: Treasury Bulletin (May 1975)*

251

# where you can get information and data on a continuous basis

**E**

## ECONOMIC NEWS AND ANALYSES

### Advertising Age
Weekly publication of:
   Advertising Age
   740 Rush Street
   Chicago, Illinois 60611
Regular features include "Advertising Marketplace," "Advertising Stocks," "Radio-TV Buys" and "This Week in Washington."

### Barron's
Weekly publication of:
   Dow Jones & Co., Inc.
   22 Cortlandt Street
   New York, N.Y. 10007
Statistics on stock quotations for the New York Stock Exchange, Over-the-Counter market, other securities exchanges, options trading, bond quotations, Dow-Jones hourly averages, Dow-Jones weekly averages, Dow-Jones price-earnings ratios, other stock market indicators, foreign stock indexes, coming financings, as well as other statistical data. In addition, there are special articles, interviews, and regular coverage of the business and financial world.

## Business News and Trends

Weekly publication of:
  Pittsburgh National Bank
  P.O. Box 340777-P
  Pittsburgh, Pennsylvania 15230
Coverage of national and international economic developments. Some issues focus on Pittsburgh and the State of Pennsylvania.

## Business Statistics

Weekly publication of the U.S. Department of Commerce obtained from:
  U.S. Government Printing Office
  Washington, D.C. 20402
A supplement to the U.S. Department of Commerce's *Survey of Current Business.*

## Business Week

Weekly publication of:
  McGraw-Hill Publishing Co., Inc.
  McGraw-Hill Building
  1221 Avenue of the Americas
  New York, N.Y. 10020
Truly outstanding coverage of economic news, money, credit, corporate developments, unions, markets, investments, finance, and related areas.

## Changing Times

Monthly publication of:
  The Kiplinger Washington Editors, Inc.
  Editors Park, Maryland 20782
Practical advice about how to use and spend your money.

## Dun's (Dun's Review)

Monthly publication of:
  Dun & Bradstreet Publications Corp.
  666 Fifth Avenue
  New York, N.Y. 10019
Excellent articles on investments, investment potentials, and corporate, industrial, and financial developments.

## Economic Indicators

Monthly publication of the Council of Economic Advisers. It is available from:
  Superintendent of Documents

U.S. Government Printing Office
Washington, D.C. 20402
This publication is prepared for the Joint Economic Committee to indicate U.S. economic developments.

## Financial Times

Daily publication of:
The Financial Times
Bracken House
Cannon Street
London EC4P 4BY, United Kingdom
Excellent daily coverage of British and international financial developments.

## First Chicago Report

Monthly publication of:
Business and Economic Research Division
The First National Bank of Chicago
One First National Plaza
Chicago, Illinois 60670
Coverage of U.S. business and economic developments.

## First National City Bank Monthly Economic Letter

Publication of:
First National City Bank
399 Park Avenue
New York, N.Y. 10022
Very valuable publication covering national and international economic developments.

## Fortune

Monthly publication of:
Time Inc.
541 North Fairbanks Court
Chicago, Illinois 60611
Excellent and often profound articles on corporate and economic developments. Especially valuable are the annual issues containing the following:
For the U.S.:
"The 500 Largest Industrial Corporations"
"The Second 500 Largest Industrial Corporations"
"The Fifty Largest Commercial Banking Companies"

"The Fifty Largest Life-Insurance Companies"
"The Fifty Largest Financial Companies"
"The Fifty Largest Retailing Companies"
"The Fifty Largest Transportation Companies"
"The Fifty Largest Utilities Companies"
Outside the U.S.:
"The 300 Largest Industrial Corporations Outside the U.S."
"The Fifty Largest Commercial Banking Companies Outside the U.S."
"The Fifty Largest Industrial Companies in the World"

## Historical Chart Book

Annual publication of:
Board of Governors of the Federal Reserve System
Washington, D.C. 20551
Issued annually in September covering economic changes.

## Manufacturers Hanover Trust—Economic Report

Monthly publication of:
Manufacturers Hanover Trust Company
350 Park Avenue
New York, N.Y. 10022
Each month a different economic subject is covered intensively. Its coverage centers on U.S. economic developments.

## MBA (Master in Business Administration)

Published eleven times per year, January through June, July/August and September through December by:
MBA Communications, Inc.
555 Madison Avenue
New York, N.Y. 10022
This publication has special articles dealing with economics, finance, and advice on how to use your money.

## Monthly Chart Book

Publication of:
Board of Governors of the Federal Reserve System
Washington, D.C. 20551
Excellent broad coverage of business and economic developments presented in a series of graphs.

## Nation's Business

Monthly publication of:
Nation's Business
1615 H Street, N.W.
Washington, D.C. 20062
Fine coverage of broad areas relating to economic matters of the individual, business community and the country.

## Newsweek

Weekly publication of:
Newsweek
The Newsweek Building
Livingston, New Jersey 07039
Excellent coverage of business and economic developments, with special articles by economists Prof. Milton Friedman and Prof. Paul A. Samuelson.

## Road Maps of Industry

Published twice monthly by:

| | |
|---|---|
| The Conference Board | The Conference Board |
| 845 Third Avenue | 333 River Road |
| New York, N.Y. 10022 | Ottawa, Ontario K1L8B9, Canada |

Intensive information and data about industries.

## Survey of Current Business

Monthly publication of the U.S. Department of Commerce. It provides statistical data of past business and economic developments, as well as information on possible future developments and presents specific future projections. An annual subscription can be obtained from:
Superintendent of Documents
U.S. Government Printing Office
Washington, D.C. 20402

## The Accountant

Weekly publication of:
The Accountant
151 Strand
London WC2R 1JJ, United Kingdon
Coverage of this publication is international in scope, but it is particularly valuable for developments concerning the United Kingdom.

## The Economist

Weekly publication of:
    The Economist Newspaper Limited
    25 St. James's Street
    London SW1A 1HG, United Kingdom
Exceptionally fine coverage of investment and economic developments around the world, as well as developments of political and social significance.

## The Journal of Commerce

Published daily except Saturdays, Sundays, and holidays by:
    Twin Coast Newspapers, Inc.
    99 Wall Street
    New York, N.Y. 10005
Outstanding daily coverage of monetary, trade and commodity developments.

## The Morgan Guaranty Survey

Monthly publication of:
    Morgan Guaranty Trust Company of New York
    23 Wall Street
    New York, N.Y. 10015
Very valuable publication covering U.S. business and financial conditions, with regular presentation of monetary indicators.

## The New York Times

Daily publication of:
    The New York Times Company
    229 West 43rd Street
    New York, N.Y. 10036
Excellent coverage of economic news, the stock market, the bond market, and other areas.

## The Washington Post

Daily publication of:
    The Washington Post Company
    1150 15th Street, N.W.
    Washington, D.C. 20071
Excellent coverage of economic news, the stock market, the bond market, and other areas.

### The Wall Street Journal

Published daily except Saturdays, Sundays, and general legal holidays by:
  Dow Jones & Company, Inc.
  22 Cortlandt Street
  New York, N.Y. 10007
A must for keeping up with daily developments in the business and financial world.

### The Wall Street Journal Index

Monthly publication of:
  Dow Jones Books
  P.O. Box 60
  Princeton, New Jersey 08540
An index that is separated into two sections for coverage of *The Wall Street Journal:*
  *First Section:* "Corporate News"
  *Second Section:* "General News"

### Time

Weekly publication of:
  Time Inc.
  541 Fairbanks Court
  Chicago, Illinois 60611
Excellent coverage of business and economic developments, as well as many other areas.

### U.S. News & World Report

Weekly publication of:
  U.S. News & World Report, Inc.
  2300 N Street, N.W.
  Washington, D.C. 20037
Fine coverage of business and economic news, with often excellent exclusive interviews.

## MONEY MARKETS

### Federal Reserve Bank of New York. Monthly releases on the Bankers' Acceptances Market

Obtained at:
  Federal Reserve Bank of New York

33 Liberty Street
New York, N.Y. 10045
Intensive coverage of developments in the bankers' acceptances market, with very valuable data.

### Federal Reserve Bank of New York. Weekly and monthly releases on the Commercial Paper Market

Obtained at:
Federal Reserve Bank of New York
33 Liberty Street
New York, N.Y. 10045
Intensive coverage of the commercial paper market, with very valuable data.

### Financial Data

Weekly publication of:
Pittsburgh National Bank
P.O. Box 340777-P
Pittsburgh, Pennsylvania 15230
Excellent coverage of the money markets, as well as the capital markets and banking developments. Graphs are often used that illustrate points very well.

### Fitch Commercial Paper Report

Publication of:
Fitch Investors Service, Inc.
12 Barclay Street
New York, N.Y.
Valuable coverage of the commercial paper market, with ratings of particular issues.

### Maturity Distribution of Outstanding Negotiable Time Certificates of Deposit

Monthly publication of:
Board of Governors of the Federal Reserve System
Washington, D.C. 20551
Released on the 24th of each month. The data refer to the last Wednesday of the previous month.

### Open Market Money Rates and Bond Prices

Monthly publication of:
Board of Governors of the Federal Reserve System
Washington, D.C. 20551
Released on the 6th day of each month. The data refer to the previous month.

## The Fixed Income Investor

Standard & Poor's Corporation
345 Hudson Street
New York, N.Y. 10014
Weekly coverage of the various fixed income securities together with specific ratings.

## Treasury Bulletin

Monthly publication of:
U.S. Department of the Treasury
Washington, D.C. 20226
It presents statistical data on U.S. government securities, U.S. government Agency securities, U.S. government-sponsored Agency securities, bonds, currency in circulation, Federal fiscal operations and developments in related areas.

## U.S. Financial Data

Weekly publication of:
Federal Reserve Bank of St. Louis
P.O. Box 442
St. Louis, Missouri 63166
This publication presents statistical data and graphs on: the monetary base, the multiplier, Federal Reserve credit, the money stock, yields on selected securities (i.e., 90-day CDs, prime commercial paper, 4 to 6 months prime bankers' acceptances, corporate AAA bonds, municipal bonds), selected short-term interest rates (i.e., Federal funds, 3-month Treasury bills, 3- to 5-year government securities, long-term Government securities), net time deposits, the demand deposit component of the money stock, CDs, borrowings from Federal Reserve Banks, and business loans (commercial and industrial).

## U.S. Government Security Yields and Prices

Weekly and monthly publication of:
Board of Governors of the Federal Reserve System
Washington, D.C. 20551
Releases presenting important data on U.S. Government securities. Yields are averages of those computed by the Federal Reserve Bank of New York on the basis of closing bid prices. Yields on Treasury bills are computed on a bank discount basis. The weekly publication is released on Monday and reports data for the week ended the previous Friday. The monthly publication is released on the 4th of each month and reports data for the previous month.

## STOCKS & BONDS

### *America's Fastest Growing Companies*

Monthly publication of:
John S. Herold, Inc.
35 Mason Street
Greenwich, Conn. 06830
Coverage of what are held to be growth stocks.

### *Babson's Reports*

Weekly publication of:
Babson's Reports, Inc.
Wellesley Hills, Mass. 02181
Provides specific buy, hold, and sell advice on stocks.

### *Chartcraft*

Monthly publication of:
Chartcraft, Inc.
Dept. B-644
Larchmont, N.Y. 10538
Provides over 2700 charts of New York Stock Exchange and American Stock Exchange stocks.

### *Crosscraft*

Monthly publication of:
Dines Chart Corporation
18 East 41st Street
New York, N.Y. 10017
Graphs of stock action of various companies.

### *Dow Theory Forecasts*

Weekly publication of:
Dow Theory Forecasts, Inc.
Dept. B 5-12
P.O. Box 4550
Grand Central Station
New York, N.Y. 10017
It provides an interpretation of the Dow Theory, originally developed by Charles H. Dow at the beginning of the twentieth century, and then applies that interpretation to specific buy, hold, and sell stock recommendations.

### Finance

Monthly publication of:
FINANCE Publishing Corp.
P.O. Box G
Lenox Hill Station
New York, N.Y. 10021
National and international coverage of the world of finance.

### Financial Analysts Journal

Bimonthly publication of:
The Financial Analysts Federation
219 East 42nd Street
New York, N.Y. 10017
Highly professional publication offering in-depth information about investments.

### Financial Executive

Monthly publication of:
Financial Executives Institute
633 Third Avenue
New York, N.Y. 10017
In-depth coverage of investments, investment strategies, and related areas, with many points of view presented.

### Financial World

Weekly publication of:
Butler Publishing Corp.
919 Third Avenue
New York, N.Y. 10022
Published weekly except for combined issues in the first two weeks in July and the last two weeks in December. Special feature articles on investments and regular coverage of stocks and bonds.

### Findings & Forecasts

Publication of:
Anametrics, Inc.
299 Park Avenue
New York, N.Y. 10017
Economic analyses with forecasts, including forecasts and views of the well-known analyst Edson Gould.

## Fitch Publications

"Fitch Bond Ratings"
"Fitch Corporate Bond Review"
"Fitch Institutional Report"
Publications of:
Fitch Investors Service, Inc.
12 Barclay Street
New York, N.Y. 10007

## Forbes

Published twice monthly by:
Forbes, Inc.
60 Fifth Avenue
New York, N.Y. 10011
Good coverage of stocks, bonds, the money markets, and corporate and economic developments.

## Form 10-K

An annual report required by the Securities and Exchange Commission of corporations whose stock is listed on securities exchanges, as well as for many corporations whose stocks are unlisted. Some corporations make their Form 10-K reports available to stockholders and nonstock-holders. Write to the Treasurer of the corporation to find out if you can obtain a copy. Some corporations charge a fee. Form 10-K reports are available at Securities and Exchange Commission libraries for use in the libraries. Form 10-K reports provide a wealth of information about a corporation, usually a lot more than can be obtained from a regular annual report.

## Institutional Investor

Monthly publication of:
Institutional Investor Systems, Inc.
488 Madison Avenue
New York, N.Y. 10022
Gives you a chance to find out what the financial institutional experts are thinking about and what their investment strategies may be.

## Investment Companies

Annual publication of:
Arthur Wiesenberger & Company, Inc.
One New York Plaza

New York, N.Y. 10004
Information and data on the performances of open-end investment companies ("mutual funds") and closed-end investment companies.

## Investment Dealers' Digest

Weekly publication of:
Investment Dealers' Digest
150 Broadway
New York, N.Y. 10038
Regular coverage of securities markets, the credit market, mutual funds, and related areas.

## Investment Strategy

Publication of:
Kidder, Peabody & Co., Inc.
10 Hanover Square
New York, N.Y. 10005
Offers specific stock analyses.

## Investments for a Changing Economy

Monthly publication of:
Merrill Lynch, Pierce, Fenner & Smith, Inc.
Merrill Lynch Service Center
Box 700
Nevada, Iowa 50201
Coverage of the stock market, bond market, and money markets. It attempts to provide investment strategies and offers specific recommendations.

## Johnson's Investment Company Charts

Annual publication of:
Hugh Johnson & Company, Inc.
110 Wall Street
New York, N.Y. 10005
Information, data and graphs about open-end investment companies ("mutual funds").

## List of OTC Margin Stocks

Semi-annual publication of:
Board of Governors of the Federal Reserve System
Washington, D.C. 20551
Released June 30 and December 31 of each year and covers data on the release date. The report deals with the Over-the-Counter market.

## Market Interpretations

Weekly publication of:
Harris, Upham & Co., Inc.
120 Broadway
New York, N.Y. 10005
Analysis of the stock market.

## Moody's Bond Record

Monthly publication of:
Moody's Investors Service, Inc.
99 Church Street
New York, N.Y. 10007
Covers the bond market, as well as providing specific ratings on municipals, corporates, convertibles, and preferred stock.

## Moody's Bond Survey

Weekly publication of:
Moody's Investors Service, Inc.
99 Church Street
New York, N.Y. 10007
Review of developments in the bond market, together with an index and ratings of specific bond issues.

## Moody's Publications

"Bank & Finance Manual"
"Dividend Record"
"Handbook of Common Stocks"
"Industrial Manual"
"Municipal & Government Manual"
"OTC Industrial Manual"
"Public Utility Manual"
"Stock Survey"
"Transportation Manual"
Publications of:
Moody's Investors Service, Inc.
99 Church Street
New York, N.Y. 10007

## Open Market Money Rates and Bond Prices

Monthly publication of:
Board of Governors of the Federal Reserve System
Washington, D.C. 20551
Released on the 6th day of each month. The data refer to the previous month.

## Past-Present-Future

Weekly publication of:
Kidder, Peabody & Co., Inc.
10 Hanover Square
New York, N.Y. 10005
Coverage of the municipal bond market.

## Poor's Register of Corporations, Directors and Executives

Annual publication of:
Standard & Poor's
345 Hudson Street
New York, N.Y. 10014
Presents alphabetical listings of corporations, biographical sketches of directors and executives, and indexes.

## Research Spotlight

Weekly publication of:
Hornblower & Weeks-Hemphill, Noyes, Inc.
8 Hanover Street
New York, N.Y. 10004
Emphasis is placed on the analysis of specific stocks and corporations.

## Sales, Revenue, Profits, and Dividends of Large Manufacturing Corporations

Quarterly publication of:
Board of Governors of the Federal Reserve System
Washington, D.C. 20551
Released on the 10th of April, June, September and December. The data refer to the second previous quarter.

## Standard & Poor's Publications

"Corporation Records"
"Dividend Record"
"Industry Surveys"
"Stock Reports"
"Trade and Securities Statistics"
Publications of:
Standard & Poor's
345 Hudson Street
New York, N.Y. 10014

## Statistical Bulletin

Monthly publication of:
Securities and Exchange Commission

Washington, D.C. 20549

Valuable statistics dealing with stocks, bonds and stock exchanges.

## Summary of Equity Security Transactions

Monthly publication of:
Board of Governors of the Federal Reserve System
Washington, D.C. 20551
Released the last week of each month. The data refer to the release date.

## The Analysts' Commentary

A publication appearing every other week and published by:
Dean Witter & Co.
45 Montgomery Street
San Francisco, California 94106
It presents a view of economic developments along with analyses of specific companies.

## The Commercial and Financial Chronicle

Weekly publication of:
The Chronicle
110 Wall Street
New York, N.Y. 10005
Presents articles, feature stories about industries, and developments in the bond and stock markets.

## The M/G Financial Weekly

Publication of:
The M/G Financial Weekly
P.O. Box 26565
Dept. B-28
Richmond, Virginia 23261
Analyses of securities markets, industries, and economic developments.

## The New York Stock Exchange Monthly Review

Publication of:
New York Stock Exchange, Inc.
11 Wall Street
New York, N.Y. 10005
Information and data on market activity, securities prices, and credit.

## The O-T-C Market Chronicle

Weekly publication of:
Wiliam B. Dana Company

25 Park Avenue
New York, N.Y. 10007
A must for keeping up with developments in the Over-the-Counter market.

## The Stock Picture

Monthly publication of:
M.C. Horsey & Co., Inc.
79 Wall Street
New York, N.Y. 10005
Graphs of stock action of various companies.

## The Value Line Convertible Survey

Monthly publication of :
Arnold Bernhard & Co., Inc.
5 East 44th Street
New York, N.Y. 10017
Provides information about convertible bonds and preferred stocks, as well as information on Chicago Board Options Exchange (CBOE) and American Stock Exchange (Amex) options.

## The Value Line Investment Survey

Weekly publication of:
Arnold Bernhard & Co., Inc.
5 East 44th Street
New York, N.Y. 10017
Periodic updating of information and data regarding specific industries and companies within an industry group. It is published in three parts:
Part I   : "Summary Index"
Part II : "Selection and Opinion"
Part III: "Ratings and Reports"

## The Wall Street Transcript

Weekly publication of:
Wall Street Transcript Corporation
120 Wall Street
New York, N.Y. 10005
Provides a collection of fundamental and technical analyses of stocks and investment possibilities. Especially valuable are the panel discussions it presents, in which experts present their views on investment potentials in various industries.

## The Weekly Bond Buyer

Publication of:
The Weekly Bond Buyer
One State Street Plaza
New York, N.Y. 10004
A must for keeping up with developments in the bond markets and related areas.

## Trendline

Weekly publication of:
Trendline
345 Hudson Street
New York, N.Y. 10014
Provides charts of stocks and stock market indicators, together with comparative earnings and dividends for many companies.

## Wall Street Week

Weekly television program.
An outstanding program for keeping up with the world of stocks and bonds. Although the emphasis is on the world of stocks and bonds, the money markets, gold and other areas of investment are covered. The members of the panel are very knowledgeable and the guests are of very high caliber. Louis Ruckeyser, the host, adds much to the effectiveness of the program.

## MONEY AND INTEREST RATES

## Automobile Installment Credit Developments

Monthly publication of:
Board of Governors of the Federal Reserve System
Washington, D.C. 20551
Released on the sixth working day of each month. The data refer to the second previous month.

## Automobile Loans by Major Finance Companies

Monthly publication of:
Board of Governors of the Federal Reserve System
Washington, D.C. 20551
Released on the seventh working day of each month and reports data for the second previous month.

### Consumer Credit

Monthly publication of:
   Board of Governors of the Federal Reserve System
   Washington, D.C. 20551
Released on the third working day of each month. The data refer to the second previous month.

### Consumer Installment Credit at Commercial Banks

Monthly publication of:
   Board of Governors of the Federal Reserve System
   Washington, D.C. 20551
Released on the fourth working day of each month. The data refer to the second previous month.

### Finance Companies

Monthly publication of:
   Board of Governors of the Federal Reserve System
   Washington, D.C. 20551
Released on the fifth working day of each month. The data refer to the second previous month.

### Finance Rate and Other Terms on New and Used Car Installment Credit Contracts Purchased from Dealers by Major Auto Finance Companies

Monthly publication of:
   Board of Governors of the Federal Reserve System
   Washington, D.C. 20551
Released on the 30th of each month. The data refer to the previous month.

### Finance Rates and Other Terms on Selected Categories of Consumer Installment Credit Extended by Finance Companies

Monthly publication of:
   Board of Governors of the Federal Reserve System
   Washington, D.C. 20551
Released on the 20th of each month and reports data for the second previous month.

### Flow of Funds

Quarterly publication of:
   Board of Governors of the Federal Reserve System
   Washington, D.C. 20551
Released on the 15th of February, May, August, and November, with data for the previous quarter. Data are given on an adjusted and

unadjusted basis. The publication covers the financial assets and liabilities of all sectors of the U.S. economy.

### Foreign Exchange Rates

Weekly and monthly publications of:
Board of Governors of the Federal Reserve System
Washington, D.C. 20551
The weekly publication is released on Monday of each week and reports data for the week ended the previous Friday. The monthly publication is released on the 1st of each month and reports data for the previous month.

### Interest Rates Charged on Selected Types of Bank Loans

Monthly publication of:
Board of Governors of the Federal Reserve System
Washington, D.C. 20551
Released on the 15th of each month and covers data for the second previous month.

### Money

Monthly publication of:
Time Inc.
541 North Fairbanks Court
Chicago, Illinois 60611
Presents coverage of stocks, bonds, and investment policies and offers practical advice about how to use and spend your money.

### Money Stock Measures

Weekly publication of:
Board of Governors of the Federal Reserve System
Washington, D.C. 20551
Released on Thursday of each week and reports data for the week ended Wednesday of the previous week. Provides invaluable data of the monetary aggregates.

### Selected Interest & Exchange Rates

Weekly publication of:
Board of Governors of the Federal Reserve System
Washington, D.C. 20551
A compilation of graphs and tables of the following:

Spot Exchange Rate Indexes
3-Month Forward Exchange Rates
Gold Price (London)

Call Money Rates
3-Month Interest Rates
Euro-dollar Deposit Rates
Selected Euro-dollar and U.S. Money Market Rates
Interest Arbitrage: 3-Month Funds
Long-term Government Bond Yields
Industrial Stock Indexes

This publication is released on Thursday of each week. The data refer to the week ended the previous Saturday for the United States and other countries.

## Volume and Composition of Individuals' Saving

Quarterly publication of:
    Board of Governors of the Federal Reserve System
    Washington, D.C. 20551
Released on the 15th of February, May, August, and November. The data refer to the previous quarter.


## COMMERCIAL BANKING


### American Banker

Daily publication of:
    American Banker, Inc.
    525 West 42nd Street
    New York, N.Y. 10036
Published daily except Saturdays, Sundays, and holidays. Provides intensive coverage of U.S. and international banking developments.

### Assets and Liabilities of all Commercial Banks in the United States

Weekly publication of:
    Board of Governors of the Federal Reserve System
    Washington, D.C. 20551
Released on Wednesday of each week. The data refer to Wednesday 2 weeks earlier.

### Assets and Liabilities of all Commercial Banks by Class of Bank

Semi-annual publication of:
    Board of Governors of the Federal Reserve System
    Washington, D.C. 20551

Released on May and November of each year. The data refer to the end of the previous December and June, respectively.

## Assets, Liabilities, and Capital Accounts of Commercial and Mutual Savings Banks—Reports of Call

Semi-annual joint release of the Federal Deposit Insurance Corporation (FDIC), the Board of Governors of the Federal Reserve System and the Office of the Comptroller of the Currency. The release is actually published by the FDIC, but can be obtained from:

Board of Governors of the Federal Reserve System
Washington, D.C. 20551

Released in May and November of each year. The data refer to the end of the previous December and June, respectively.

## Bank Debits, Deposits, and Deposit Turnover

Monthly publication of:

Board of Governors of the Federal Reserve System
Washington, D.C. 20551

Released on the 25th of each month. The data refer to the previous month.

## Bank Rates on Short Term Business Loans

Quarterly publication of:

Board of Governors of the Federal Reserve System
Washington, D.C. 20551

Released on the 18th of March, June, September, and December. The data refer to the first 15 days of February, May, August, and November.

## Banking

Monthly publication of:

American Bankers Association
350 Broadway
New York, N.Y. 10013

Valuable coverage of the U.S. banking industry.

## Barclays Review

Quarterly publication of:

Barclays Bank Limited
Group Economic Intelligence Unit
54 Lombard Street
London EC3P 3AH, United Kingdom

Valuable coverage of developments concerning investments, finance, banking, and related areas, with statistical tables and graphs.

## Changes in Status of Banks and Branches

Monthly publication of:
  Board of Governors of the Federal Reserve System
  Washington, D.C. 20551
Released on the 25th of each month. The data refer to the previous month.

## Commercial and Industrial Loans Outstanding by Industry

Weekly publication of:
  Board of Governors of the Federal Reserve System
  Washington, D.C. 20551
Released on Wednesday of each week. The data refer to Wednesday one week earlier.

## Commercial and Industrial Term Loans Outstanding by Industry

Monthly publication of:
  Board of Governors of the Federal Reserve System
  Washington, D.C. 20551
Released on the second Wednesday of each month. The data refer to the last Wednesday of each month.

## Condition Report of Large Commercial Banks and Domestic Subsidiaries

Weekly publication of:
  Board of Governors of the Federal Reserve System
  Washington, D.C. 20551
Released on Wednesday of each week. The data refer to Wednesday of one week earlier.

## Condition Report of Large Commercial Banks in New York and Chicago

Weekly publication of:
  Board of Governors of the Federal Reserve System
  Washington, D.C. 20551
Released on Thursday of each week. The data refer to the previous Wednesday.

## End of Month Demand Deposits Except Interbank and U.S. Government Accounts

Annual publication of:
   Board of Governors of the Federal Reserve System
   Washington, D.C. 20551
   Released on March 25 of each year. The data refer to the previous year.

## The Bankers Magazine

Quarterly publication of:
   Warren, Gorham & Lamont, Inc.
   89 Beach Street
   Boston, Mass. 02111
   In-depth coverage of many aspects of banking.

## Weekly Summary of Banking and Credit Measures

Publication of:
   Board of Governors of the Federal Reserve System
   Washington, D.C. 20551
   Released on Thursday of each week. The data refer to the week ended the previous Wednesday and the week ended Wednesday of the previous week.


## FEDERAL RESERVE SYSTEM

## Annual Report of the Federal Reserve System

Publication of:
   Board of Governors of the Federal Reserve System
   Washington, D.C. 20551
   Covers previous year's operations of the Federal Reserve System.

## Aggregate Reserves and Member Bank Deposits

Weekly publication of:
   Board of Governors of the Federal Reserve System
   Washington, D.C. 20551
   Released on Tuesday of each week. The data refer to the week ended the previous Wednesday and deal with Federal Reserve member banks.

## Assets and Liabilities of All Member Banks by Districts

Monthly publication of:
   Board of Governors of the Federal Reserve System
   Washington, D.C. 20551

Released on the 14th of each month and reports data for the last Wednesday of the previous month for all member banks of the Federal Reserve System.

### Changes in State Member Banks

Weekly publication of:
Board of Governors of the Federal Reserve System
Washington, D.C. 20551
Released on Tuesday of each week and covers data for the week ended the previous Saturday. The data refer to state banks that are members of the Federal Reserve System.

### Deposits, Reserves, and Borrowings of Member Banks

Weekly publication of:
Board of Governors of the Federal Reserve System
Washington, D.C. 20551
Released on Wednesday of each week and reports data for the week ended 3 Wednesdays earlier.

### Factors Affecting Bank Reserves and Condition Statement of Federal Reserve Banks

Weekly publication of:
Board of Governors of the Federal Reserve System
Washington, D.C. 20551
Released on Thursday of each week and reports data for the week ended the previous Wednesday.

### Federal Reserve Bank of Atlanta

Atlanta, Georgia 30303
Numerous publications providing data about the area or jurisdiction of the Federal Reserve Bank of Atlanta, as well as articles of national and international significance.

### Federal Reserve Bank of Boston

Boston, Mass. 02110
Numerous publications providing data about the area of jurisdiction of the Federal Reserve of Boston, as well as articles of national and international significance.

### Federal Reserve Bank of Chicago

Box 834
Chicago, Illinois 60690

Numerous publications providing data about the area of jurisdiction of the Federal Reserve Bank of Chicago, as well as articles of national and international significance.

### Federal Reserve Bank of Cleveland

P.O. Box 6387
Cleveland, Ohio 44101
Numerous publications providing data about the area of jurisdiction of the Federal Reserve Bank of Cleveland, as well as articles of national and international significance.

### Federal Reserve Bank of Dallas

Dallas, Texas 75222
Numerous publications providing data about the area of jurisdiction of the Federal Reserve Bank of Dallas, as well as articles of national and international significance.

### Federal Reserve Bank of Kansas City

Kansas City, Missouri 64198
Numerous publications providing data about the area of jurisdiction of the Federal Reserve Bank of Kansas City, as well as articles of national and international significance.

### Federal Reserve Bank of Minneapolis

Minneapolis, Minnesota 55480
Numerous publications providing data about the area of jurisdiction of the Federal Reserve Bank of Minneapolis, as well as articles of national and international significance.

### Federal Reserve Bank of New York

33 Liberty Street
New York, N.Y. 10045
Numerous publications providing data about the area of jurisdiction of the Federal Reserve Bank of New York, as well as articles of national and international significance.

### Federal Reserve Bank of New York Monthly Review

Monthly publication of:
Federal Reserve Bank of New York
33 Liberty Street
New York, N.Y. 10045

This publication regularly presents a monthly review of the business situation and the money and capital markets. Its coverage of the money and capital markets is truly outstanding.

### Federal Reserve Bank of Philadelphia

Philadelphia, Pennsylvania 19101
Numerous publications providing data about the area of jurisdiction of the Federal Reserve Bank of Philadelphia, as well as articles of national and international significance.

### Federal Reserve Bank of Richmond

Richmond, Virginia 23213
Numerous publications providing data about the area of jurisdiction of the Federal Reserve Bank of Richmond, as well as articles of national and international significance.

### Federal Reserve Bank of San Francisco

400 Sansome Street
San Francisco, California 94120
Numerous publications providing data about the area of jurisdiction of the Federal Reserve Bank of San Francisco, as well as articles of national and international significance.

### Federal Reserve Bank of St. Louis

St. Louis, Missouri 63102
Numerous publications providing data about the area of jurisdiction of the Federal Reserve Bank of St. Louis, as well as articles of national and international significance.

### Federal Reserve Bulletin

Monthly publication of:
Board of Governors of the Federal Reserve System
Washington, D.C. 20551
This publication regularly presents the latest official statistical tables of monetary, fiscal, banking, financial, industrial, and consumer data. In addition, economic analyses and special articles are provided.

### Federal Reserve Chart Book on Financial and Business Statistics

Monthly publication of:
Board of Governors of the Federal Reserve System
Washington, D.C. 20551
Excellent presentation of financial and business developments in a series of graphs.

## Reserve Positions of Major Reserve City Banks

Weekly publication of:
Board of Governors of the Federal Reserve System
Washington, D.C. 20551
Released on Friday of each week and reports data for the week ended
Wednesday of the previous week.

## State Member Banks of Federal Reserve System and Nonmember Banks that Maintain Clearing Accounts with Federal Reserve Banks

Monthly publication of:
Board of Governors of the Federal Reserve System
Washington, D.C. 20551
Released in the first week of each month. The data refer to the previous
month.

## EURODOLLAR MARKET, EUROCURRENCY MARKET, AND INTERNATIONAL ECONOMICS

### Euromoney

Monthly publication of:
Euromoney Publications Limited
14 Finsbury Circus
London EC2M 7AB, United Kingdom
Outstanding coverage of the Eurocurrency market and related areas.

### Finance & Development

A quarterly publication of the International Monetary Fund and the
World Bank Group. It is available in English, French, and Spanish and
is published by:
International Monetary Fund and the International Bank
for Reconstruction and Development
Washington, D.C. 20431

A German-language edition is published by the International Monetary
Fund and the International Bank for Reconstruction and Development
in collaboration with HWWA-Institut für Wirtschaftforschung-
Hamburg and is produced by Verlag Weltarchiv GmbH. The German
edition can be obtained by writing to:
*Finanzierung und Entwicklung*
HWWA-Institut
2 Hamburg 36
Neuer Jungfernstieg 21, Germany

A selection of the contents of *Finance & Development* is published annually in Rio de Janeiro, Brazil, in cooperation with the United Nations Information Center, in Portuguese.

### IMF Survey

Bimonthly publication (except for December, when a single issue is published), which may be obtained from:
The Secretary
International Monetary Fund
Washington, D.C. 20431
Extremely valuable and well-presented coverage of international monetary and economic developments.

### International Letter

Weekly publication of:
Federal Reserve Bank of Chicago
Box 834
Chicago, Illinois 60690
This publication spotlights important international monetary and financial developments.

### The International Executive

Published three times a year by:
The Foundation for the Advancement of International
    Business Administration, Inc.
64 Ferndale Drive
Hastings-on-Hudson, N.Y. 10706
Very valuable coverage of current books and periodicals dealing with international business.

## TAXATION

### Commerce Clearing House, Inc., Publications

"Excise Tax Reporter"
"Federal Estate and Gift Tax Reporter"
"Individuals' Filled-in Tax Return Forms"
"Standard Federal Tax Reporter"
"Tax Court Memorandum Decisions"
"Tax Court Reporter"
"U.S. Tax Cases"

Publications of:
Commerce Clearing House, Inc.
522 Fifth Avenue
New York, N.Y. 10036

### Monthly Tax Features

Publication of:
Tax Foundation, Inc.
50 Rockefeller Plaza
New York, N.Y. 10020
Current developments in taxation.

### Prentice-Hall Publications

"American Federal Tax Reports"
"Executive Report"
"Federal Tax Citator"
"Federal Tax Guide"
"Federal Taxes Report Bulletin"
"Government Control of Business"
"Oil and Gas Taxes Report Bulletin"
"Securities Regulations"
"State and Local Taxes"
"Tax Ideas"
Publications of:
Prentice-Hall, Inc.
Englewood Cliffs, New Jersey 07632

### Tax Coordinator

Annual publication of:
The Research Institute of America, Inc.
589 Fifth Avenue
New York, N.Y. 10017
Intensive coverage of the tax field.

### Taxes—The Tax Magazine

Monthly publication of:
Commerce Clearing House, Inc.
4025 West Peterson Avenue
Chicago, Illinois 60646
Presents very valuable information on developments relating to taxes.

### The Journal of Corporate Taxation

Quarterly publication of:
Warren, Gorham & Lamont, Inc.
210 South Street
Boston, Mass. 02111
In-depth coverage of tax accounting and judicial decisions.

### The Tax Adviser

Monthly publication of:
American Institute of Certified Public Accountants
1211 Avenue of the Americas
New York, N.Y. 10036
Presents intensive coverage of planning, trends and techniques relating to taxation.

### U.S. Tax Week

Publication of:
Matthew Bender & Company, Inc.
235 East 45th Street
New York, N.Y. 10017
Regular coverage of the numerous areas relating to taxes.

# bibliography

The author has made great use of the following publications.

ANGLE, ELIZABETH W., *Keys for Business Forecasting* (Third Edition; Richmond, Virginia: Federal Reserve Bank of Richmond, August 1969).

AXILROD, STEPHEN H., and RALPH A. YOUNG, "Interest Rates and Monetary Policy," *Federal Reserve Bulletin* (September 1962), pp. 1110-1137.

BANK FOR INTERNATIONAL SETTLEMENTS, *45th Annual Report* (Basle: June 9, 1975).

BECK, DARWIN, and JOSEPH SEDRANSK, "Revision of the Money Stock Measures and Member Bank Reserves and Deposits," *Federal Reserve Bulletin* (February 1974), pp. 81-95.

BLACK, ROBERT P., *The Federal Reserve Today* (Federal Reserve Bank of Richmond, 1968).

BOARD OF GOVERNORS OF THE FEDERAL RESERVE SYSTEM, "Federal Fiscal Policy, 1965-72," *Federal Reserve Bulletin* (June 1973), pp. 383-402.

———, "Financial Developments in the Second Quarter of 1974," *Federal Reserve Bulletin* (August 1974), pp. 533-541.

———, *Flow of Funds, Assets and Liabilities Outstanding 1974, Preliminary* (February 1975).

———, "Money Supply in the Conduct of Monetary Policy," *Federal Reserve Bulletin* (November 1973), pp. 791-798.

——, "Numerical Specifications of Financial Variables and Their Role in Monetary Policy," *Federal Reserve Bulletin* (May 1974), pp. 333-337.

——, "SDR's in Federal Reserve Operations and Statistics," *Federal Reserve Bulletin* (May 1970), pp. 421-424.

——, *Selected Interest & Exchange Rates,* numerous issues.

——, "Some Problems of Central Banking," *Federal Reserve Bulletin* (June 1973), pp. 417-419.

——, *The Federal Reserve System: Purposes and Functions* (5th Ed., November 1967).

BOLTZ, PAUL W., "Changes in Bank Lending Practices, 1973," *Federal Reserve Bulletin* (April 1974), pp. 263-267.

BURNS, ARTHUR F., *Statement Before the Committee on Banking, Housing and Urban Affairs,* United States Senate (February 27, 1973).

EDMONSON, NATHAN, "Capacity Utilization for Major Materials: Revised Measures," *Federal Reserve Bulletin,* pp. 246-251.

FEDERAL NATIONAL MORTGAGE ASSOCIATION, *Federal National Mortgage Association Charter Act* (December 1, 1972).

FEDERAL RESERVE BANK OF ATLANTA, *Monthly Review,* numerous issues.

FEDERAL RESERVE BANK OF BOSTON, *New England Business Review,* numerous issues.

FEDERAL RESERVE BANK OF CHICAGO, *Business Conditions* (November 1971, September 1973, October 1974, January, February, and March 1975).

——, "Interbank Lending—An Essential Function," *Business Conditions* (November 1974), pp. 3-7.

——, *International Letter,* numerous issues.

——, *Modern Money Mechanics* (publication originally written by Dorothy M. Nichols in May 1961 and revised September 1971).

——, "The New Federal Financing Bank," *Business Conditions* (May 1974), pp. 9-15.

——, *Two Faces of Debt* (October 1972).

FEDERAL RESERVE BANK OF CLEVELAND, *Economic Review* (April 1970).

——, *Money Market Instruments* (August 1970).

FEDERAL RESERVE BANK OF DALLAS, *Business Review,* numerous issues.

FEDERAL RESERVE BANK OF KANSAS CITY, *The Federal Budget and Economic Activity,* by Glenn H. Miller, Jr. (June 1969).

FEDERAL RESERVE BANK OF MINNEAPOLIS, *Making Peace With Gold* (September 1968).

FEDERAL RESERVE BANK OF NEW YORK, *Auction of $1.5 Billion of Federal Financing Bank Bills,* circular No. 7419 (July 12, 1974).

————, *Basic Information on Treasury Bills* (September 1974).

————, *Composite Closing Quotations for U.S. Government Securities,* numerous issues.

————, *Essays in Domestic and International Finance* (August 1969).

————, *Glossary: Weekly Federal Reserve Statements* (September 1972).

————, *Information Concerning the Purchase of U.S. Treasury Notes and Bonds* (April 1973).

————, *Money: Master or Servant?* (6th Ed., 1971).

————, *Monthly Review,* numerous issues.

FEDERAL RESERVE BANK OF PHILADELPHIA, *Defending the Dollar* (Sepember 1970).

————, *50 Years of The Federal Reserve Act* (1964).

————, *Monetary Policy* (April 1961).

————, *The Four Hats of the Federal Reserve* (no date).

————, *The Quest for Stability* (February-May 1950).

FEDERAL RESERVE BANK OF RICHMOND, *Economic Review* (September/October 1974).

————, *Instruments of the Money Market* (August 1970).

————, *Monthly Review* (August 1972).

————, *Monthly Review* (September 1973).

FEDERAL RESERVE BANK OF SAN FRANCISCO, *Business & Financial Letter,* numerous issues.

————, *Monthly Review* (August 1972).

FEDERAL RESERVE BANK OF ST. LOUIS, *Federal Budget Trends,* numerous issues.

————, *Monetary Trends,* numerous issues.

————, *National Economic Trends,* numerous issues.

————, *Review,* numerous issues.

————, *U.S. Financial Data,* numerous issues.

FRY, EDWARD R. "Measures of Member Bank Reserves," *Federal Reserve Bulletin* (July 1963), pp. 890-903.

HOLMES, ALAN R., "Open Market Operations," *Federal Reserve Bulletin* (May 1974), pp. 338-350.

HULL, DAVID, and LINDA DAVIDSON, "Rates on Consumer Loans," *Federal Reserve Bulletin* (September 1973), pp. 641-645.

KICHLINE, JAMES L., P. MICHAEL LAUB, and BERUL DECK, "Yields on Recently Offered Corporate Bonds," *Federal Reserve Bulletin* (May 1973), pp. 336-337.

KIDDER, KAREN, *Wall Street: Before the Fall* (Federal Reserve Bank of San Francisco, *Monthly Review Supplement,* 1970).

MEEK, PAUL, *Open Market Operations* (Federal Reserve Bank of New York, May 1973).

NISSEN, ANTON, DARWIN BECK, NEVA G. VAN PESKI, and EDWARD R. FRY, "Revision of the Money Stock Measures and Member Bank Reserves and Deposits," *Federal Reserve Bulletin* (February 1973), pp. 61-79.

OFFICE OF THE FEDERAL REGISTER, NATIONAL ARCHIVES AND RECORDS SERVICE, GENERAL SERVICES ADMINISRATION, *United States Government Manual 1973/1974* (Washington, D.C.: U.S. Government Printing Office, July 1973).

OFFICE OF THE FEDERAL REGISTER, NATIONAL ARCHIVES AND RECORDS SERVICE, GENERAL SERVICES ADMINISTRATION, *United States Government Manual 1974-75* (Washington, D.C.: U.S. Government Printing Office, September, 1974).

PRUITT, ELEANOR M., "State and Local Borrowing Anticipations and Realizations," *Federal Reserve Bulletin* (April 1973), pp. 257-260.

PUBLIC LAW 93-224 (93rd Congress, H.R. 5874, December 29, 1973).

SCANLON, MARTHA S., "Changes in Time and Savings Deposits at Commercial Banks, *Federal Reserve Bulletin* (September 1973), pp. 627-635.

U.S. DEPARTMENT OF THE TREASURY, *Treasury Bulletin,* numerous issues.

# index